LINDA LIGHTON

LOVE & WAR

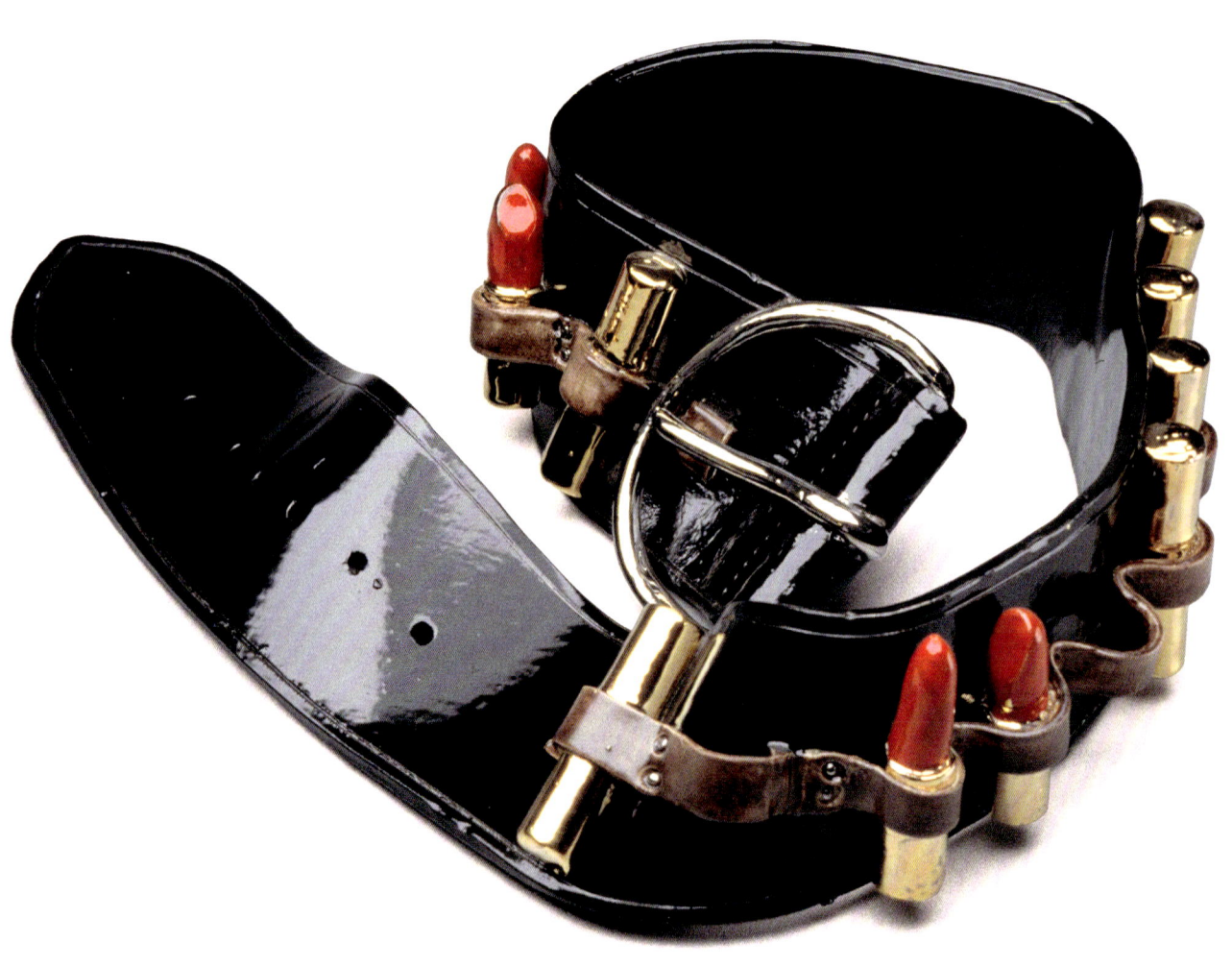

LINDA LIGHTON

LOVE & WAR

A FIFTY-YEAR SURVEY
1975—2025

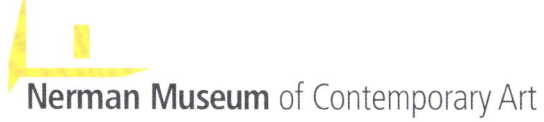

Nerman Museum of Contemporary Art

HIRMER

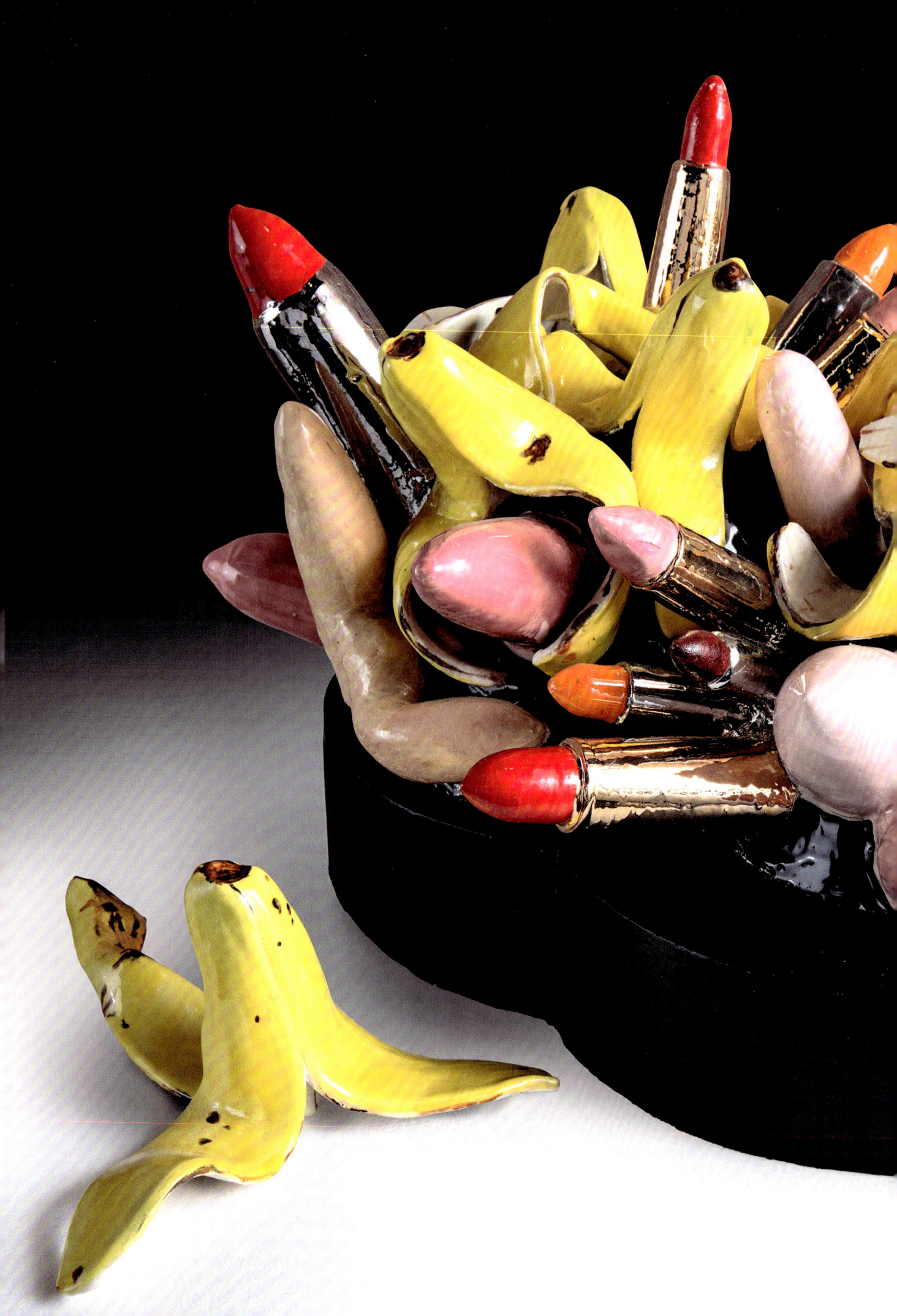

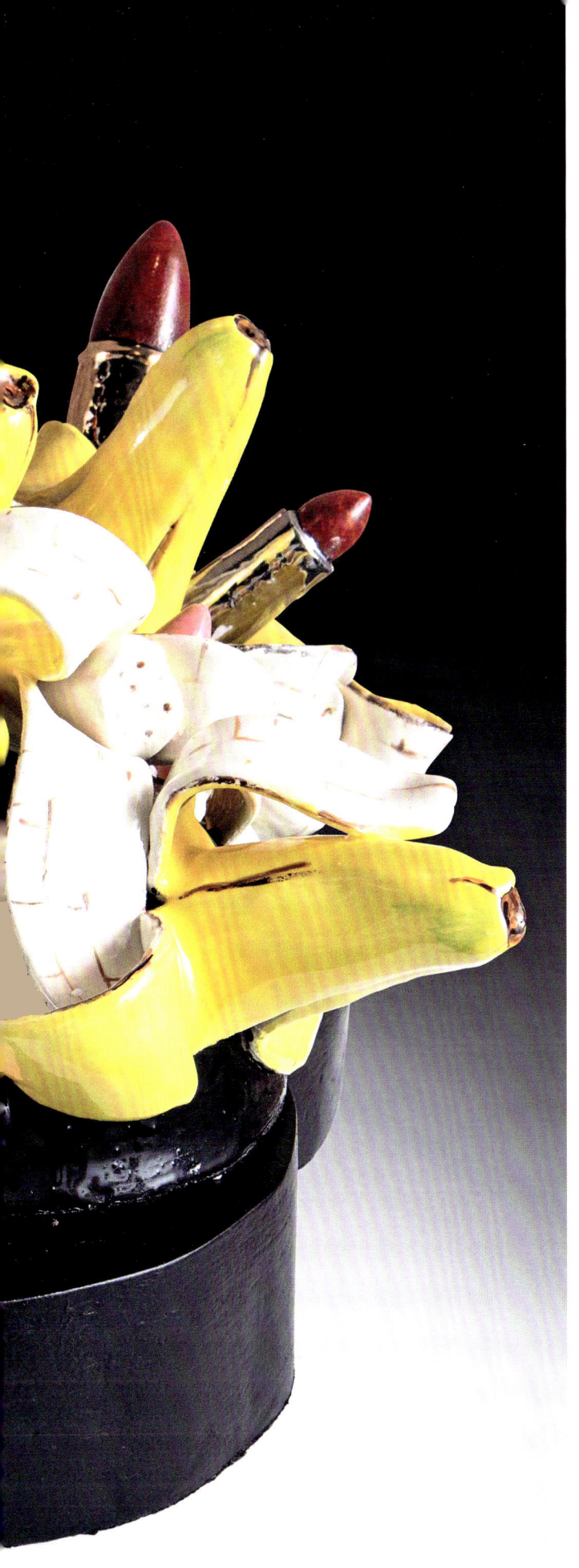

TABLE OF CONTENTS

SPONSORS

Jeffrey D. Byrne

J. Scott Francis, Francis Family Foundation

Dennis and Carol Hudson Family Foundation

R.C. Kemper, Jr. Charitable Trust and Foundation

DIRECTOR'S FOREWORD

The Kansas City area is blessed with visual arts institutions in abundance, including the Nelson-Atkins Museum of Art, the Kemper Museum of Contemporary Art, and the Nerman Museum of Contemporary Art. Notable alumni of the Kansas City Art Institute, an undergraduate art and design school, include contemporary art luminaries Nick Cave and Roberto Lugo. Thanks to an abundance of buildings with artist studio space, graduates of KCAI and other programs tend to stay in the area, and plentiful artist-run galleries and spaces have emerged as a result.

When I relocated to Kansas City from the West Coast in 2021, I was impressed with the rich cultural ecosystem. I embarked on a series of studio visits, and Linda Lighton was among the first artists I met. Her ceramic sculptures thrilled with their luscious forms and feminist themes—this was a world-class artist whose work deserved broader recognition. In 2022, I proposed that the Nerman Museum of Contemporary Art give Lighton the retrospective she deserves. This exhibition would not have been possible without Sydney Stutterheim, PhD, and Rose Dergan, who lent their intellectual and critical skills to this endeavor.

In 1995, The Nelson-Atkins mounted a retrospective of the work of ceramic artist Ken Ferguson. Not since then has a Kansas City institution given a local artist similar scholarly attention. I can think of no individual more worthy than Lighton, for her extraordinary work spanning 50 years. I acknowledge her passion and devotion to her craft with enormous gratitude.

JoAnne Northrup
Executive Director and Chief Curator
Nerman Museum of Contemporary Art

IN FULL BLOOM:
THE STORY OF LINDA LIGHTON

by Glenn Adamson

There's nothing Linda Lighton won't tell you. In the space of one conversation, she'll happily discuss—if not necessarily in chronological order—her upbringing in a wealthy Kansas City family, her early exposure to the avant-garde, her father's decision to institutionalize her in an asylum, and her subsequent escape from familial confines. Then her youthful adventures: plunging into the Bay Area counterculture, just as it was embarking on its psychedelic trip; living communally on a Native American reservation in Washington state. Then the first stages of professionalism—becoming a painter and then a ceramicist, falling in with the West Coast Funk movement, learning how to do china painting. Becoming a feminist. Returning to Kansas City after a stint in Idaho. Becoming an anti-gun activist. Sponsoring an international artist exchange program. And working, always working, the ideas pouring out of her in a warm, swirling flood, white clay infused with vibrant polychromatic life, so that it speaks of her irrepressible sense of humor and her moral outrage, giving material form to the seductive, subversive, and sublime.

It's enough to take your breath away. Yet despite the fact that her work has been included in hundreds of exhibitions over the course of her long career, Lighton is not all that widely known—or at least not as widely known as she ought to be. Partly, no doubt, this is because she has worked chiefly in a marginalized medium. Partly it's because she spent most of her career in the Midwest, away from major art centers. Partly it's because, despite the brilliance of her conversation, she is no self-promoter. And partly—OK, maybe mostly—it is because she has marched to the beat of her own proverbial drum, creating a supremely individualistic oeuvre which can only be taken on its own terms and has fit only intermittently into surrounding currents. She is an art movement of one. Fortunately, the time for a full appraisal is at hand, in the shape of this book and the exhibition that it accompanies. So let's jump in, shall we?

As mentioned above, Lighton was born in Kansas City, in 1948, to a Jewish family of considerable means (fig. 1). Right at the end of the Civil War, her great-grandfather, Alfred Woolf, and his brother, Samuel, had moved from New York City to what then still qualified as the frontier. They established a shirt-making business off the back of a sizable contract at Fort Leavenworth, and in 1879 relocated to Kansas City, where they established themselves as one of the region's leading garment manufacturers and retailers (among their customers were Buffalo Bill Cody and Wild Bill Hickok—Lighton has the receipts). Woolf Brothers would remain a family enterprise for over a century, closing only in 1986. Linda's father, Alfred, began working there in 1937 at the age of twenty, eventually rising to become the company's president. His mother (Linda's grandmother), Gertrude Woolf Lighton (fig. 2), was an amateur painter, a trustee of the Kansas City Art Institute, a major donor to the Nelson-Atkins Museum, and co-founder of the Kansas City Society of Artists—an organization headquartered at Lighton Studios, which she also founded, in 1930. The site had formerly been a house of prostitution with the wonderfully gothic name of the Bloody Bucket. Gertude, showing a sense of humor unusual within the patrician class, paid tribute to the building's ill-reputed history by calling its elegant tea room the Red Lantern.

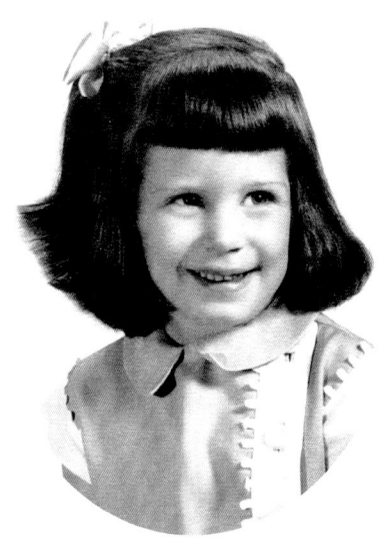

1 Linda Lighton, c. 1953

Thanks to her family background, art was always around for Linda, always accessible. Her first memorable aesthetic experience was dusting her grandmother's Sèvres porcelains. By the time she was a teenager, a Wayne Thiebaud and a Diego Rivera hung in the kitchen. She seems never to have doubted that she herself would be an artist, but for a young woman of her generation, that was never going to be easy. When she graduated from high school, a meeting was arranged for her to meet the director of the Kansas City Art Institute (she was, after all, a Lighton). Instead of letting her enroll, though, he asked, "Honey, don't you have a boyfriend?" She was duly packed off to Centenary College for Young Women in New Jersey in 1966. This proved to be a disaster, due to her wayward and unbiddable spirit, but she did get over to Manhattan to see a lot of art. She remembers being bowled over by both Minimalism and Pop: Ellsworth Kelly, Roy Lichtenstein, Claes Oldenburg, Andy Warhol. She was even invited to swing by a party at Warhol's Factory, though she was too intimidated to go.

The East Coast experiment lasted less than a year, and she found herself back in Kansas City, getting hired and fired by a florist ("I wanted to put yellow and purple together," she explains). It was at this juncture that Lighton's relations with her family reached a breaking point. Already cast in the role of black sheep, she refused to attend the Jewel Ball, a debutante gala that her grandmother had a hand in organizing. Her father, furious, became physically abusive, then had her committed to a mental institution—the sort of place where shock treatments were regularly administered. Without any legal means of proving her own sanity, she was trapped there for four months: no going outside, no phone calls, no visitors. It seems legitimate to make a connection between this event and the latent violence and claustrophobia that would later recur in her work. As soon as she was released, Lighton sought a more permanent freedom, moving to Lawrence, Kansas. And that is where her adventures in radical living began.

It was now the late 1960s. The Civil Rights Movement was on, and the conflict in Vietnam was spiraling out of

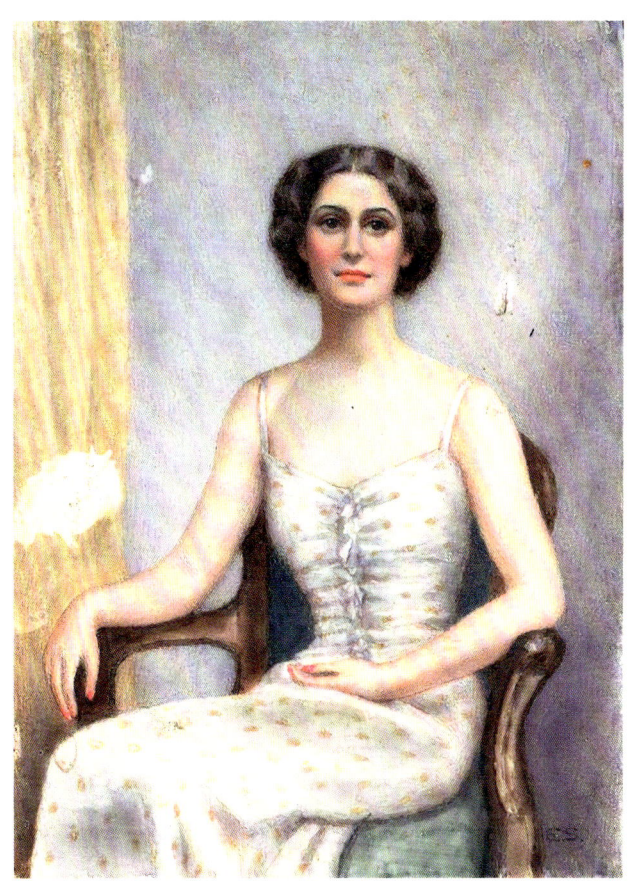

2 **Portrait of Gertrude Woolf Lighton, c. 1932–36 by Emma Siboni, a resident artist at Lighton Studios**

control. In this febrile political atmosphere, Lighton fell in with a group of anti-war activists and progressives, helping to publish a leftist newspaper called *The Screw: A Twisted Device for Holding Things Together* (later renamed *Vortex*, it was published until 1973) **(fig. 3)**. On one occasion, the editorial team interviewed a draft dodger for a profile, conducting the whole conversation through a hung bedsheet to preserve his anonymity. Then, like so many other young and idealistic Americans, she and her husband headed to Haight-Ashbury, arriving just in time to witness flower power in full bloom. They arrived in 1968, a year after the Summer of Love, but even at her impressionable age she could see that all was not well in paradise. Drug dealers were mov-

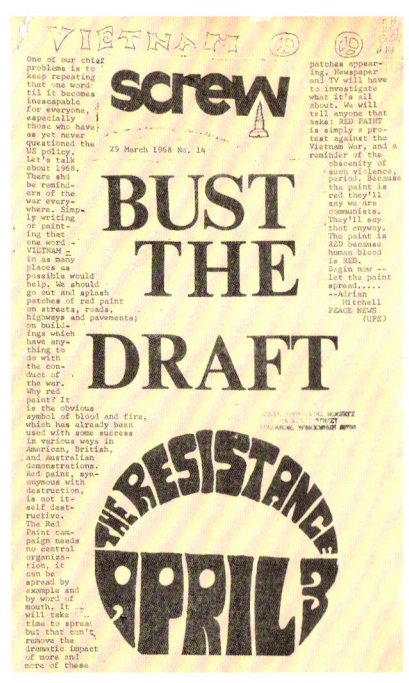

3 *The Screw: A Twisted Device for Holding Things Together*, cover, March 29, 1968

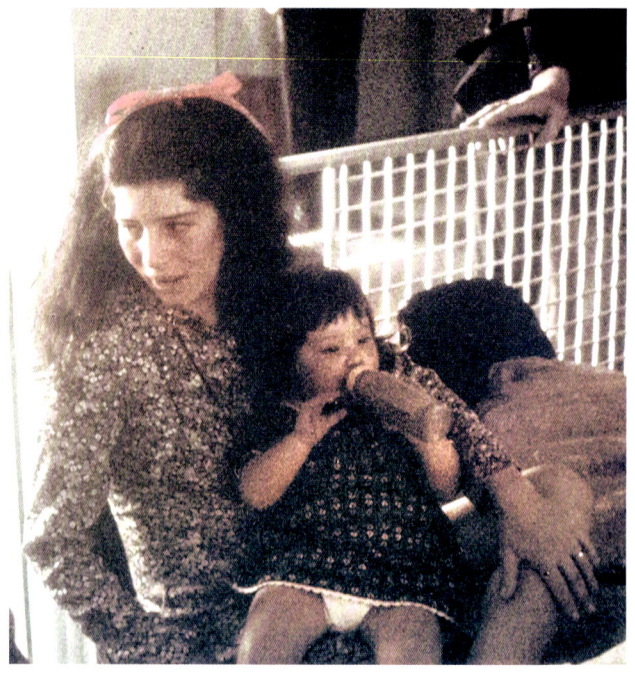

4 *Linda and Rose in New Mexico*, 1970

ing into the Haight, and most of the people around her were broke (as indeed was Lighton herself; she was effectively in hiding from her own family). Nonetheless, it was a time of discovery. The psychedelic bluesman Steve Miller lived upstairs from her; another neighbor was a girl who made clothing for Jimi Hendrix. Lighton took it all in: the music, the drugs, the mind-expanding imaginativeness. On one occasion she even helped build geodesic domes in Berkeley; when asked what that was like, she says, "can't remember. I was too stoned."

Having arrived in San Francisco at its bohemian peak, Lighton soon joined the exodus of those dismayed by its rapid descent and eager to try a new experiment: that of living off the land. She went up to Washington state, where her daughter Rose was born, in February of 1969. Linda turned 21 a month later (**fig. 4**). Linda and Rose soon joined a commune on a 200-acre piece of land situated on the Colville Native American Reservation, home to the Nimíipuu tribe (the "Nez Percé" in white

settler terminology). "There was no running water, no electricity," she says, "but it was gorgeous up in the high mountains. There were a dozen of us, some from the Rainbow Commune in Oregon. We had horses, goats, chickens, a turkey and a goose. Raised animals, hunted and tanned hides. Dug a garden and a well, and made an eight-sided log house. We dragged all standing dead timber with a horse, tried making soap. And worked hard to get in with the Indians."

In the summers, Lighton worked for the Forest Service and in a logging camp, to make a little money. Meanwhile, she was becoming an artist. She still has some watercolors that she painted at this formative moment, and they show her responding both to the scenery around her and to then-prevalent ideas about the holistic unity of nature, humanity, and the spirit. One painting depicts a figure rising from the ground, a tree emerging from the shoulders; another, a utopian landscape glimpsed through a keyhole, as if it were a place one could actually go if one could just open the right lock. During this period of austerity and freedom, Lighton had just enough of a sense of professional ambition that she sought out an institutional attachment. Prior to decamping to the reservation, she'd begun taking classes at a non-degree-granting art school called The Factory in Seattle (no relation to Warhol's). Though she was initially interested in painting, the minute she walked into the ceramics studio she was smitten: "I thought I would make dishes for the house, but ended up making art right away." It was a fortuitous encounter. At the time, Seattle was the second city of Funk, which (unbeknownst to her) had gotten its rambunctious, raunchy start in the Bay Area, where she'd just been. It had been a missed connection, but now she found out all about it through its reception in the Pacific Northwest.

The progenitors of Funk ceramics, including its perpetually bemused, anti-authoritarian leader, Robert Arneson, were reacting against the dominant strain in Californian clay during the 1950s: the gestural abstraction of Peter Voulkos, John Mason, and their circle, initially centered at the Otis Art Institute in Los Angeles and then, with Voulkos' move to Berkeley in 1960, the Bay Area. Arneson briefly tried to inhabit this style, but it was never going to be for him—he was too sly, too subversive, to take himself so seriously. By 1961, he was feeling his way into a whole new language, figurative and slapstick. His work had affinities to contemporaneous Pop Art, but it was—well, funkier, wallowing in the inherent earthiness of the medium.

Arneson's jokes were intentionally broad, but they had a cutting edge, too, particularly when he addressed ceramics' lowly place in the art hierarchy—a disregard he merrily mocked, even as it placed constraints on his career. He created a whole narrative around the idea of second-class citizenship, using such typologies as toilets and bricks to emphasize the least exalted aspects of the discipline (fig. 5). Other Funk artists in his immediate circle, like Clayton Bailey, David Gilhooly, Chris Unterseher and Peter VandenBerge, tended to be more light-hearted, expressing a healthy appetite for the absurdities of American daily life: the human comedy of scatology,

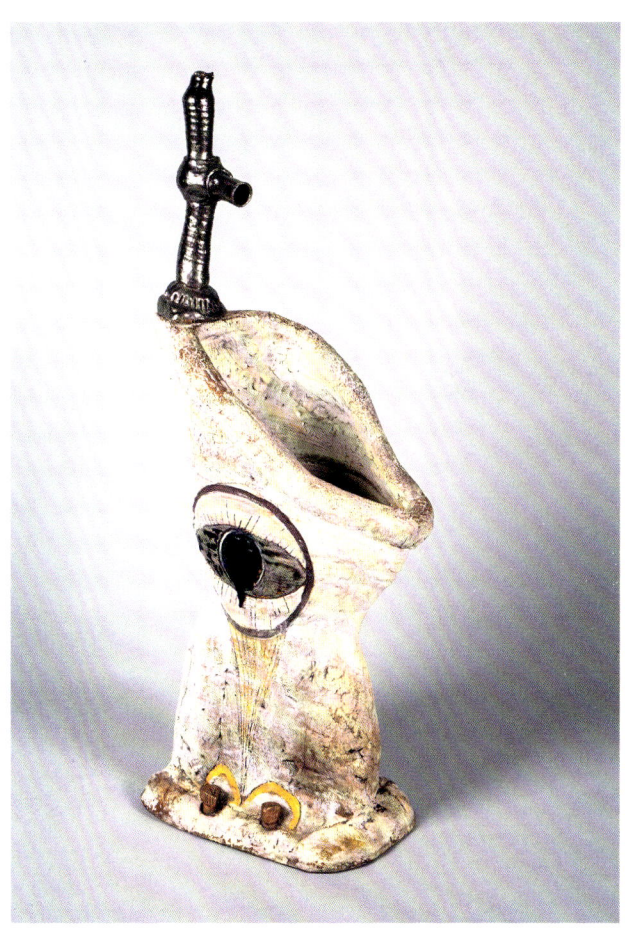

5 **ROBERT ARNESON,** Untitled (Urinal) 1963
Glazed ceramic
46 ¾ × 23 × 13 ½ in. (118.7 × 58.4 × 34.3 cm)
Collection of San José Museum of Art

sex, and suburbia. Their works were typically made not of glazed stoneware, but of low-fire white earthenware colored with china paints, a purposeful allusion to "little old lady" amateurism which also opened up a brighter, more flexible palette. It was a material vocabulary that Lighton would adopt in turn.

Funk had become a nationwide phenomenon by the late 1960s, but nowhere outside California was its presence more strongly felt than the Pacific Northwest, especially at the University of Washington. The primary vec-

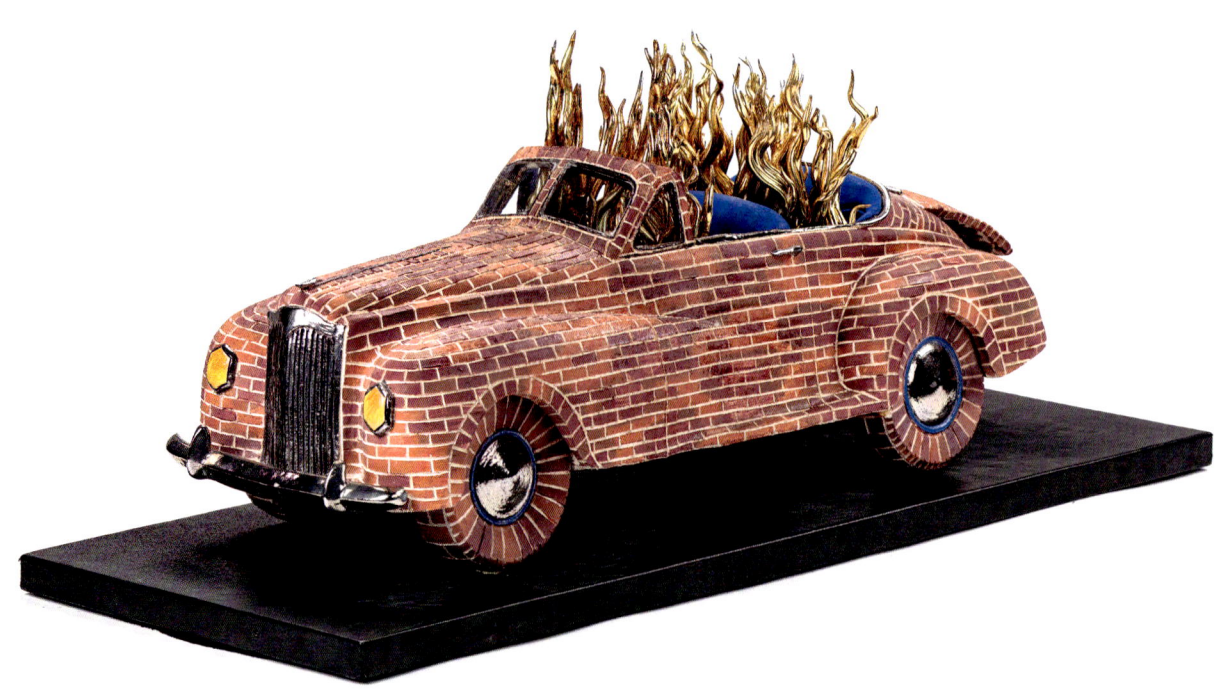

6 **PATTI WARASHINA, Convertible Car Kiln** c. 1971
Earthenware, gold and silver luster glaze, and Plexiglas
14 ½ × 35 ½ × 14 ½ in. (36.8 × 90.2 × 36.8 cm)
Smithsonian American Art Museum, Washington, DC

tors of transmission were Howard Kottler and Patti Warashina, both of whom began teaching there in the mid-1960s. They anchored an impressive group who also included Fred Bauer (who was married to Warashina at the time), Mark Burns, Anne Currier, Margaret Ford, David Furman, and Robert Sperry. Lighton says it never even occurred to her to attend the university, given everything going on in her life. But its faculty often did guest teaching at the Factory, so she had a great deal of exposure to their work and thinking. Given that Lighton had been living out the idea that "the personal is the political" on a daily basis, it is no surprise that Warashina would have made a particularly indelible impression. She is one of those women artists who, when faced with white male patriarchy, simply laughs in its face. Her best-known works, like *Car Kiln*, are hilarious sendups of the

machismo then so prevalent in American ceramics **(fig. 6)**. Warashina's work was also inspiring for its technical mastery, with brickwork that makes even Arneson's look crude in comparison, and flames executed with gleaming metallic luster.

Lighton discovered feminism and ceramic art more or less simultaneously; her first encounters with the medium were already politically charged. In addition to Warashina, she was well aware of Viola Frey, whose monumental figural sculptures explored the panoramic, problematic theater of American gender relations; and of Judy Chicago, who incorporated china painting into a bold and beautiful pageant of liberationist craftsmanship. Lighton also remembers being extremely impressed by Mark Burns, then a graduate student at the University of Washington, when he gave an artist's talk at

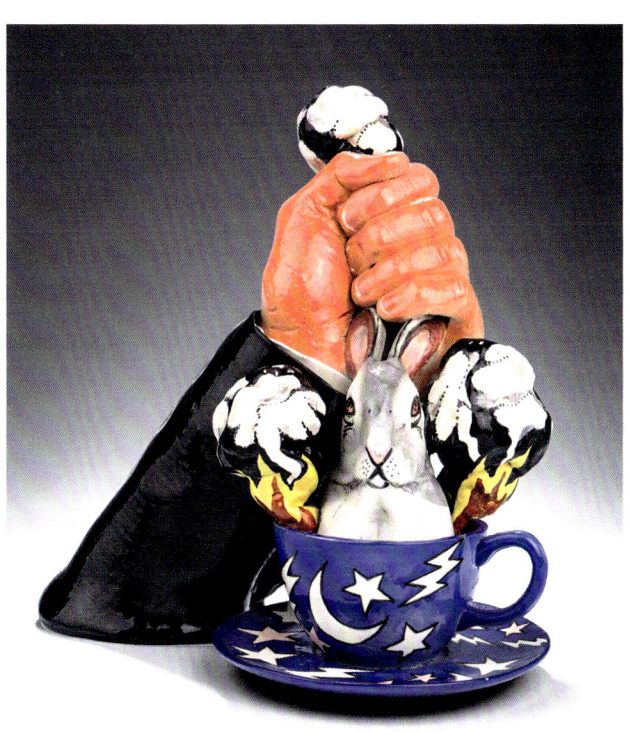

7 **MARK BURNS, Magician's Cup** 1973
Ceramic
8 ⅞ × 9 × 7 in. (22.5 × 22.9 × 17.8 cm)
Smithsonian American Art Museum, Washington, DC

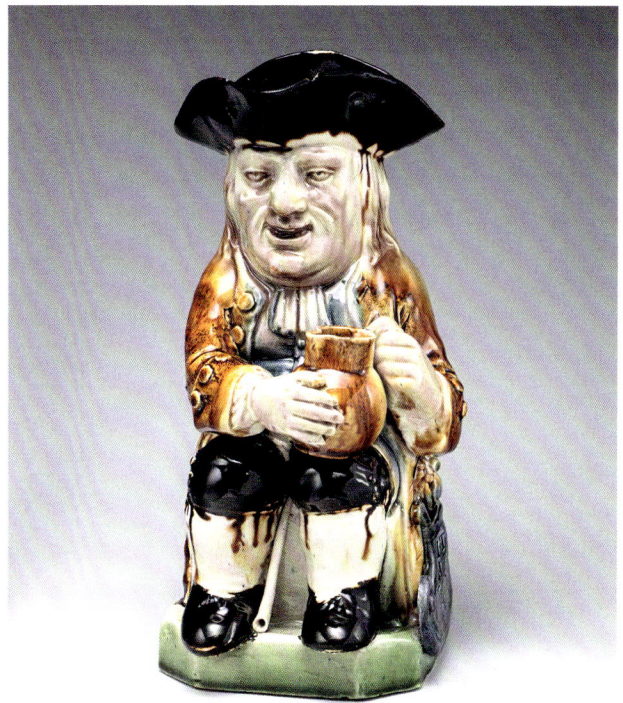

8 **RALPH WOOD THE YOUNGER (1748–1795), Toby jug** c. 1780
Lead-glazed earthenware
Height 9 ¾ in. (24.8 cm)
The Metropolitan Museum of Art, New York, NY

the Factory about his unbridled, queer-positive iconography (fig. 7). With such examples before her, and having decided that "living your life as art leaves little time for making any art," Lighton left the reservation and moved to Bellingham, Washington, committing herself more fully to her studio practice. In 1976 she would move again, this time near the University of Idaho, to take advantage of their ceramic facilities; then in the 1980s she came back home and attended the Kansas City Art Institute. That brought her early years of experimental living to a close. As far as her work was concerned, though, the wild imagination was just beginning.

By 1979, Lighton was exploring several directions in parallel. She made small, funky, organic *Globes*, which anticipated her later botanicals and owe something to Chicago's overtly sexual iconography. She created a se-

ries incorporating fat phallic pencil forms, humorously arranged into crystalline and mountainscape formations. Arguably her most significant early body of work—an appropriate phrase, in this context—combined figuration with wry social commentary. Having learned the process of making and decorating vessel forms, such as teapots, she now used them as a vehicle to depict certain typically American characters: the businessman; the athlete; the upper-class huntsman, with his leather kneepads for riding (a piece, she says, that has something of her father in it); and, drawing on her summer employment experiences, the logger. These portrayals have something in common, perhaps, with the historic ceramics that Lighton had known since childhood, like the "Toby jugs" with which the eighteenth-century British affectionately mocked their own swelling middle

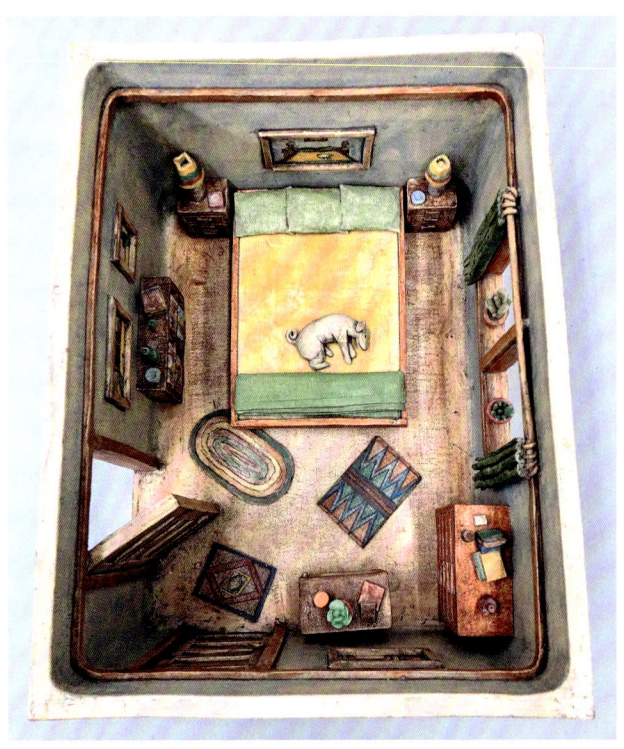

9 **DAVID FURMAN**, The Bedroom 1970
Ceramic, glaze, luster
7 × 9 × 12 in. (17.8 × 22.9 × 30.5 cm)
Private collection

which artists like Arneson, Richard Shaw, and Robert Hudson were embracing both as a technical challenge and a means of evoking the poetry of the physical. The leading exponent of this impulse in Seattle was David Furman, who made beguiling, quietly Surrealist still-life works as well as architectural dioramas—a barber shop, a diner, his own living room. Each is a downbeat little marvel of observation (fig. 9).

Also important in defining the style was the Canadian artist Marilyn Levine, who studied under Voulkos in Berkeley, but took a totally different direction in her work. Her astonishingly convincing imitations of leather objects helped to bring the phenomenon of Superrealism, then enjoying a brief vogue in painting, into ceramics; beyond their wizardly effect, they were also quietly moving tributes to the texture of everyday life and the way that material artifacts register the passage of time and hard use (fig. 10). Levine showed Lighton how to mix fibers into her clay, both strengthening it and giving it a flexible, fabric-like quality. Lighton exploited the technique in works like *Doctor's Bag*—made in 1980 while her mother was sick with cancer. She also made many depictions of clothing, among them *Denim Shirt*, based on a garment that had belonged to her first husband, and *The Secretary*, based on one of her own blouses (the one she wore to her second wedding). These were effectively an indirect form of portraiture—an idea that Levine had also explored— but also relics of Lighton's own experience: reminders of the time when the heiress to a garment business chose to make her life among the denim-clad, footloose and free. "After all," she says, "clothes define the person!"

Over the next decade, she would develop her figural forms further, eventually arriving at a series she called *Building People*. Inspired by specific people—both real and imagined—these works take the form of torsos bearing architectural fragments in place of heads; occasionally they have other apertures, like a stepped porch out front. When she first started making them, the ceramic faculty at KCAI told her they were "trite, insipid and meaningless." Her reaction was to move to the sculpture department. And in fact, they are perhaps Lighton's most

class (fig. 8). Relatively small in scale and simple in execution, they lack the force of Frey's gargantuan polychrome personages, Arneson's savagely satirical portrait busts, Burns' over-the-top parodies, or indeed the coruscating intensity of Lighton's own later politically oriented works. But they compensate with offbeat charm. They are about the small-mindedness of cliché identity, yet are not without sympathy. There isn't a hint of cruelty in them. Rather, a feeling of gentle teasing, of cutting stereotype down to size: "I feel that using humor is a good way to get into someone's head more easily."

With their delight in depicting clothing and other character attributes or "props," Lighton's character vessels also connect to another current in West Coast ceramics of the 1970s, which ran in parallel to the gutbucket materiality of Funk. This was an interest in *trompe l'œil*,

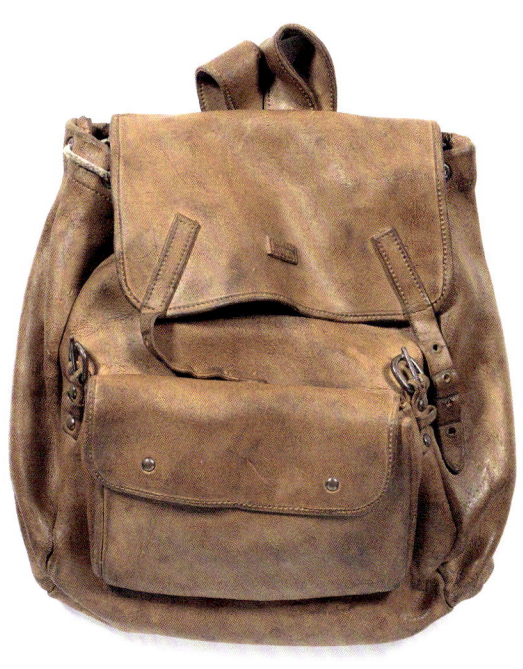

10 **MARILYN LEVINE**, Sand Backpack 1974
Stoneware
20 × 16 ¾ × 5 ⅞ in. (50.8 × 42.5 × 14.9 cm)
The Nelson-Atkins Museum of Art, Kansas City, MO

The circumspect vision of mainstream America that Lighton offers in these figural works has found a more straightforwardly critical pendant in a long series she has made on the theme of garbage. This idea originally came about through her friendship with Bob Berkebile, the founder of Seattle's first recycling center. Moved by his environmental concern, she began to address the detritus of consumer culture through the unexpected means of replicating it, with impressive verisimilitude, as if to say: *just look at this mess.* Lighton's series of works also reflects an important insight of hers: by using clay as a stand-in for other materials, and by arranging objects into a vignette, even one showing random rubbish, she found that she could create a space of suspended disbelief and hence an implied narrative. This was a crucial breakthrough in her artistic development, for it made her not just a sculptor, but also a storyteller, a role that she has occupied ever since.

It all came together in an exhibition she held in 1987, poignantly entitled *And She Did Not Live Happily Ever After… but She Did Live.* By this time, she was at the Kansas City Art Institute, pursuing a mid-career degree. ("My daughter was going away to college," she notes, "so I did, too.") (fig. 11). The exhibition was built around a fic-

psychologically sophisticated works. The first impression one has is of a certain personality type—a general, a housewife, an executive—simply *thinking* about architecture. But then you begin to notice the way that the building is taking over, windows and doors taking the place of eyes and mouths, to dehumanizing and claustrophobic effect. "We talk about spontaneity but we crave conformity," Lighton has written of these works. "Some people are bound so tightly by their habits and the mores of society that they become institutionalized. They are bricked into the death throes of our culture by the trappings, strappings of society." Nor does she exempt herself from this judgment; the most haunting of the *Building People* features the same blouse that appeared in *The Secretary*; the head is an open cage with a noose dangling within.

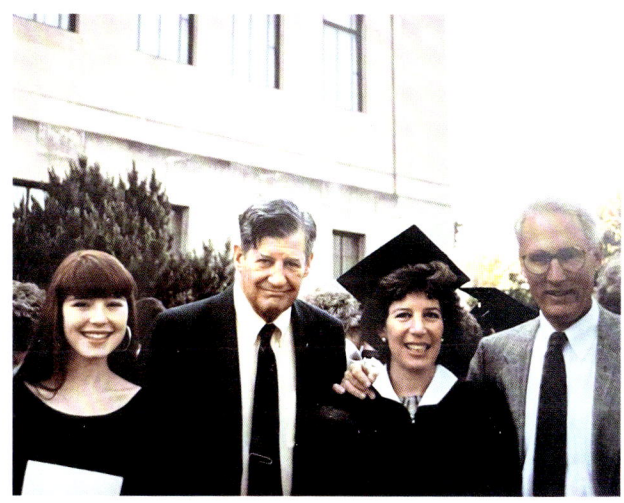

11 Linda's graduation from the Kansas City Art Institute, 1989, with her daughter, Rose; her father, Alfred; and her husband, Lynn

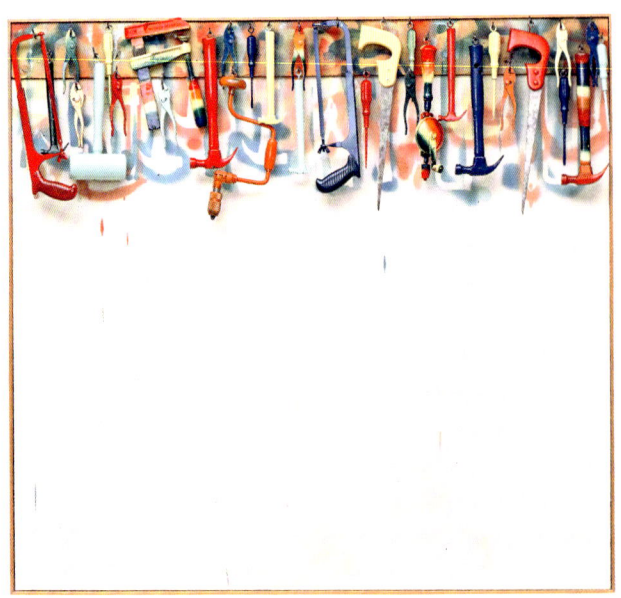

12 **JIM DINE, Five Feet of Colorful Tools** 1962
Oil on unprimed canvas surmounted by a board
on which painted tools hang from hooks
55 ⅝ × 60 ¼ × 4 ⅜ in. (141.3 × 153 × 11.1 cm)
The Museum of Modern Art, New York, NY

tional construct, which at first appears to be that of a long-suffering housewife. Tableaus like *What the Bridal Consultant Never Tells You* have the elliptical compression of a good short story; stylistically, they allude both to classical statuary and to Meissen porcelain centerpieces, implying a combination of nobility and domesticity. That sense of a miniature monument is further enhanced by the furl of cloth that overspills the base, legible as an ordinary rag, but also as a scroll awaiting some proclamation.

Lighton's intentions here were certainly explicitly feminist—the ceramic equivalent of activist efforts to get housework properly recognized and financially compensated (a political project no closer to being realized today than it was then, unfortunately). Other works she made at the time would seem to reinforce this message, like *Laundry*, a simple pile of clothing, rendered in exquisite folds like the drapery of some baroque statue, and the heavily ironic *First Lady*, with its celebratory red-

white-and-blue swags. Nor were these abstract political gestures on Lighton's part; she was putting her own experience as a wife and mother into her art. But matters are also more complicated than that, as we can see from related works like *S&M Cleaning* and *Daddy's Hungry* (both 1987) with their shiny black glaze and constricting belts. These sculptures are—there's no other word for it—kinky, and they unsettle any idea of Lighton's work of the 1980s as earnestly didactic. Like a lot of other feminist art of this period, it is possessed of a devilish sense of humor, a desire not only to critique the oppressive ways of the patriarchy, but also to offer more permissive and more pleasurable, as well as more equitable, alternatives. If that means rubber gloves and squeeze bottles gleaming like patent leather, so be it.

Like a lot of really good storytellers, then, Lighton often says one thing while implying a whole bunch of others. As her work has matured compositionally and technically, it has also deepened in its mechanisms of meaning. She often employs visual puns and double entendre, or treats certain motifs as punchlines while also assigning them allegorical significance. Gas pumps are a good example. They entered her iconographical repertoire in the wake of the 1979 Iranian oil embargo, which had triggered a brief but alarming economic crisis. Lighton lit upon the symbol both as an insignia of environmental degradation and, relatedly, as a would-be emblem of power that could also be read as limp and ineffective, a phallic symbol in the grip of stagflation.

She used monkey wrenches in a similar way, using them to dismantle masculine gender norms. An important sculpture from 1981 shows five of them, variously colored and in black monochrome, radiating from a green-glazed octagonal nut; her skill in imitating various materials is evident in the matte surfaces of the "metal" and the smooth glossiness of the "wood." Lighton called this work *Monkey Wrench Mandala*, poking fun of the cult that some men make of their hand tools (what's going on there, one wonders), while also signaling that the composition was genuinely worthy of extended contemplation. Somewhat in the manner of the Pop artist Jim Dine,

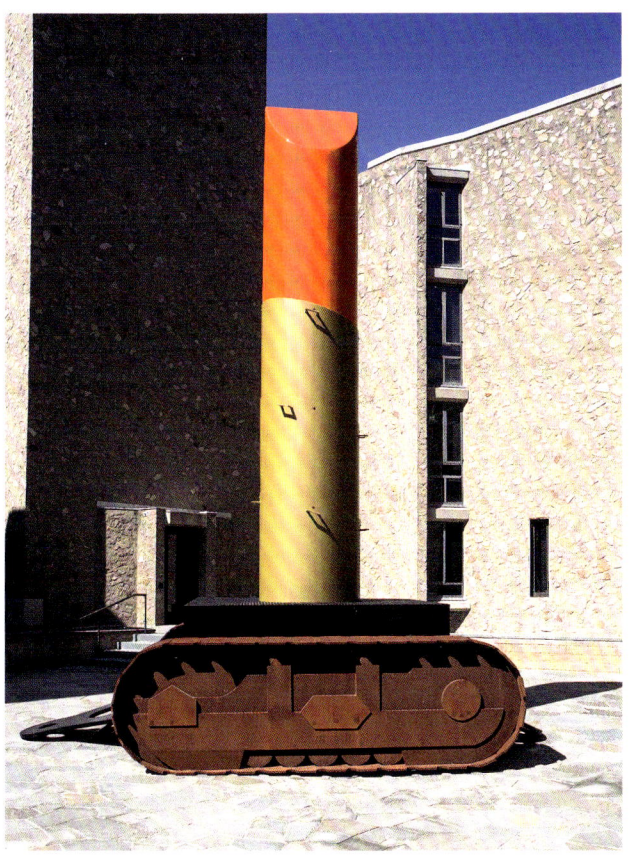

13 **CLAES OLDENBURG**, Lipstick (Ascending) on Caterpillar Tracks
1969, reworked in 1974
Painted steel, aluminum, and fiberglass
264 × 234 × 131 in. (670.6 × 594.4 × 332.7 cm)
Yale University Art Gallery, Gift of the Colossal Keepsake Foundation

juxtapose conventional emblems of masculinity and femininity (**fig. 13**). It was only when her second husband had a terrifying experience while heading to their studio one morning, though, that the subject of gun violence took on primary significance for her. He was driving along—nothing unusual—when suddenly the street exploded with gunfire on both sides: rival gang members, settling scores. He was unhurt, fortunately, but two people were killed. The frightening incident focused Lighton's attention on the ongoing tragedy of firearms in America. Kansas City, she learned, was the fifth most dangerous city in the whole country; what her husband had witnessed was so commonplace that it didn't even warrant news coverage. Something, she knew, was deeply wrong. "With this many guns," she liked to joke, "we should be the safest country on Earth!"

With her customary energy, Lighton threw herself into the cause, helping to circulate petitions in favor of gun control and using her connections to personally lobby congressional representatives. She also responded in her art. Her 2012 exhibition *Taking Aim*, held at Sherry Leedy Contemporary Art in Kansas City, was the first of a series of projects taking on the loaded subject. She created elaborate, monumental compositions that called into question Americans' tendency to worship firearms, while at the same time commemorating the victims. *I Don't Want a Bullet to Kiss Your Heart* (2012) is a sort of anti-triumphal arch, with twin piles of armament towering into the sky. A pair of works entitled *Thoughts & Prayers* (2018) adopt the format of funeral wreaths; one is glazed in sadomasochistic red and black, the other bleached like a pile of bones.

Lighton has always been attracted to the extremes; she takes things all the way, in whatever direction she travels. There is no better indication of this trait than the fact that, even as she was creating her dark and outraged works on gun violence, she was simultaneously making works that were their exact antithesis: botanical sculptures that are luxuriant, lush, and lyrical. Even if she had made nothing else in her career, this extraordinary and extensive body of work would make her one of contem-

she did indeed bestow a strangely iconic power on the wrenches, treating them as placeholders for complex, undigested issues around gender and class (**fig. 12**).

In retrospect, Lighton's gas pumps and monkey wrenches can be seen as precedents to her later, more extended exploration of another, far more problematic, item in the arsenal of masculinity: the gun. She was quite conscious of this association—in one work, she even set two "pearl-handled" wrenches like dueling pistols. A few years later, she doubled down on this gender dynamic in works like *Bullet Belt* (1985) and *Love and War: The Ammunition* (1986), which, with a nod to Claes Oldenburg,

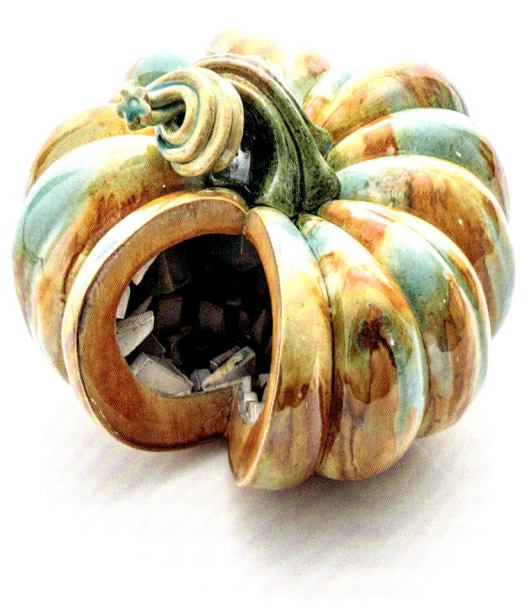

14 **KATE MALONE, Crystal Filled Pumpkin** 2023
Crystalline-glazed stoneware
Height 9 ½ in. (24.1 cm), diameter 12 ⅝ in. (32.1 cm)

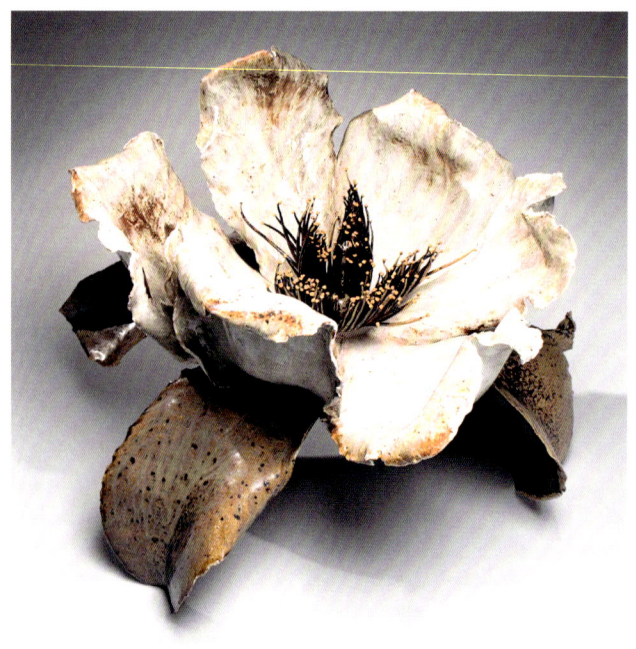

15 **SUGIURA YASUYOSHI, Pseudo Camellia** 2019
Glazed stoneware
15 ¾ × 21 ⅝ × 21 ⅝ in. (40 × 54.9 × 54.9 cm)

porary ceramics' most generative figures, an American counterpart to Britain's Kate Malone or Japan's Sugiura Yasuyoshi (figs. 14, 15). Like those artists, Lighton takes actual plant life as a point of departure; she had, after all, lived off the land, and has studied vegetal morphology closely. In the studio, though, she channels all this knowledge into a flood of fantasy. "How would I visualize desire, the life force: a dangerous beauty entailing seduction, sexual prowess and moaning hormones?" she asked herself. And here was her answer:

> I want to celebrate the spirit of life. The work two-stepping towards figuration, beckoning the viewer to come closer, come hither. Oh my God, have I gone over the line? Is this Baroque-a-go-go? I wish my work to have colors as soft and slippery as a satin quilt. Taste the effervescent tingle of pink. Succulent!

It's a brilliant passage of writing, fully in keeping with the energies of the work it describes. They do, indeed, veer in the direction of the much-too-much. Flowers, after all, are the sex organs of the botanical world; her ecstatic celebration of their forms could easily come across as quasi-pornographic, self-indulgent, or inadvertently comic. But Lighton is far too good an artist for that. Like Georgia O'Keeffe before her, she balances voluptuousness with formal intelligence (fig. 16).

Very early in her career, Lighton adopted china painting as one of her signature techniques. Rather than using underglaze colors, which are usually favored by studio potters, she would paint mineral pigments over the glaze and then re-fire the piece at a relatively low temperature. This method is usually regarded as merely decorative, and is mainly practiced by amateurs; but as mentioned above, Lighton had also seen it deployed to great effect by Judy Chicago, including in Chicago's fa-

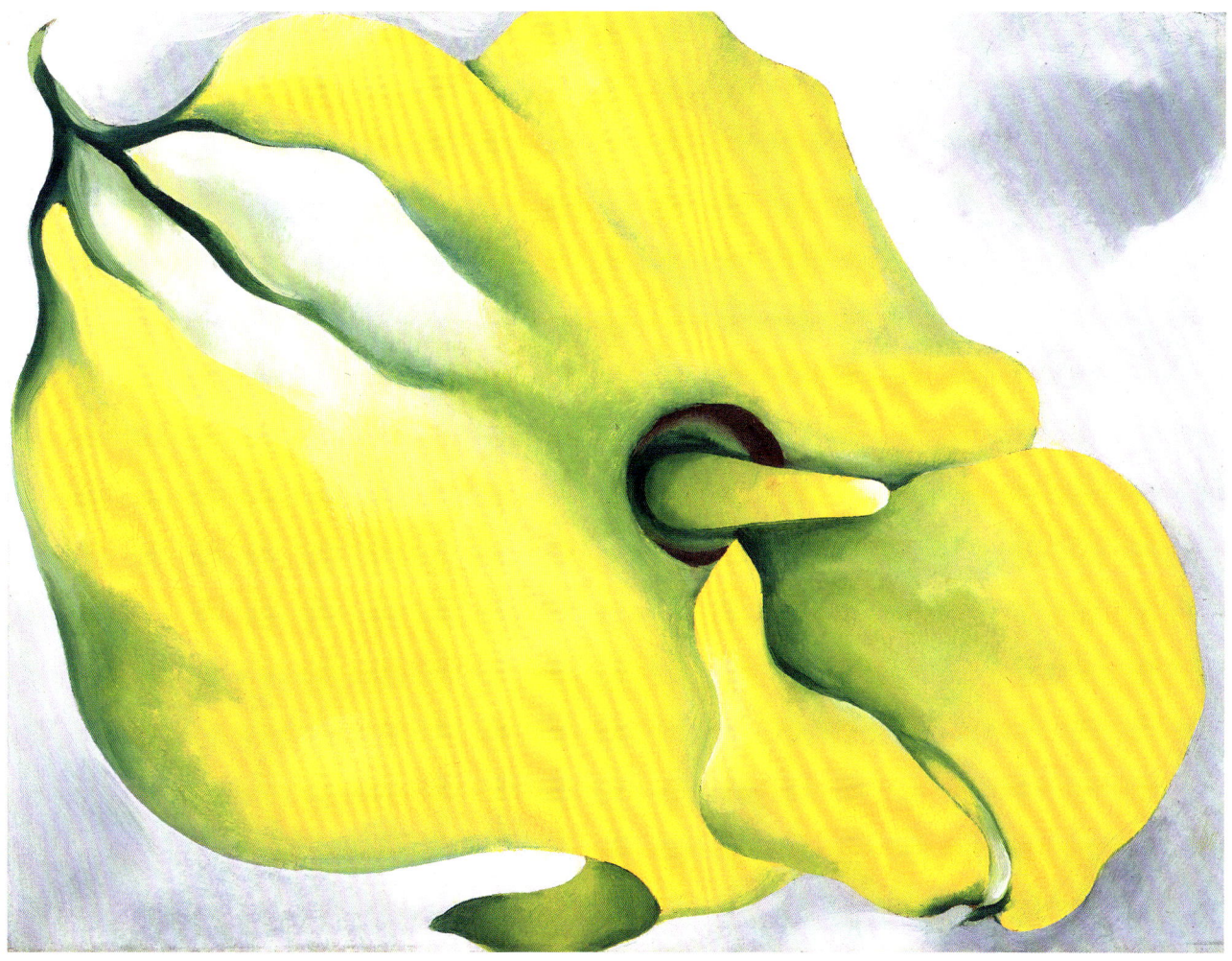

16 **GEORGIA O'KEEFFE,** Yellow Calla 1926
Oil on fiberboard
9 ¼ × 12 ½ in. (23.5 × 31.8 cm)
Smithsonian American Art Museum, Washington, DC

mous (and infamous) *Dinner Party*. Lighton saw in it a great potential to achieve luminosity—a light that seems to come from within—and subtle polychromatic effects. ("I can snuggle into a sensuous pink," she has written, "as if it were a soft, rose-scented satin quilt.") She made a study both of the history and technical repertoire of china painting, looking at everything from imperial Chinese wares to Limoges porcelains to the American Arts and Crafts Movement. Many of these precedents them-

selves featured floral iconography, an additional prompt to explore.

Lighton's work certainly is impressive in its technical wizardry—she layers paints, lusters, and glazes to achieve her subtle surfaces, firing each piece up to ten times to achieve the effects she is after—but what makes her work unique in the ceramic tradition is its gutsy, primordial energy, alive to the complex, multisensory landscape of desire. "I have tried to make my work smell," she

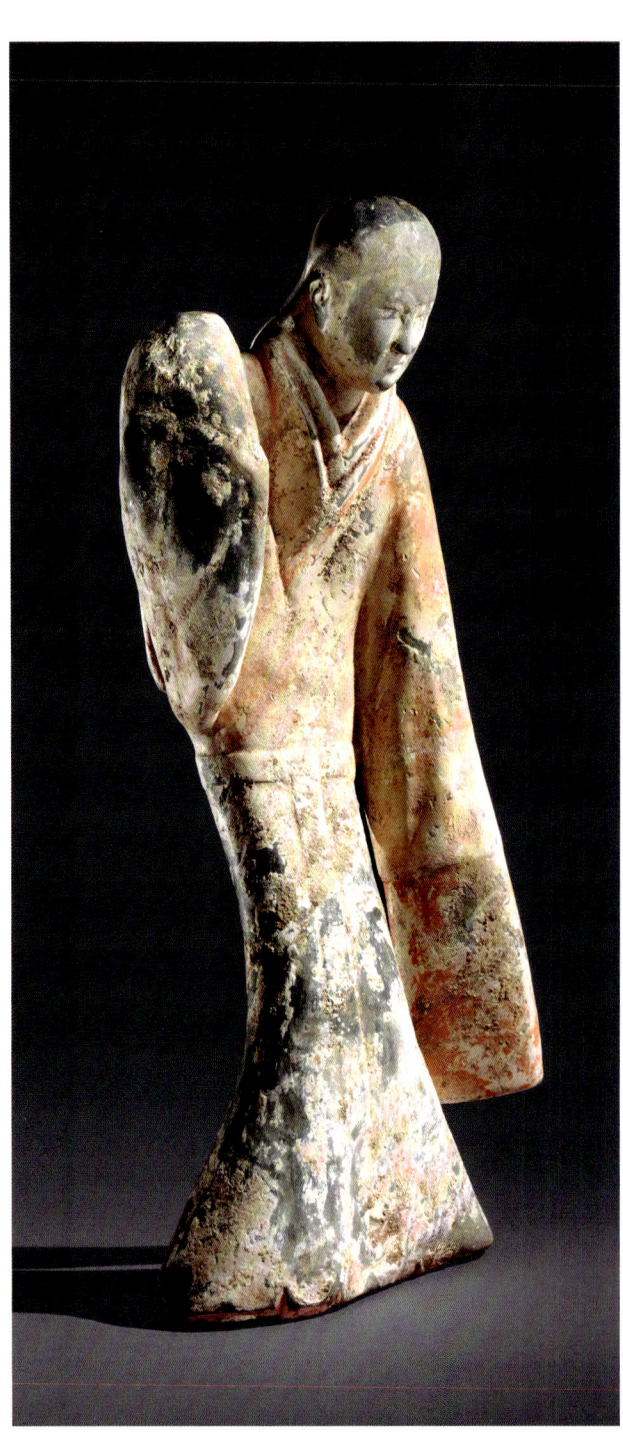

17 **Female Dancer, Western Han dynasty** 2nd century BCE
Earthenware with slip and pigments
Height 21 in. (53.3 cm)
The Metropolitan Museum of Art, New York, NY

has written. "Oysters, seaweed, the salty metallic taste of blood and rusted iron are scents I have in mind… the depth of a plum red, the languid pulsing of purple, the lustful heat and dank smell of moldering red, pulsing blood and muscle underneath. The satin quilted lofted softness of creamy peach, with just a bit of tartness." Steamy stuff, this—she has even added a custom-made scent to an exhibition to reinforce the sensory impression—and the sculptures that Lighton has made more than live up to it. She often plunges us headlong into a moment of apparent transformation, as in her wonderful *Divas*, which call to mind the unfurling forms of ancient Chinese tomb figures, but replace their chaste formality with explicit seductiveness **(fig. 17)**. They perform for us, preening and prancing, alternately veiling themselves and opening themselves to our prying eyes. Leaves and arms, stamens and tongues, lips and petals, tendrils and fingers are all conflated, conjuring a pan-species exploration of the sensual.

In related works, Lighton incorporates more unsettling elements—pointed spikes, tumescent shafts, bumpy accretions—equally redolent of a sea bed and a sex shop. She clearly loves making these works, and has been prolific in doing so, giving them a wondrous variety of shapes and scales. Some lie horizontally like odalisques, others stand proud; still others hang in gardenlike profusion from the ceiling, illuminated from within. Not to get too Freudian about it, but if Lighton's confrontation with gun violence sees her contending with America's death drive, then in her botanical works, we are gifted with a manifestation of the erogenous and erotic—the instinctive impulses from which all life, that most precious of things, ultimately springs.

What else? Plenty. I have not so much as touched on Lighton's philanthropic work, which is devoted to forging cross-cultural understanding through sponsoring almost two hundred international artistic residencies, or her own extensive travels around the globe, which have done so much to nurture her artistic development. (She likes a quotation from Mark Twain: "Travel is fatal to prejudice, bigotry and narrow-mindedness.") She has

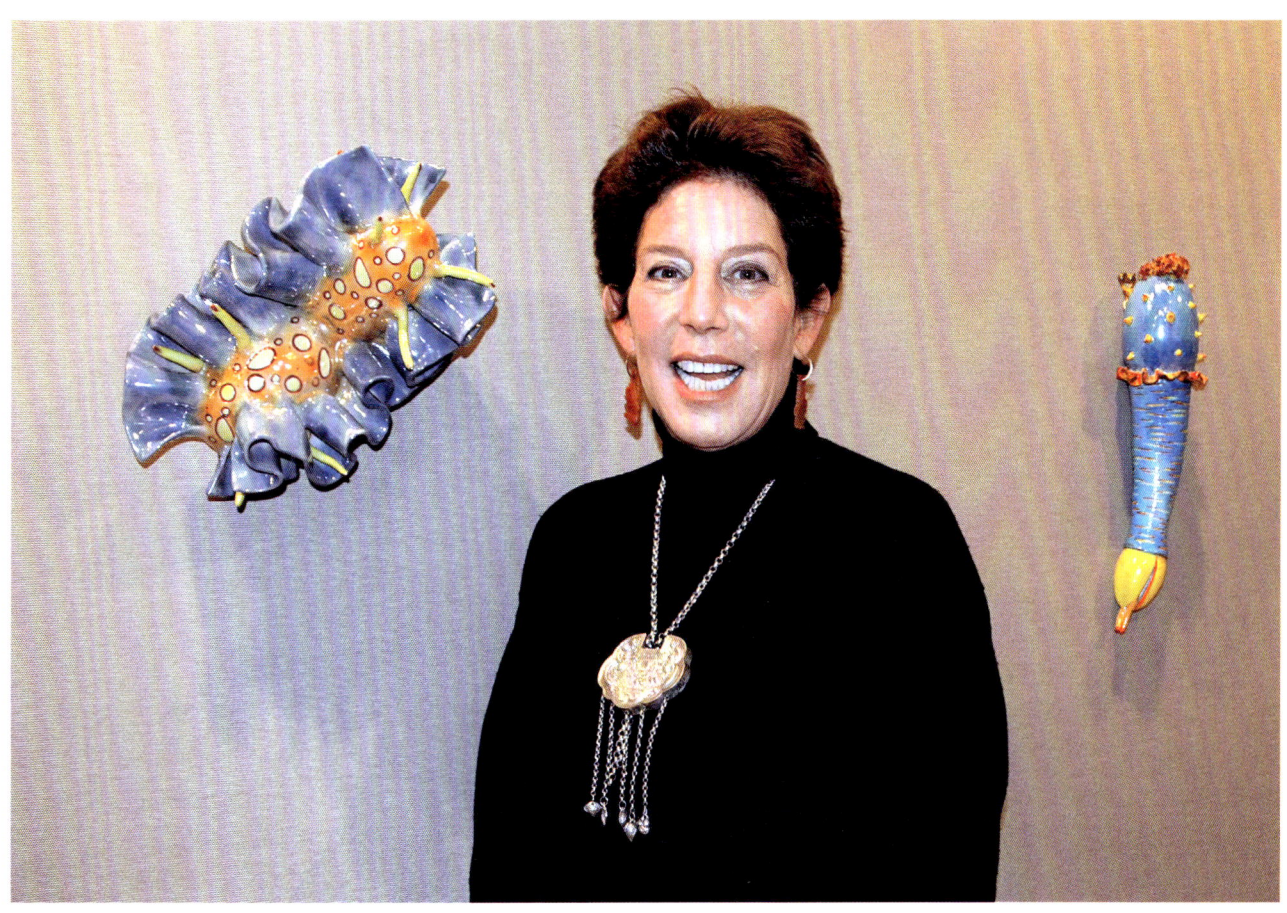

18 Lighton at her exhibition *Boundless Joy*, Carter Arts Center, Penn Valley Community College, 2008

also helped bring to fruition the One Percent for Art program in Kansas City, helped to pass the bi-state cultural tax, helped to develop the Kansas City Contemporary Art Space (later the Leedy-Voulkos Art Center), and supported Young Audiences of Kansas City, the Kansas City Ballet, and Parsons Dance Company in New York.

Nor I have said anything about her exquisite drawings in colored pencil; or the many ceramic ribbons that she has made, as if giving herself little awards for keeping going; or her beautiful, epic tile mural for the Kansas City airport, which brings the outdoors in, a breath of fresh air; or the time she started putting bananas in her sculptures, half-peeled (though perhaps this speaks for itself).

There you have it; Linda Lighton's energies cannot be so easily contained. Like all her great topics—nature, fashion, violence, sexuality—her art is in a state of constant change, growing, bursting, imagining itself anew. She's an artist who keeps no secrets, but then, she doesn't need to. "I want to make gorgeous, elegant and sublime work," she says, "but I have seen the world. I need to laugh." And she'll always have more to tell (fig. 18).

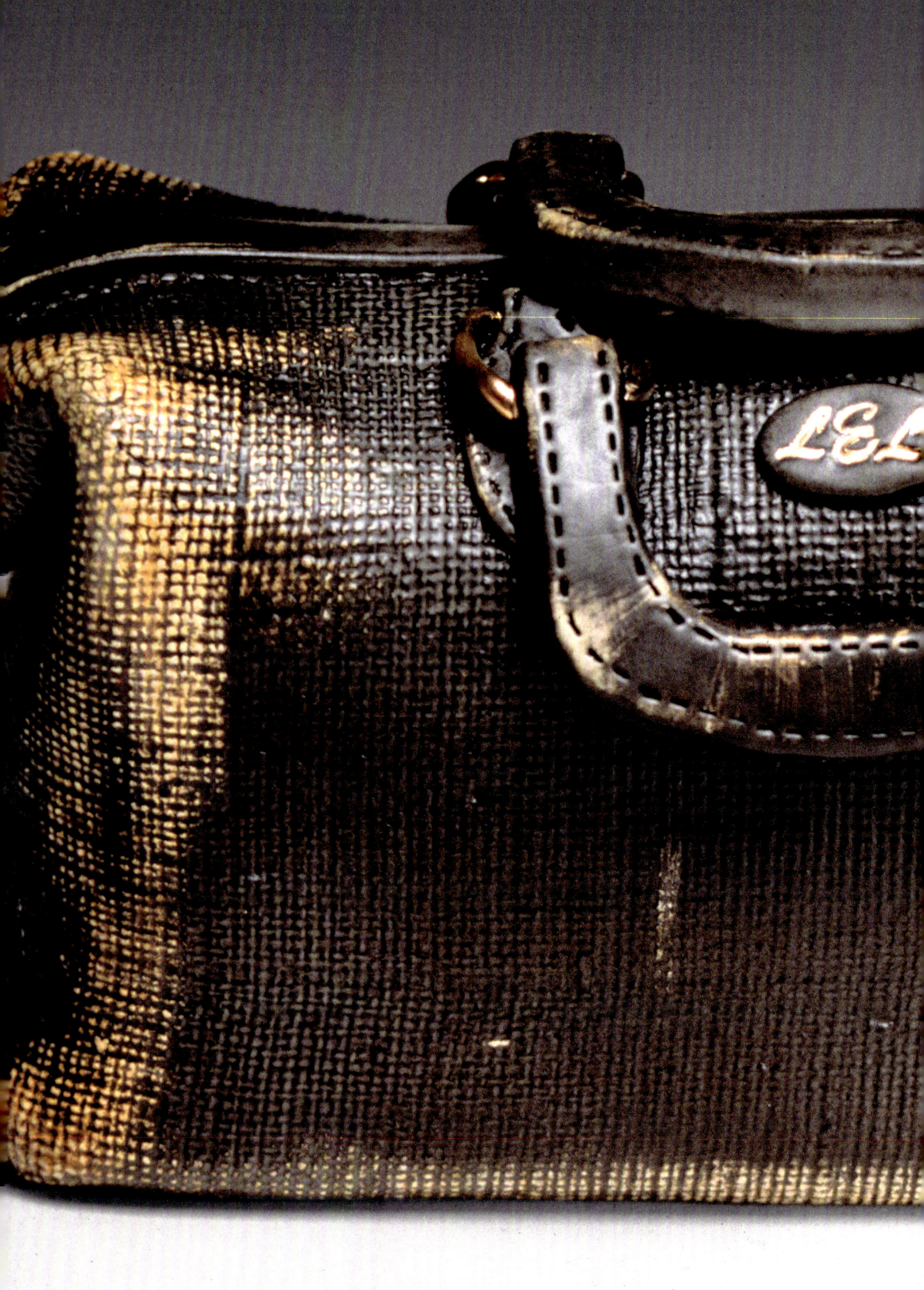

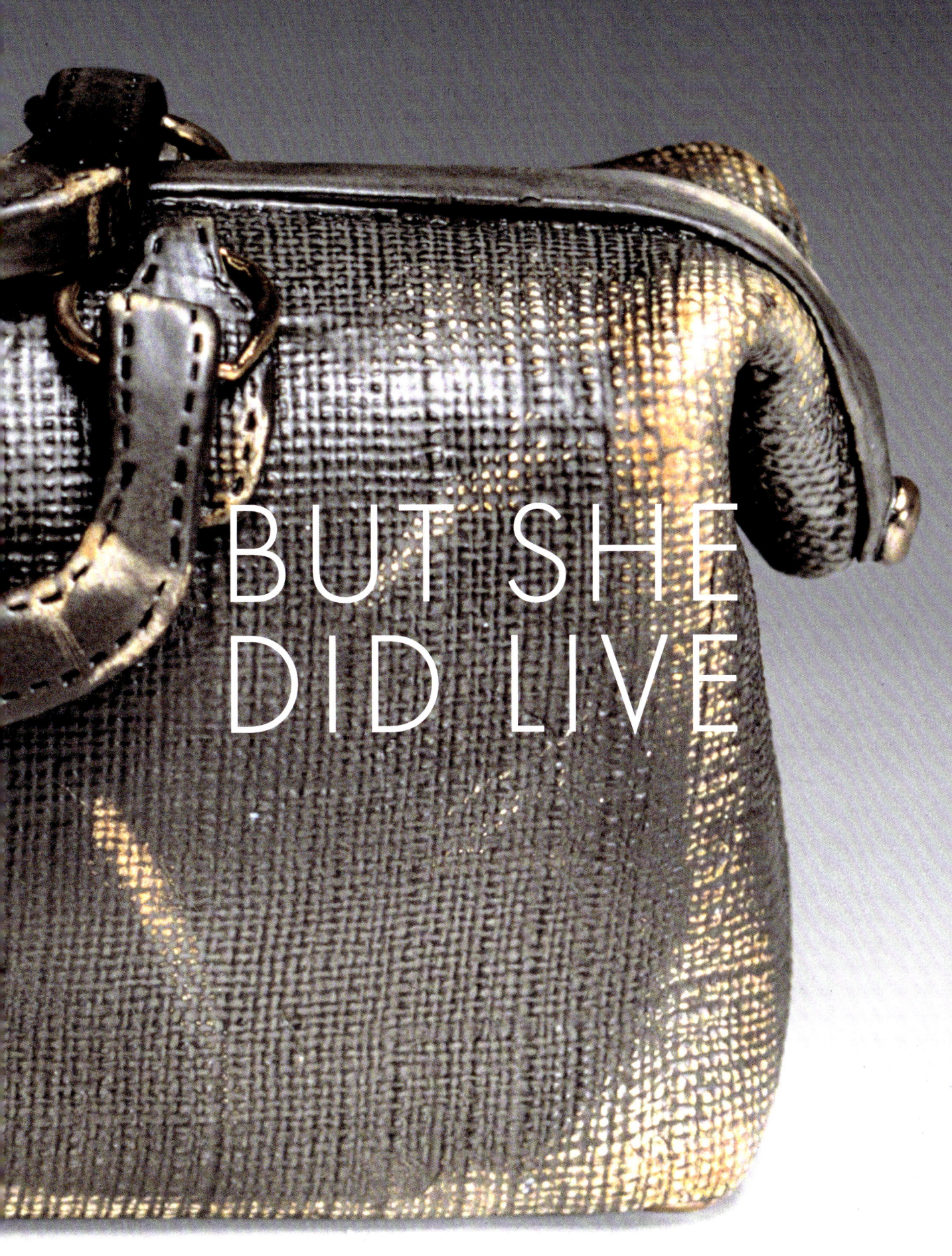

BUT SHE
DID LIVE

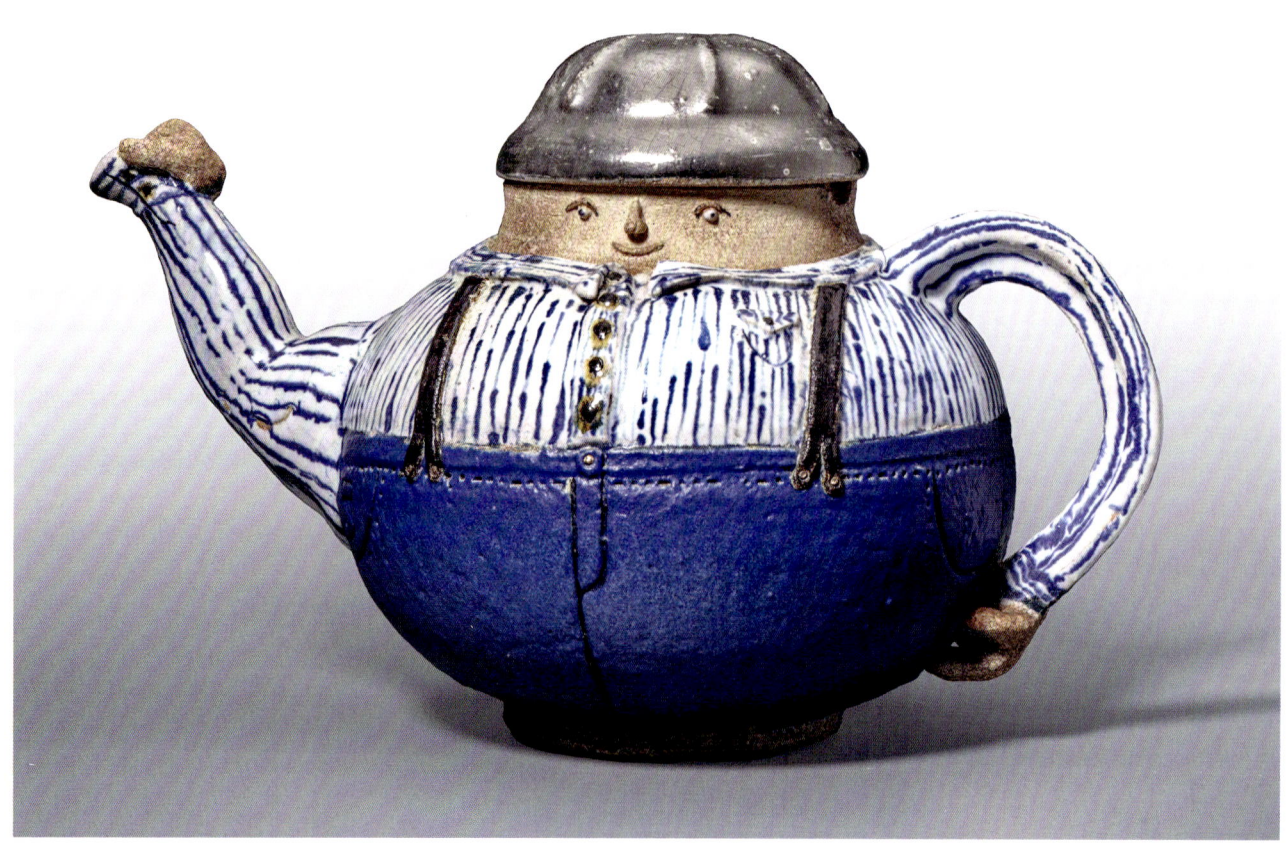

Logger Teapot 1978
Glazed stoneware with underglaze and luster
7 × 11 × 7 in. (17.8 × 27.9 × 17.8 cm)

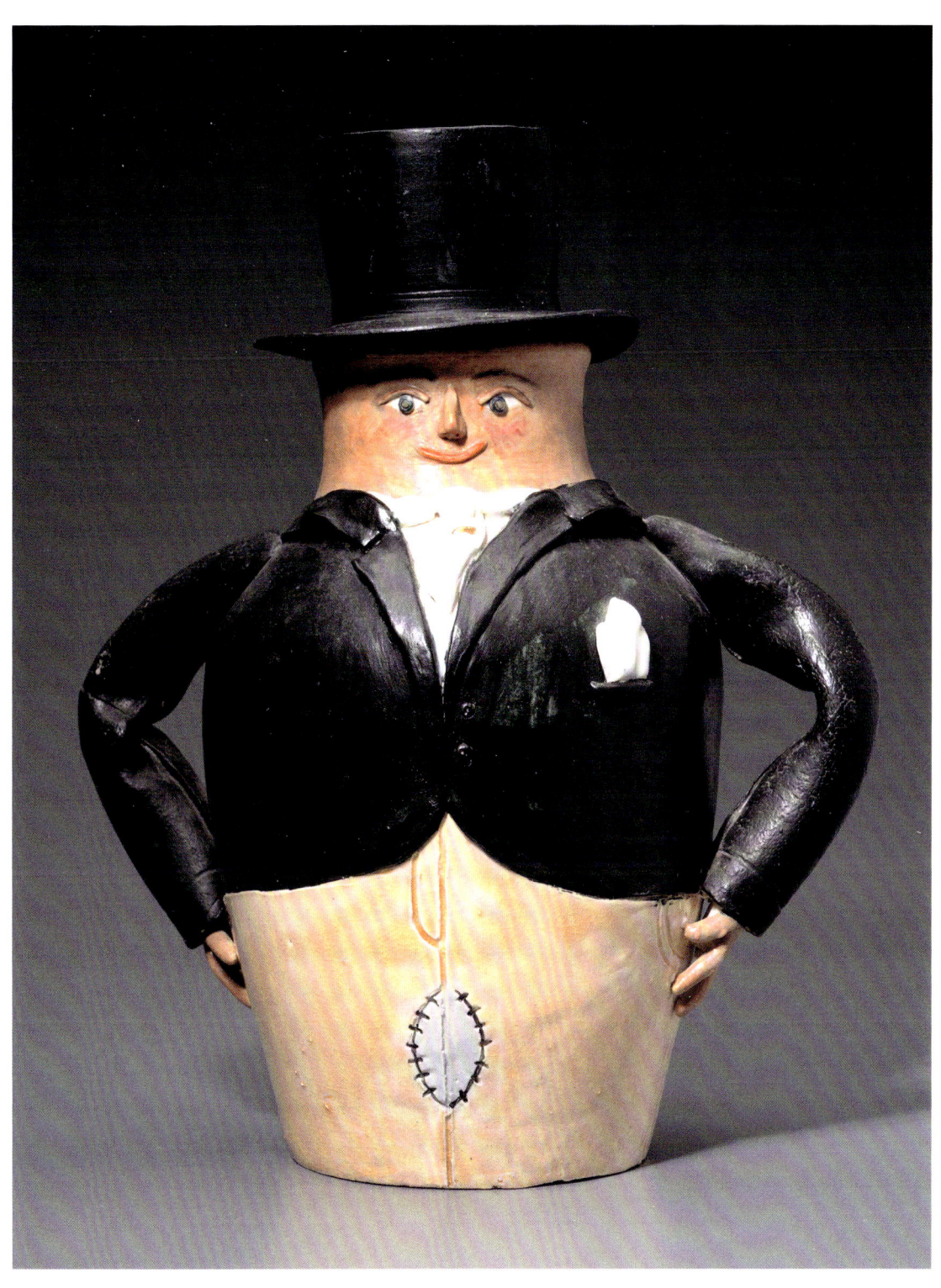

Huntsman Teapot 1979
Glazed stoneware with underglaze, china paint and luster
8 ½ × 8 × 5 in. (21.6 × 20.3 × 12.7 cm)

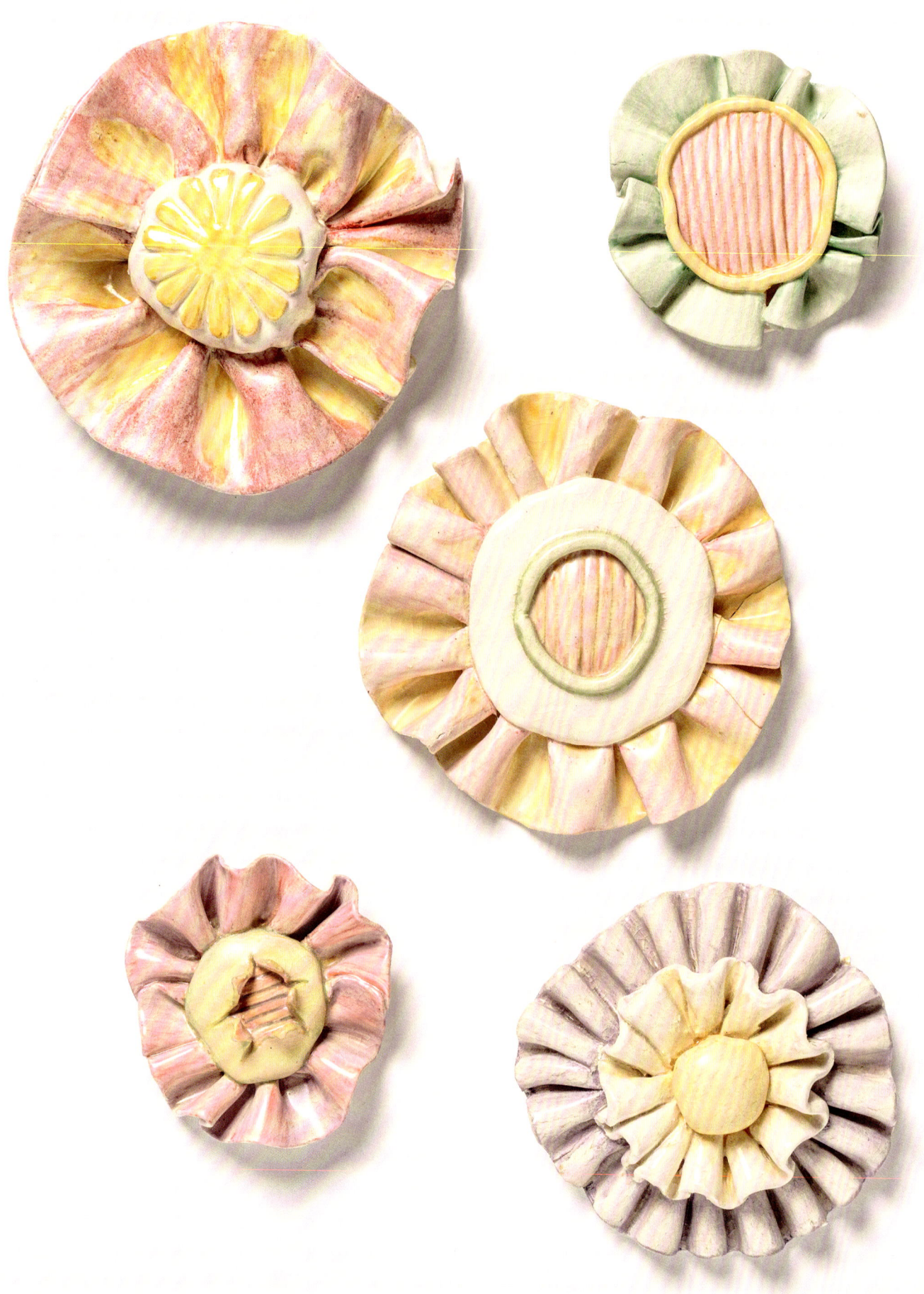

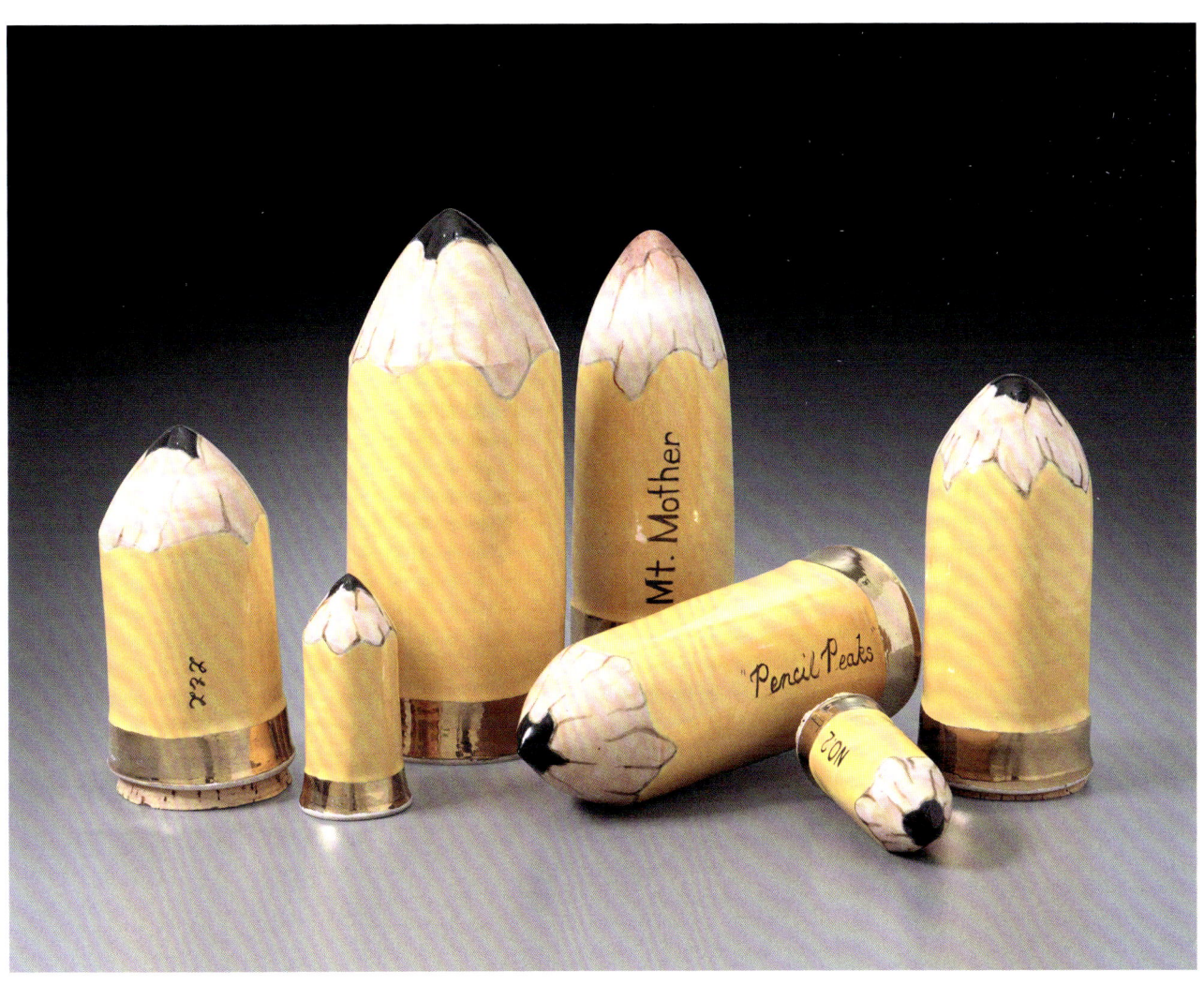

Left page
Ribbons 1978
Glazed earthenware with china paint and luster
Each approx. 5 ¼ × 5 ¼ × ½ in. (13.3 × 13.3 × 1.3 cm)

Pencil Peaks 1978
Glazed earthenware with china paint, luster and cork
Overall: 9 × 17 × 10 in. (22.9 × 43.2 × 25.4 cm)

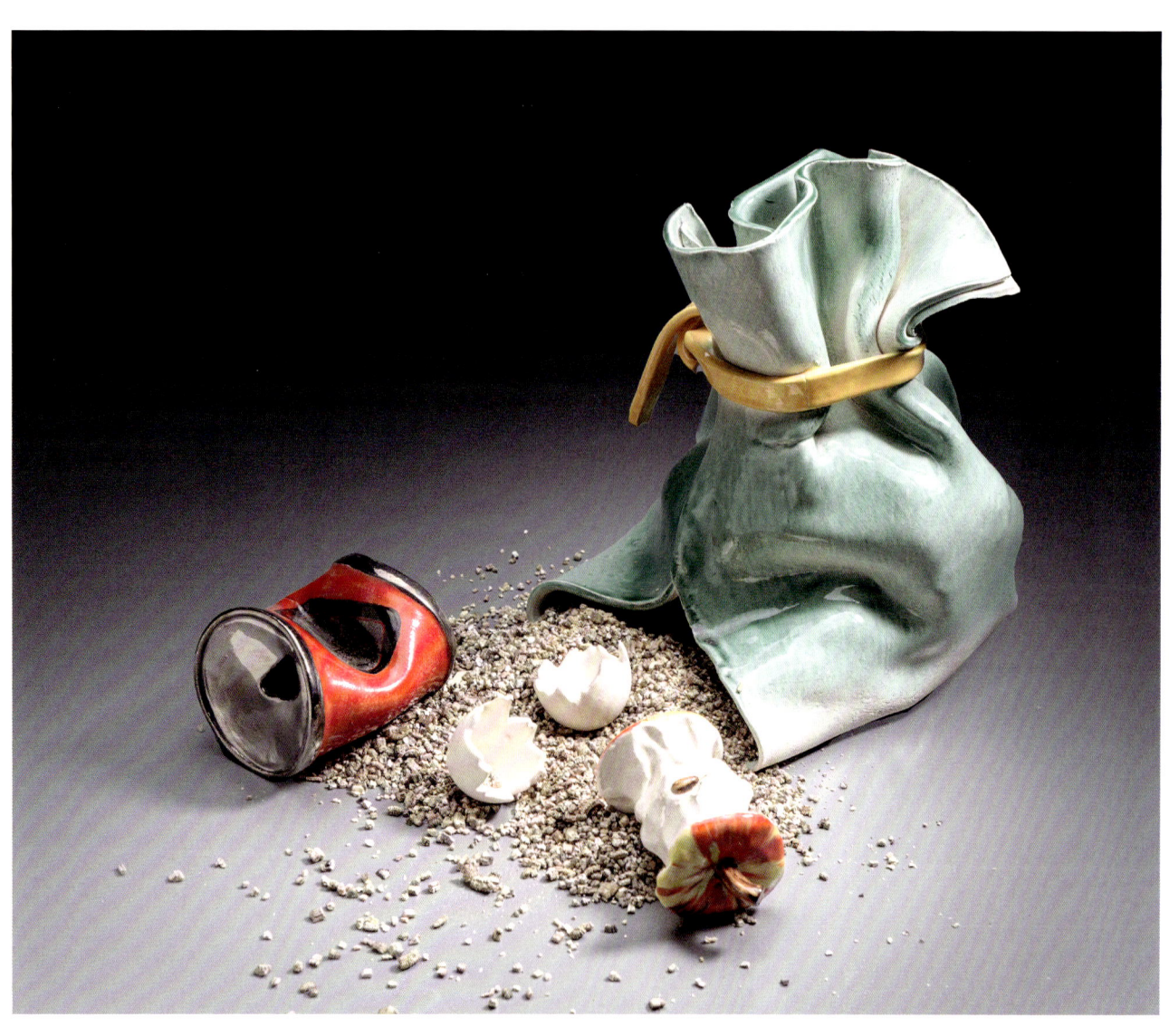

KC Trash 1980
Glazed earthenware with china paint, luster and vermiculite
Overall: 9 × 19 × 8 in. (22.9 × 48.3 × 20.3 cm)

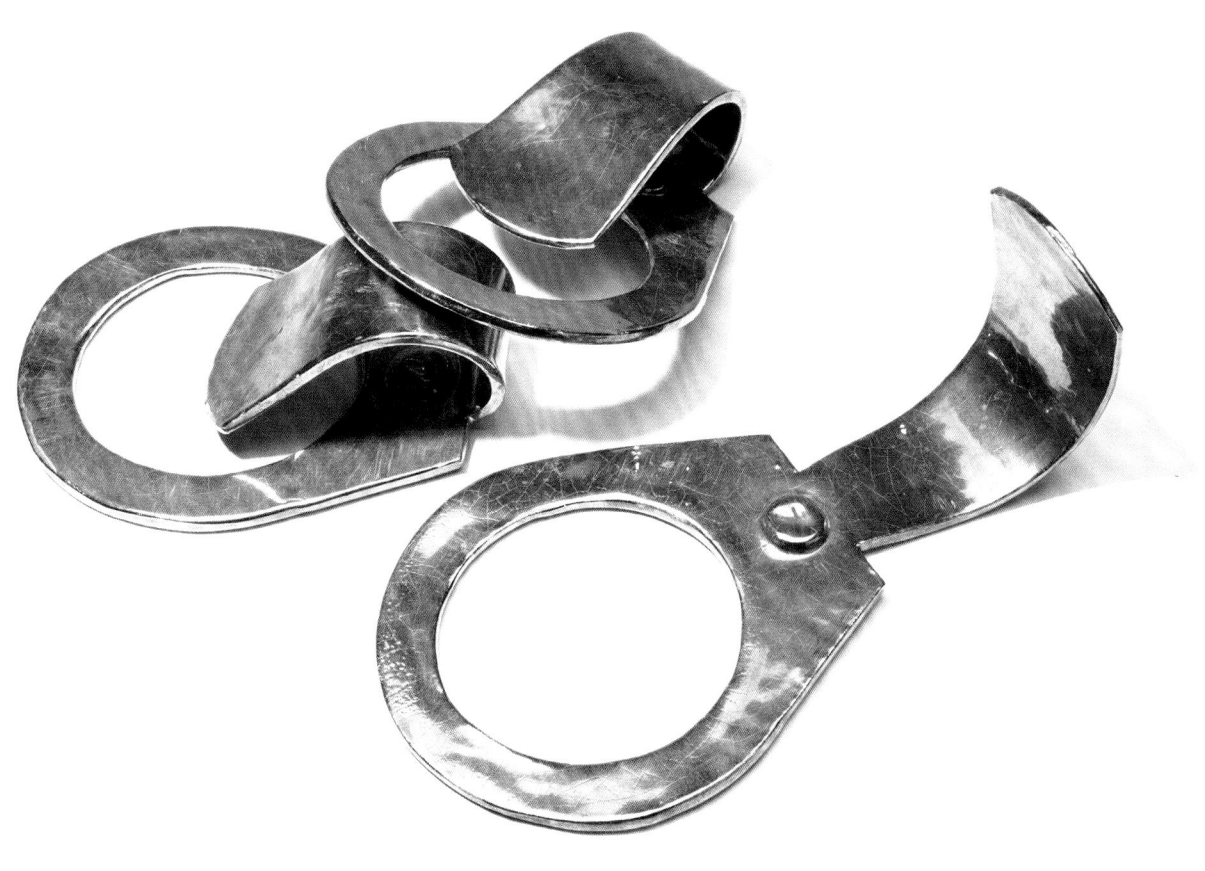

Pop Tops 1981
Glazed earthenware with luster
Largest: 3 ¾ × 5 ½ × 10 in. (9.5 × 14 × 25.4 cm)

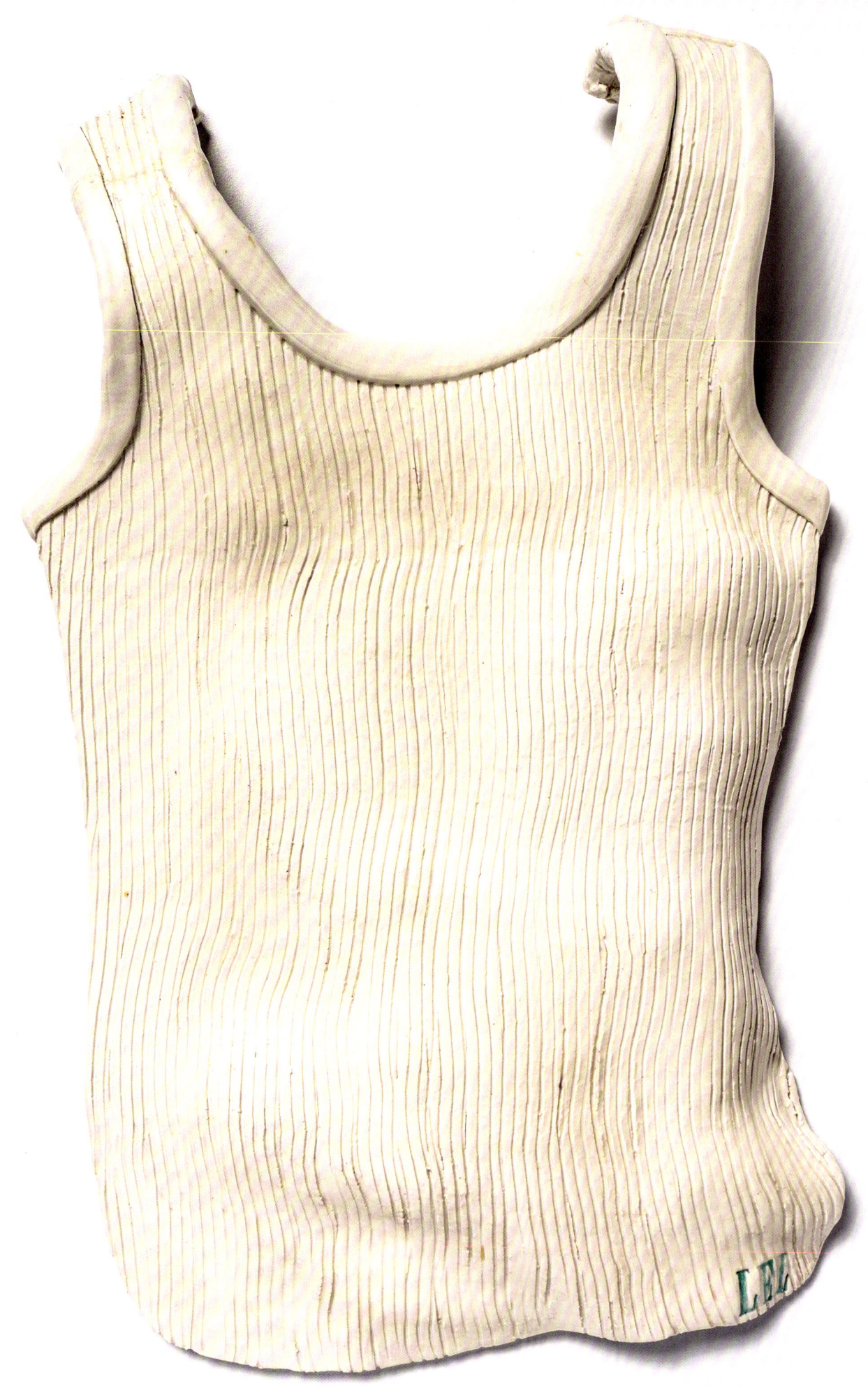

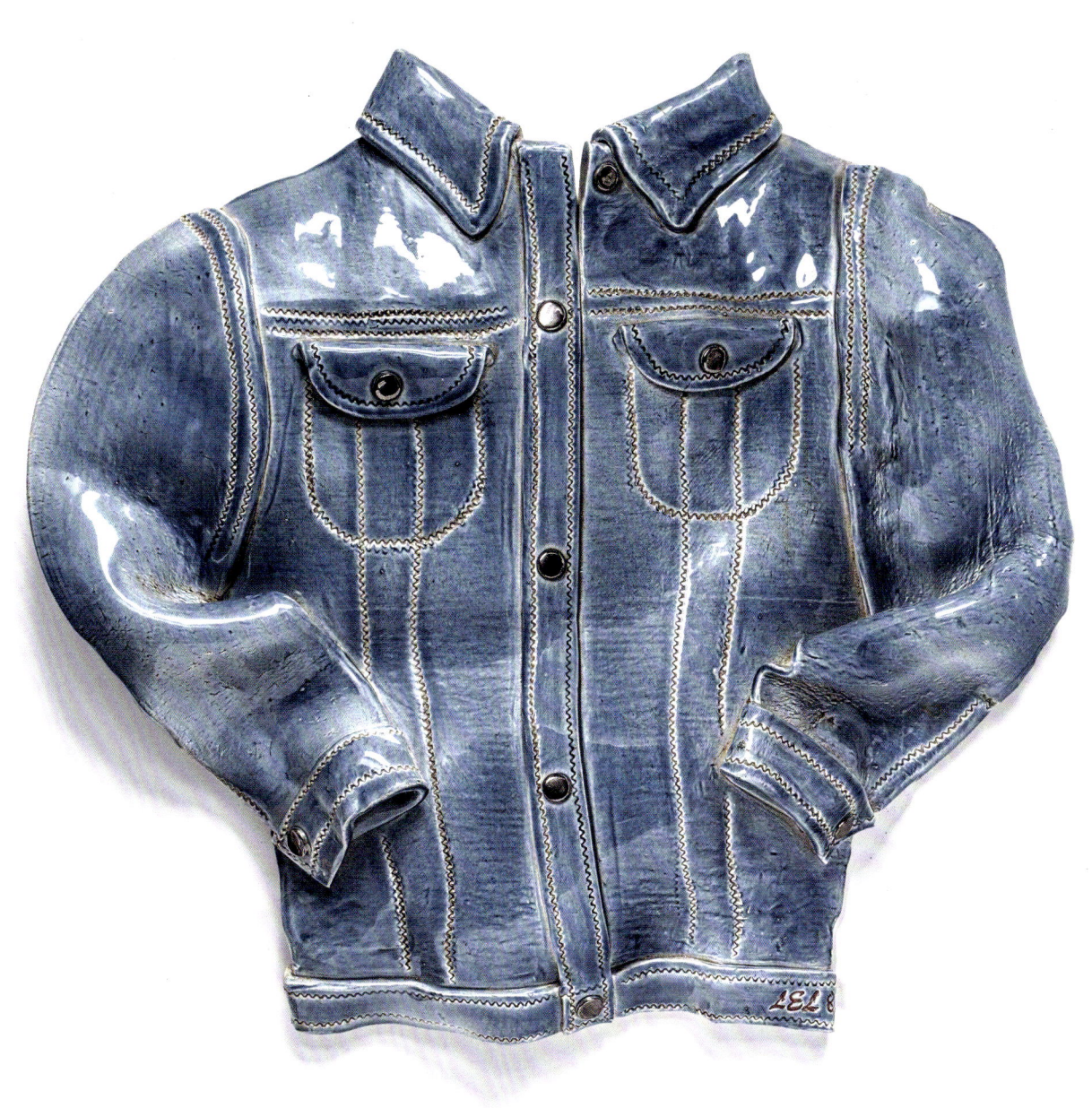

Left page
Dude 1981
Glazed earthenware
19 × 13 × 3 in. (48.3 × 33 × 7.6 cm)

Blue Jean Jacket 1981
Glazed earthenware with luster
18 × 20 × 3½ in. (45.7 × 50.8 × 8.9 cm)

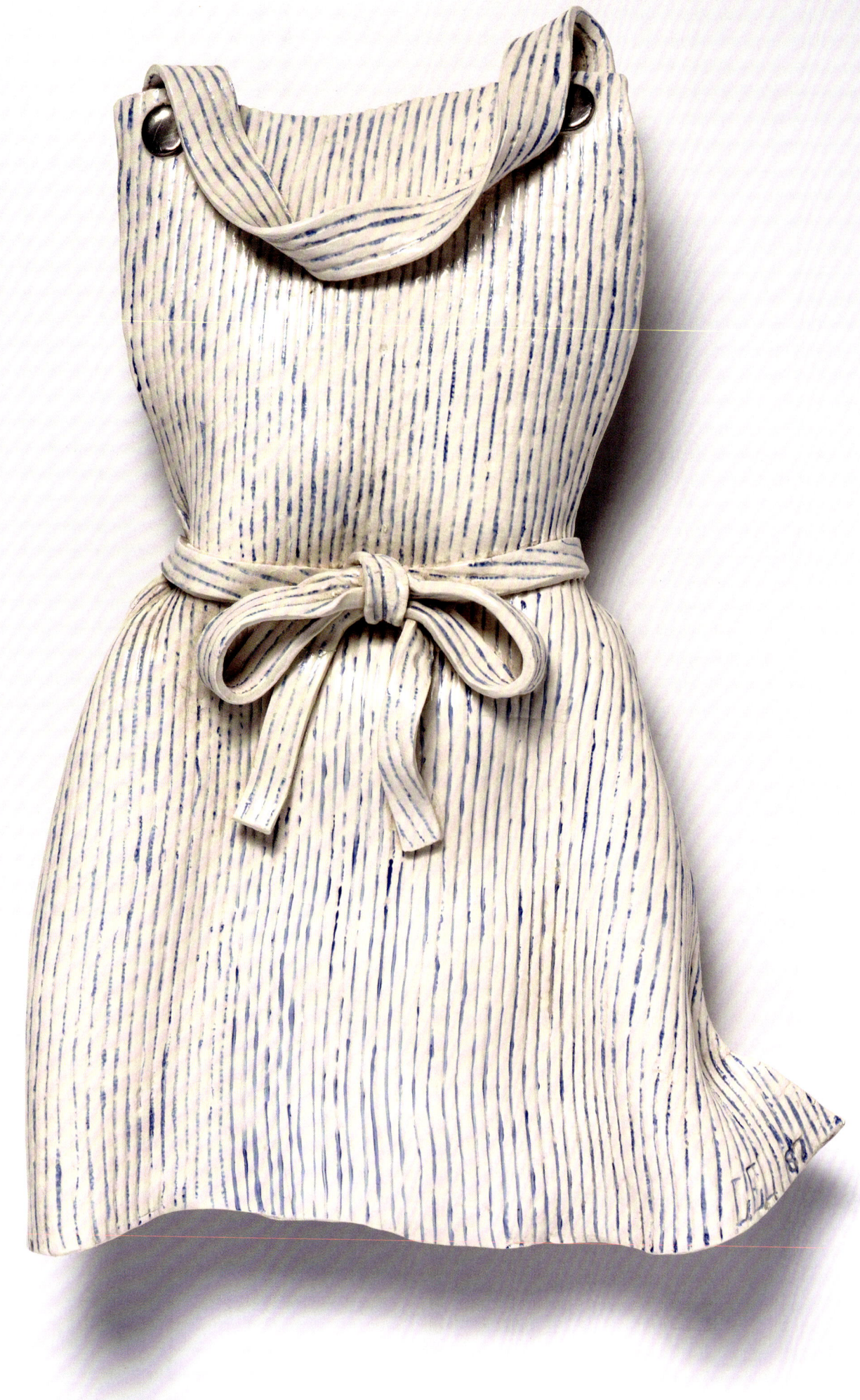

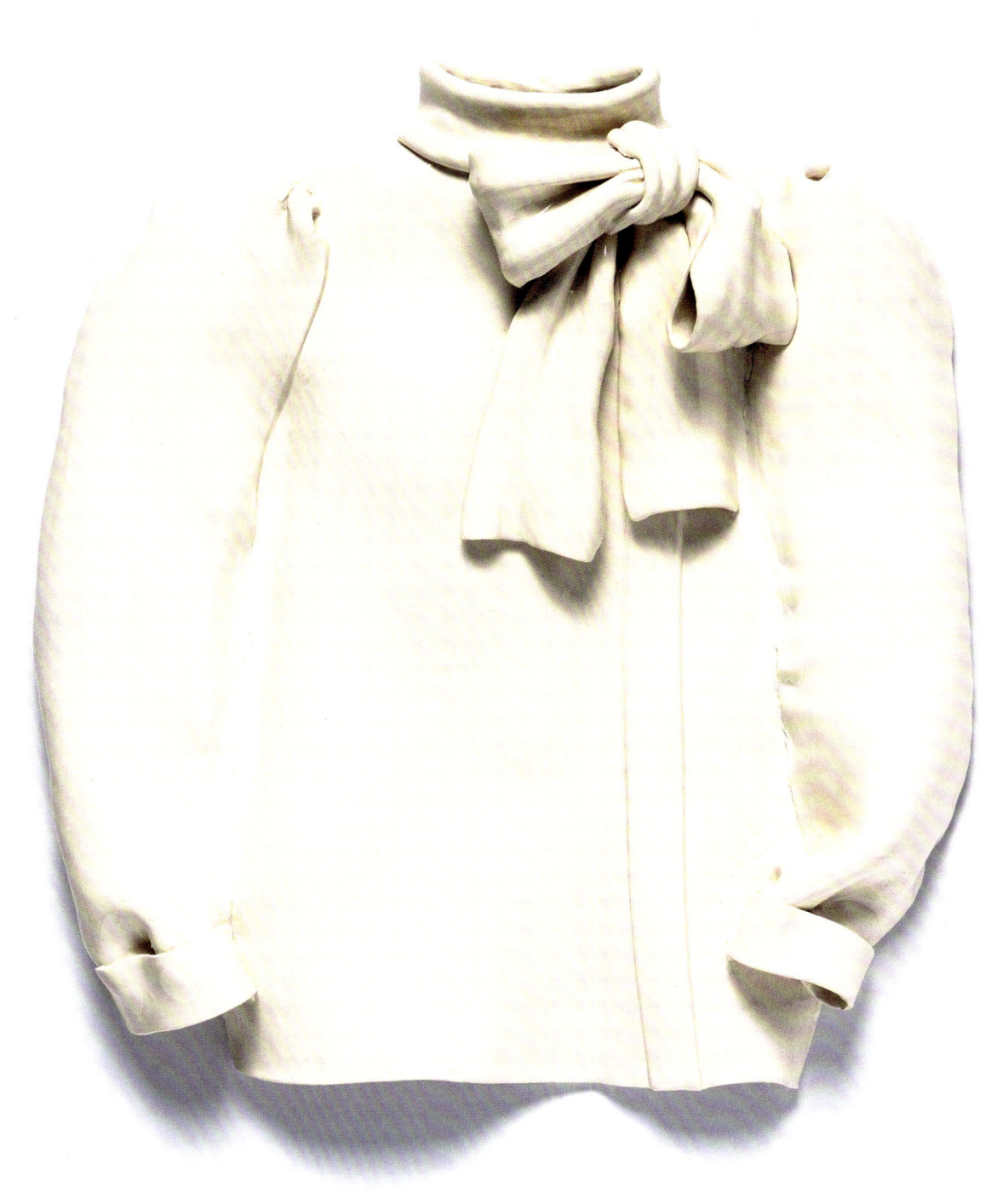

Left page
Apron 1987
Glazed earthenware with china paint and luster
21 × 14 ½ × 4 ½ in. (53.3 × 36.8 × 11.4 cm)

The Secretary 1986/2023
Glazed earthenware
20 × 18 ⅓ × 3 ½ in. (50.8 × 46.6 × 8.9 cm)

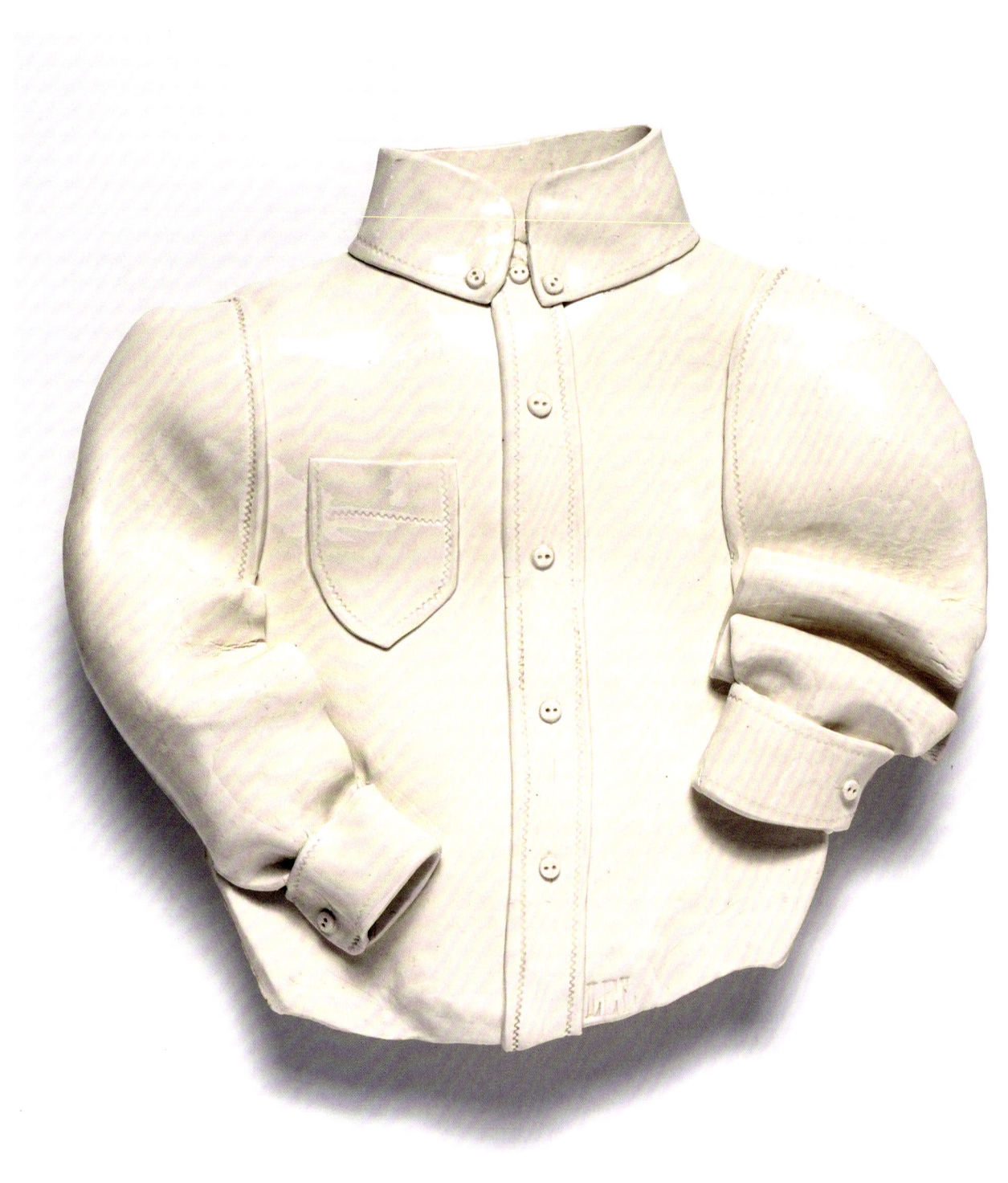

Mr. Business 1981
Glazed earthenware
17 ½ × 18 × 2 ¾ in. (44.5 × 45.7 × 7 cm)

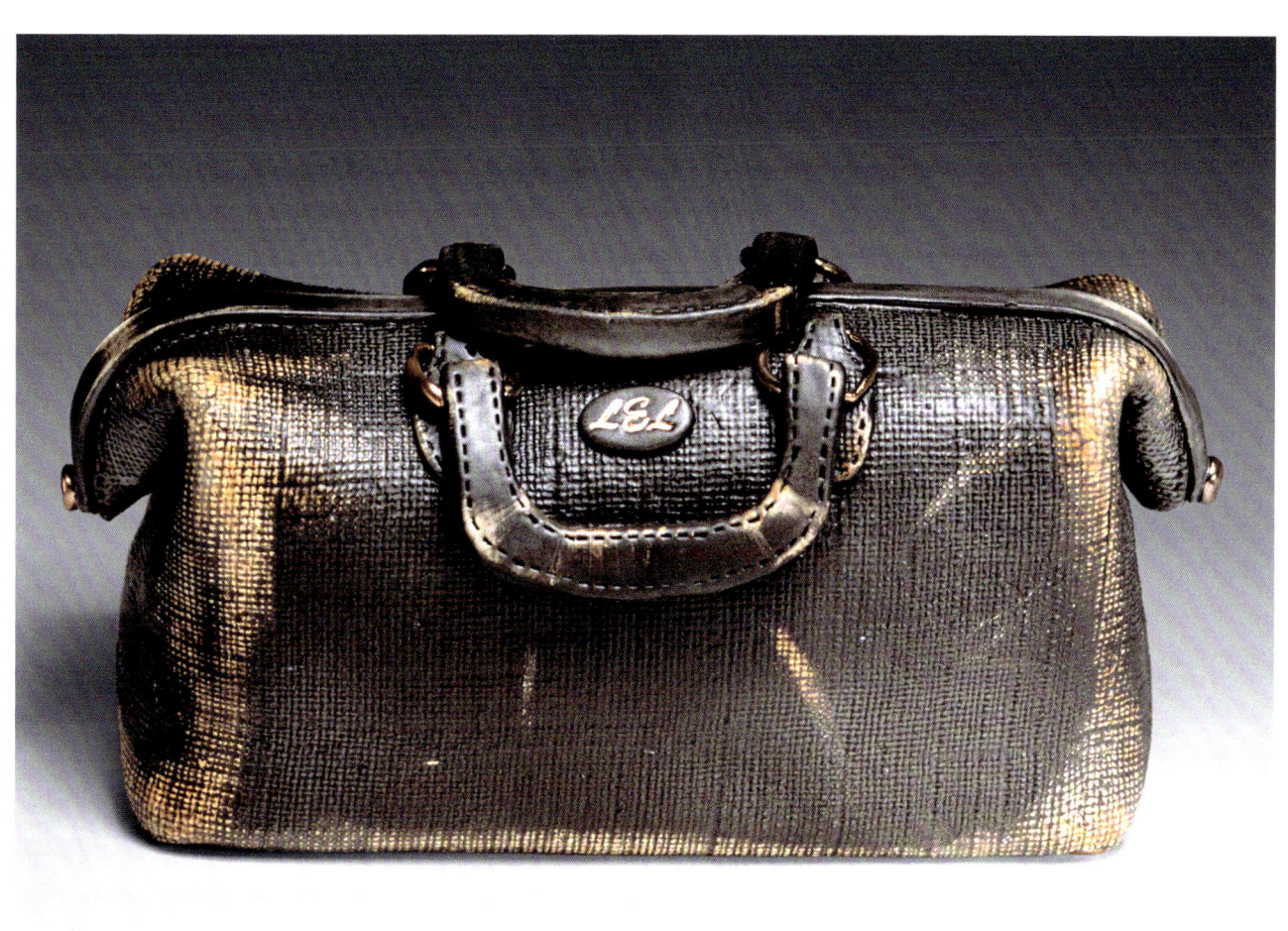

Doctor's Bag 1980
Glazed earthenware with underglaze and luster
6 × 12 × 4 ½ in. (15.2 × 30.5 × 11.4 cm)
Collection Gretchen and the late Dr. Larry Jacobson

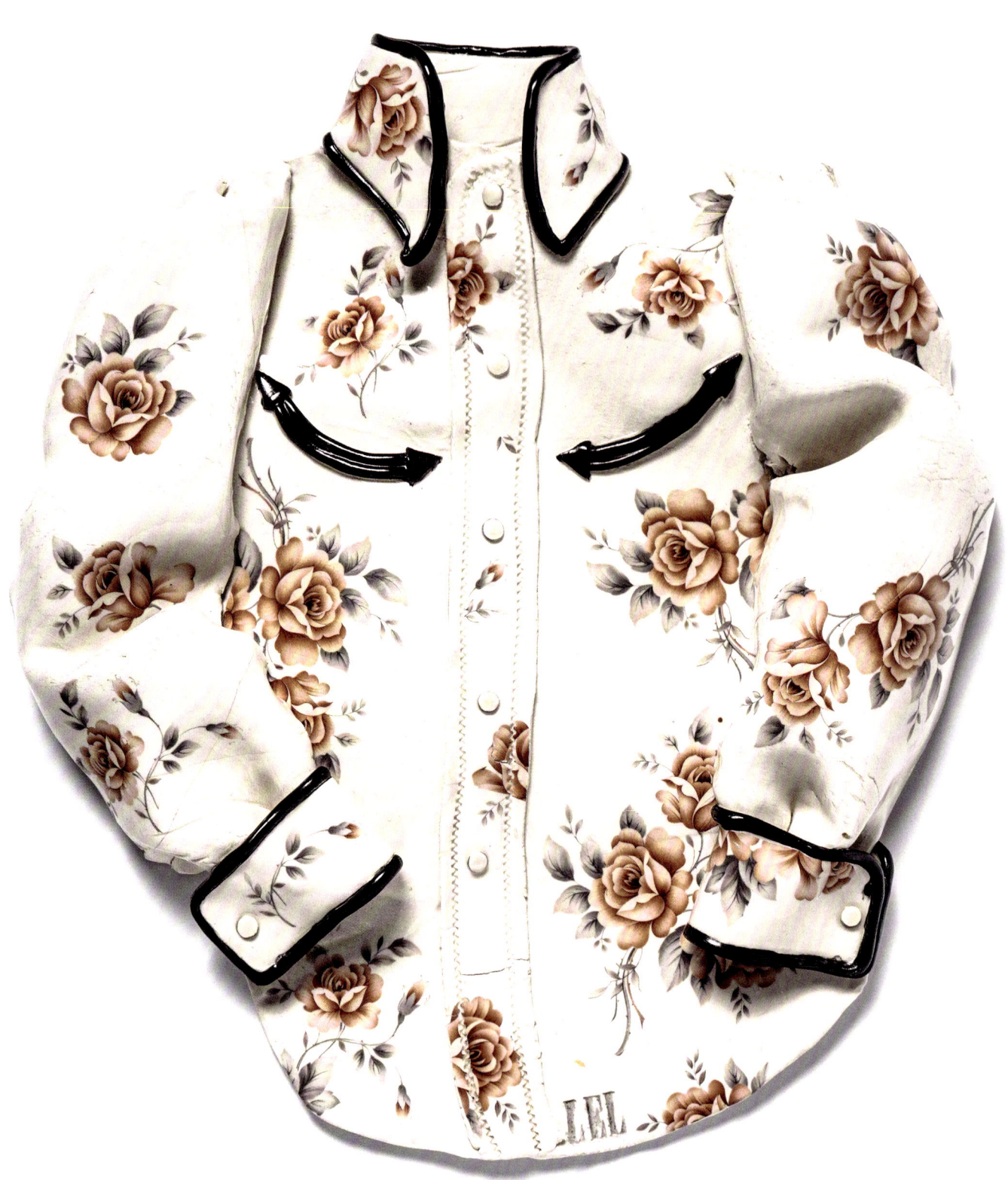

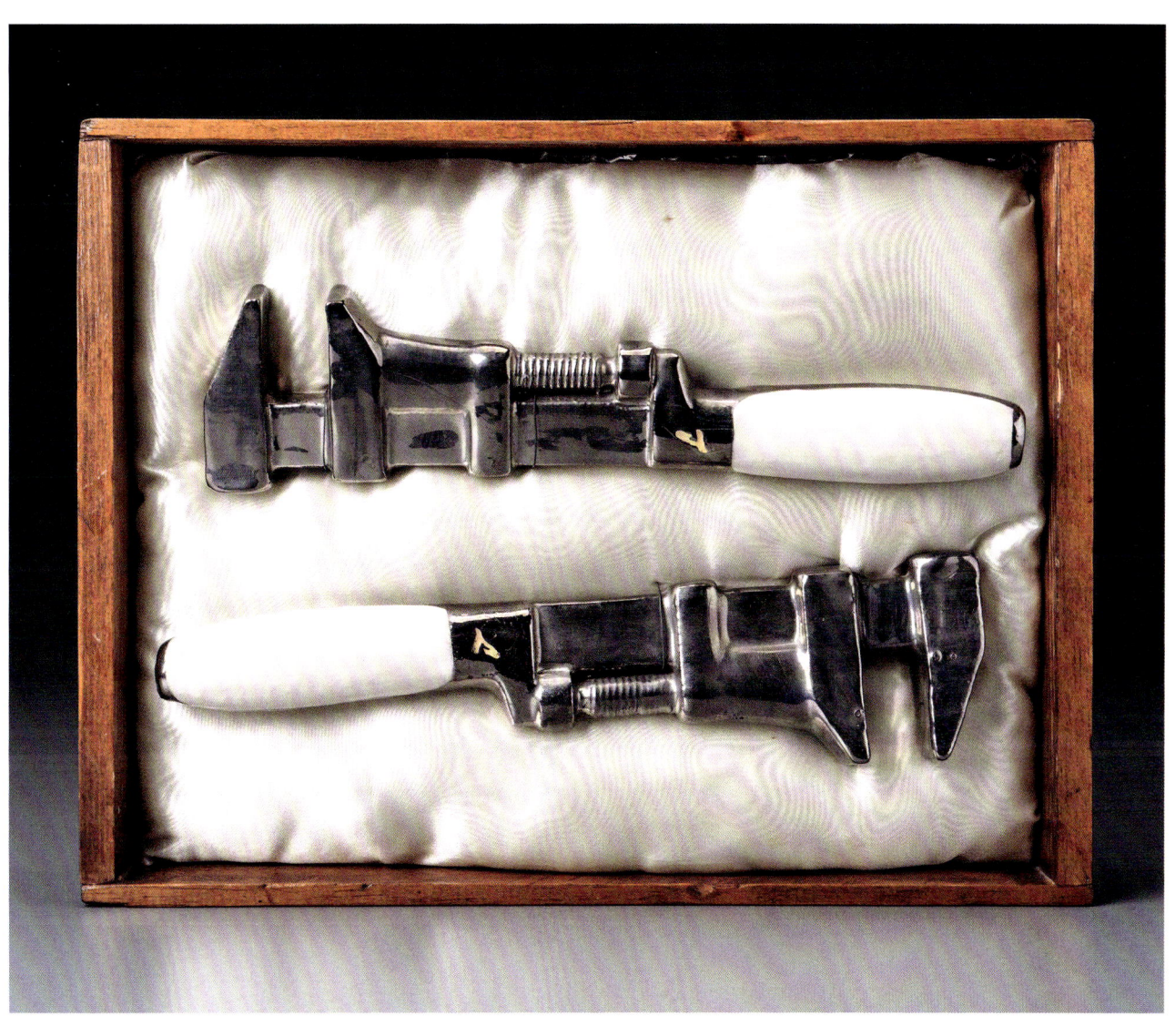

Left page
Flowered Cowboy Shirt c. 1980
Glazed earthenware and decals
18 × 16 × 2 in. (45.7 × 40.6 × 5.1 cm)
Collection Bill Popplewell

Pearl Handled Dueling Monkey Wrenches 1981
Glazed earthenware with china paint, luster, satin and wood
10¾ × 14¼ × 4 in. (27.3 × 36.2 × 10.2 cm)

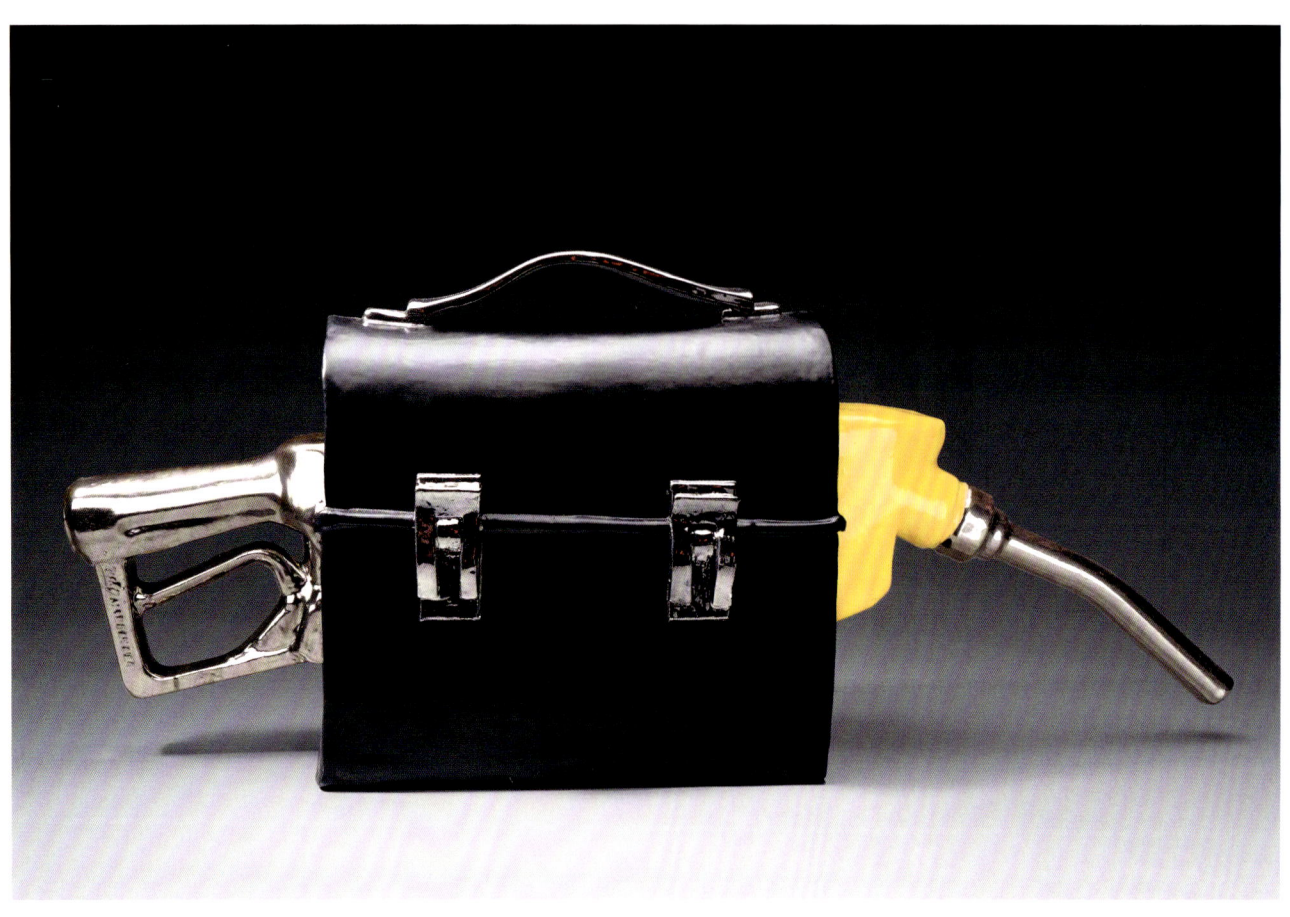

Working Man's Dilemma 1982/2023
Glazed earthenware with luster
10½ × 24 × 6 in. (26.7 × 61 × 15.2 cm)

Right page
Legal Pad 1984
Glazed earthenware with underglaze and pencil
11 × 8 × 2 in. (27.9 × 20.3 × 5.1 cm)

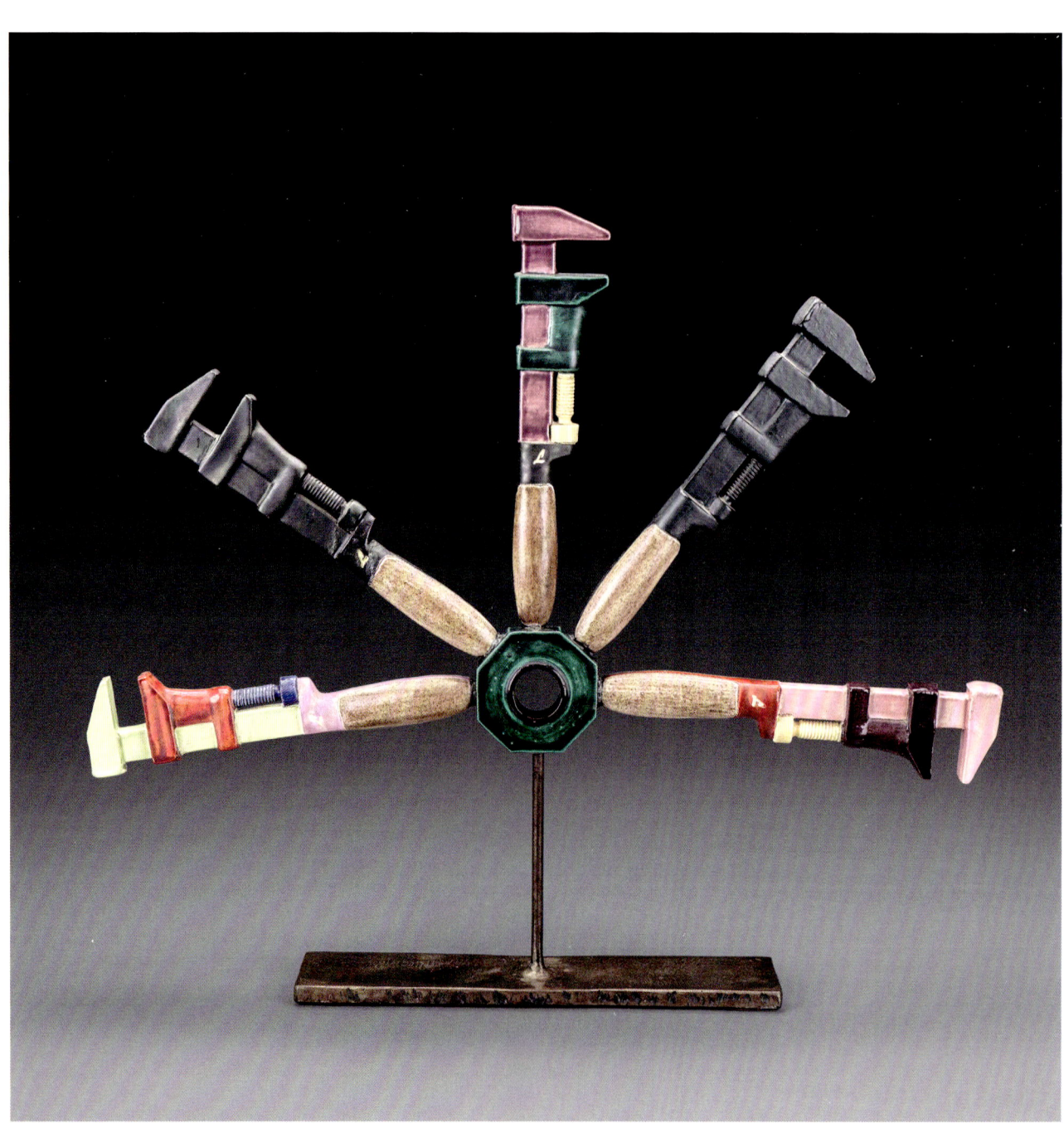

Monkey Wrench Mandala 1981
Glazed earthenware with china paint and steel
22 × 26 ½ × 2 ¾ in. (55.9 × 67.3 × 7 cm)

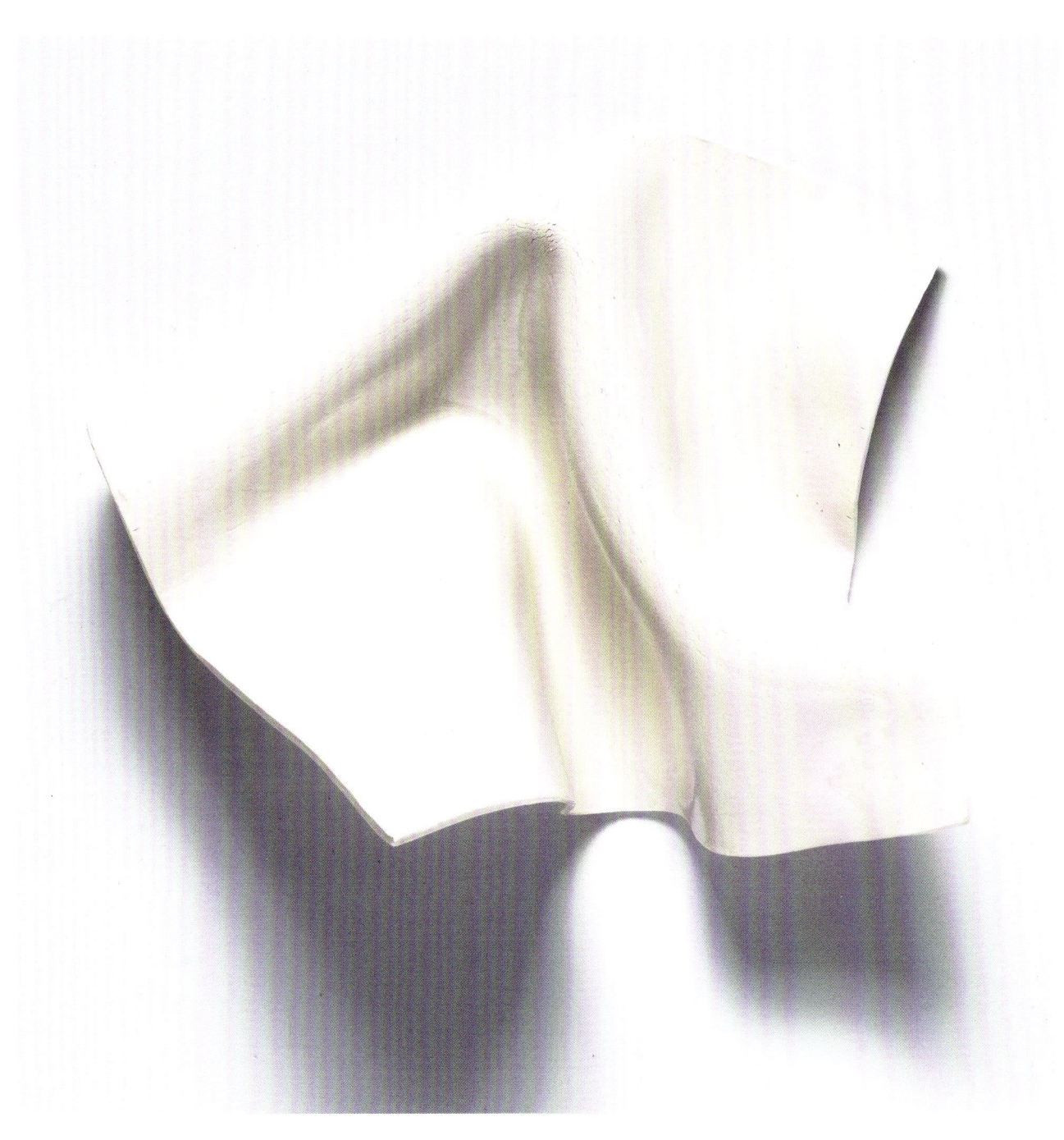

Dish Rag 1988
Glazed earthenware
13 × 13 ½ × 5 ¾ in. (33 × 34.3 × 14.6 cm)

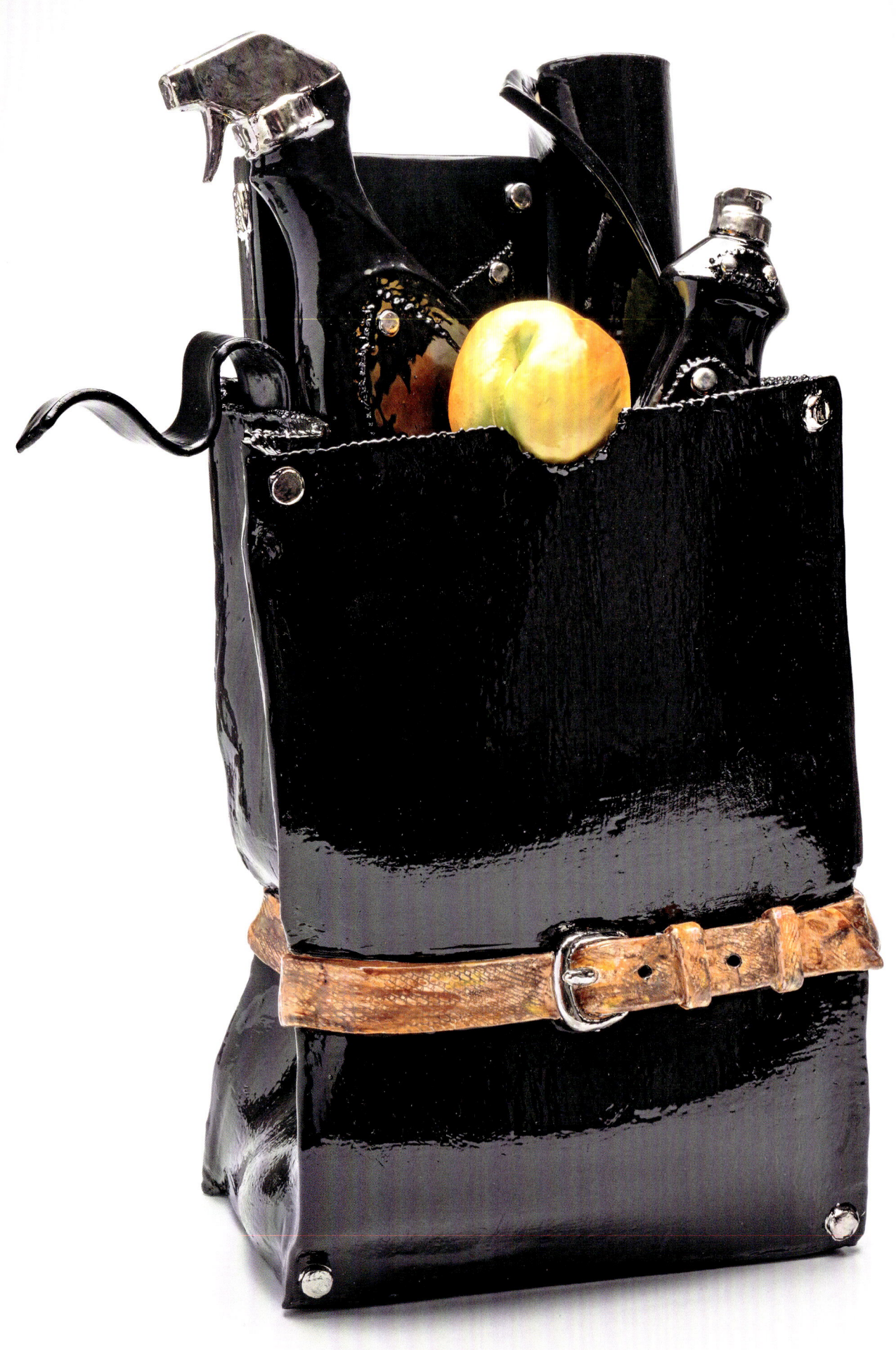

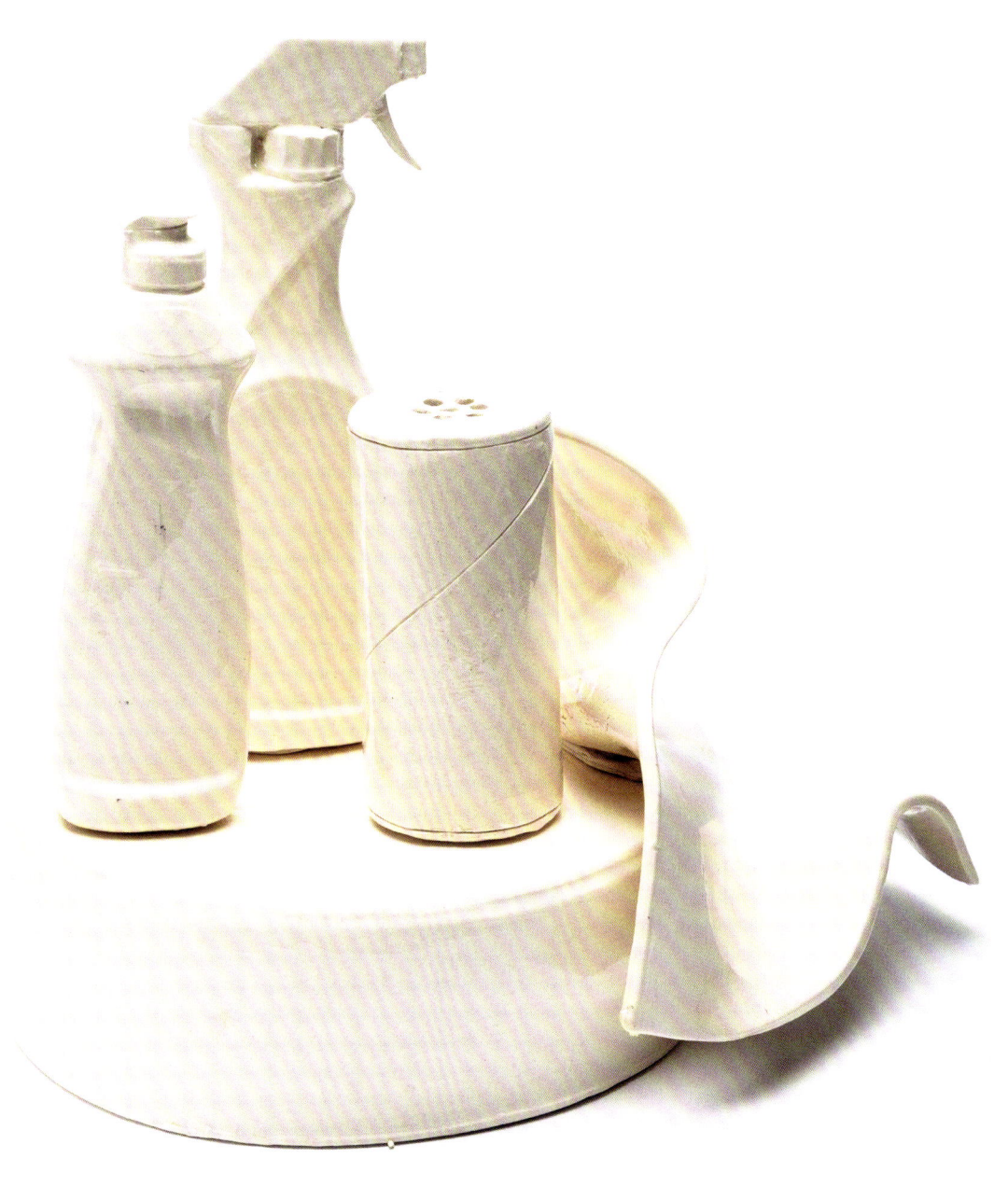

Left page
Daddy's Hungry 1987/2023
Glazed earthenware with china paint and luster
21 ½ × 17 × 8 ½ in. (54.6 × 43.2 × 21.6 cm)

What the Bridal Consultant Never Tells You 1987/2023
Glazed earthenware
10 × 12 ½ × 12 in. (25.4 × 31.8 × 30.5 cm)

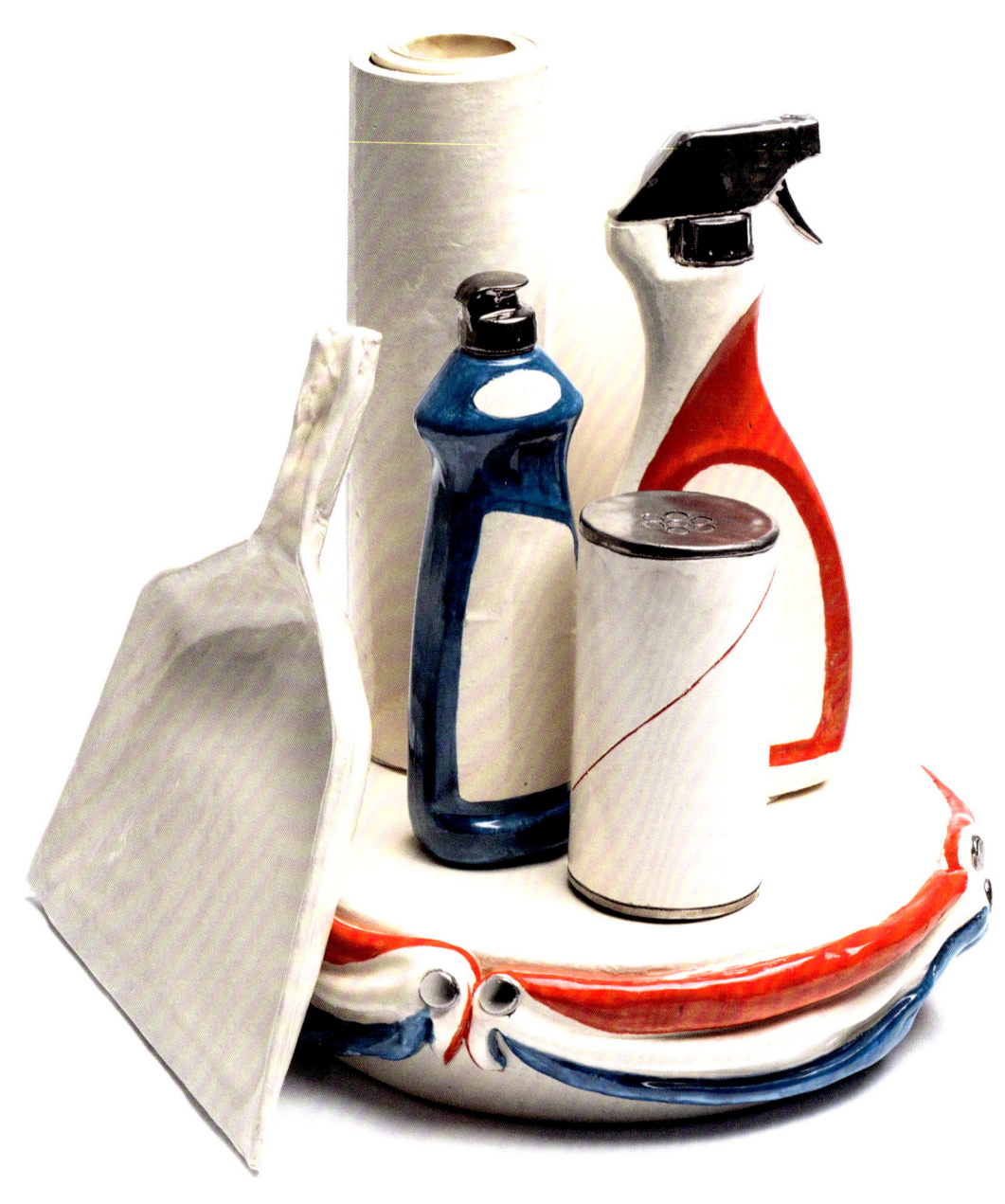

The First Lady 1986/2023
Glazed earthenware with china paint and luster
13 ¼ × 14 × 13 in. (33.7 × 35.6 × 33 cm)

Right page
S&M Cleaning 1987/2023
Glazed earthenware with china paint and luster
14 × 15 × 14 in. (35.6 × 38.1 × 35.6 cm)

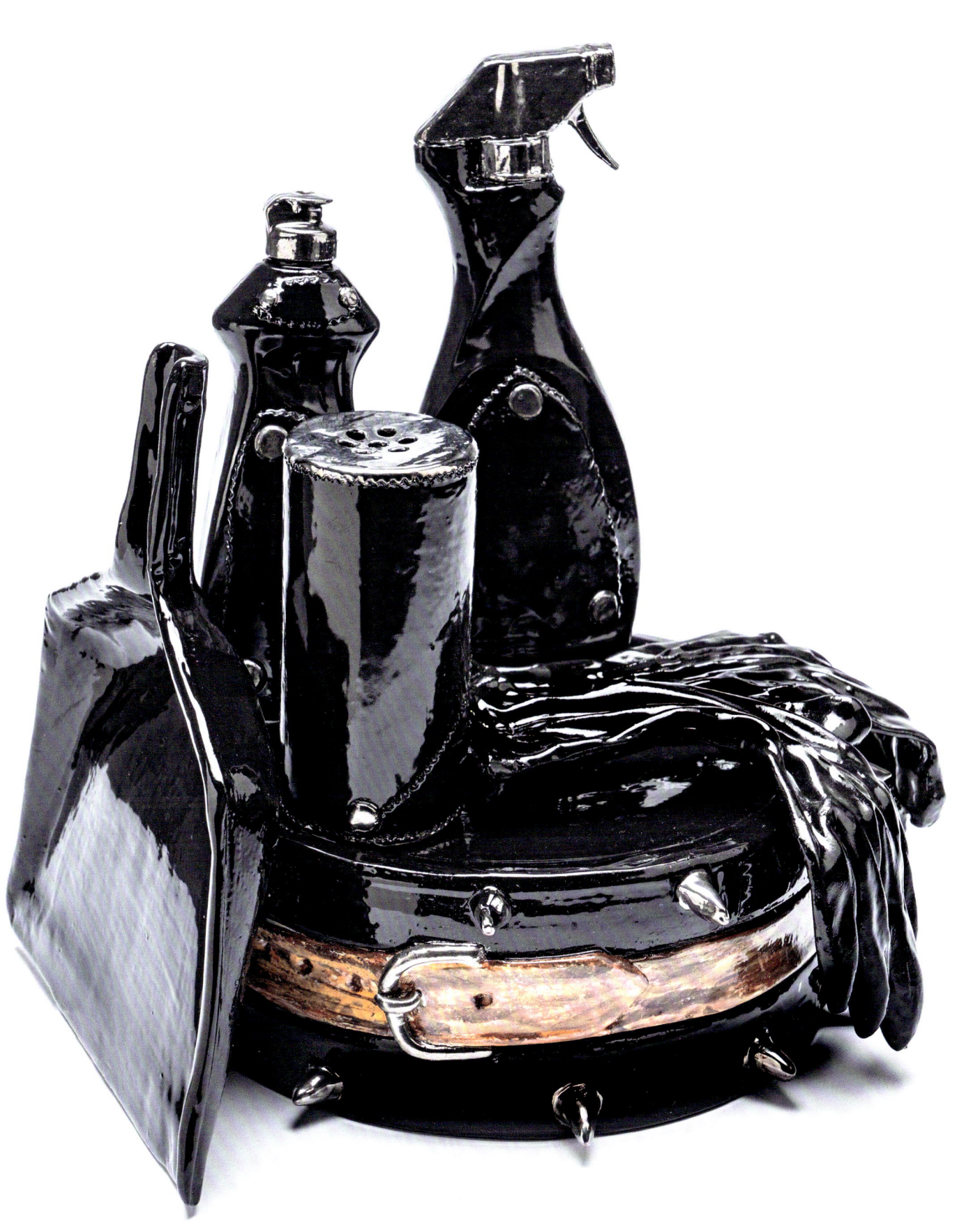

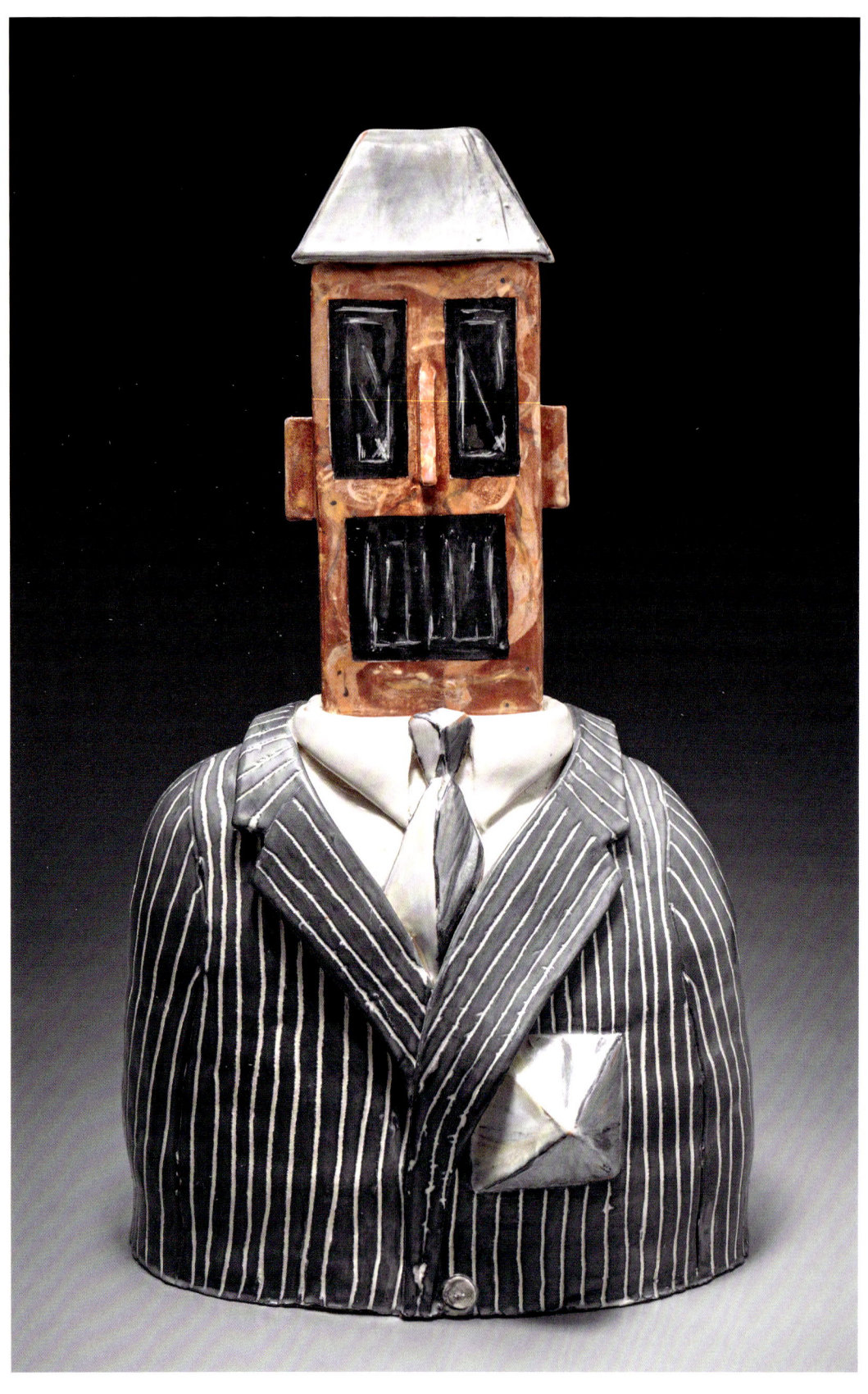

Figure in Architecture 1989
Glazed earthenware with underglaze and china paint
17 × 9 ½ × 6 in. (43.2 × 24.1 × 15.2 cm)

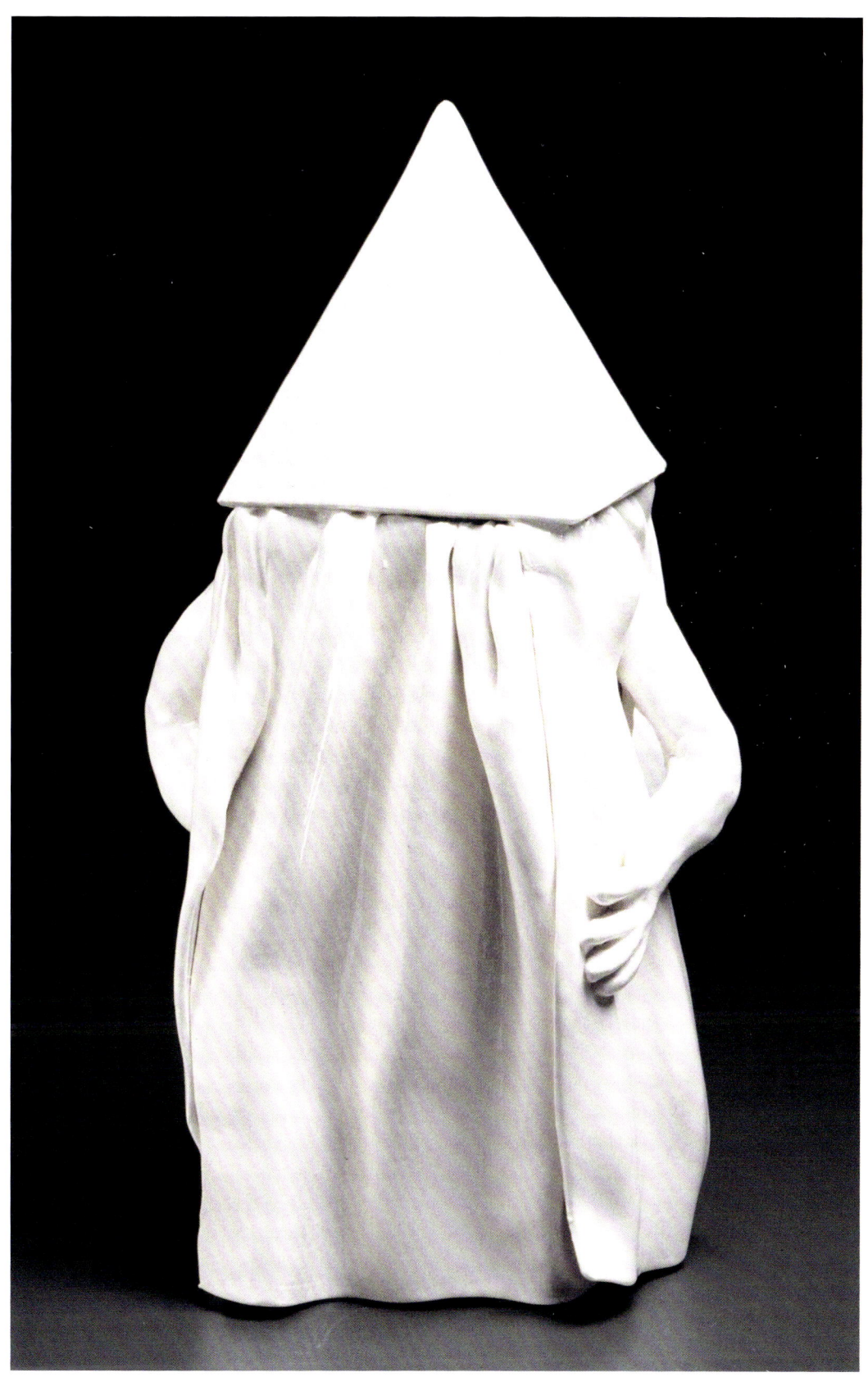

Stepford Wife 1989
Glazed earthenware
17 ½ × 6 × 7 ½ in. (44.5 × 15.2 × 19.1 cm)
Collection Gretchen and the late Dr. Larry Jacobson

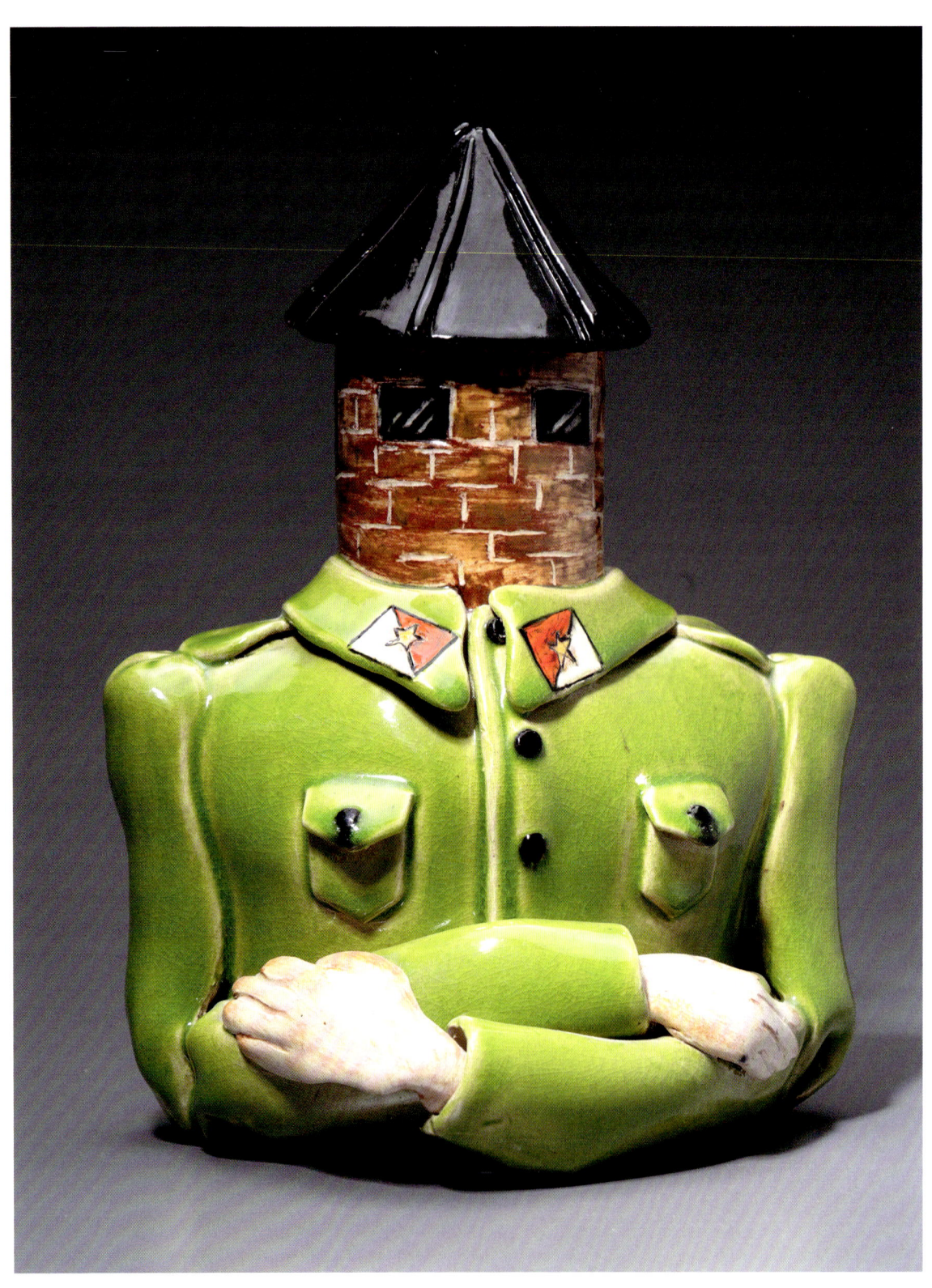

Latvian Security Guard 1993
Glazed earthenware with china paint
9 × 7 ¼ × 5 in. (22.9 × 18.4 × 12.7 cm)

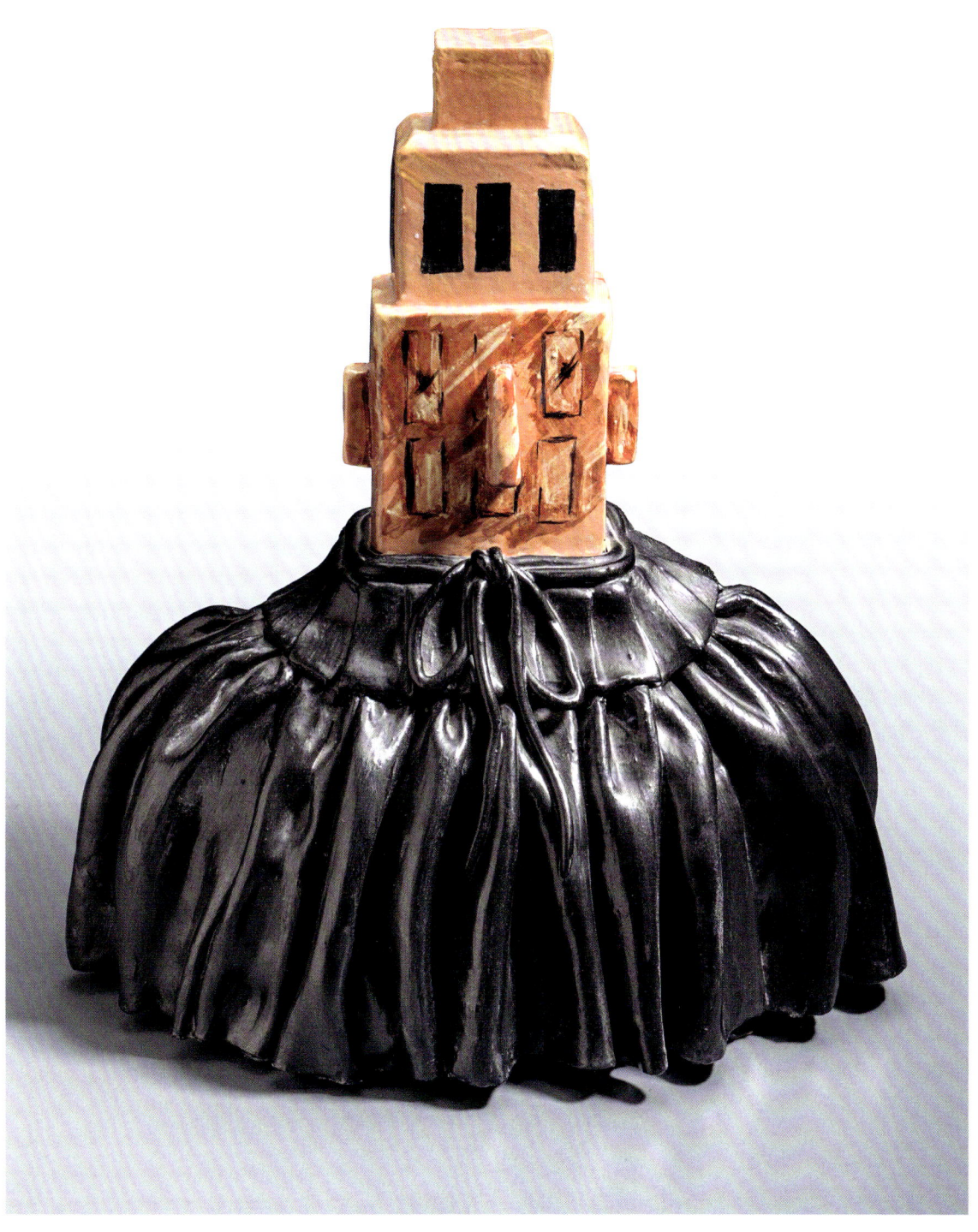

The Judge 1989
Glazed earthenware with underglaze
13 × 12 × 9 ½ in. (33 × 30.5 × 24.1 cm)

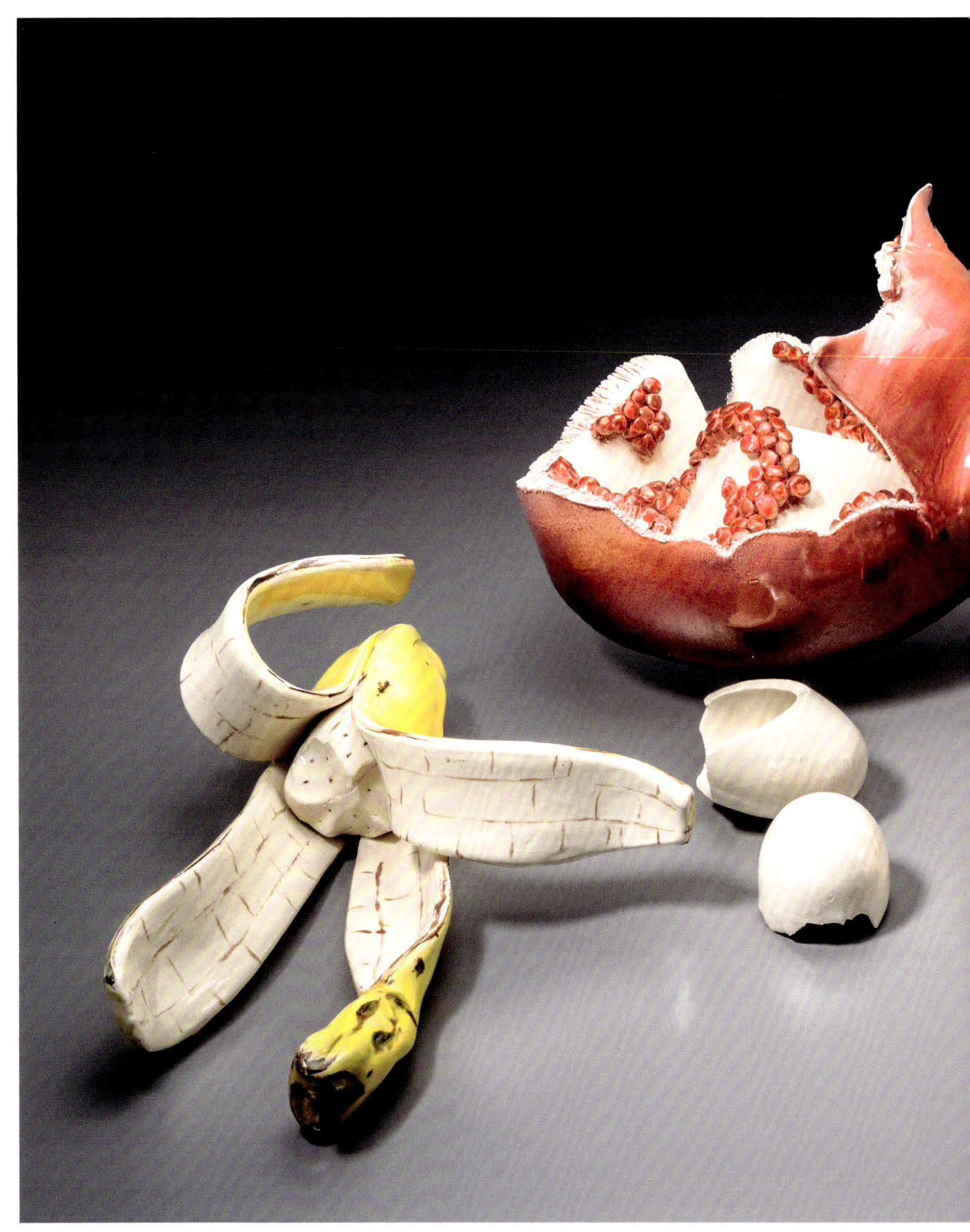

Compost 2003–4
Glazed earthenware with china paint and luster
Overall: 10 × 43 × 12 in. (25.4 × 109.2 × 30.5 cm)

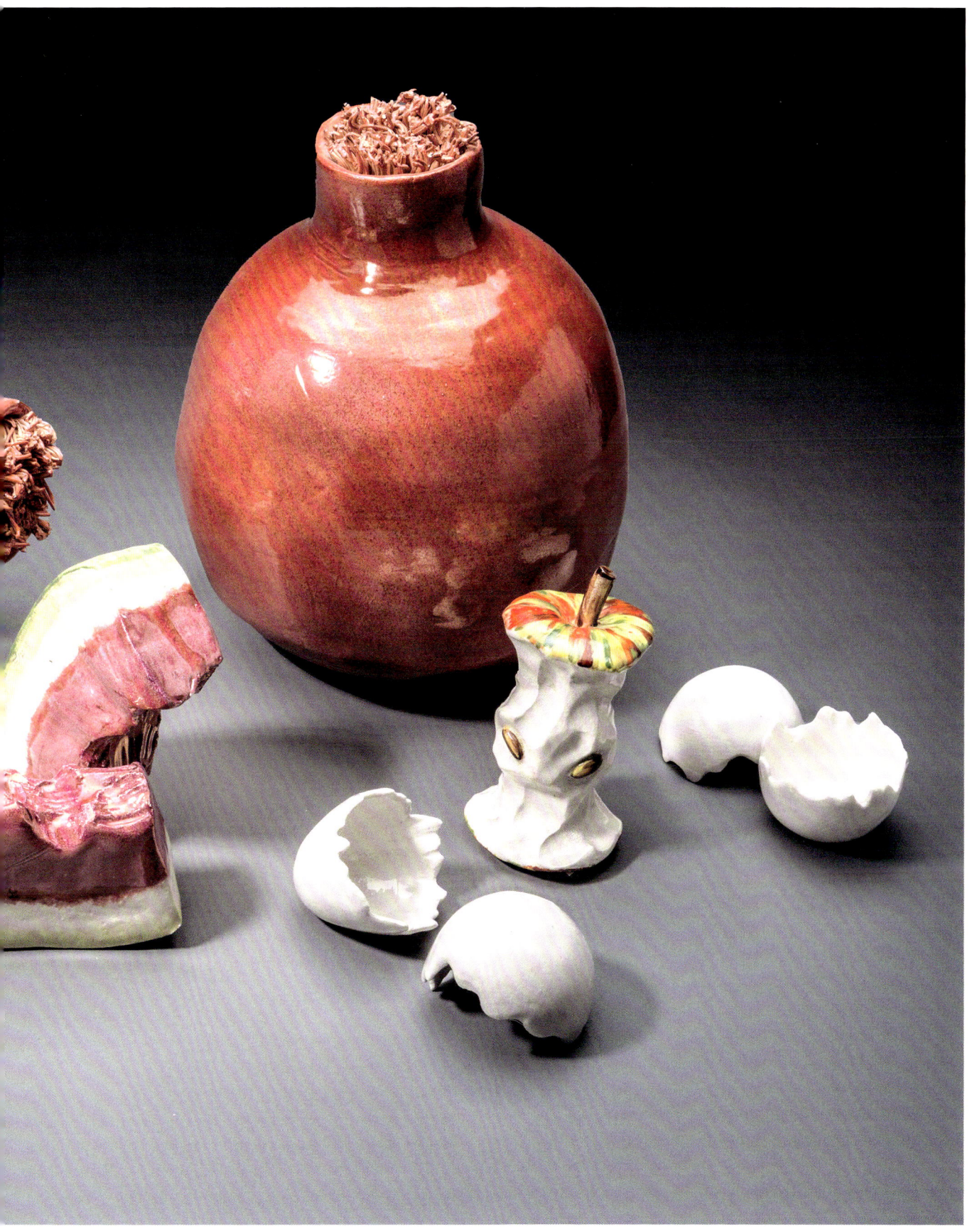

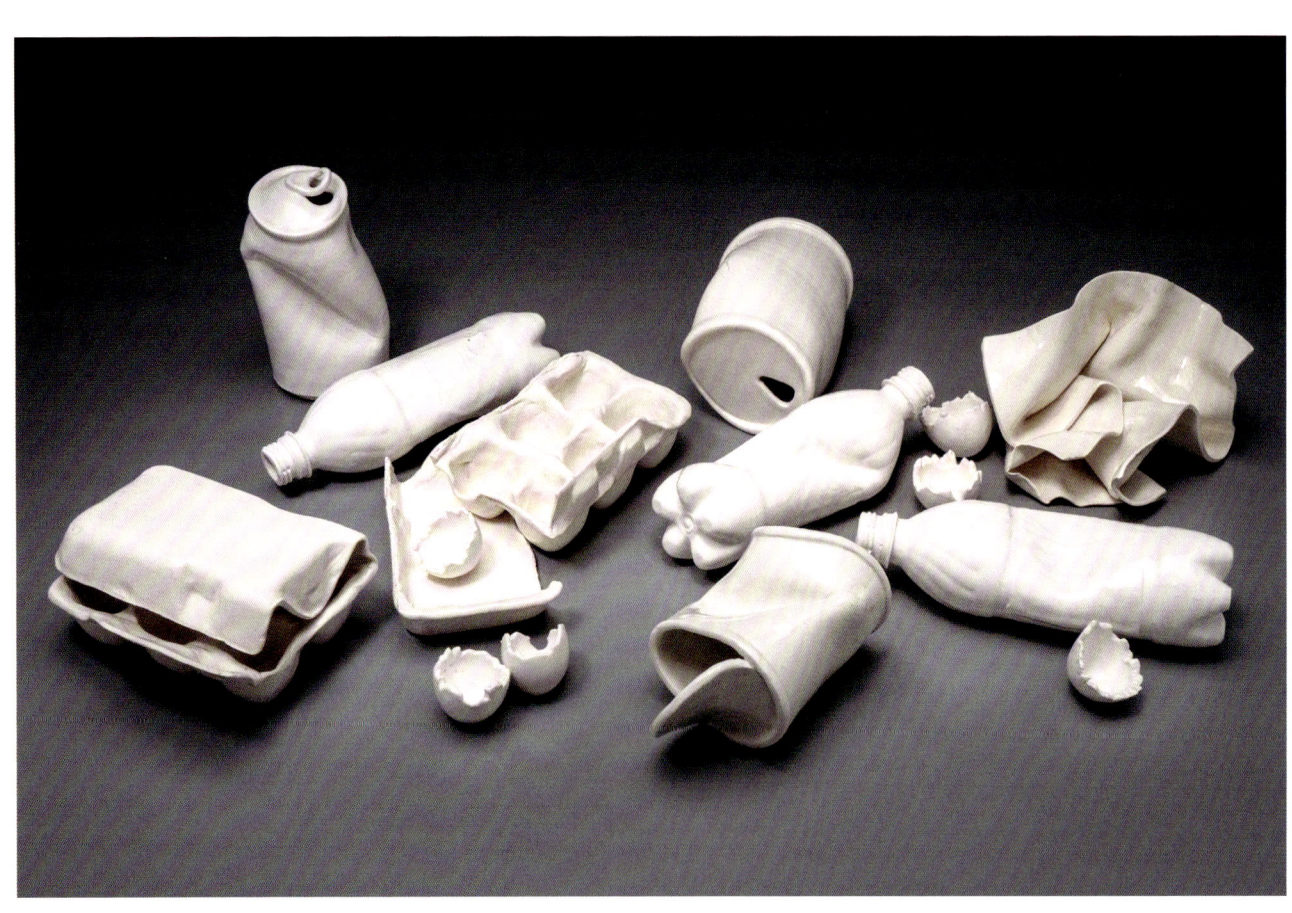

White Trash 2003
Glazed porcelain
Overall: 4 × 23 ½ × 17 ¾ in. (10.2 × 59.7 × 45.1 cm)

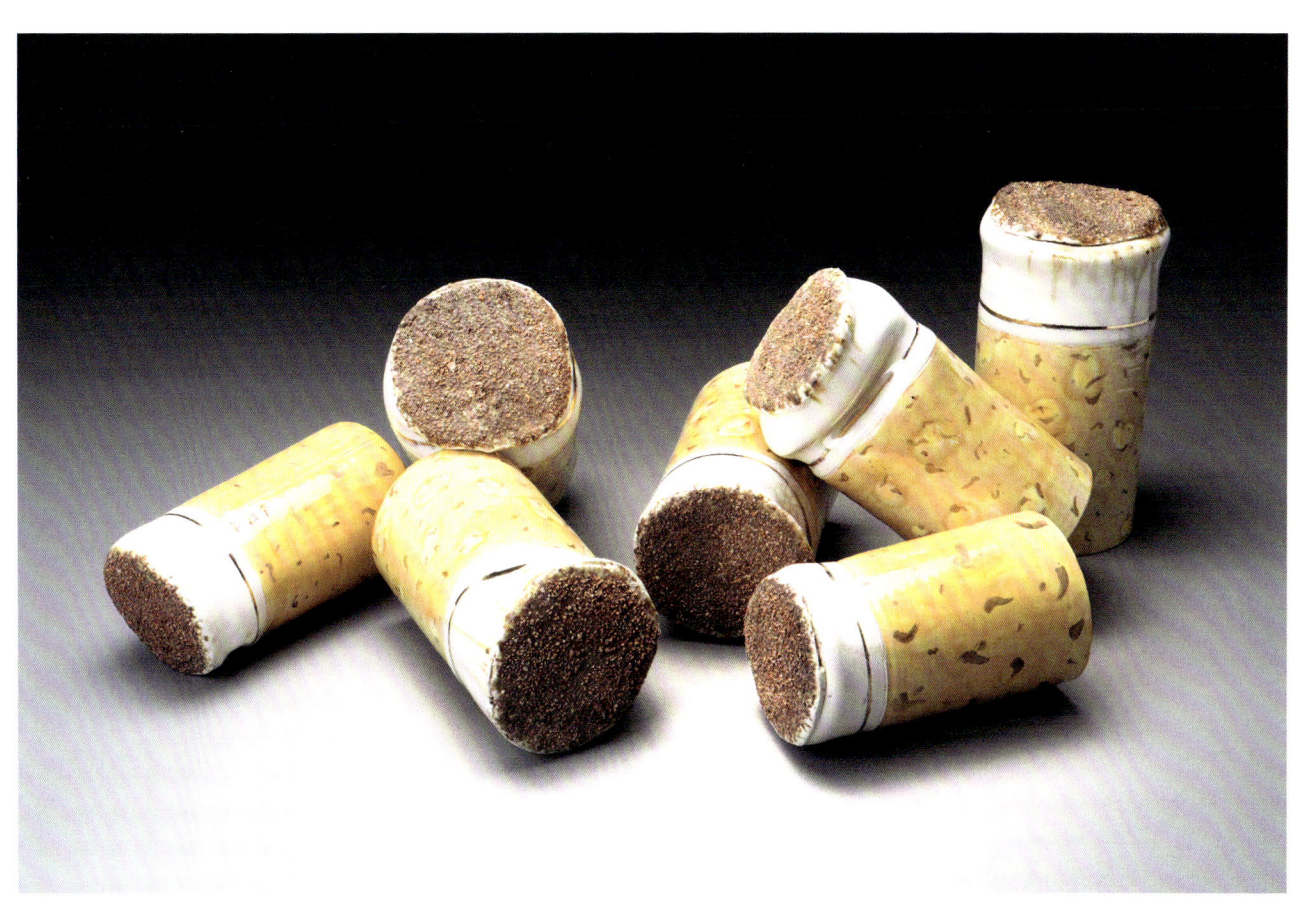

Cigarette Butts c. 1981
Glazed earthenware, luster, and vermiculite
Overall: 9 × 30½ × 12 in. (22.9 × 77.5 × 30.5 cm)

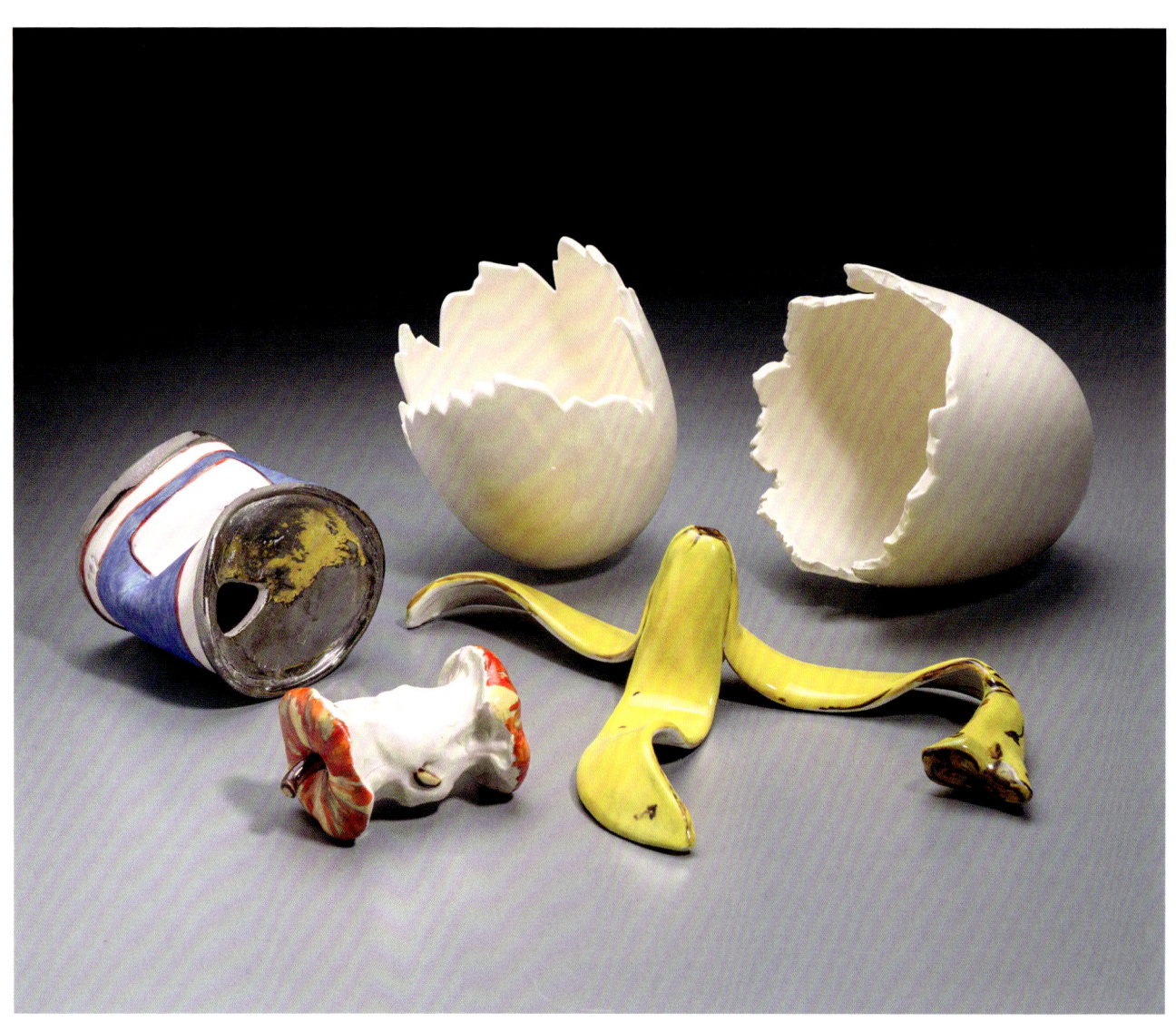

Trash 1980
Glazed earthenware with china paint and luster
Overall: 6 × 15 ½ × 12 in. (15.2 × 38.1 × 30.5 cm)
Collection Gretchen and the late Dr. Larry Jacobson

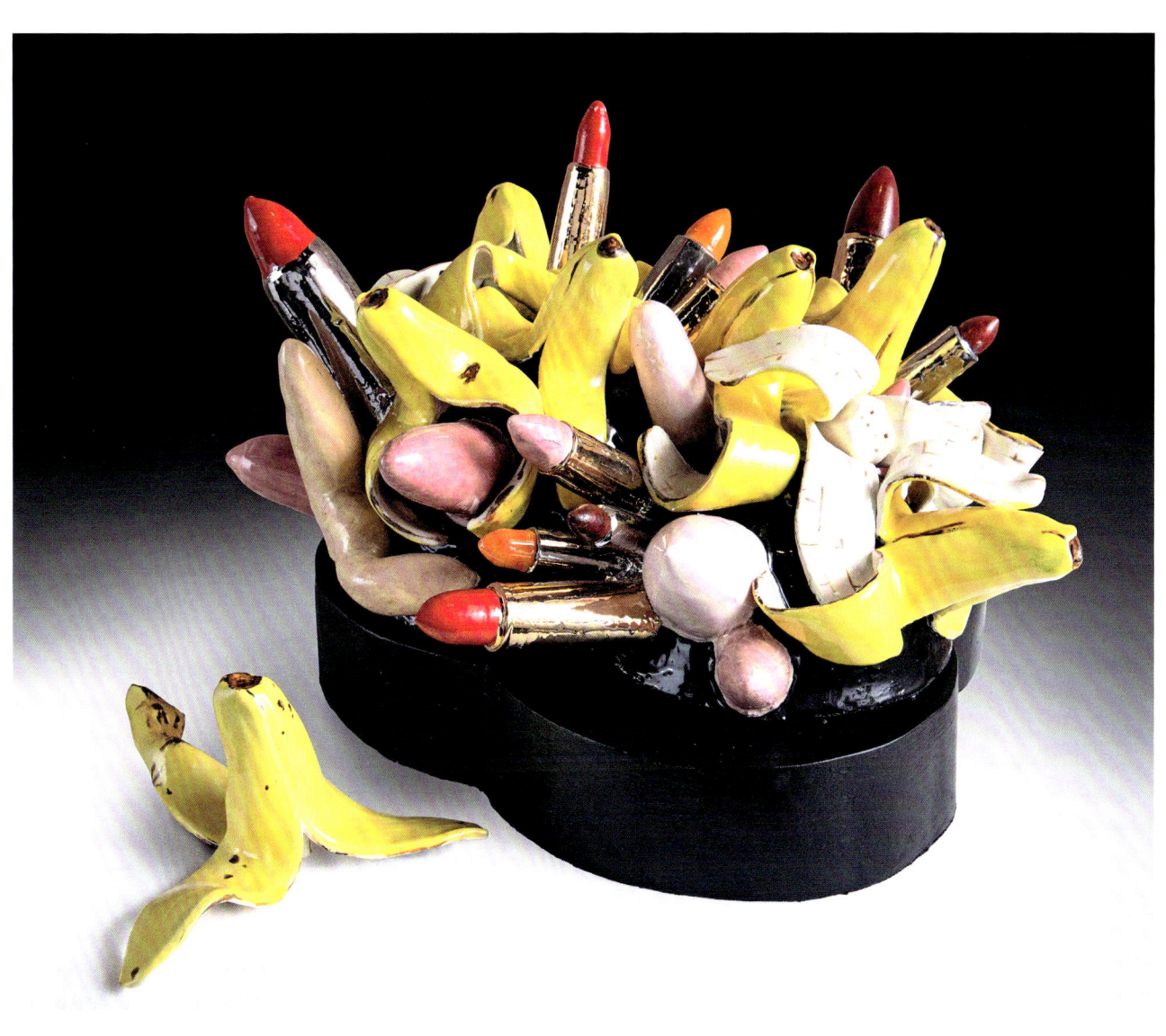

Bananascape 2020–21
Glazed earthenware with china paint, luster, wood and paint
13 × 21 × 18 in. (33 × 53.3 × 45.7 cm)

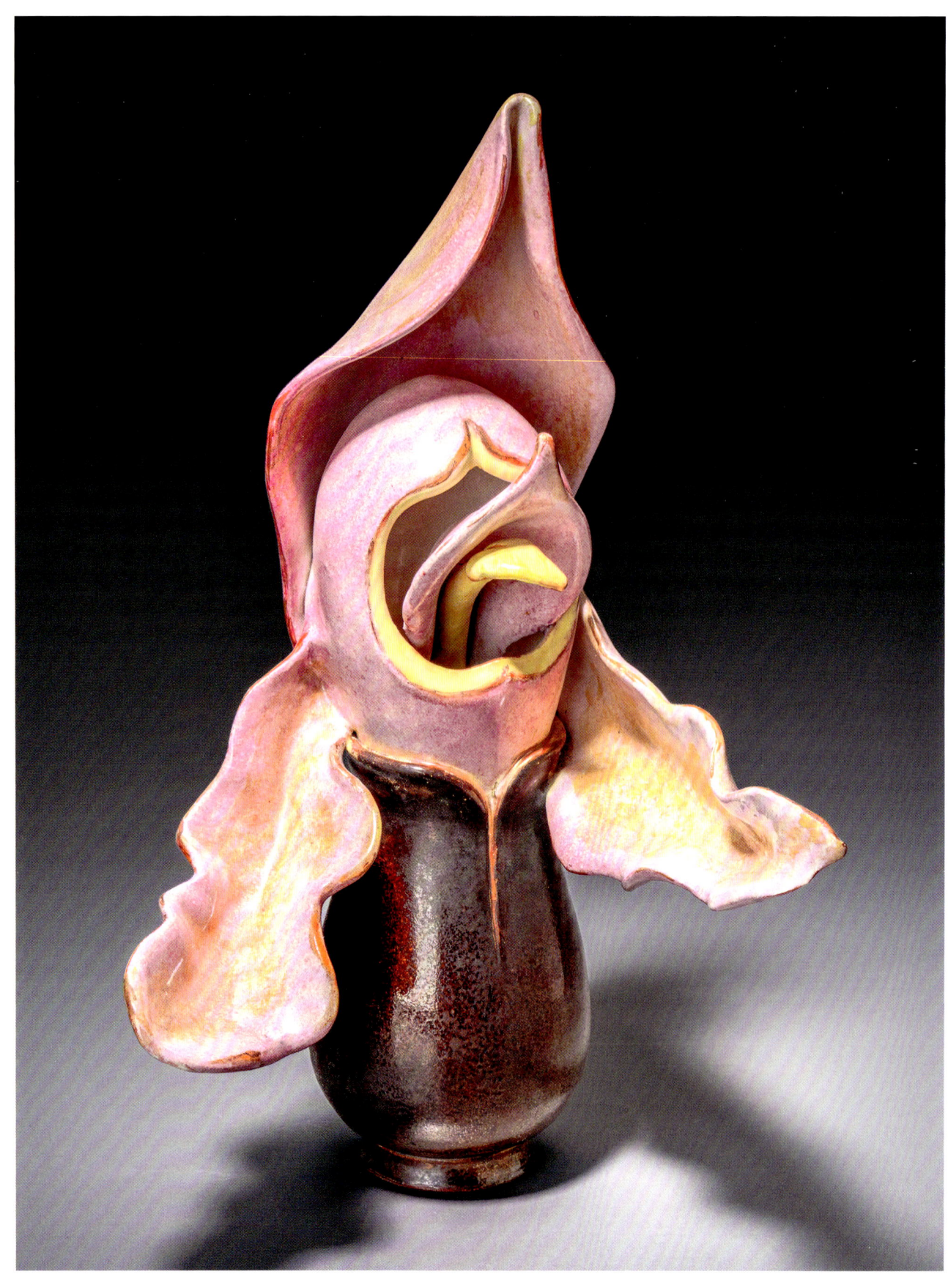

Diva Yael 2000
Glazed earthenware with china paint and luster
12 × 7 ½ × 7 in. (30.5 × 19.1 × 17.8 cm)

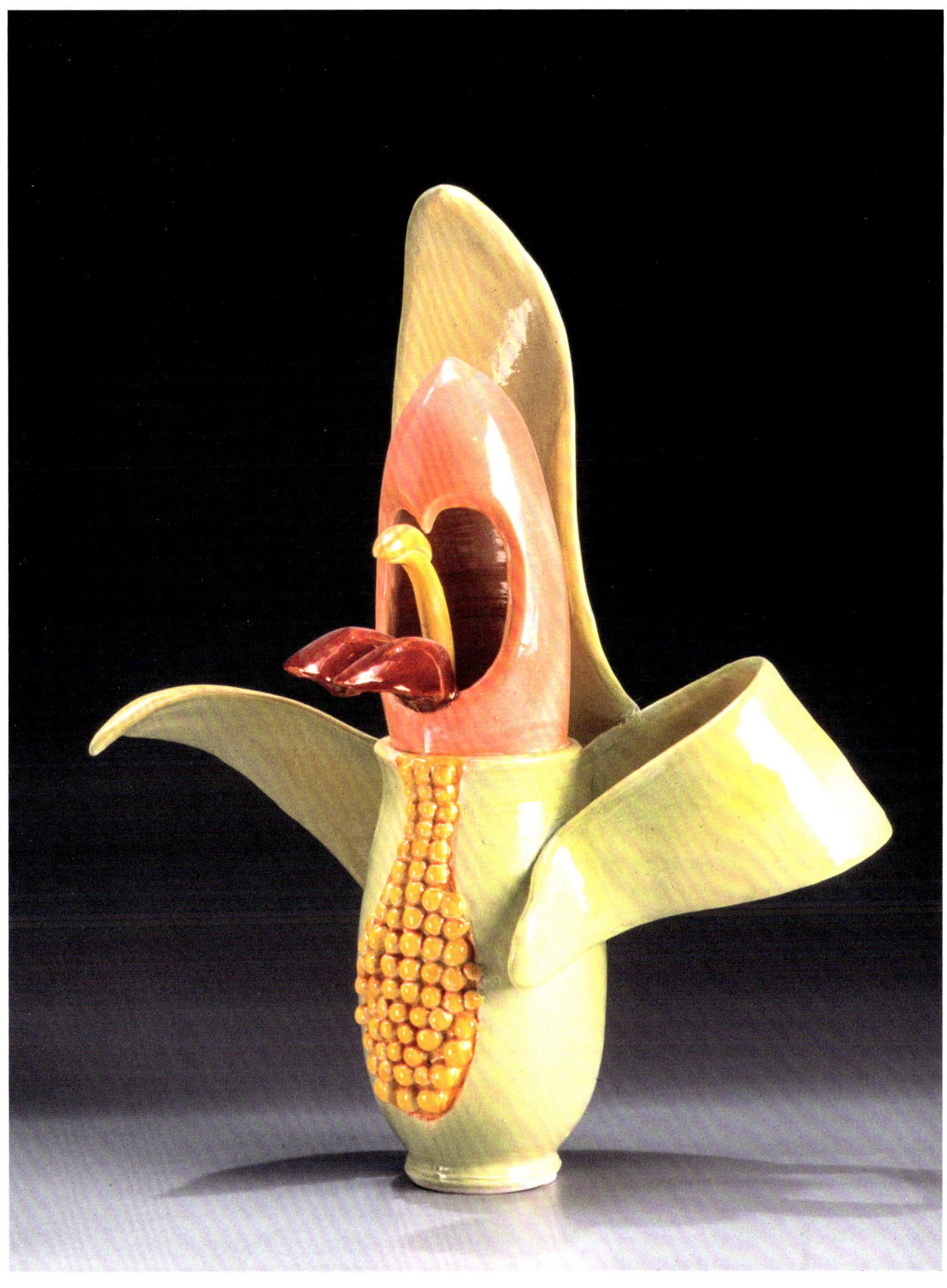

Diva Bebe 2000
Glazed earthenware with china paint and luster
10 × 7 × 5 ½ in. (25.4 × 17.8 × 14 cm)

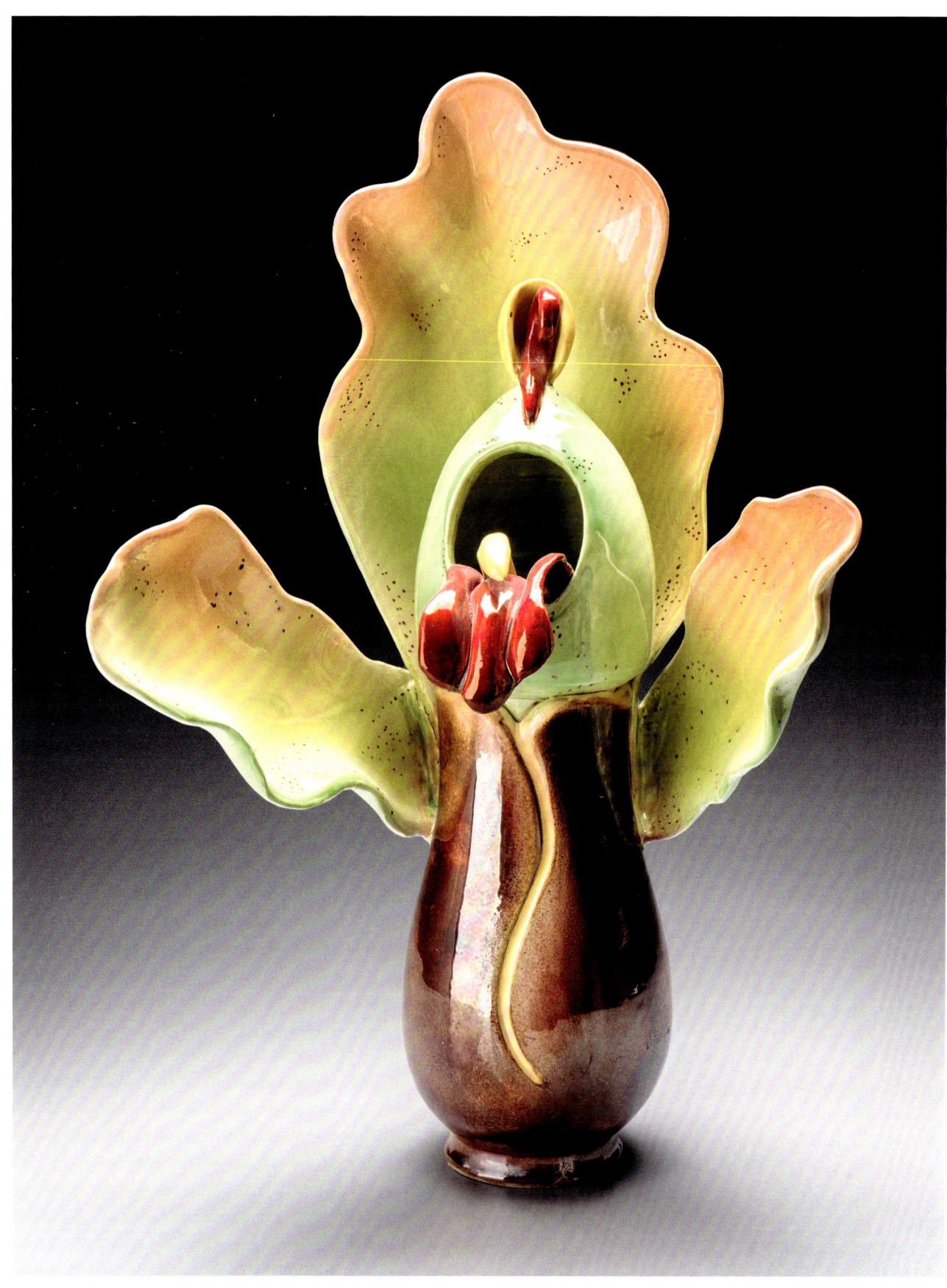

Diva Marilyn 2000
Glazed earthenware with china paint and luster
16 × 6 × 5 in. (40.6 × 15.2 × 12.7 cm)
Collection Nerman Museum of Contemporary Art,
Johnson County Community College, Overland Park, KS

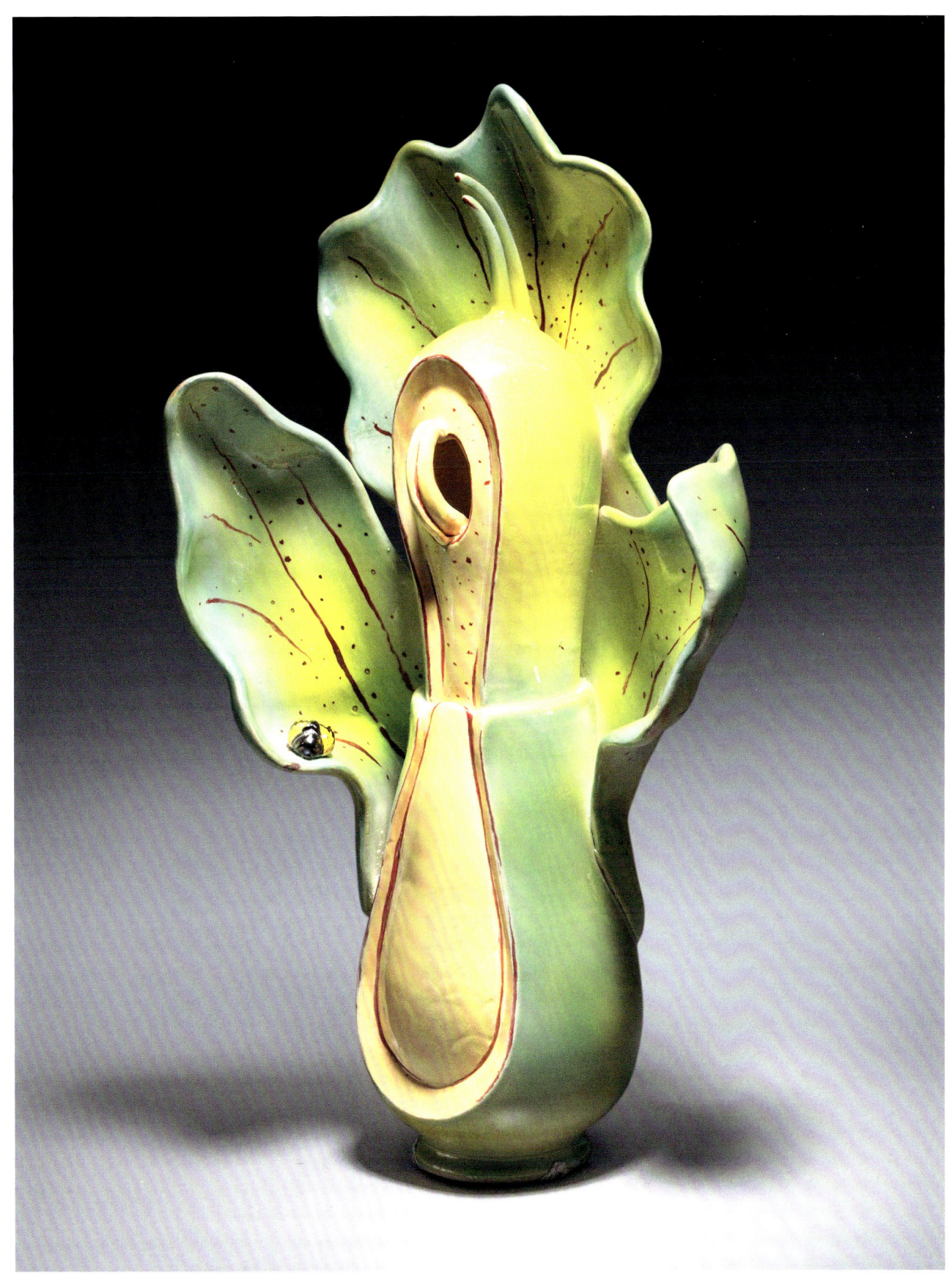

Diva 2000
Glazed earthenware with china paint and luster
14 ½ × 8 × 6 in. (36.8 × 20.3 × 15.2 cm)

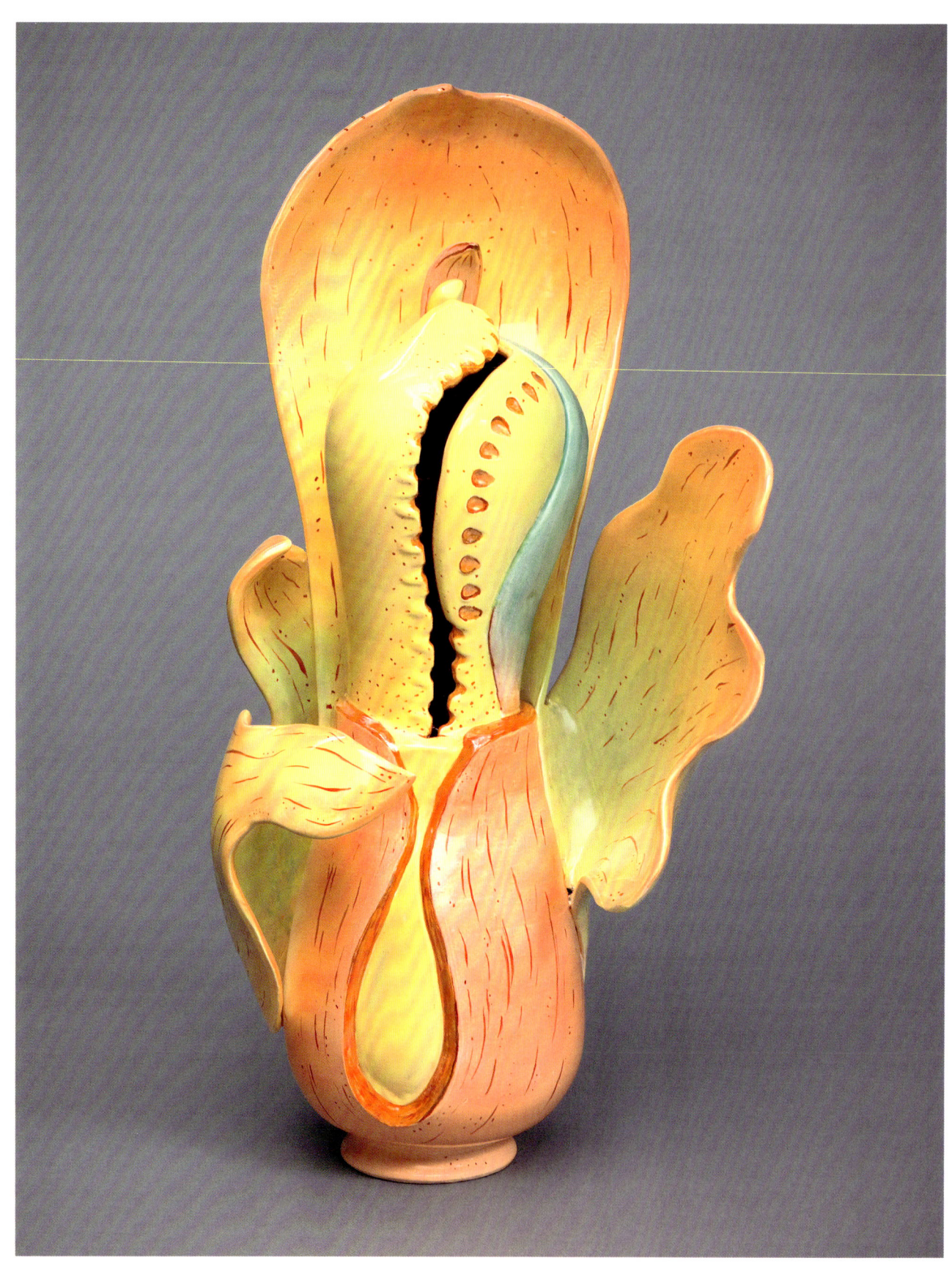

Diva Laura 2002
Glazed earthenware with china paint and luster
22 × 9 × 11 in. (55.9 × 22.9 × 27.9 cm)
Collection The Nelson-Atkins Museum of Art, Kansas City, MO

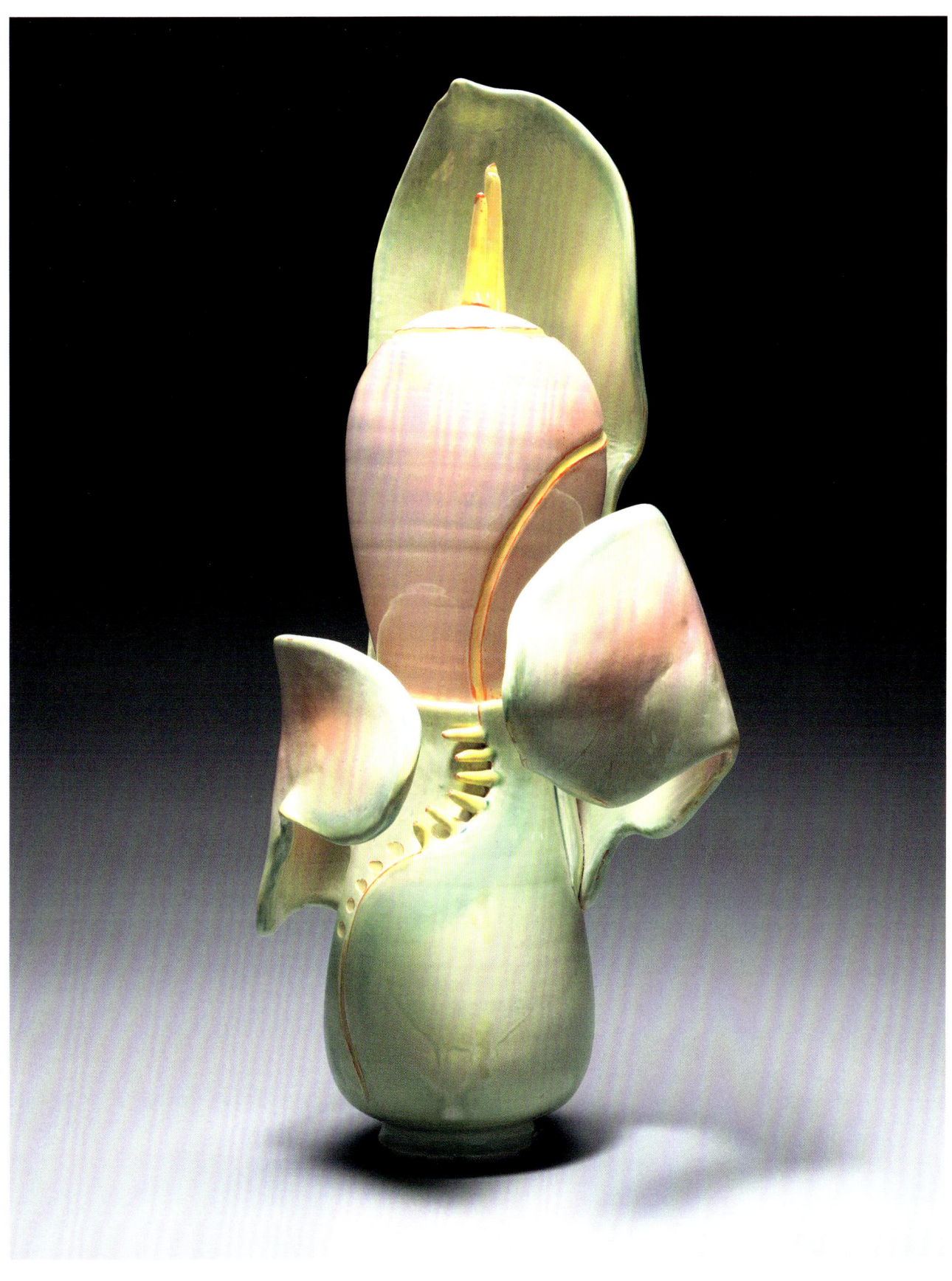

Diva 2001
Glazed earthenware with china paint and luster
20½ × 10 × 13 in. (52.1 × 25.4 × 33 cm)

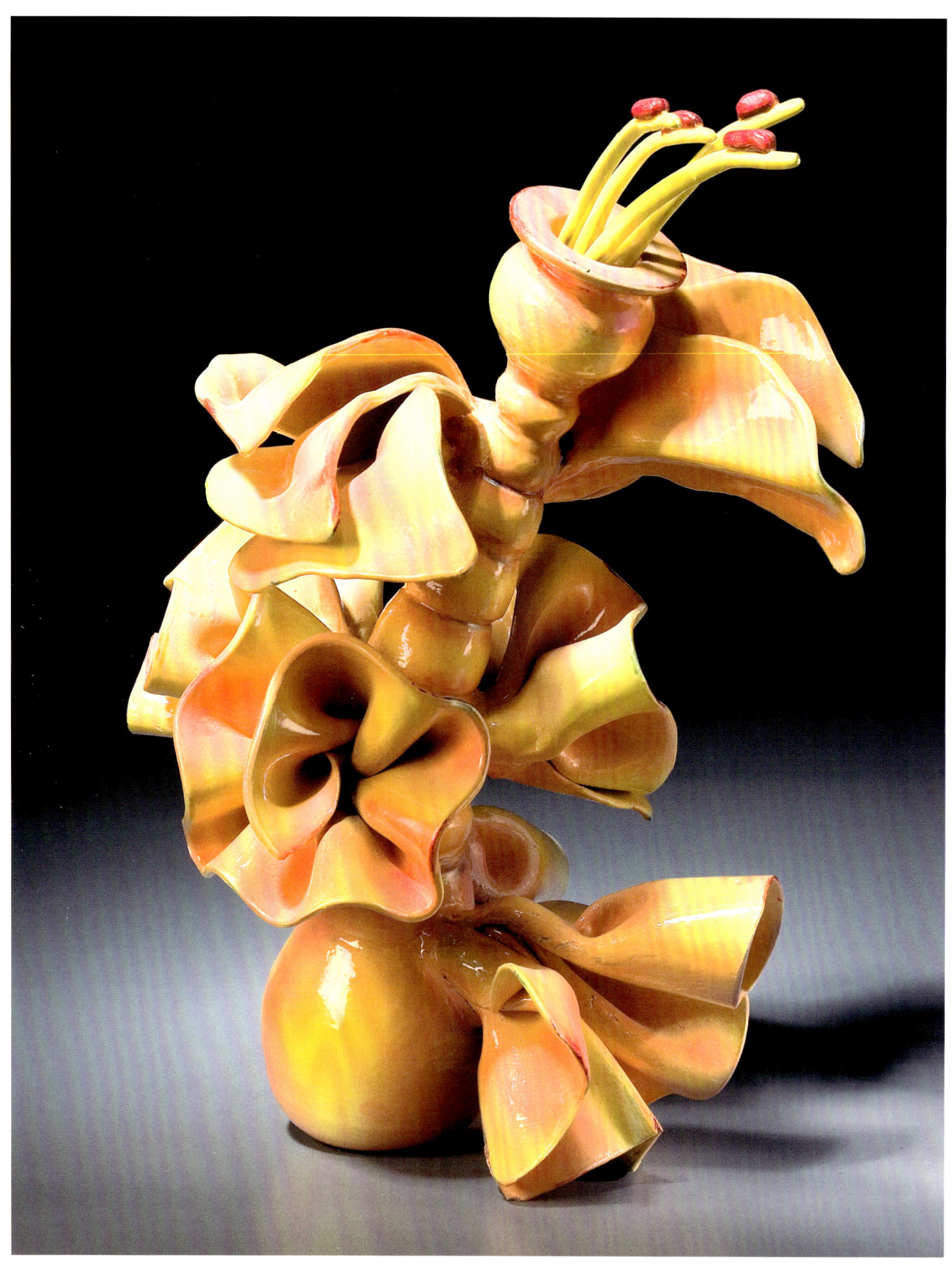

Nude Descending a Staircase 2007
Glazed earthenware with china paint and luster
18 × 11 ½ × 5 ½ in. (45.7 × 29.2 × 14 cm)
Collection Shook, Hardy, & Bacon L.L.P.

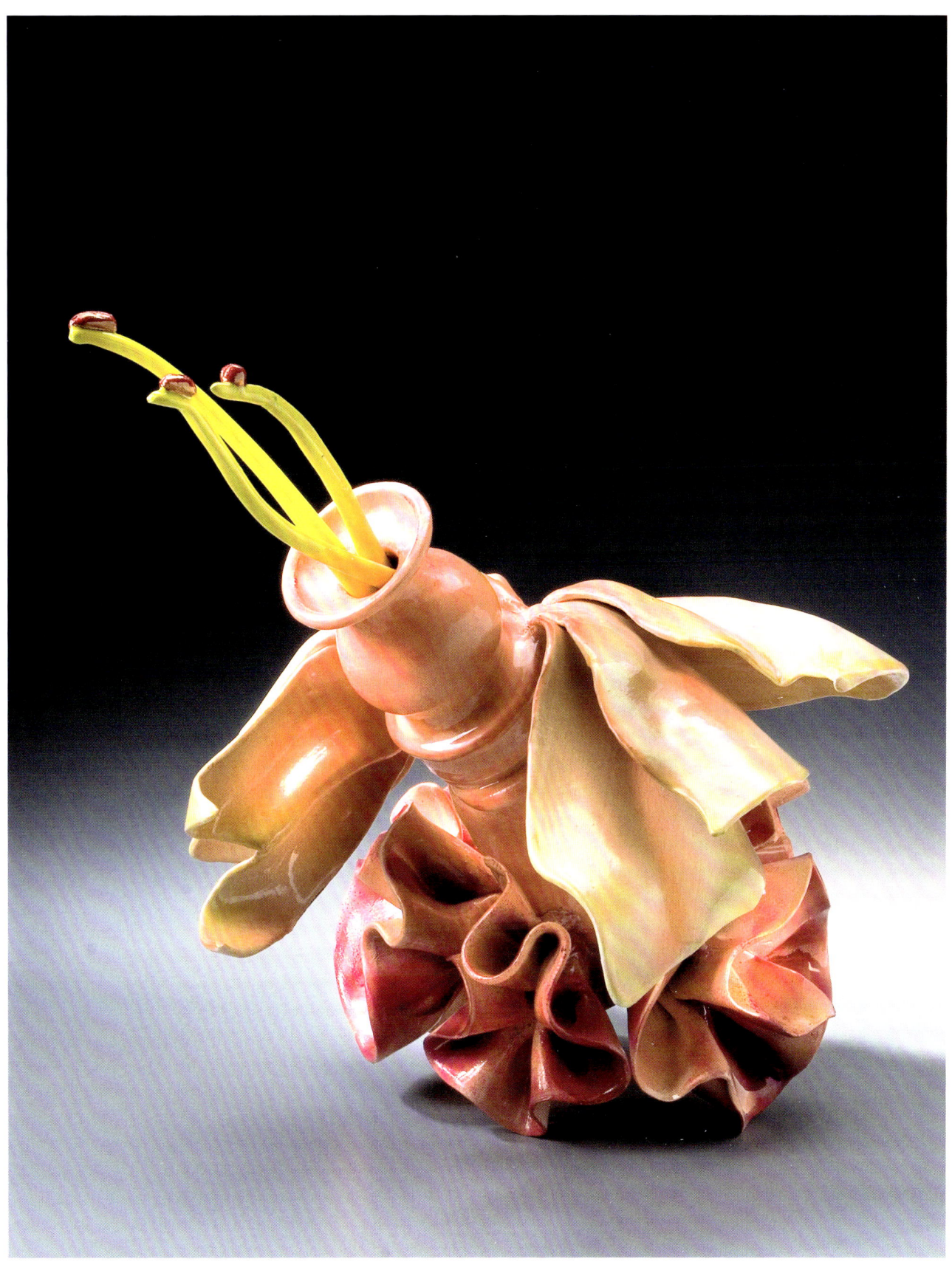

Tinkerbelle 2007
Glazed earthenware with china paint and luster
14½ × 13 × 12 in. (36.8 × 33 × 30.5 cm)

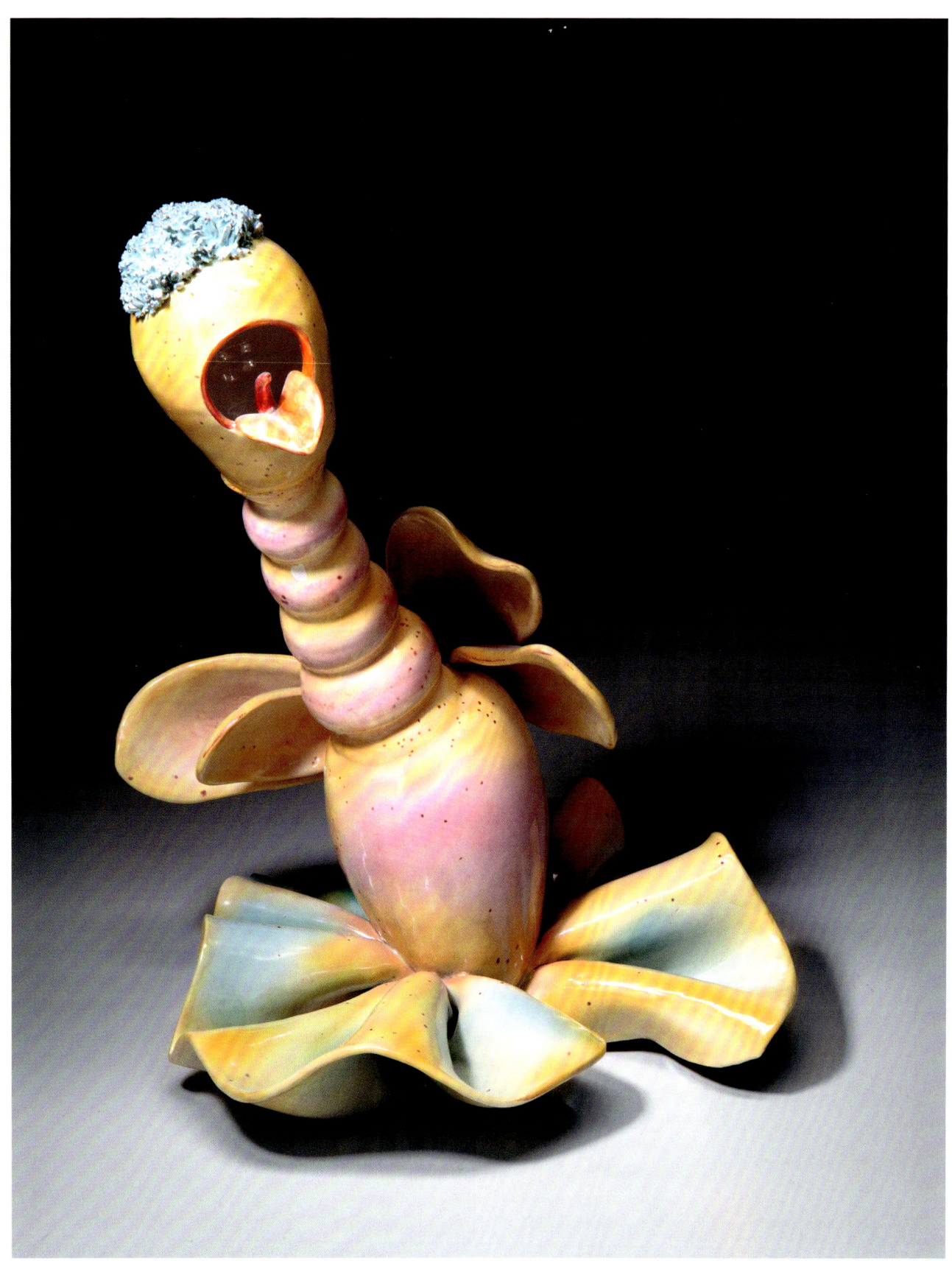

Diva Peregrine 2007
Glazed earthenware with china paint and luster
18 ⅓ × 13 × 12 in. (46.6 × 33 × 30.5 cm)

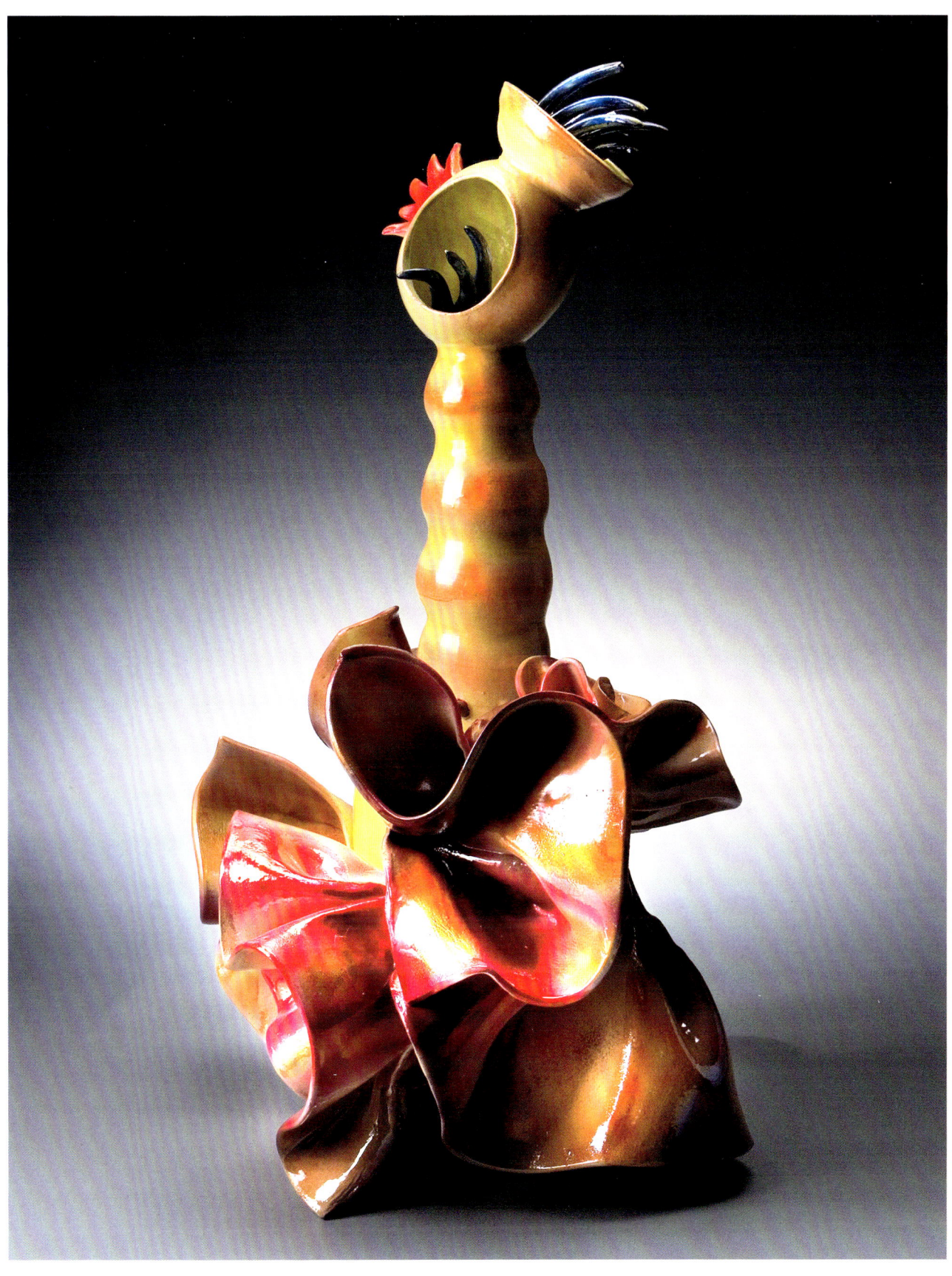

Ricci's Samba Partner 2007
Glazed earthenware with luster
20½ × 13½ × 11 in. (52.1 × 34.3 × 27.9 cm)

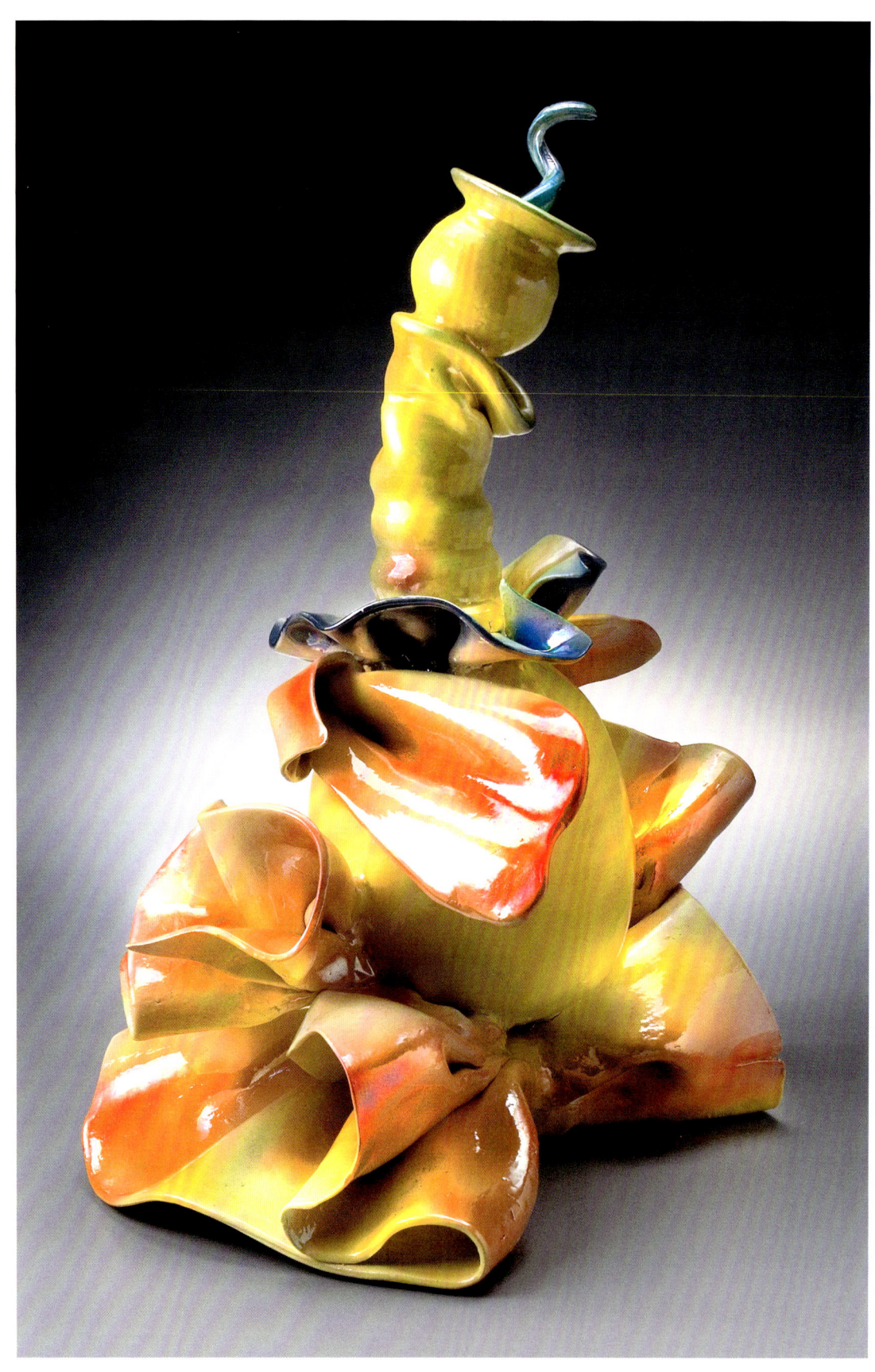

Samba Dancer 2007
Glazed earthenware with china paint and luster
17 ¾ × 14 × 10 in. (45.1 × 35.6 × 25.4 cm)

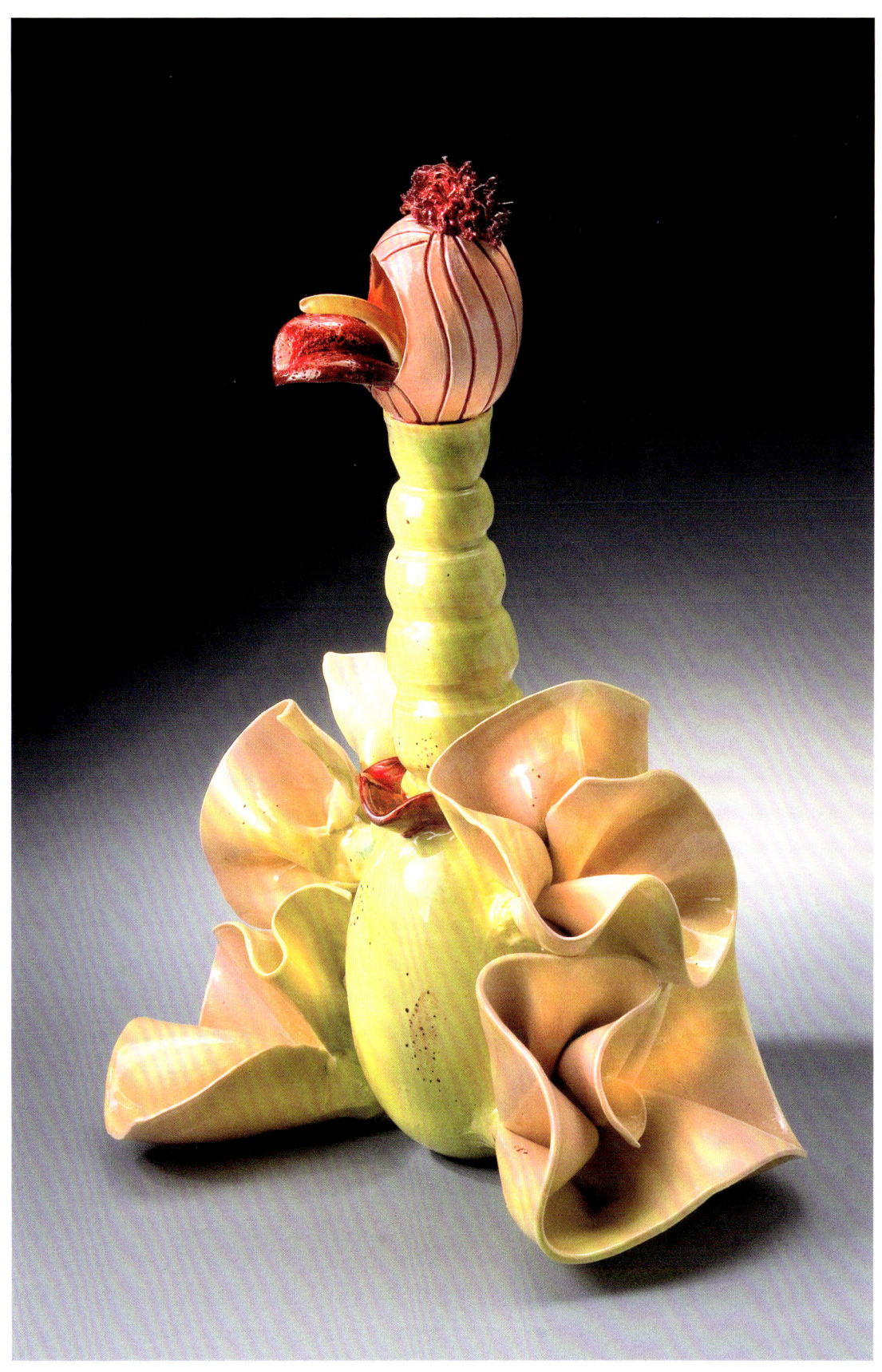

Samba Chicken 2007
Glazed earthenware with china paint and luster
18 ½ × 13 × 9 ½ in. (47 × 33 × 24.1 cm)
Collection Tom and Loretta Mentzer

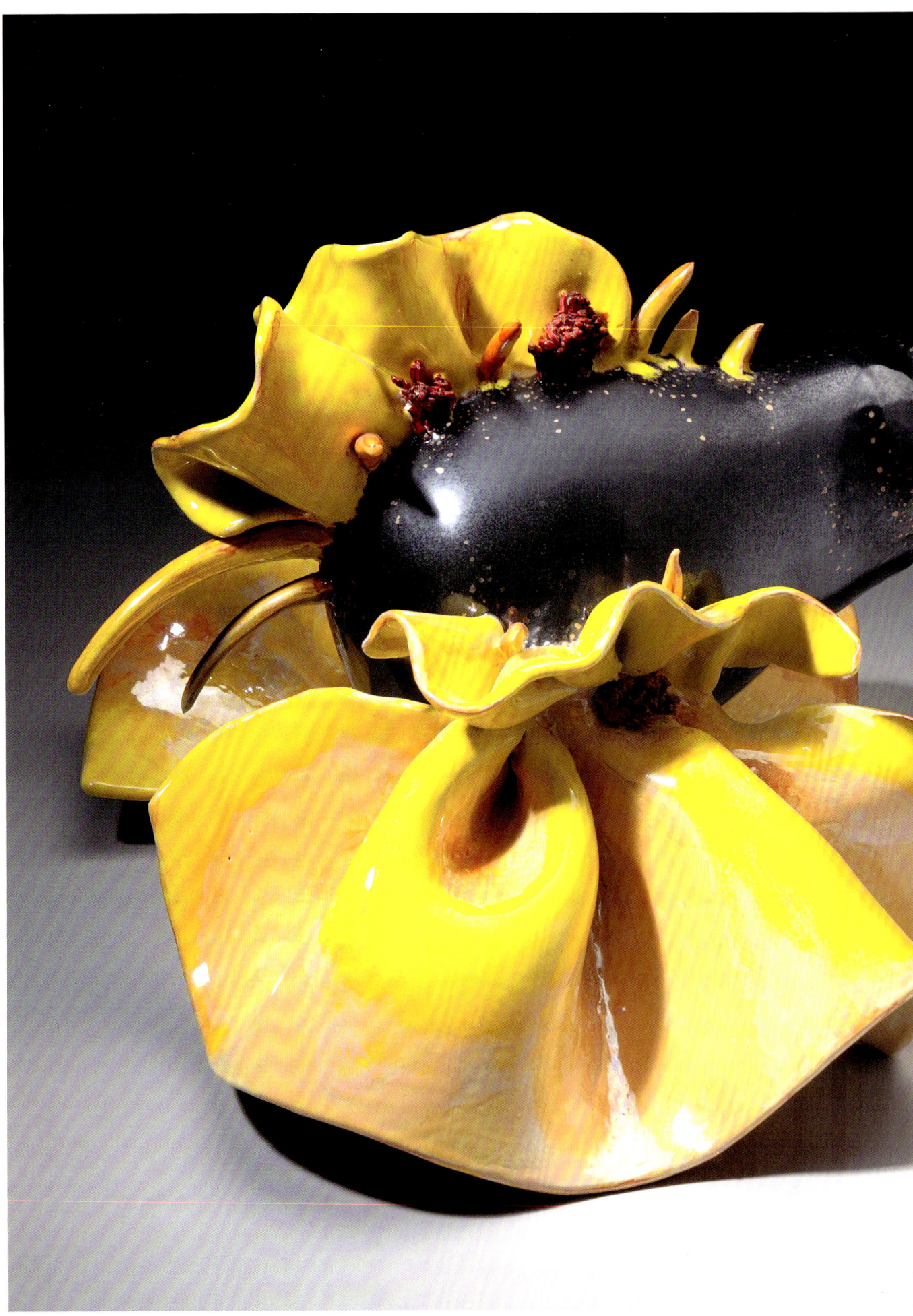

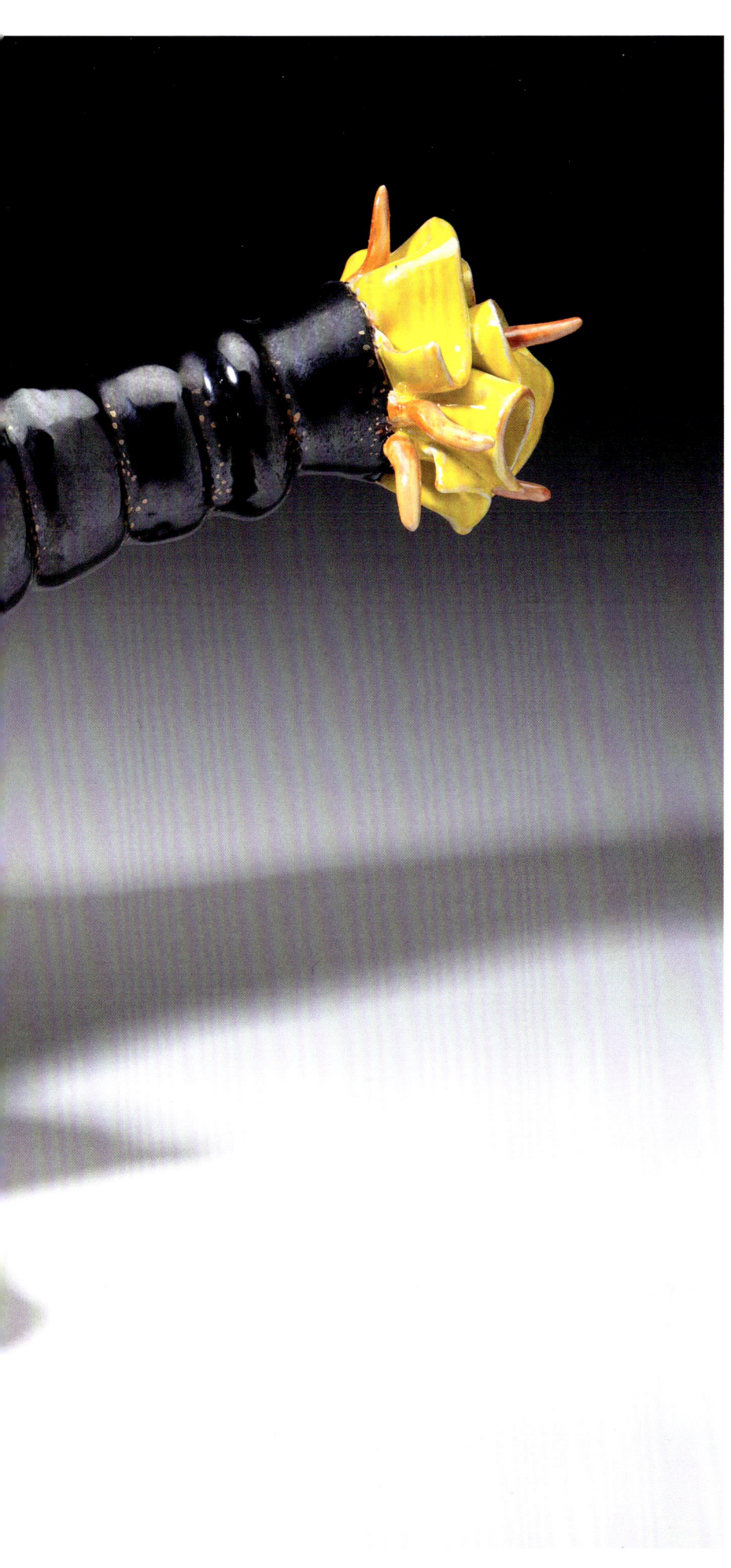

Curious Georgia 2008
Glazed earthenware with china paint
19 × 15 × 11 in. (48.3 × 38.1 × 27.9 cm)
Collection Michael Klein

LINDA LIGHTON:
SHAPES OF ABSENCE AND LONGING

by Sara Morris

Like many of Linda Lighton's ceramic sculptures, *The Secretary* (1986) (fig. 1) gives shape to absence and longing. Resembling a life-sized white silk blouse with perfectly puffed sleeves and a so-called pussy bow, this sartorial sculpture evokes a signature look of 1980s women's fashion. In the blouse's hand-modeled and glossy white surface, soft curves cling to what could be perceived as an ideal feminine form underneath. *The Secretary*, part of Lighton's *Americana* series, begun in 1981, draws inspiration from everyday articles of clothing—icons of American culture such as work shirts, denim jackets, and aprons—that serve as metaphors for gender and class. When taken together, these works reveal the notable absence of the body throughout much of Lighton's oeuvre—a lack that reflects women's exclusion within historical narratives while simultaneously amplifying women's experiences and desire for visibility on their terms.

Clothing, of course, is a powerful conveyor of identity, including sex, gender, sexuality, socioeconomic status, profession, and group affiliations. Lighton's attention to clothing, rather than the figure, exemplifies sociologist Joanne Entwistle's observation that "so signifi-

cant are clothes to our readings of the body that they can come to stand for sexual difference in the *absence* of a body."[1] Without a body to scrutinize, viewers project their own assumptions onto the garments, pulling themselves into the work, one sleeve at a time. In the case of *The Secretary*, the blouse connotes not only femininity but also the stereotype of the office secretary—a role often held by overqualified, college-educated women striving to shatter the glass ceiling, yet frequently depicted as sexy, sassy, and available.

It is fitting that *The Secretary* was created two years before the workplace drama *Working Girl* (1988), starring Melanie Griffith, Sigourney Weaver, and Harrison Ford. Griffith plays a career-driven secretary from Staten Island who works in Manhattan. To be taken seriously, Griffith's character embraces a polished corporate aesthetic characterized by a short haircut and broad-shouldered suits. In the 1980s, power dressing became a way for women to assert themselves in the workplace. In discussing clothing's connection to the body and identity, Entwistle traces the causes and effects of fashion in the twentieth century, when more people—particularly women—began working outside of the home. As interactions among strangers became daily occurrences, individuals found themselves with less time to make lasting, meaningful impressions.[2] She argues that with the rise of anonymity, one's appearance gained greater significance. In the context of the 1980s, then, it follows that the anonymity of *The Secretary* speaks to women's desire for greater visibility in professional spheres and beyond.

Paradoxically, however, this sense of anonymity also highlights a feminist critique of the objectification of women, who are reduced to mere items like a blouse or skirt, emphasizing the complex and contradictory nature of being seen. The work shares many similarities with feminist art of the 1980s, which often analyzed figurative representations of the female body as constructions of the male gaze, particularly in the context of nudity in both art and popular culture. As the British feminist film theorist Laura Mulvey writes, women's bodies "are simultaneously looked at and displayed, with their

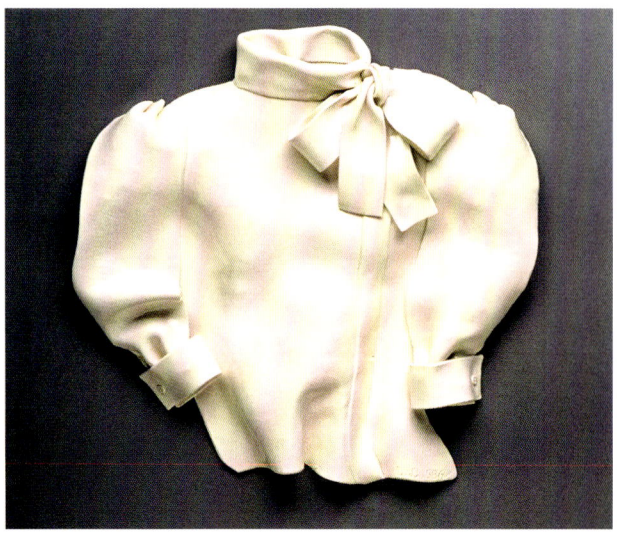

1 **LINDA LIGHTON, The Secretary** 1986
Glazed earthenware
18 × 17 × 3 in. (45.7 × 43.2 × 7.6 cm)

appearance coded for strong visual and erotic impact so that they can be said to connote *to-be-looked-at-ness*."[3] Lighton's sculpture of a blouse—deliberately portrayed without its wearer—flips the script, obscuring signs of bodily difference to some extent and turning the act of covering up into a challenge to traditional representations of the female figure in sculpture.

Men's clothing also makes appearances in Lighton's *Americana* series. For example, *Dude* (1981) (fig. 2) is a hand-formed ceramic sculpture of a sleeveless white shirt. In the early twentieth century, these affordable undershirts were marketed to working-class men. Today, however, they are colloquially known as muscle shirts or "wifebeaters"—a deeply derogatory name that links these tank tops to domestic violence against women. It is unclear if Lighton would have known of this term in the early 1980s, but what is evident is the artist's deliberate use of the comparatively subdued, yet still gendered, label "Dude." The use of male-oriented terminology here is noteworthy, especially given the evolution of its meaning in the late twentieth century. In the 1930s and 1940s, men used "dude" to describe a man particularly attentive to his attire.[4] By the 1980s, the term had loosened, evolving to refer to men who were laid-back. In the body's absence, *Dude* and *The Secretary* construct a more nuanced narrative that situates clothing as both a tool of patriarchal control and a productive marker of nonconformity and self-empowerment.

Lighton's emphasis on clothing speaks to the trail of life experiences she left behind her. The importance of dressing well was instilled in her from an early age. Born in Kansas City, Missouri, she belonged to an affluent family who owned Woolf Brothers, a high-end department store in town. Reflecting on her summers spent working at the store and the importance of dress, Lighton shared, "Every single day of my life, I was given the once-over to make sure I looked appropriate."[5] It is therefore unsurprising that some of her earliest works embody the societal expectations associated with upper- and middle-class behavior—expectations she would ultimately choose to reject in her own life.

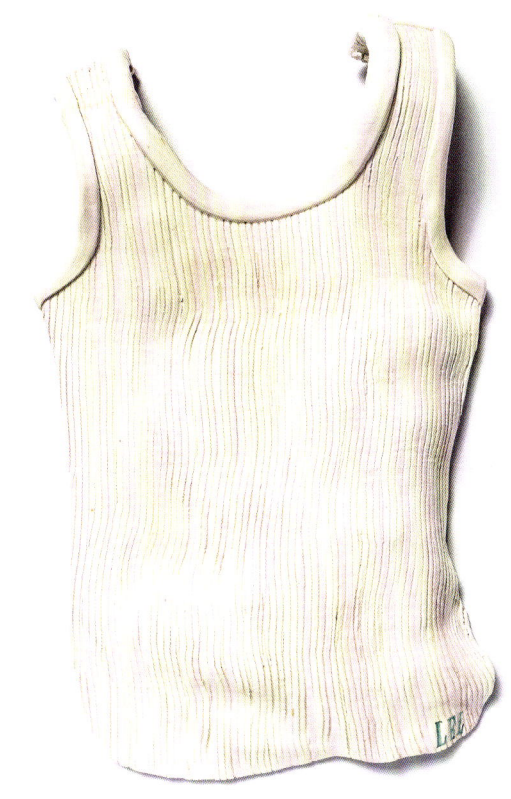

2 **LINDA LIGHTON**, Dude 1981
Glazed earthenware
19 × 13 × 3 in. (48.3 × 33 × 7.6 cm)

Lighton's desire to break with tradition and her family's expectations can be traced to a pivotal moment in 1968: her expected debut at the annual Jewel Ball, a debutante ball held at the Nelson-Atkins Museum of Art in Kansas City. Her grandmother supported the event, hoping to promote greater acceptance of Jews in society. However, Lighton sought a very different path for herself and chose not to attend. Parental retribution was swift. Her father had her committed to a mental institution against her will as punishment for her defiance. She was confined for over four months and was only allowed to leave her prison in order to attend court hearings against

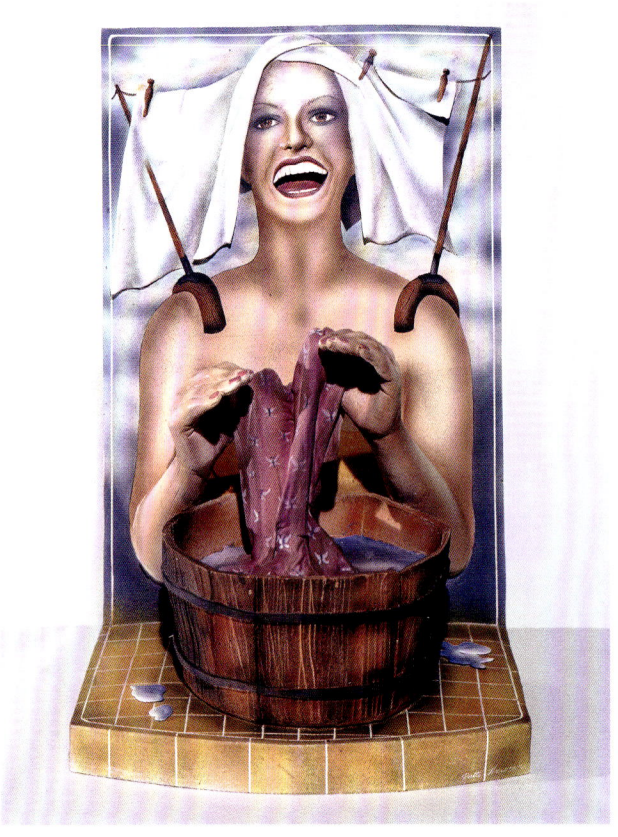

3 **PATTI WARASHINA, Wash and Wear** 1976
Glazed low-fire clay
25 ¼ × 15 ¾ × 13 ½ in. (64.1 × 40 × 34.3 cm)
Memphis Brooks Museum of Art, Memphis, TN

handling, reading, writing, and motherhood were all part of her radical new existence. So was Lighton's impulse to move, out of fear of being found by her father.

Though Lighton would eventually move back to Kansas City in the early 1980s—enrolling at the Kansas City Art Institute (KCAI) in 1987, where she studied ceramics under Ken Ferguson and sculpture under Dale Eldred—she began her ceramics training in Seattle, Washington, at the Factory of Visual Arts, a newly formed alternative art school founded by artist and architect Lin Lipetz.[6] Many ceramic artists, including Patti Warashina, Mark Burns, Anne Currier, and David Furman, taught there as part of their graduate studies at the University of Washington, Seattle. At the Factory, Lighton learned pottery techniques and was introduced to Funk ceramics—a mode of making that emerged in northern California in the 1960s and was canonized in the 1967 exhibition *Funk*, curated by Peter Selz for the Berkeley Art Museum at the University of California, Berkeley. Characterized as nonaesthetic, apolitical, ambiguous, unapologetic, and ironic, the anything-goes message of Funk ceramics spread from northern California to the Pacific Northwest.

Too often, representational and low-fire ceramics from this era are written about strictly in terms of Funk, and though Lighton credits these material, representational, and humorous artistic currents she encountered at the Factory as a major influence, her work is also informed by second-wave feminism and the broader landscape of West Coast ceramics of the 1970s. In the 1980s and 1990s, Lighton participated in a number of all-women gallery exhibitions, including *Women in Art* (1981) in Springfield, Ohio; *Women's Perspective* (1983) in Guilford, Connecticut; and *Genesis Gender* (1993) in Kansas City, Missouri. Indeed, Lighton belongs to a lineage of women artists, including Beatrice Wood (1893–1998), Viola Frey (1933–2004), Judy Chicago (b. 1939), Coille Hooven (1939–2024), and Patti Warashina (b. 1940), who engaged ceramics and a visual repertoire of feminine iconography as expressions of women's creativity and empowerment.

her father. After months of litigation, she was released. She left home, married, moved to Lawrence, Kansas, and helped publish an underground newspaper called *The Screw: A Twisted Device for Holding Things Together.* Soon after, she and her husband hitched a ride as far from her father as possible—to San Francisco.

The years between 1968 and 1977 were an intense and itinerant period in her life. It's a countercultural tale of newfound freedoms and utopian dreams set in the years following the "Summer of Love." Lighton and her husband lived in a house in the Haight-Ashbury district, down the street from Janis Joplin and Jefferson Airplane, in sharp contrast to the conformity of her former life in the Midwest. In 1969, they had a child. Sex, drugs, pan-

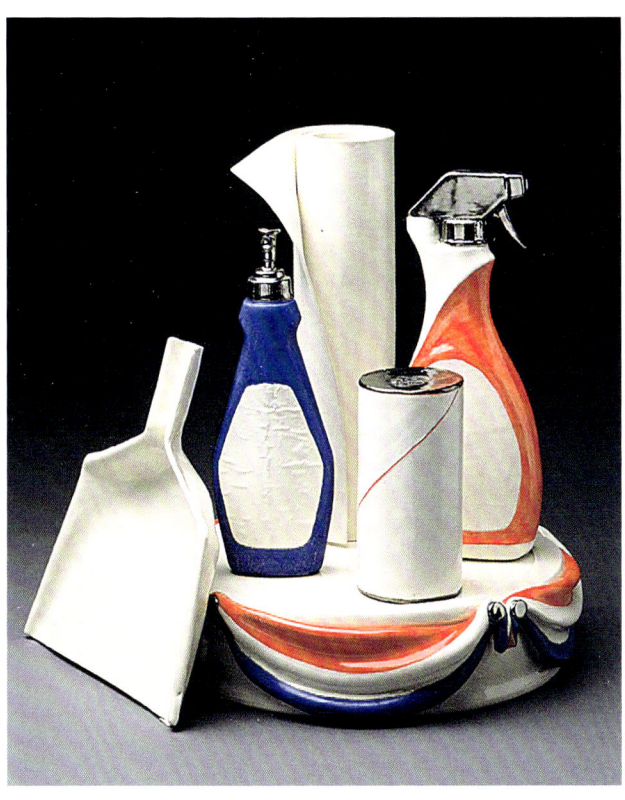

4 **LINDA LIGHTON, The First Lady** 1986
Glazed earthenware with china paint and luster
14 × 9 ½ × 13 in. (35.6 × 24.1 × 33 cm)

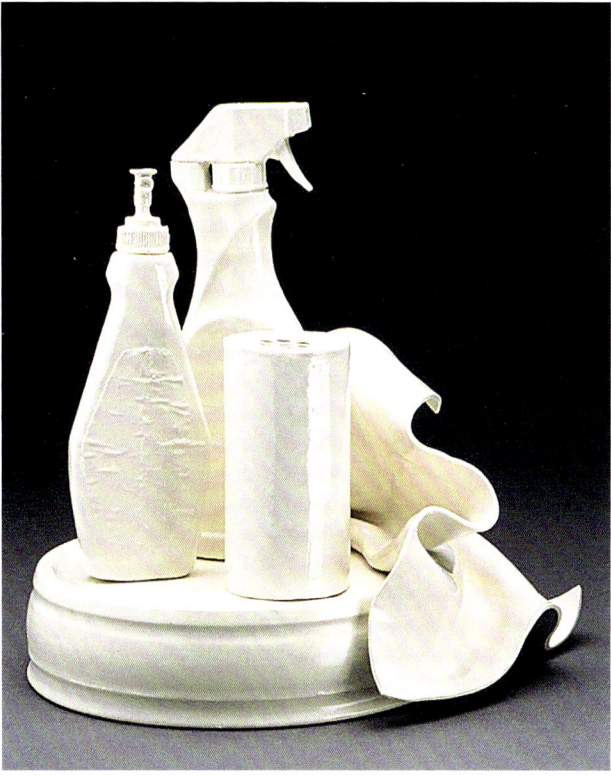

5 **LINDA LIGHTON, What the Bridal Consultant Never Tells You** 1987
Glazed earthenware
10 × 12 ½ × 12 in. (25.4 × 31.8 × 30.5 cm)
Collection Dorothy Curry

One of the most visible artists creating women-centered ceramics in the Pacific Northwest and, for several years in the mid-1960s, the Midwest was Warashina, who joined the faculty at the University of Washington, Seattle, as a professor of ceramics in 1970. Warashina is known for her work in low-fire materials and sculptures of fantastical female forms engaged in various domestic tasks. In the 1970s, she frequently depicted women playfully performing—and evading—housework, as illustrated in figurative sculptures such as *Wash and Wear* (1976) **(fig. 3)** and *Clothes Line Robbery* (1979). These works serve as commentaries on the toils of domestic labor and motherhood, while also unsettling figurative ceramic's associations with porcelain figurines, femininity, and Asian American stereotypes.

Lighton, too, embraced feminine iconography, low-fire clay bodies and glazes, such as china painting, as uniquely female expressions. In 1987, she exhibited her series *And She Did Not Live Happily Ever After... but She Did Live* at the Batz-Lawrence Gallery in Kansas City. The exhibition included still lifes of cleaning supplies like dustpans, dishrags, and other tools of domestic labor, such as *The First Lady* (1986) and *What the Bridal Consultant Never Tells You* (1987) **(figs. 4, 5)**. Both pieces resemble cleaning kits of sorts, glazed with colors that nod to the women referenced in their titles. Take *The First Lady*, for example: a red spray bottle, a blue bottle of dish soap, and a roll of white paper towels echo the colors of the American flag. In an artist statement from 1987, Lighton explained her feelings about traditional, gen-

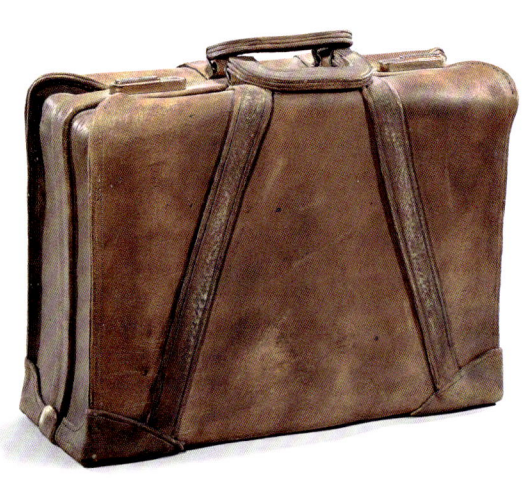

6 **MARILYN LEVINE, Suitcase** 1971
Ceramic
18 × 21 ½ × 8 ½ in. (45.7 × 54.6 × 21.6 cm)
Crocker Art Museum, Sacramento, CA

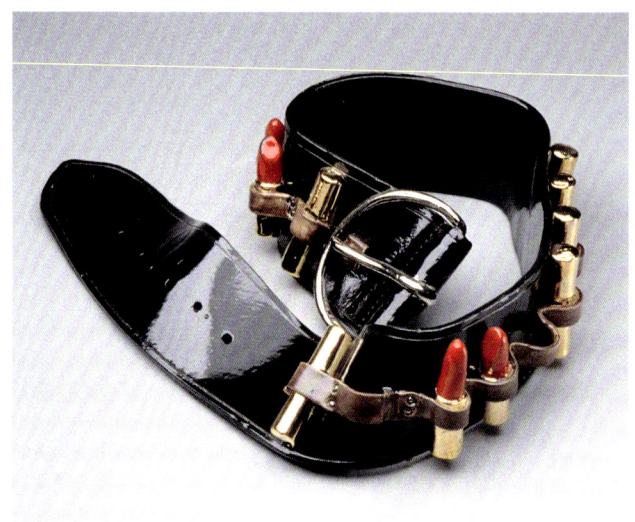

7 **LINDA LIGHTON, Bullet Belt** 1985
Glazed earthenware with china paint, luster and wood (not pictured)
4 × 15 × 15 in. (10.2 × 38.1 × 38.1 cm)
Crocker Art Museum, Sacramento, CA

der-based divisions of labor regarding domesticity and homelife:

I'm sure we no longer lie to ourselves about the creativity of housework. We clean from a different viewpoint now. It is no longer an end in itself. We are trying to explode the myth of these roles.[7]

In the context of second-wave feminism, Lighton engages with themes of sexual liberation and gender non-conformity through a lexicon of explicitly feminine iconography.

Lighton is also preceded by Canadian artist Marilyn Levine (1935–2005), whose hyper-realistic ceramic sculptures of worn-out brown leather objects, such as *Suitcase* (1971) **(fig. 6)**, offer clues about the object's life, such as age, use, and relationship with the body. When asked about her choice of subject matter in an interview, Levine explained that she was drawn to leather articles because "they tell you something about the wearer."[8] Beyond the intricacy of her sculptures, the effectiveness of the illusion in *Suitcase* stems from the careful atten-

tion to surface treatments that often incorporated non-ceramic materials, like oil paint and shoe polish. The wear patterns and signs of use that characterize Levine's works are also self-reflexive in that they speak to her own laborious artistic practice.

Although Lighton's works are exquisitely modeled, they are not meant to deceive the eye of the viewer like Levine's illusionist ceramics. Lighton's sculptures, particularly from the series *And She Did Not Live Happily Ever After... but She Did Live*, are more politically charged and boldly assert the power of female sexuality and the erotic. For instance, the shiny surface of *Bullet Belt* (1985) **(fig. 7)** resembles black patent leather. Lighton's rendition of a wide leather belt blends elements of an 1880s western holster with 1980s BDSM subcultures. In place of bullets, ammo loops hold gold-luster cartridges of red lipstick, offering a sex-positive critique distinct from other sartorial works, as both lipstick and belts make connections between bodily pain and pleasure.

Examining Lighton's early works from the 1980s reveals how her ceramics serve as provocative counterpoints to sculptures depicting women's experiences through literal, figurative representations, thereby expanding the narrative possibilities of clay in the 1970s and 1980s.

Since the late 1980s, Lighton has created entirely new emblems for female expression, moving from everyday articles of clothing and cleaning supplies to fantastical and erotic creations of flamboyant flowers and sea creatures. For example, the hand-modeled ceramic folds and sensuous petals of *Wondrous Kiss* (2005) (fig. 8) are particularly sexual in their glistening rose-pink references to female genitalia. A single flower emerges from a glistening bed of green leaves. Unlike the anthropomorphized floral sculptures in Lighton's *Diva* series (1999–2009 and 2014)—named after women she admires—these china-painted sculptures are inspired by "the sex of flowers."[9]

Sculptures like *Wondrous Kiss* recall feminist erotic art of the 1970s, which employed vaginal imagery as a means to counter the sexual objectification and domination of women's bodies in art. Art historian Rachel Middleman has highlighted how women artists in the mid-1960s and 1970s, such as Hannah Wilke (1940–1993), used clay in the creation of abstract representations of genitalia, resisting clear-cut interpretations of biological differences and issues of determinism. This abstract approach to overtly erotic and bodily art challenged biological essentialism and critiqued traditional heterosexual and gender norms. While not abstract, Lighton's *Wondrous Kiss* resonates with Middleman's observations on erotic genital imagery that transcends normative male/female dichotomies. The sculpture takes the form of a "perfect flower," exposing the flower's male and female sex organs. From its center extend stylized evocative yellow structures that resemble stamens with slender filaments, and the pistil, which includes the flower's ovary, style, and stigma. In addition to her floral sculptures, Lighton's sculptures of fleshy, erect tubeworms (figs. 9, 10) act as stand-ins for the body. With tubeworms as their subject—organisms that often possess both male and female reproductive organs—these works use eroticism as a lens through which to interrogate binary notions of sex

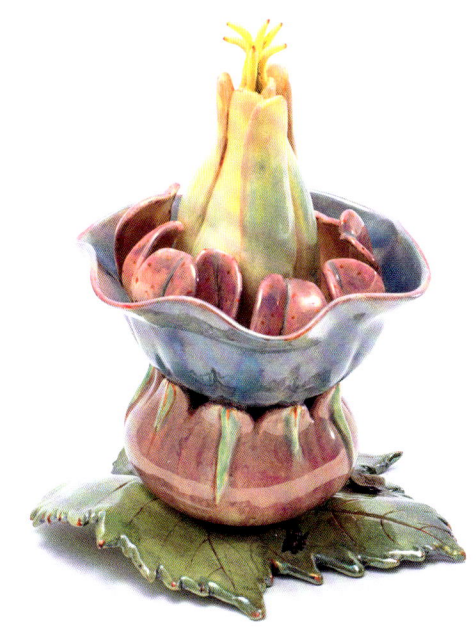

8 **LINDA LIGHTON, Wondrous Kiss** 2005
Glazed earthenware with china paint and luster
12 × 9 ½ × 9 ¼ in. (30.5 × 24.1 × 23.5 cm)

and gender, reflecting a shift toward a more fluid and unfixed way of seeing and being in the world.

What is particularly captivating about Lighton's use of the erotic is her ability to bring to the surface feelings and desires that are often left unexpressed in both social and personal relationships. In feminist writer and civil rights activist Audre Lorde's revolutionary essay "The Uses of the Erotic: The Erotic as Power," she understands the erotic as a female source of power, knowledge, and energy which exudes an internal sense of satisfaction.[10] For Lorde, unleashing the erotic in women dismantles the dominant power structures that forbid women from truly feeling joy in what they do. She articulates the pursuit of the erotic in all aspects of life as a crucial responsibility, one that requires a refusal to accept "the convenient, the shoddy, the conventionally expected, or the merely safe."[11] In a similar vein, Lighton has

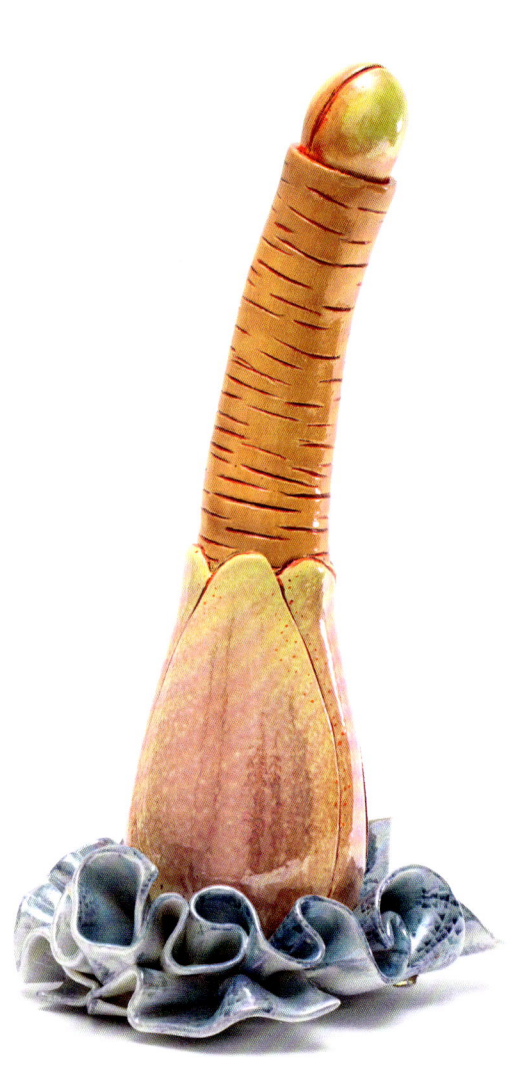

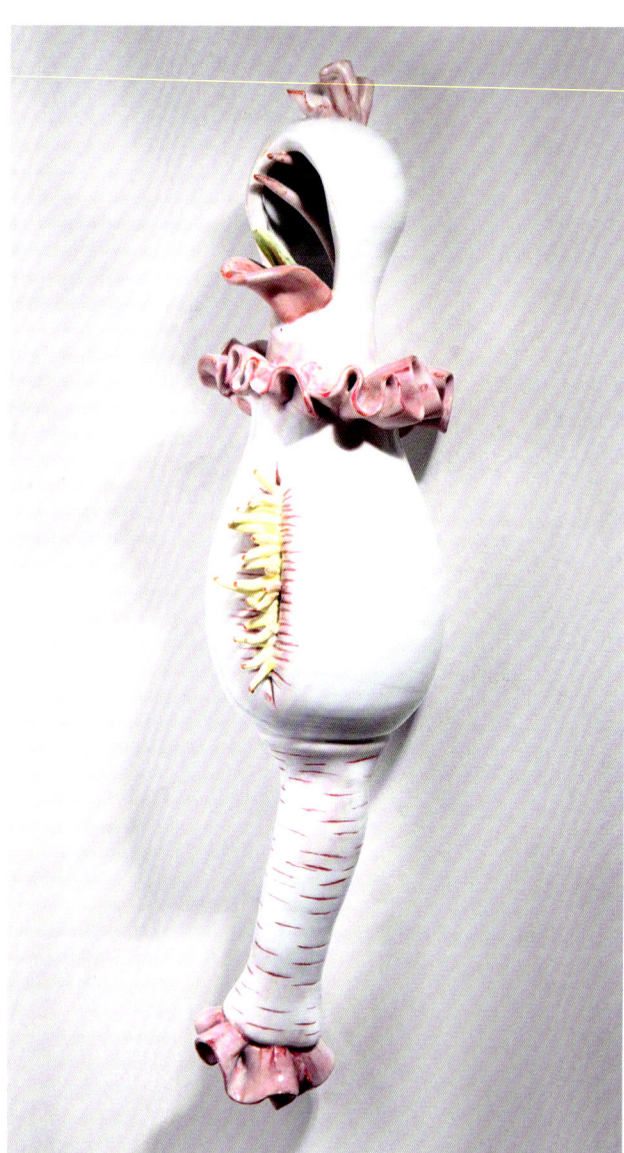

9 **LINDA LIGHTON**, Tubeworm 2004
Glazed earthenware with china paint and luster
17 × 5 × 6½ in. (43.2 × 12.7 × 16.5 cm)
Collection Rose Dergan, New York

10 **LINDA LIGHTON**, Tenacious Tubeworm 2003–5
Glazed earthenware with china paint
18 × 5 × 4½ in. (45.7 × 12.7 × 11.4 cm)

persistently challenged conventional expectations, playing on themes of bodily presence and absence in her art in order to explore the erotic within herself and quell the profound ache of unfulfilled desires. "My desire," she explains in her artist statement, "is to embrace the life force, hope and strive for a better future and world."[12] By giving shape to the themes of absence, longing, and the erotic, Lighton not only countered sexist exclusion by reimagining sculpture as both ceramic and feminine, but also introduced the possibility of transforming nonfigurative representational imagery into unfixed expressions of joy, fulfillment, and hope for the future.

Notes

1 Joanne Entwistle, "Fashion and Gender," in *The Fashioned Body: Fashion, Dress, and Modern Social Theory* (Cambridge: Polity Press, 2000), 141.

2 Ibid., 112–139.

3 Laura Mulvey, "Visual Pleasure and Narrative Cinema," in *The Feminism and Visual Culture Reader*, ed. Amelia Jones (New York: Routledge, 2003), 60.

4 Sarah Diamond, "Hey, Dude, What's the History of Dude?," *The New York Times*, March 23, 2024, https://www.nytimes.com/2024/03/23/insider/hey-dude-whats-the-history-of-dude.html.

5 Linda Lighton, e-mail to the author, September 26, 2024.

6 LaMar Harrington, *Ceramics in the Pacific Northwest: A History* (Seattle and London: University of Washington Press, 1979), 48.

7 Linda Lighton, Artist Statement, "And She Did Not Live Happily Ever After... but She Did Live," Batz-Lawrence Gallery, Inc. (November 6, 1987).

8 N. Foote, "Photo-Realists: 12 Interviews," *Art in America* 60 (November 1972): 84.

9 Linda Lighton, Artist Statement, "Tubeworm Tango," accessed October 31, 2024, https://www.lindalighton.com/#/new-gallery/.

10 Audre Lorde, "Uses of the Erotic: The Erotic as Power" (Trumansburg: The Crossing Press, 1978). https://www.proquest.com/books/uses-erotic-as-power/docview/2138587327/se-2. Lorde originally delivered her views on the erotic in a speech at the Fourth Berkshire Conference on the History of Women at Mount Holyoke College in Massachusetts in 1978. It was first published in a private edition of 250 copies for distribution at the Conference on Feminist Perspectives on Pornography, San Francisco, November 1978.

11 Lorde, 7.

12 Linda Lighton, Artist Statement, accessed November 7, 2024, https://www.lindalighton.com/bioandstatement.

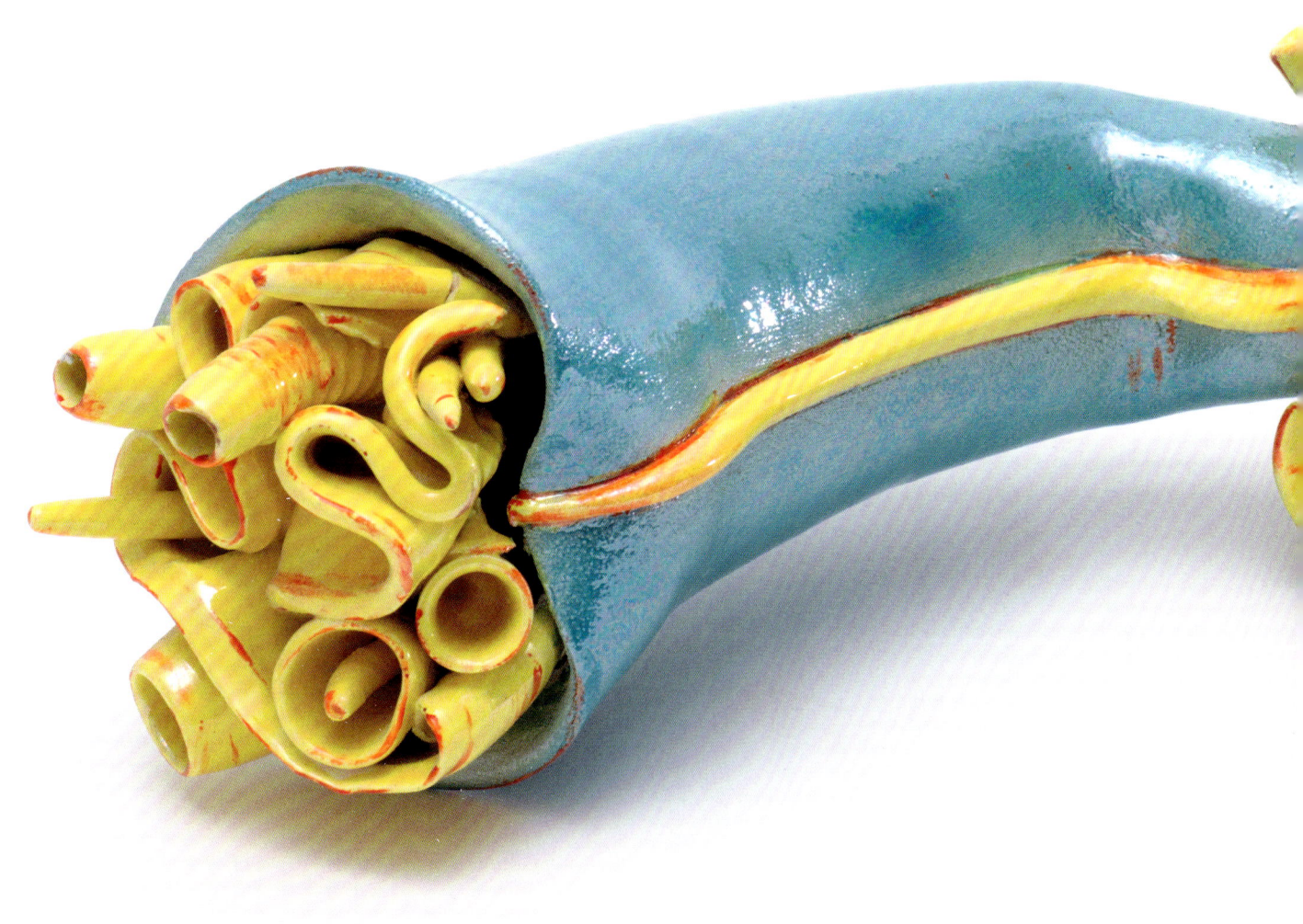

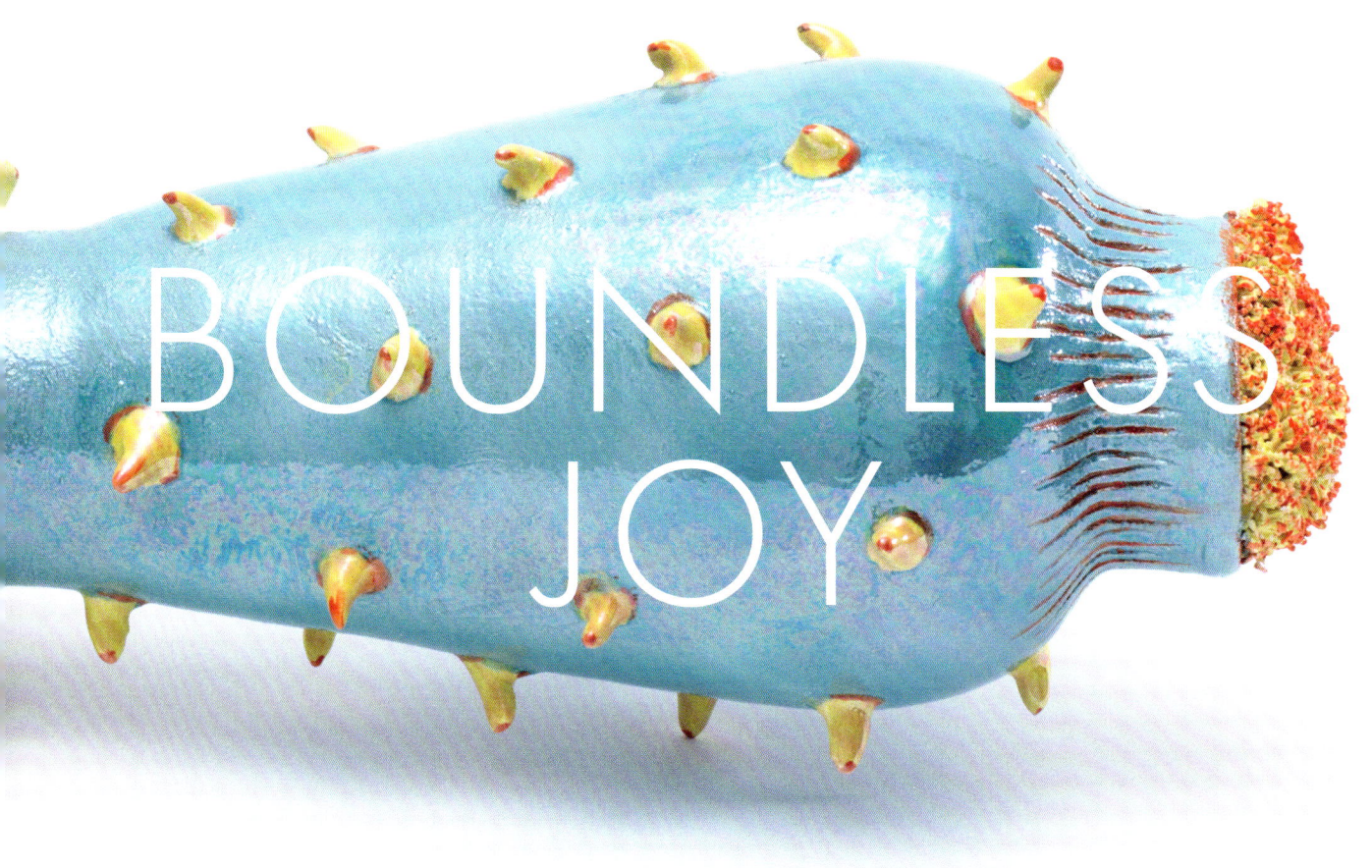

BOUNDLESS
JOY

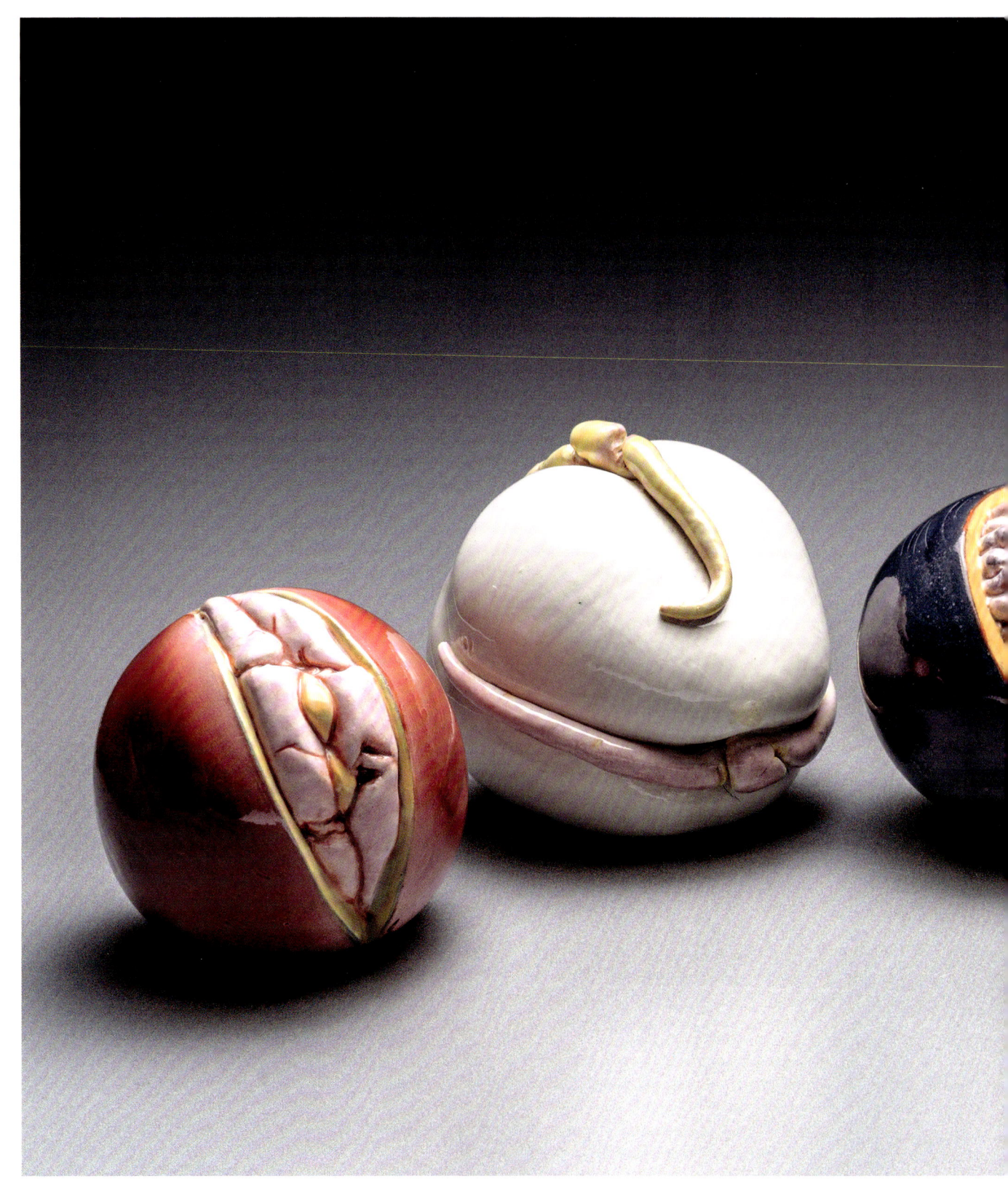

Globes 1979
Glazed earthenware with china paint and luster
Each approx. 6 × 6 × 6 in. (15.2 × 15.2 × 15.2 cm)

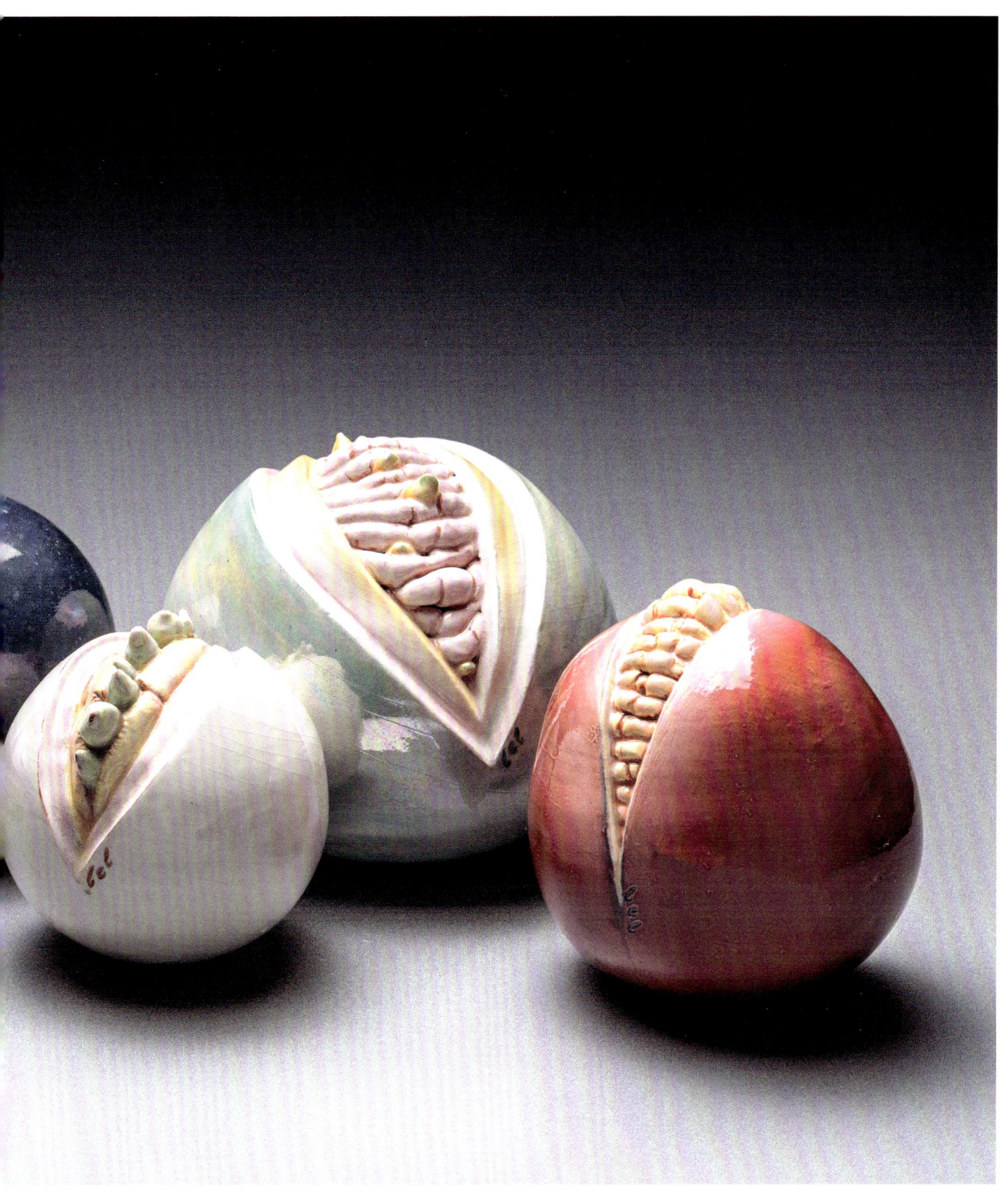

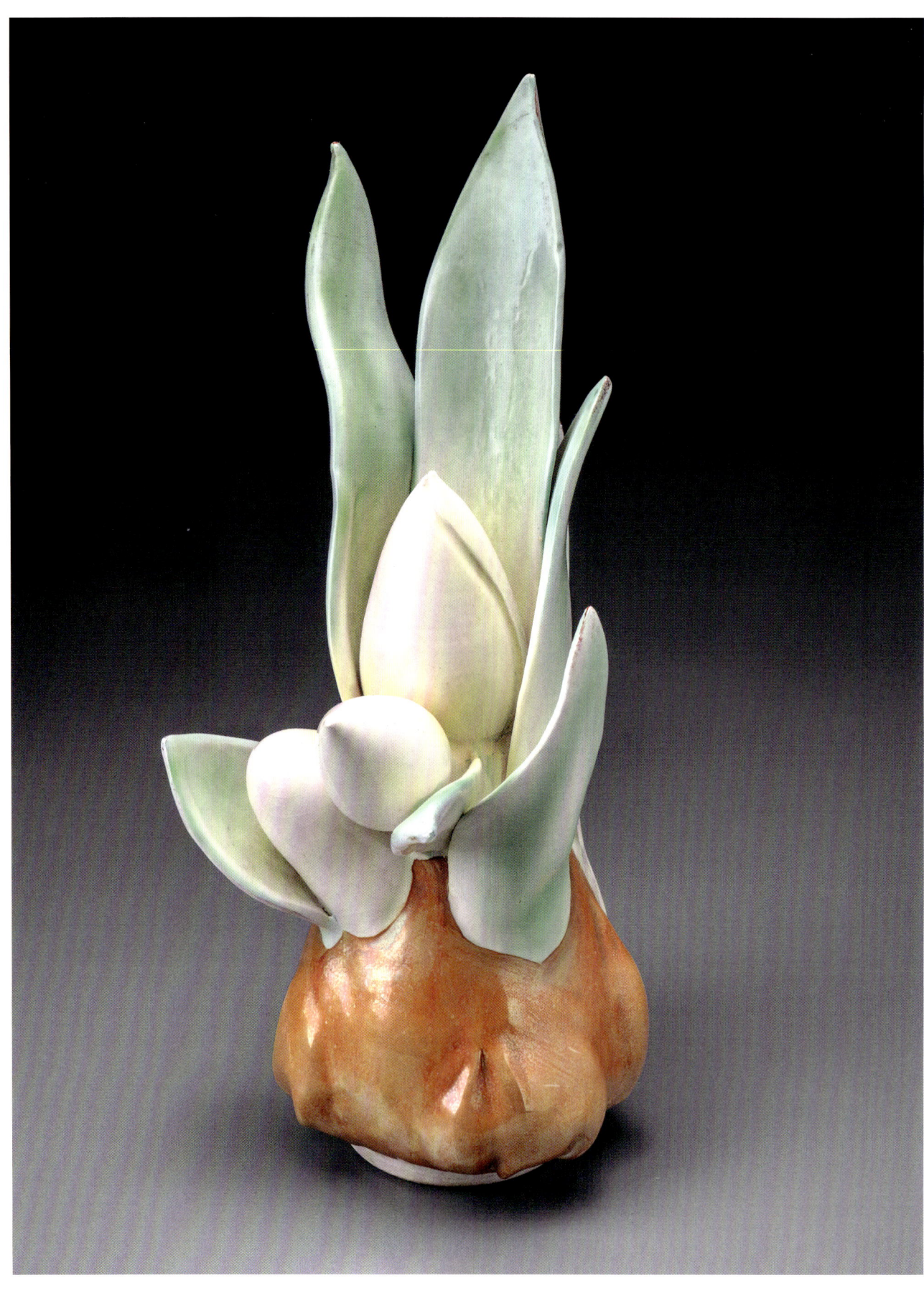

Flowering Bulb 1985
Glazed earthenware with china paint and luster
19 × 8 ½ × 8 in. (48.3 × 21.6 × 20.3 cm)

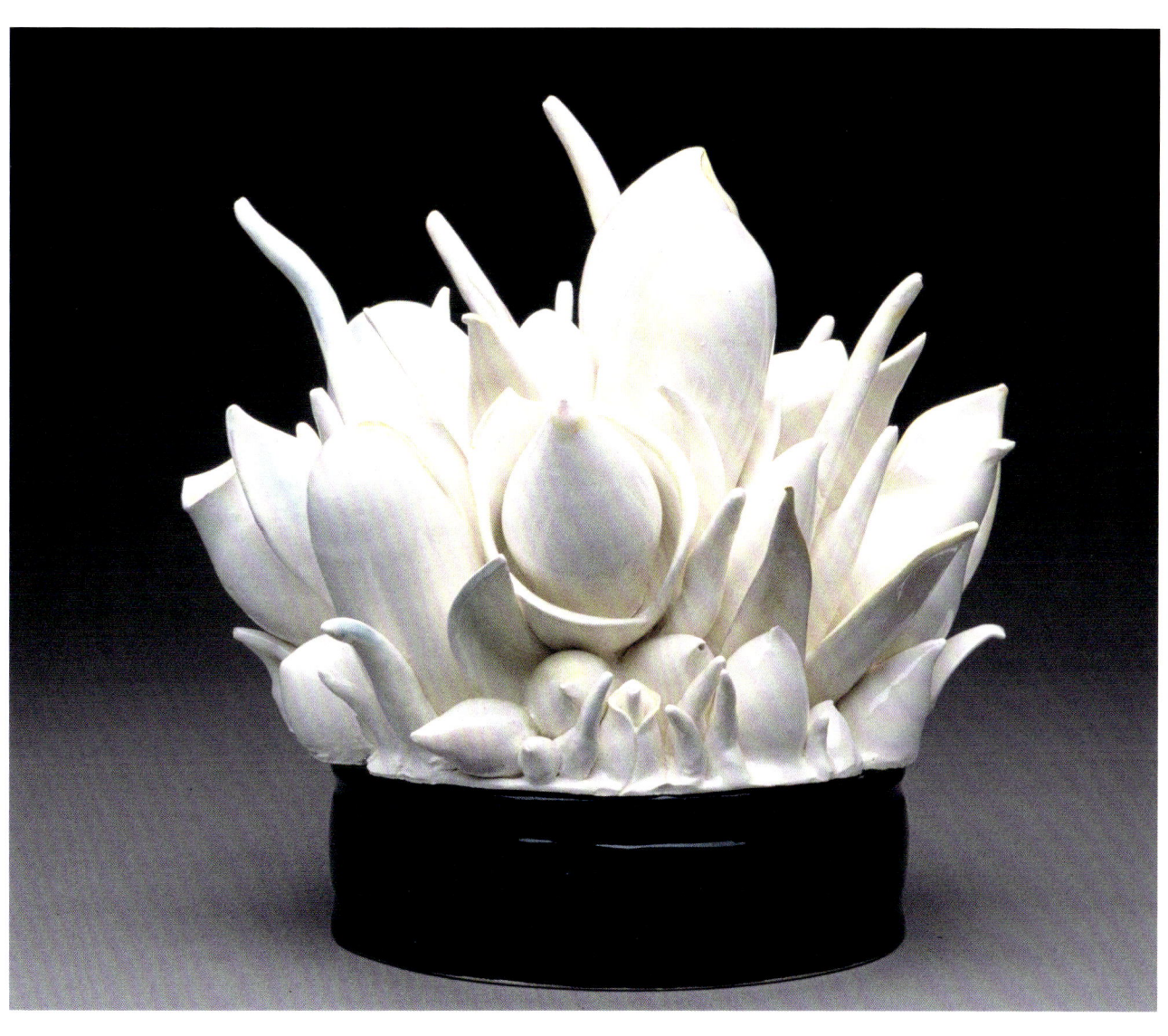

Flowering Bulbs 1986–96
Glazed earthenware with china paint
13 ½ × 14 × 14 in. (34.3 × 35.6 × 35.6 cm)

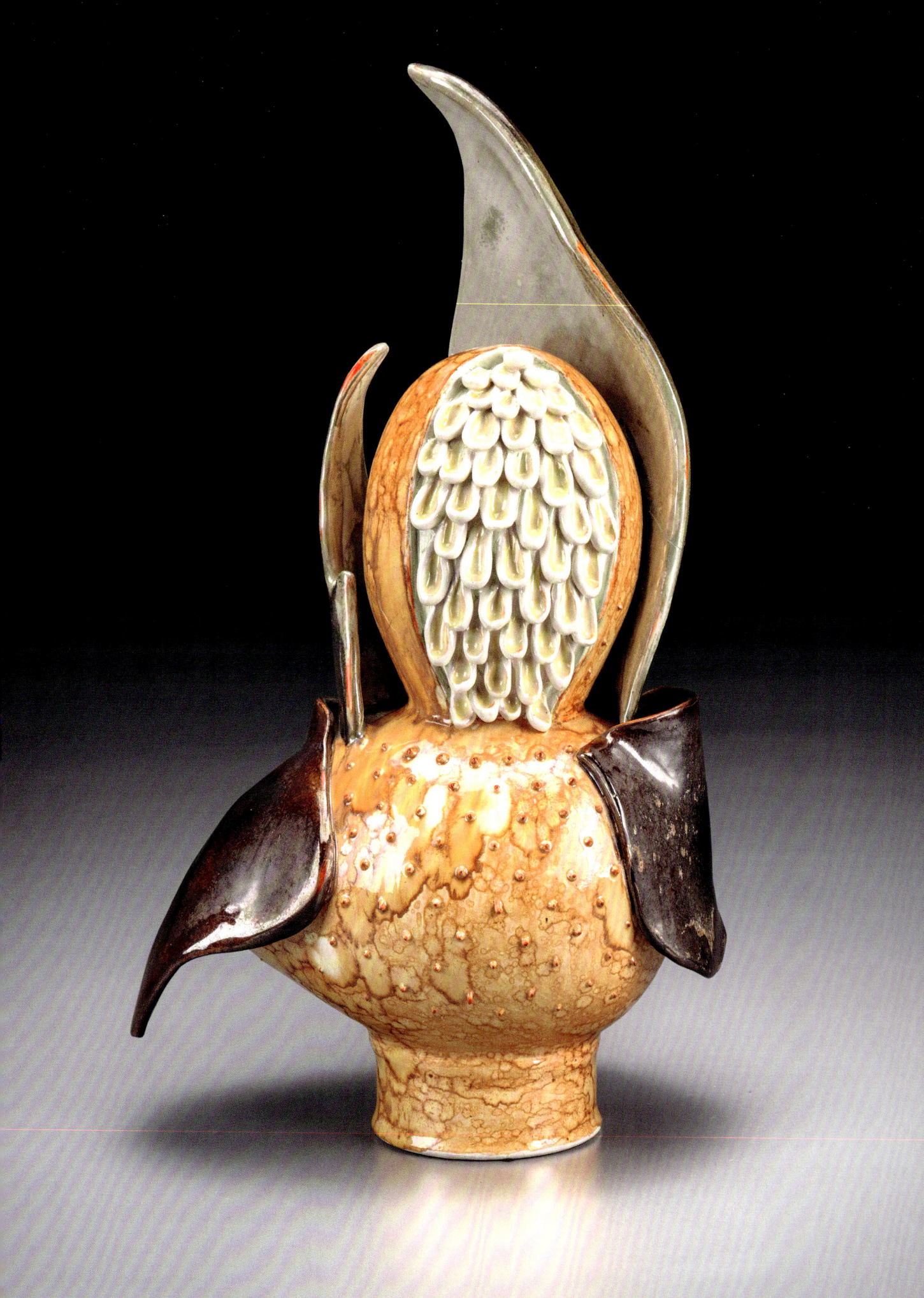

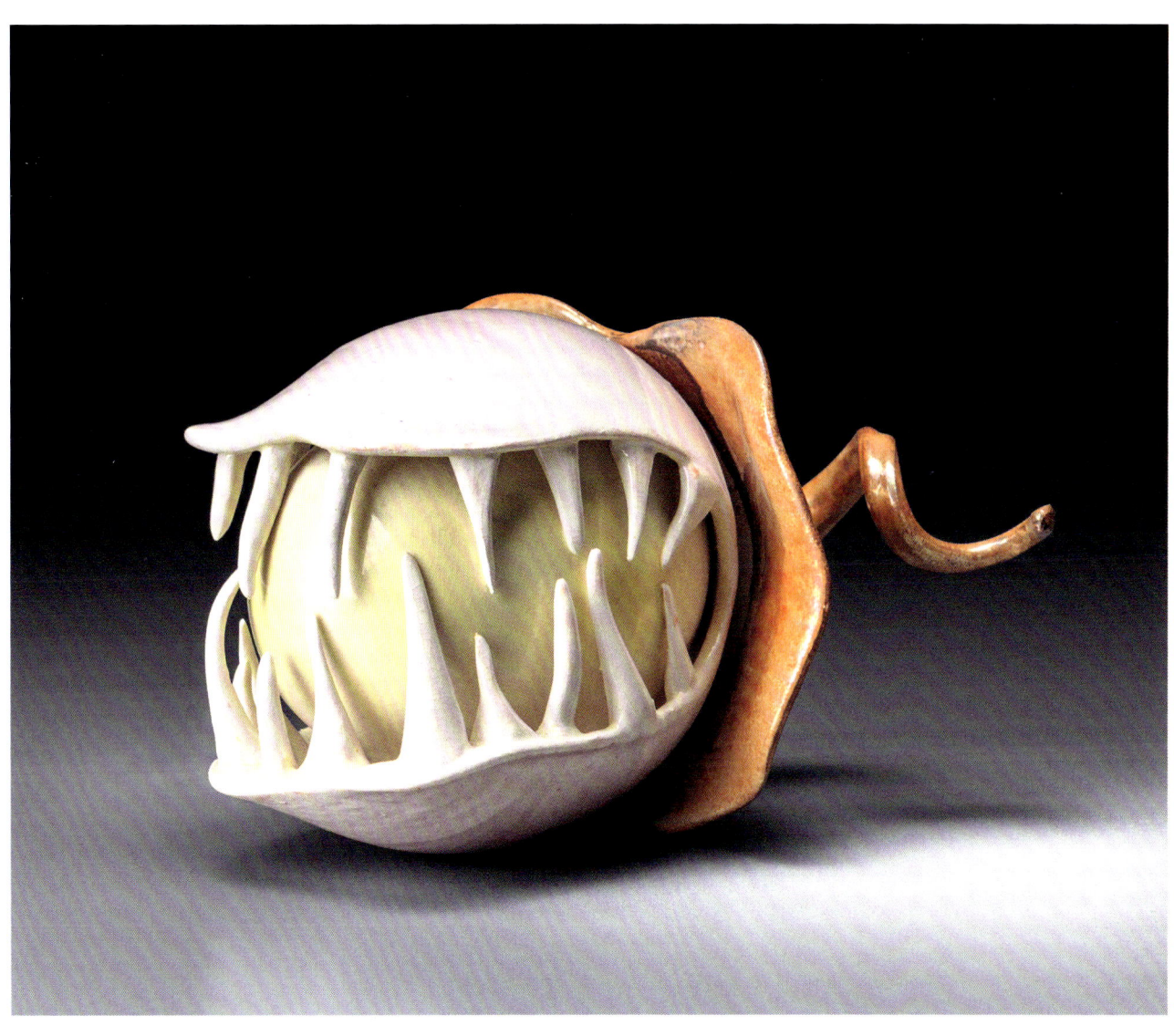

Left page
Untitled 1987
Glazed earthenware with china paint and luster
19 × 11 × 9 in. (48.3 × 27.9 × 22.9 cm)

The Iron of a Mother's Love 1987
Glazed earthenware with china paint and luster
5 ½ × 7 ½ × 9 in. (14 × 19.1 × 22.9 cm)

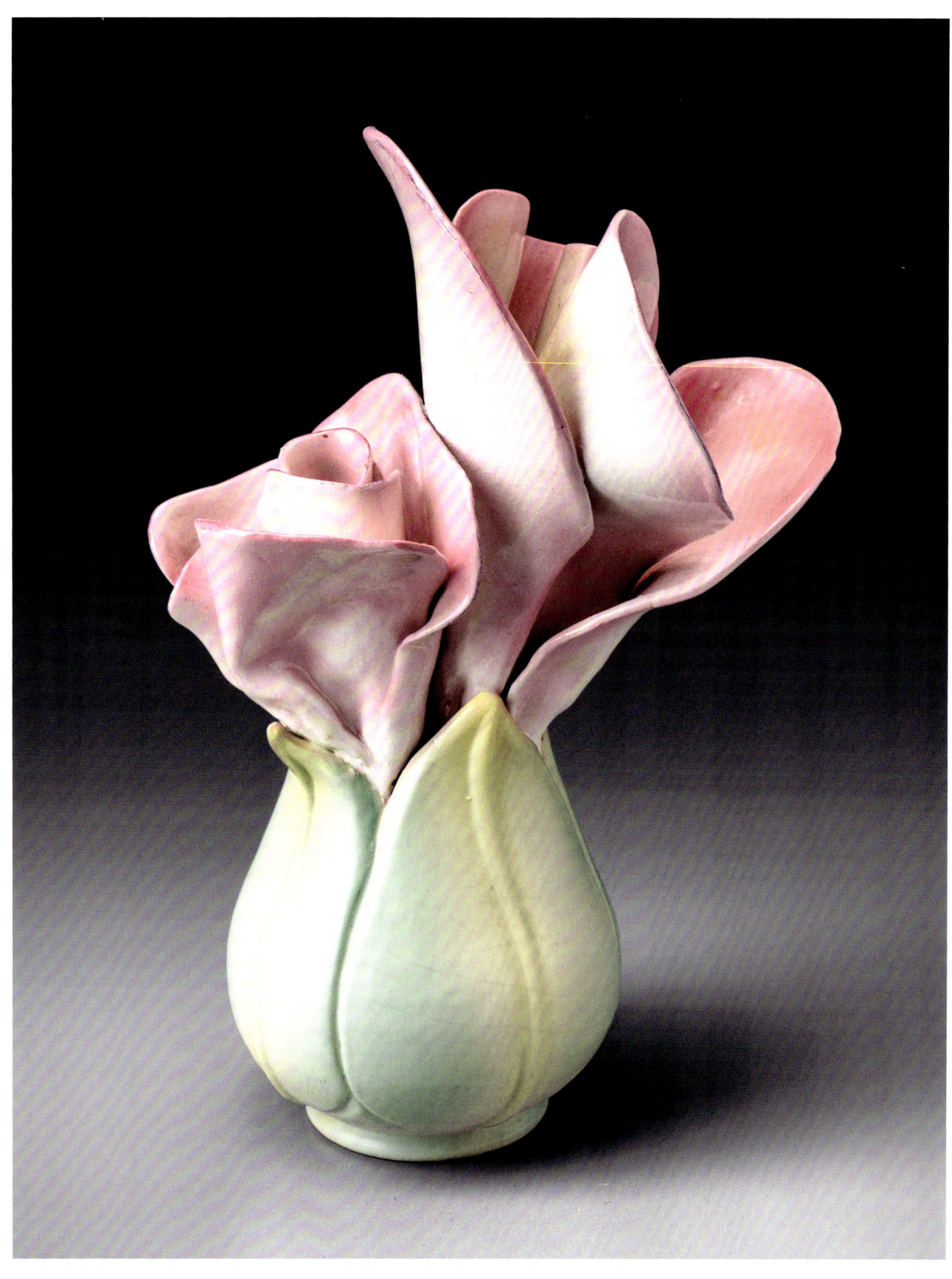

Flowering Bulb 1985
Glazed earthenware with china paint and luster
12 ½ × 9 ½ × 8 in. (31.8 × 24.1 × 20.3 cm)

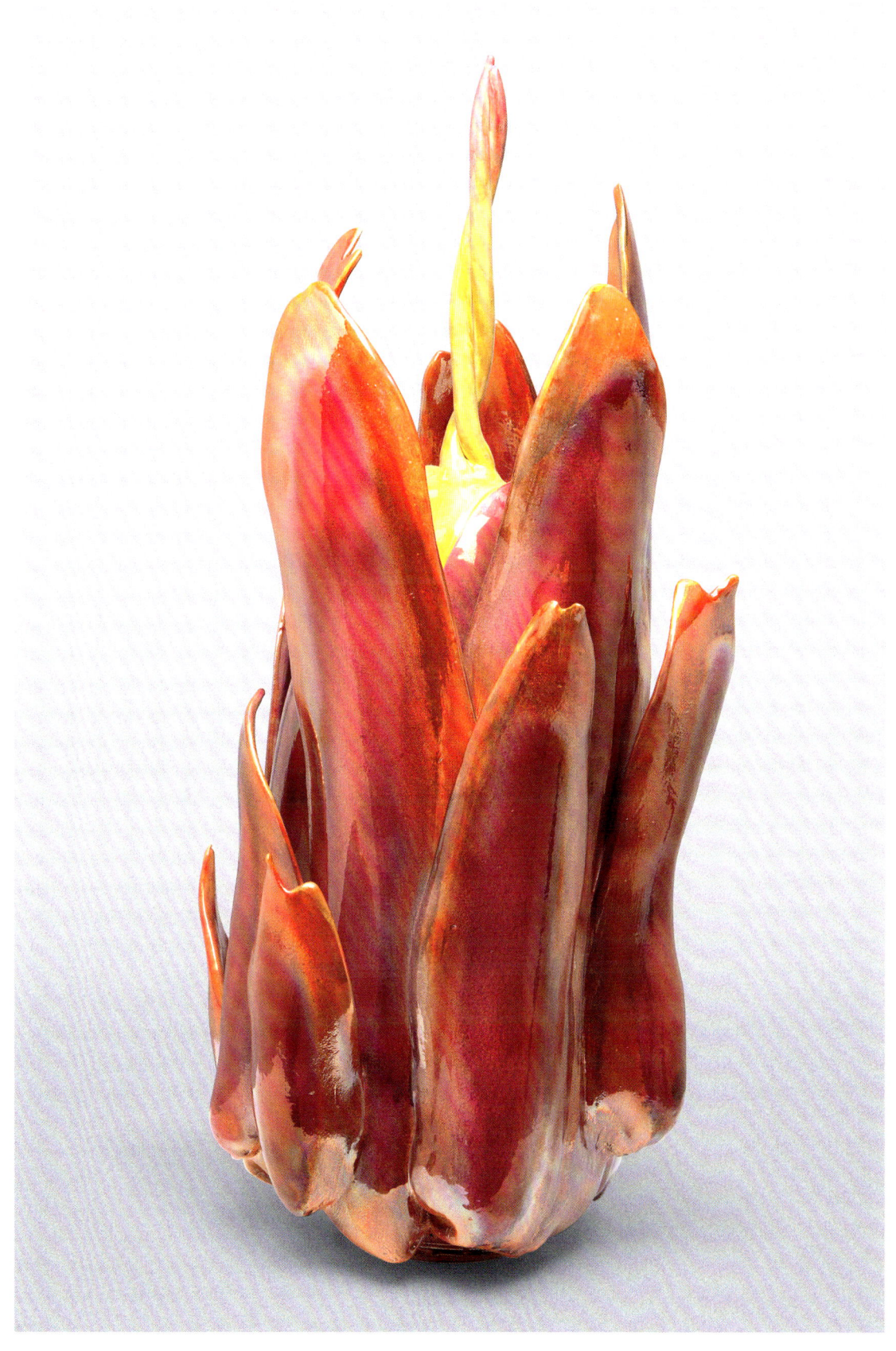

Transition 1998
Glazed earthenware with china paint and luster
23 × 10 × 12 in. (58.4 × 25.4 × 30.5 cm)

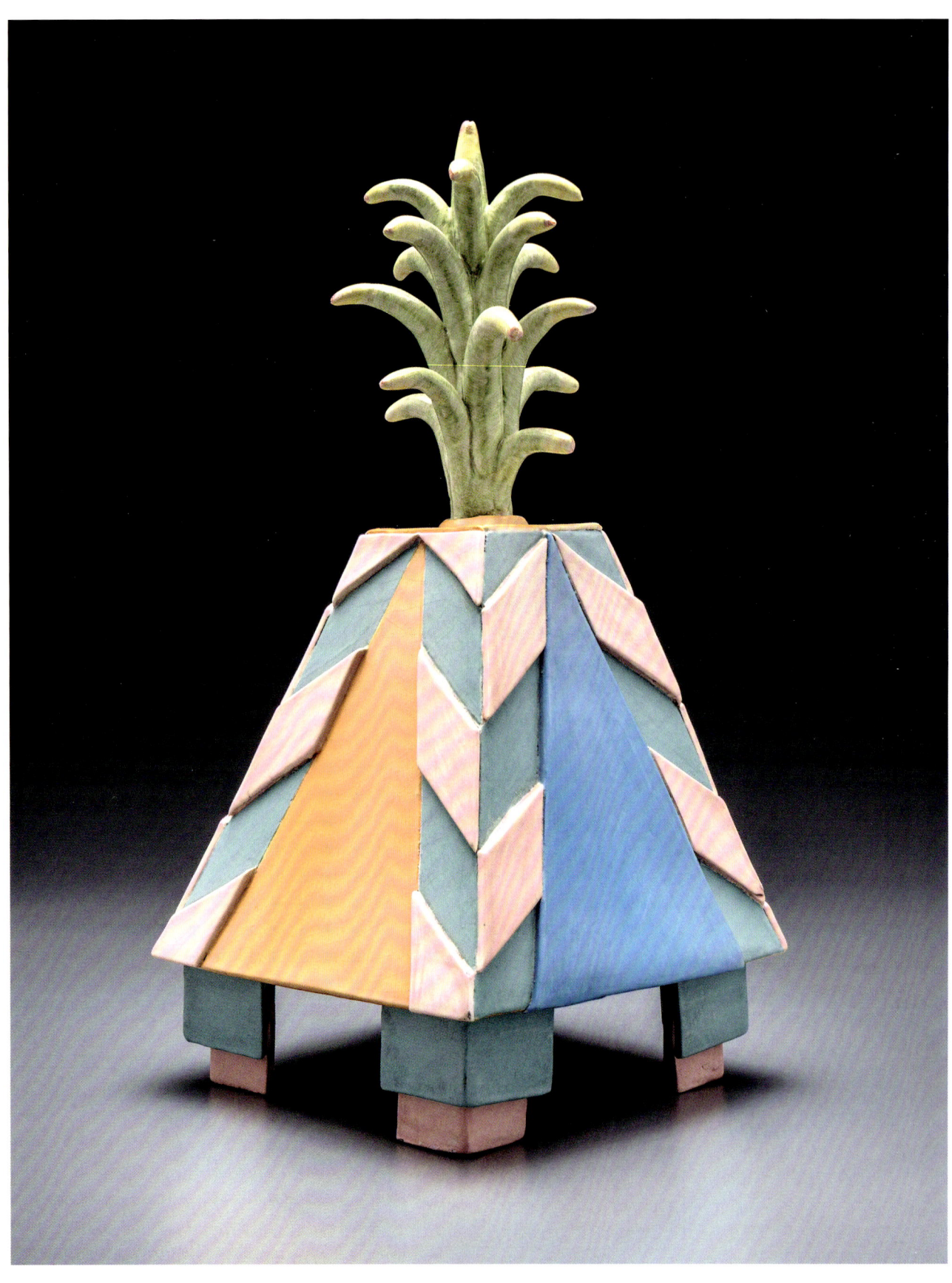

Untitled 1985
Glazed earthenware with china paint
16½ × 8½ × 8 in. (41.9 × 21.6 × 20.3 cm)

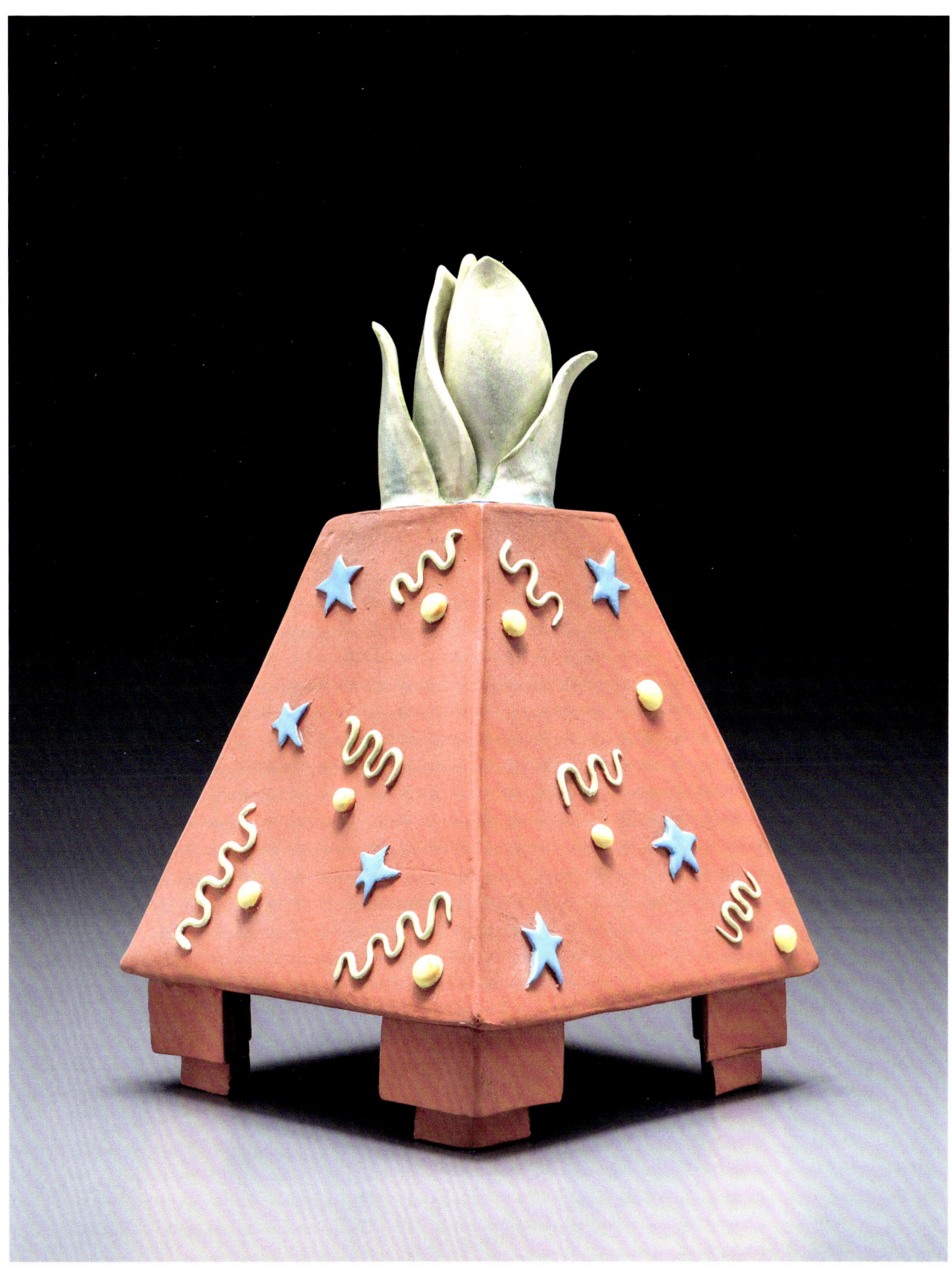

Untitled 1985
Glazed earthenware with china paint
13 ½ × 8 × 8 in. (34.3 × 20.3 × 20.3 cm)

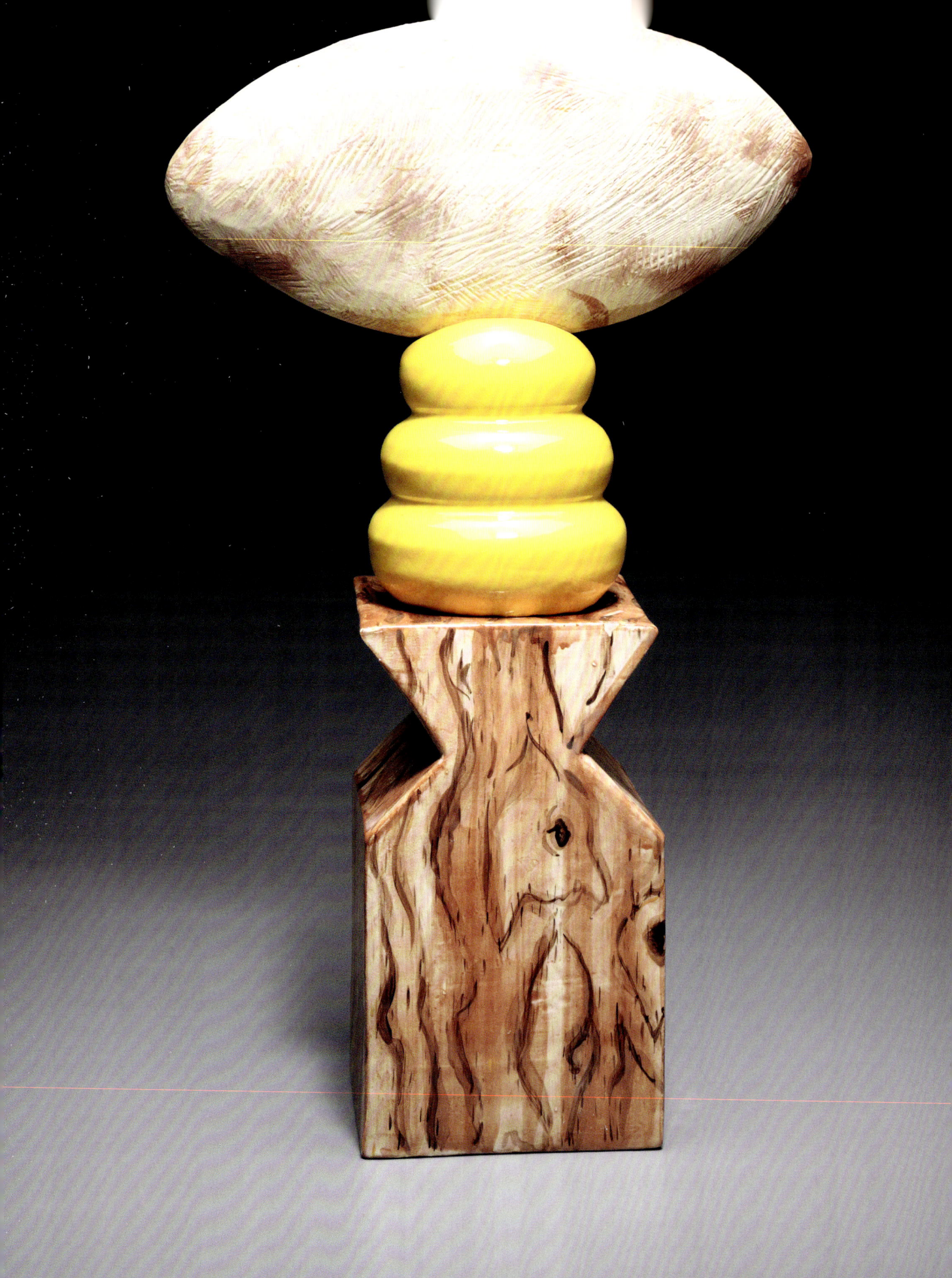

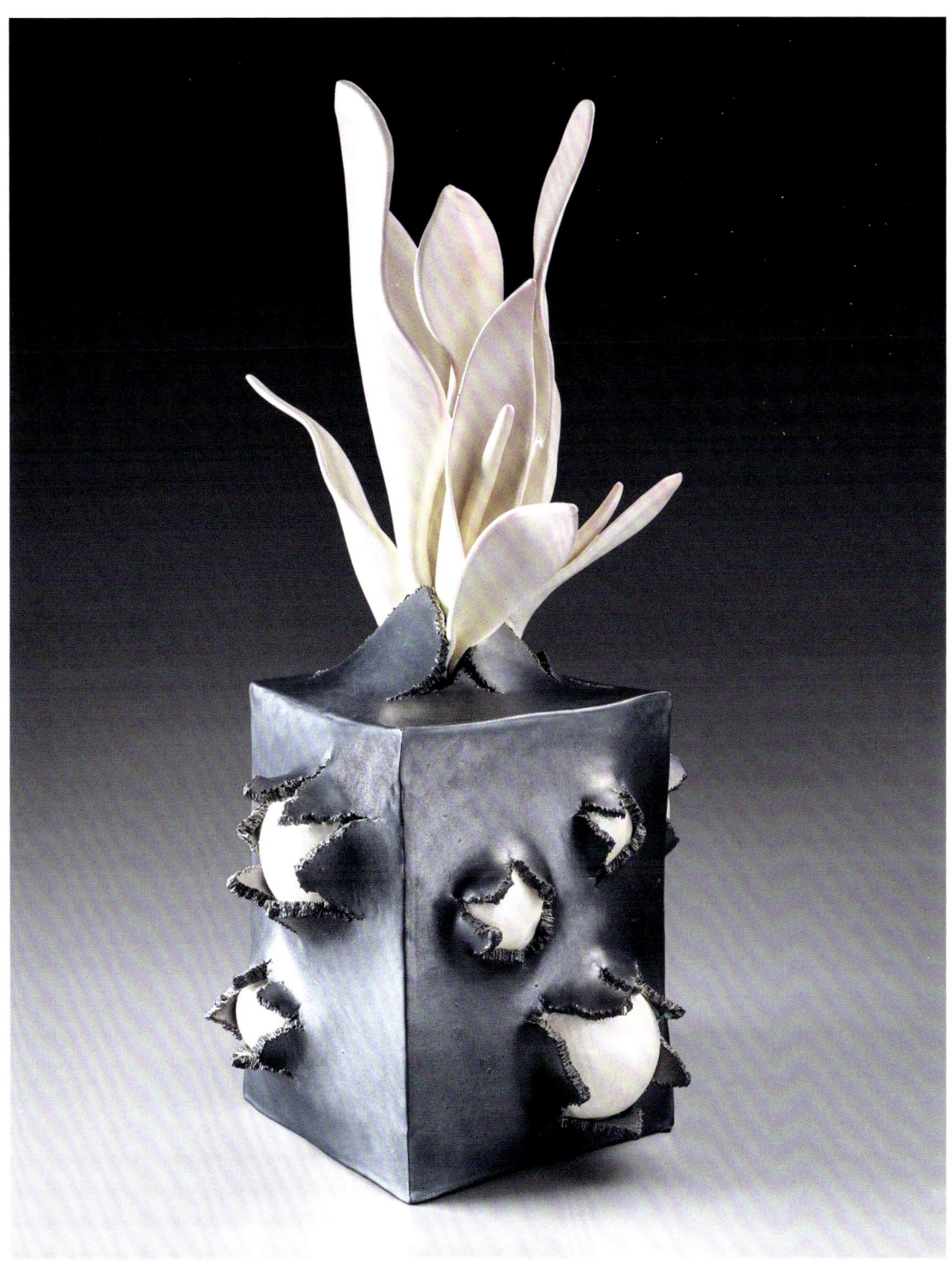

Left page
Untitled 1985
Glazed earthenware with underglaze
22 × 13 ½ × 6 ¼ in. (55.9 × 34.3 × 15.9 cm)

Transition 1987
Glazed earthenware with china paint
26 × 13 × 13 in. (66 × 33 × 33 cm)

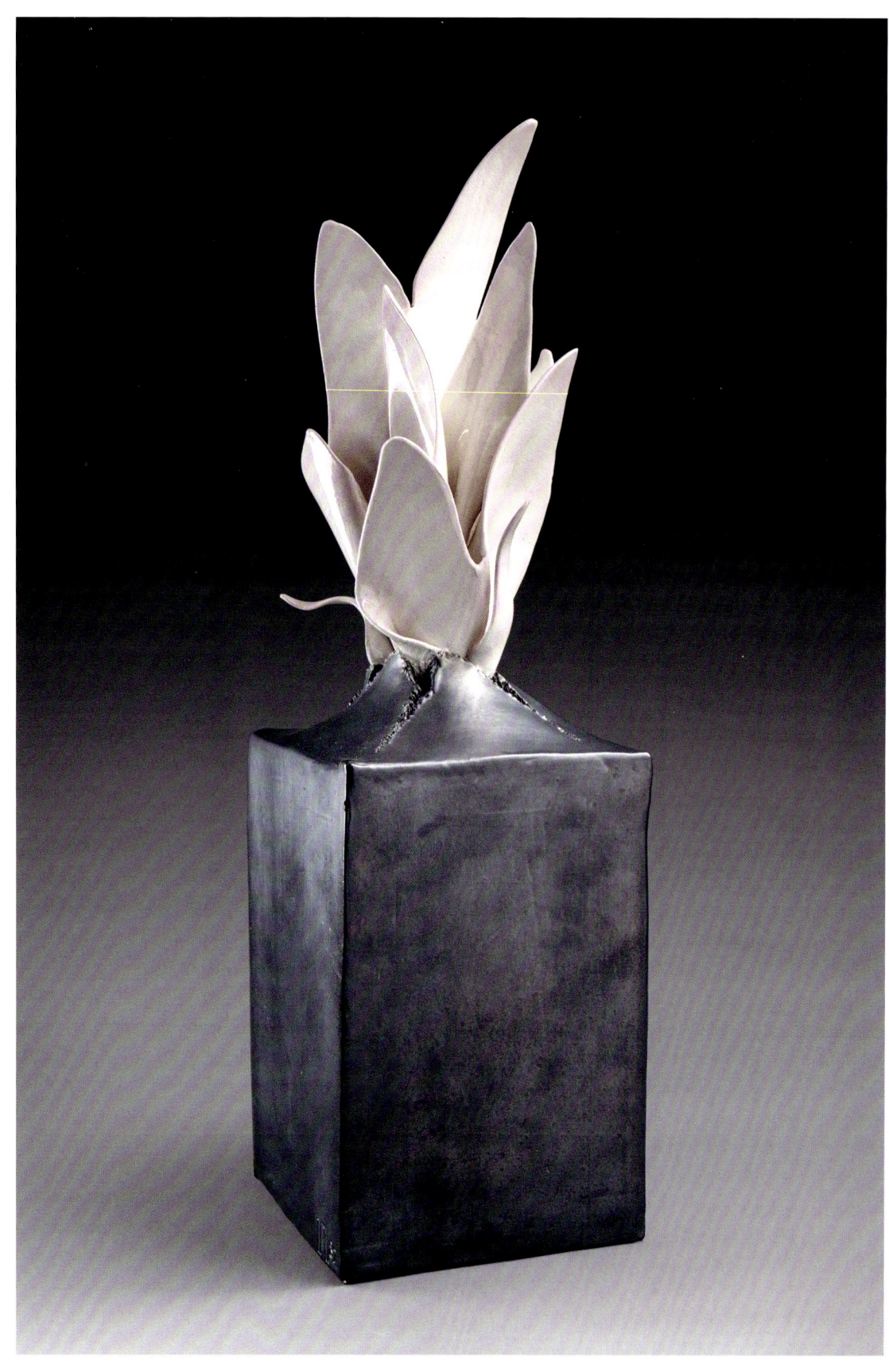

Transition 1988
Glazed earthenware with china paint
23 × 7 ¼ × 7 ¼ in. (58.4 × 18.4 × 18.4 cm)

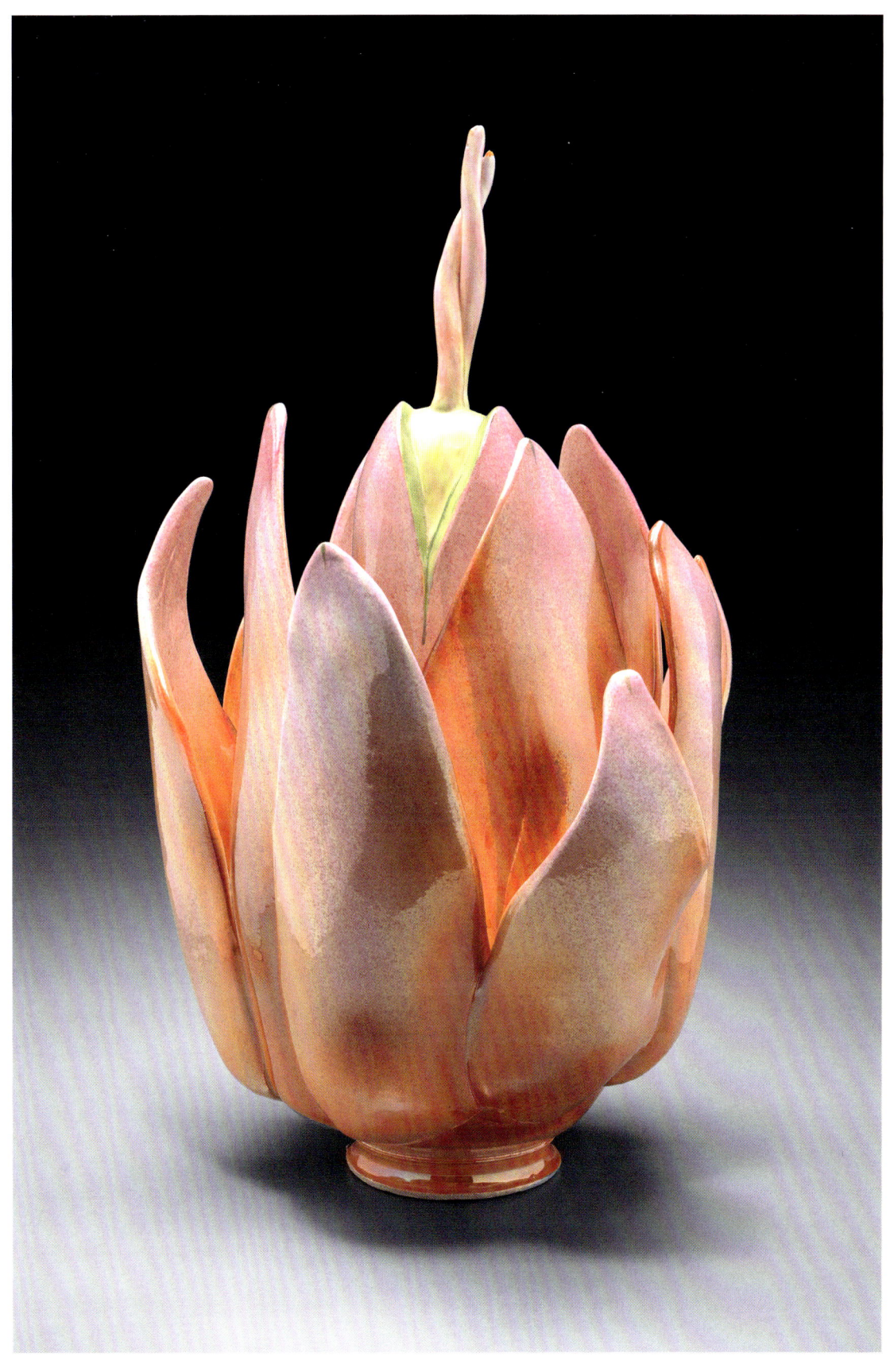

Transition 1998
Glazed earthenware with china paint and luster
18 × 12 × 12 in. (45.7 × 30.5 × 30.5 cm)

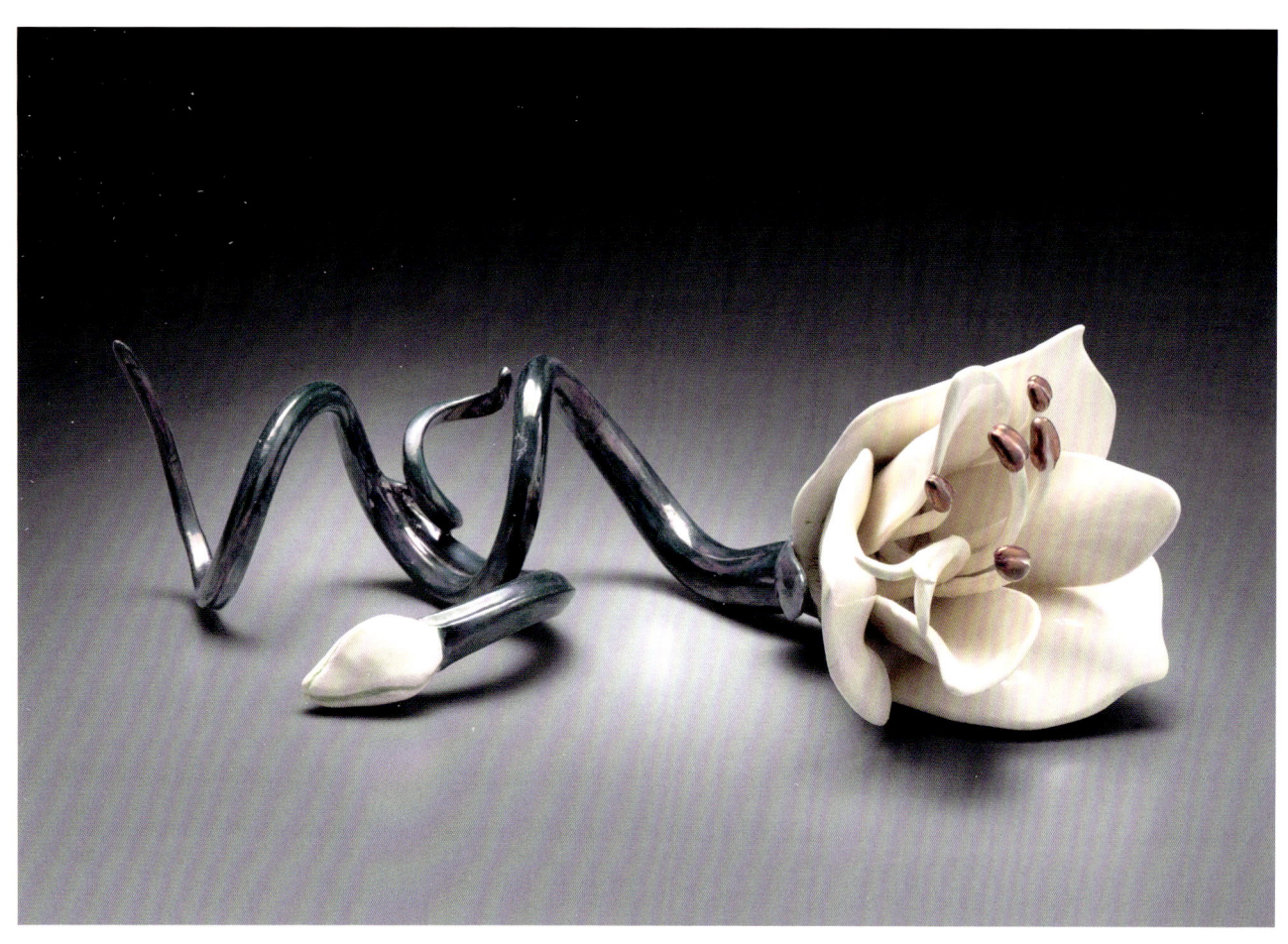

Peruvian Lily 1994
Glazed earthenware with luster
5 × 18 × 14 in. (12.7 × 45.7 × 35.6 cm)
Collection William Fowks

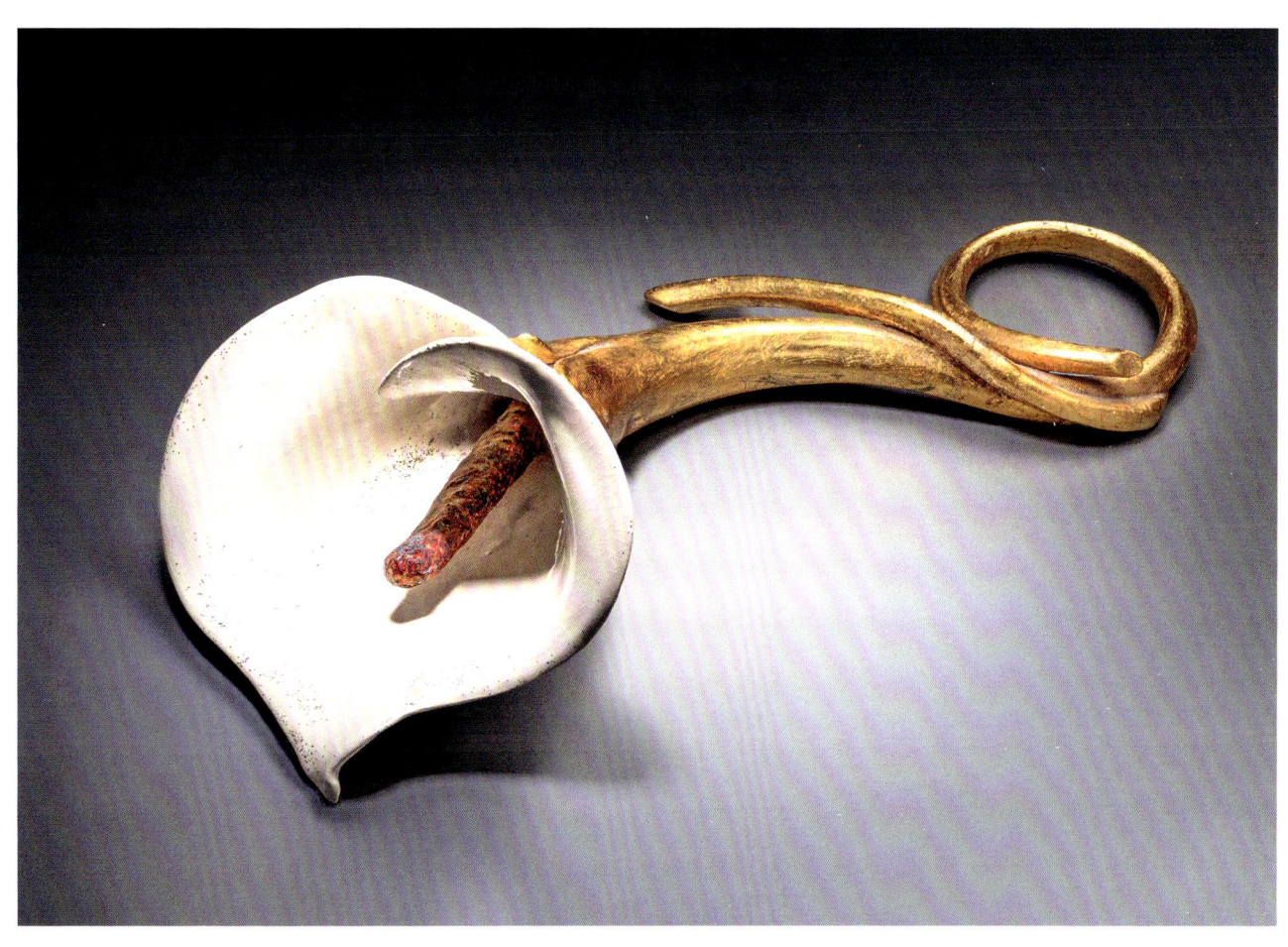

Calla Lily 1994
Glazed earthenware with luster and gold leaf
6 × 19 ½ × 8 ¼ in. (15.2 × 49.5 × 21 cm)
Collection Terry Anderson and Michael Henry

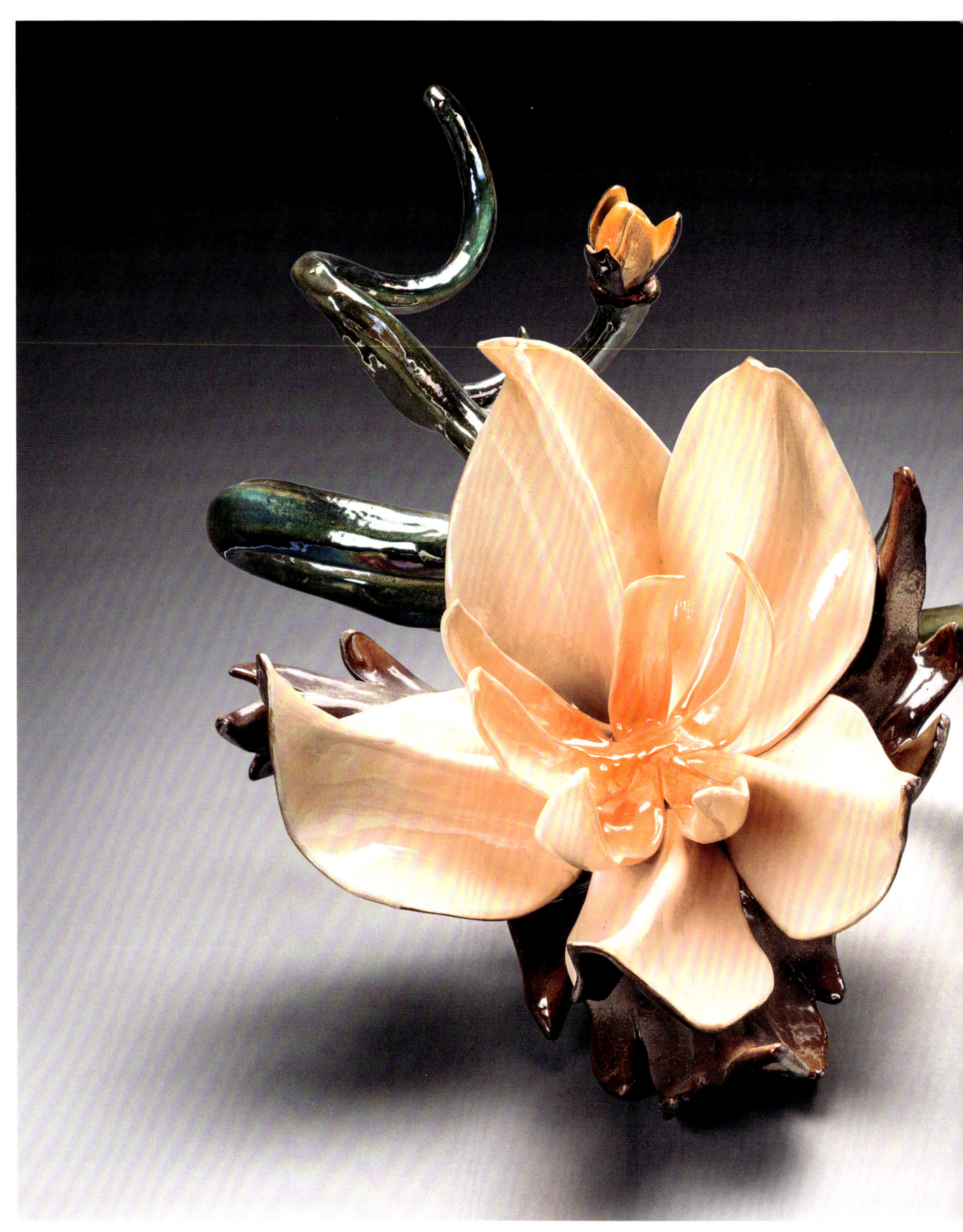

Cotton Boll 2007
Glazed earthenware with china paint and luster
36 × 29 × 16 in. (91.4 × 73.7 × 40.6 cm)

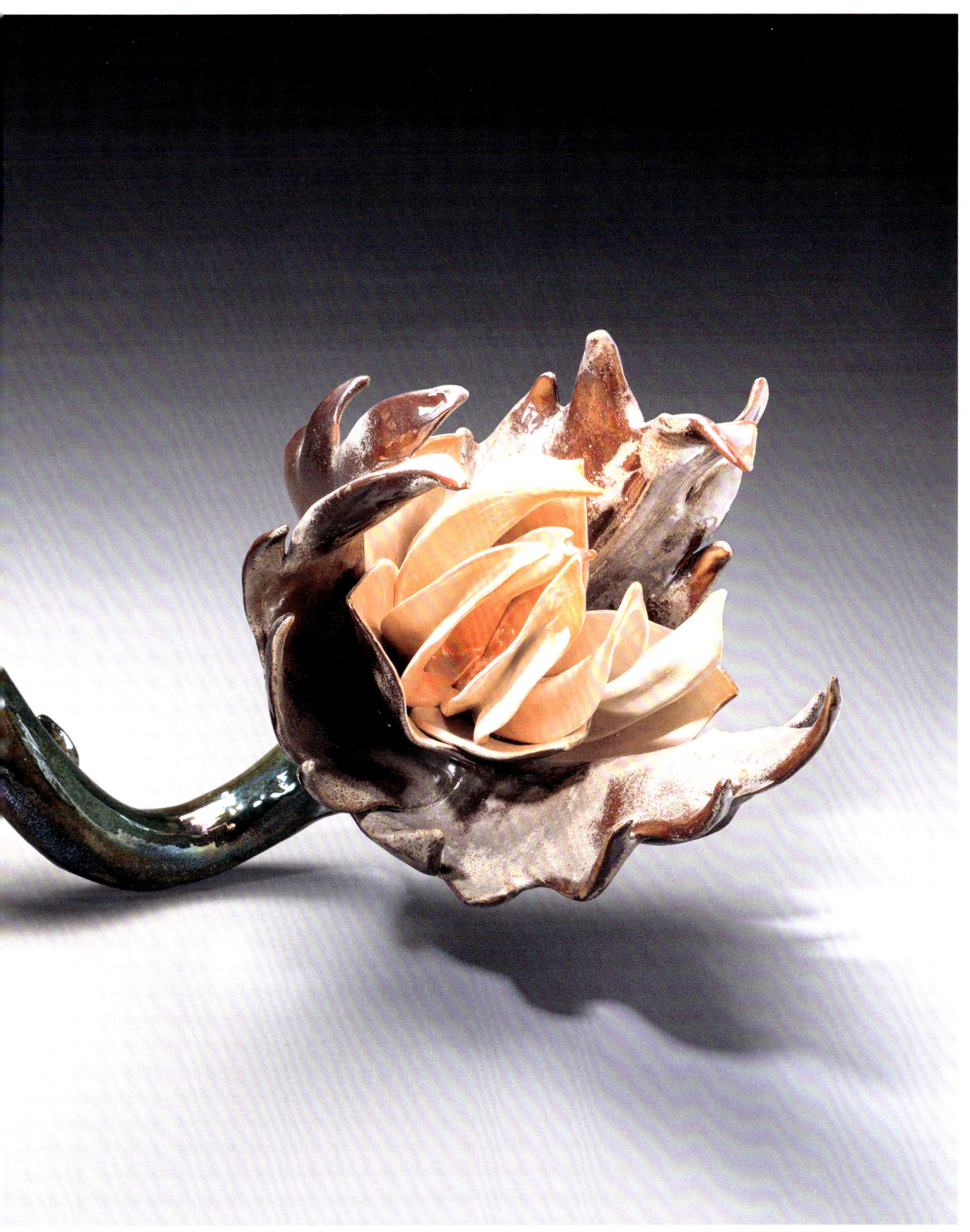

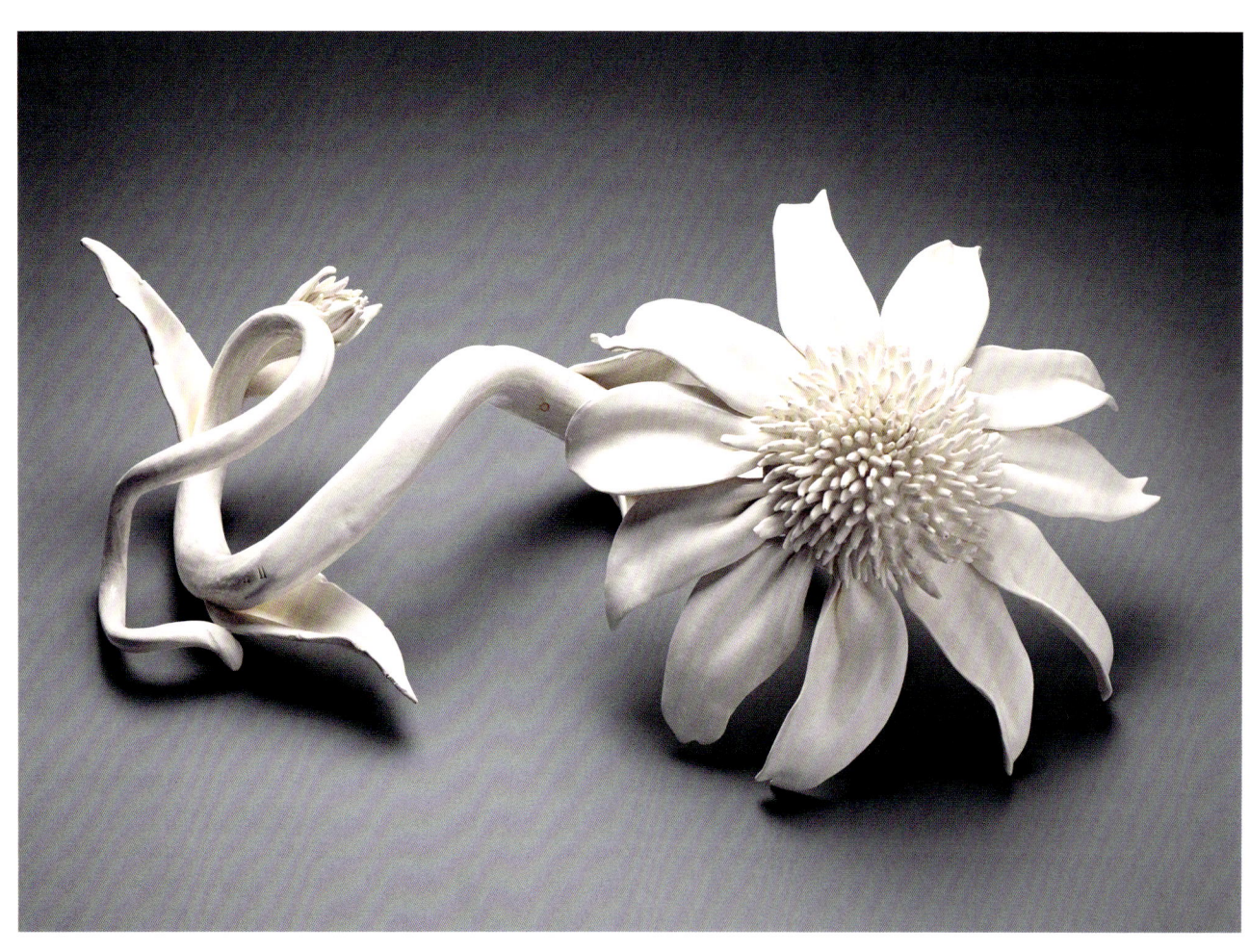

Echinacea 1998
Glazed earthenware
12 ½ × 37 ½ × 21 in. (31.8 × 95.3 × 53.3 cm)
Collection The Nelson-Atkins Museum of Art, Kansas City, MO

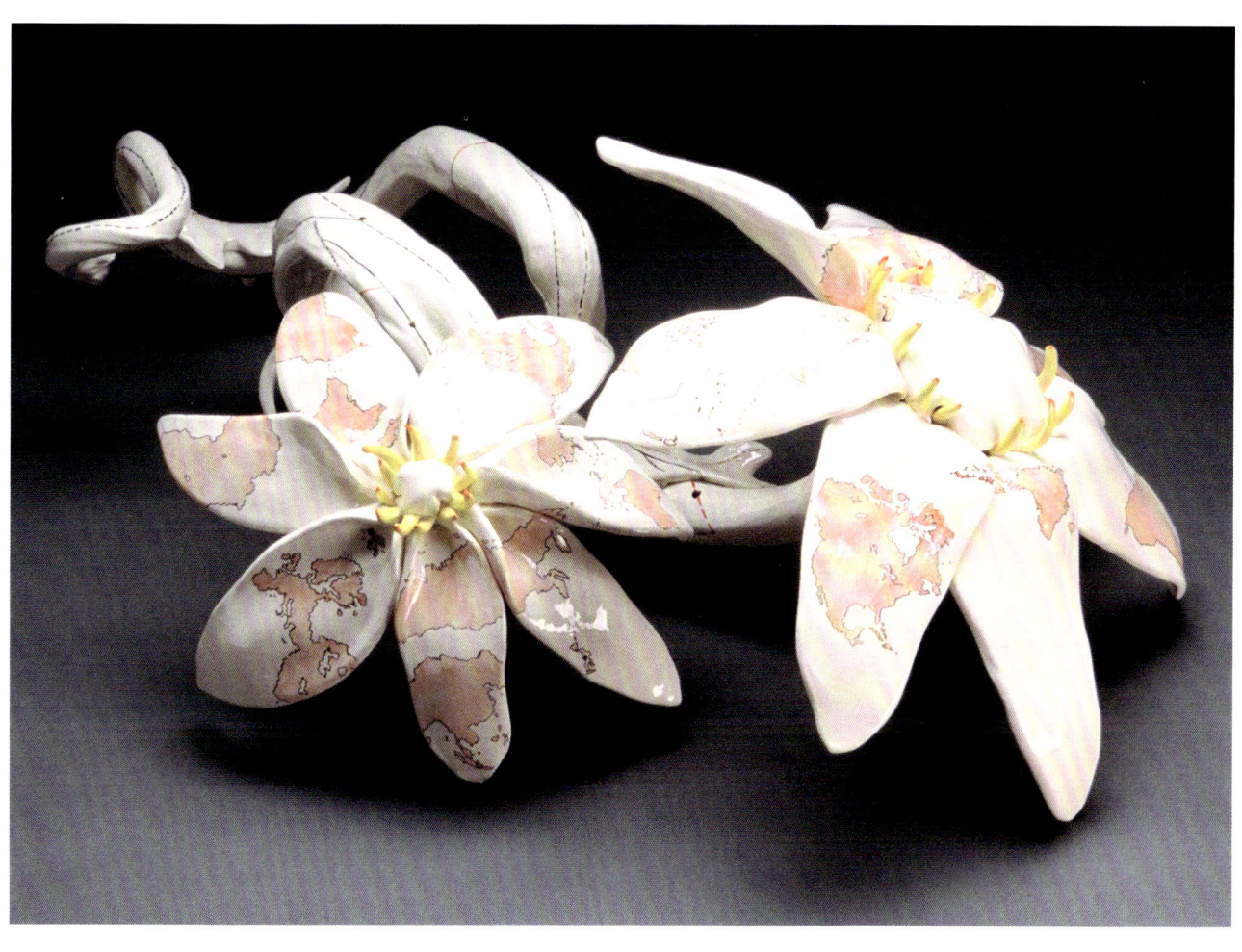

Mapped Flower 1995
Glazed earthenware with china paint
11 ¼ × 31 × 22 in. (28.6 × 78.7 × 55.9 cm)
Collection Kemper Museum of Contemporary Art, Kansas City, MO

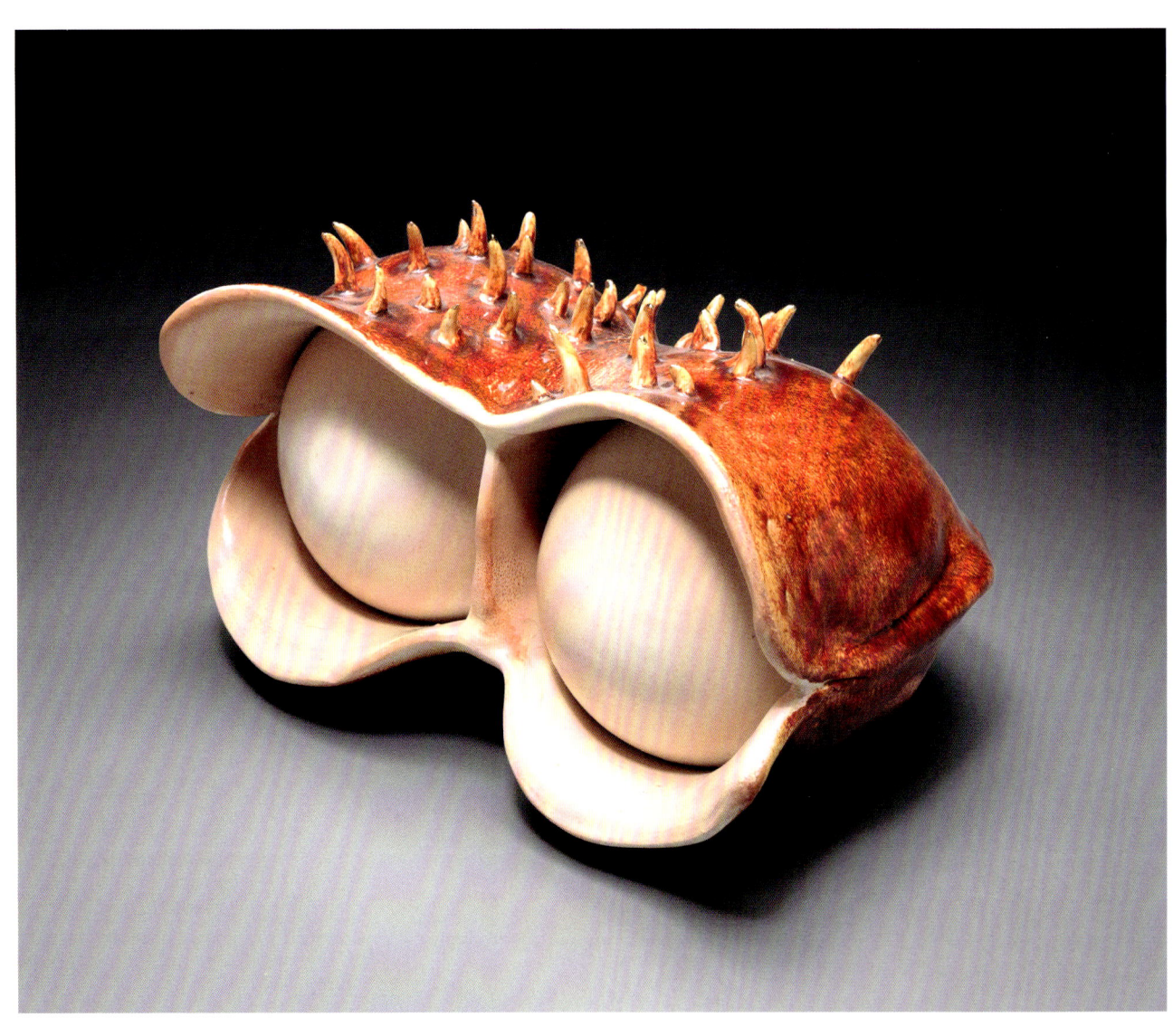

Chestnut 1996
Glazed earthenware with china paint
5 ½ × 9 × 8 in. (14 × 22.9 × 20.3 cm)

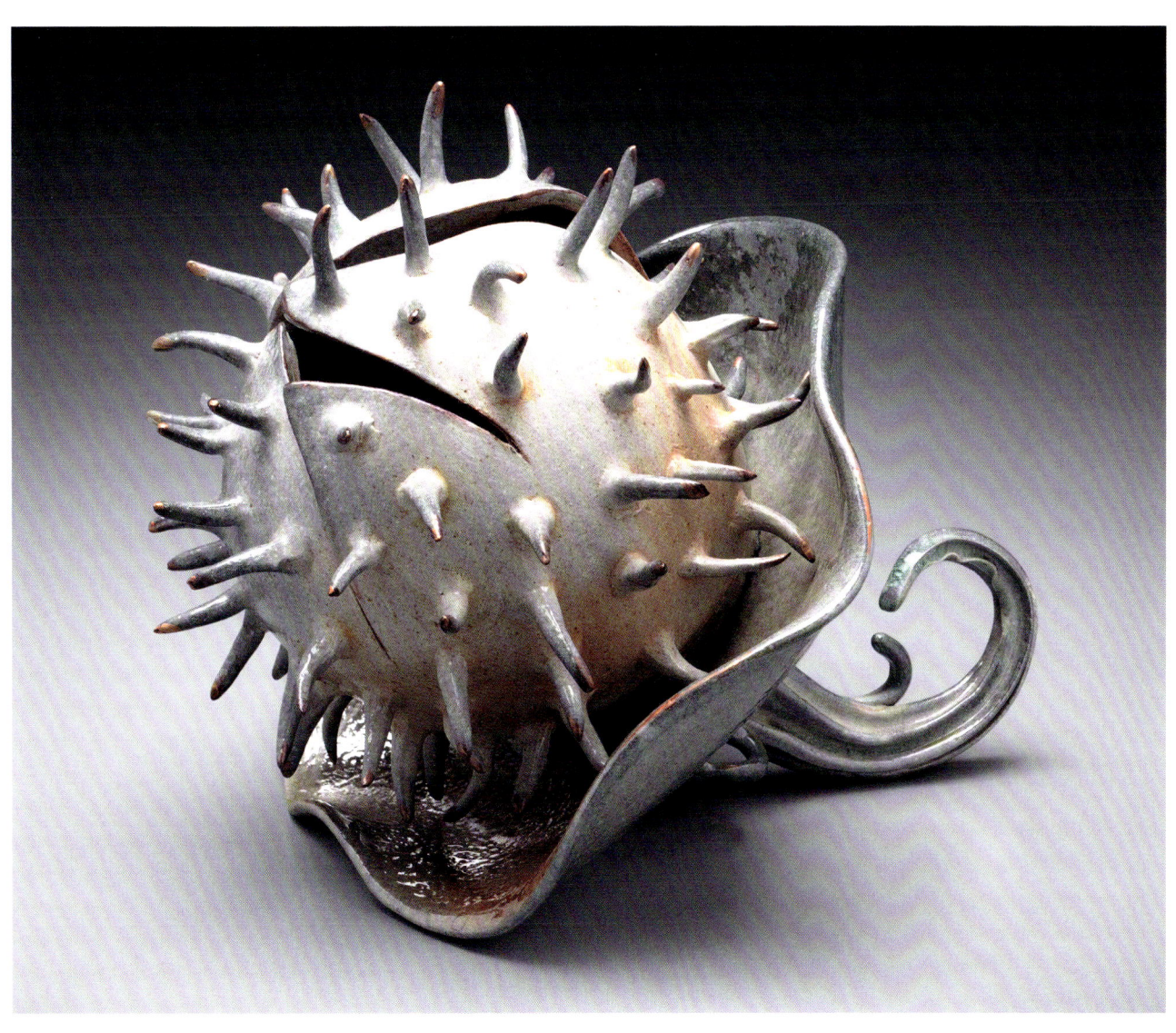

Horse Chestnut 2003
Salt fired stoneware with luster
10 × 9 × 14 in. (25.4 × 22.9 × 35.6 cm)

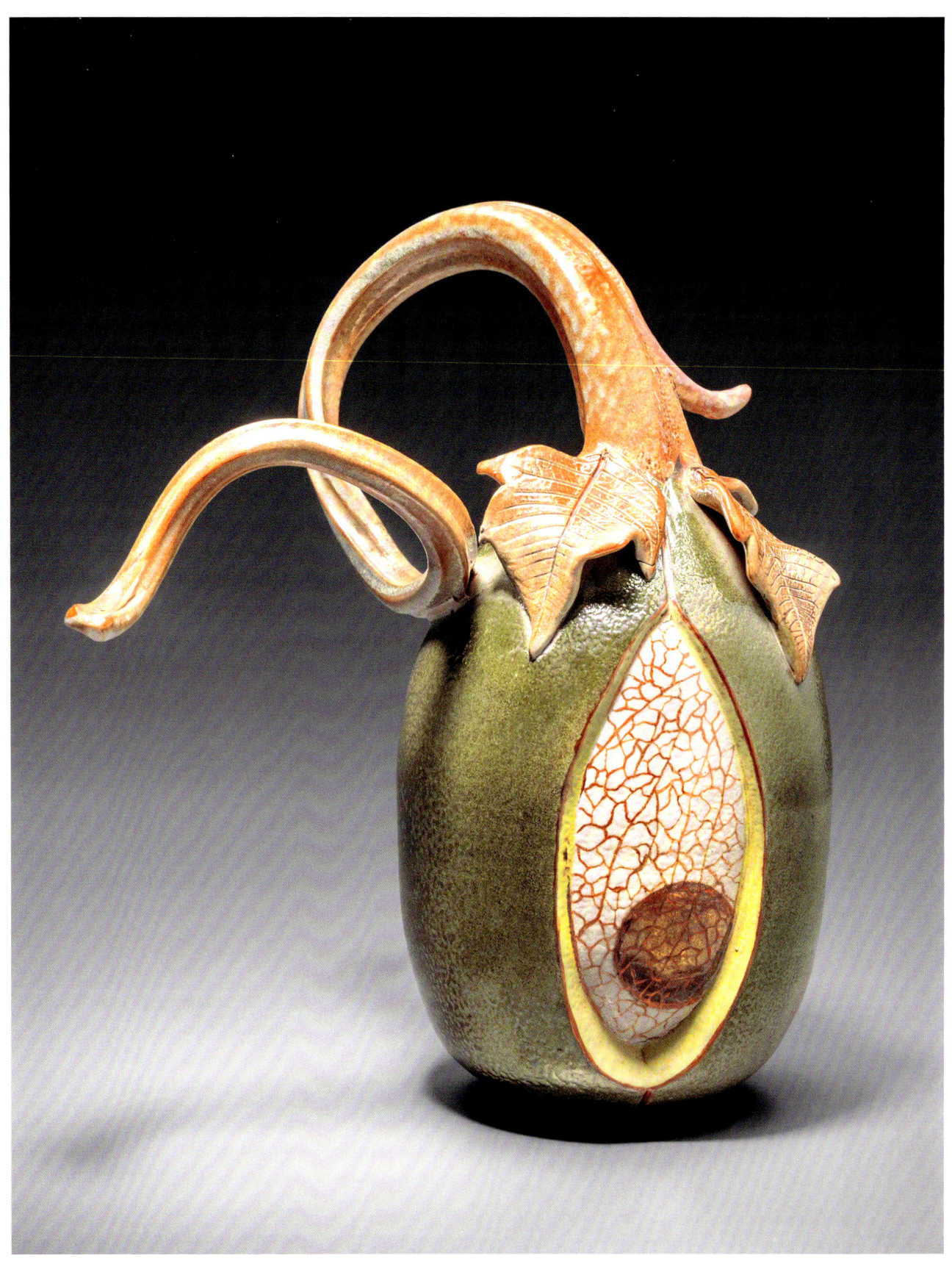

Salt Fired Bulb 2003
Salt fired porcelain with china paint and luster
11 × 9 × 8 in. (27.9 × 22.9 × 20.3 cm)

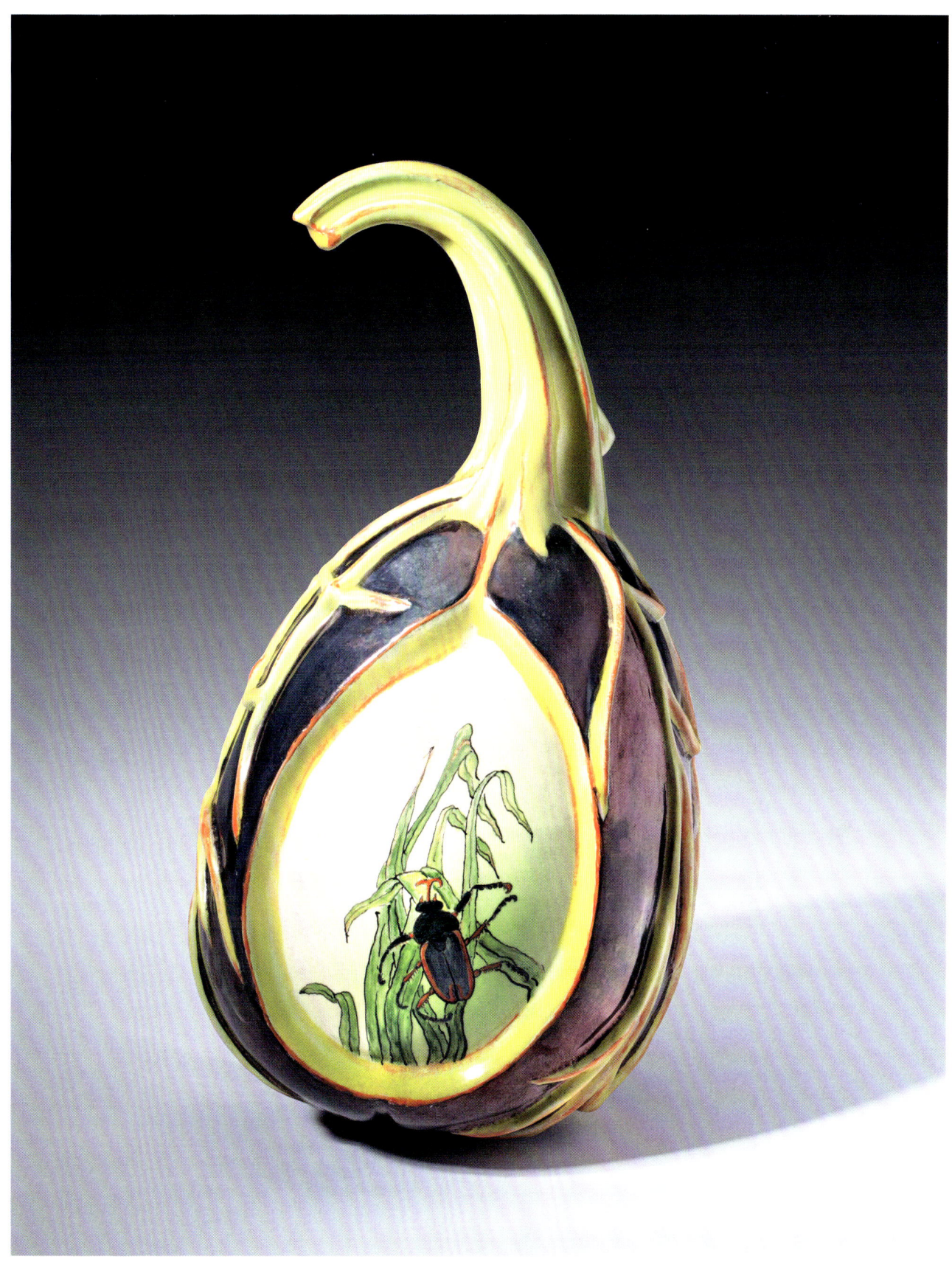

Bulb with Beetle 2000
Glazed earthenware with china paint and luster
11 × 5 ¼ × 5 in. (27.9 × 13.3 × 12.7 cm)

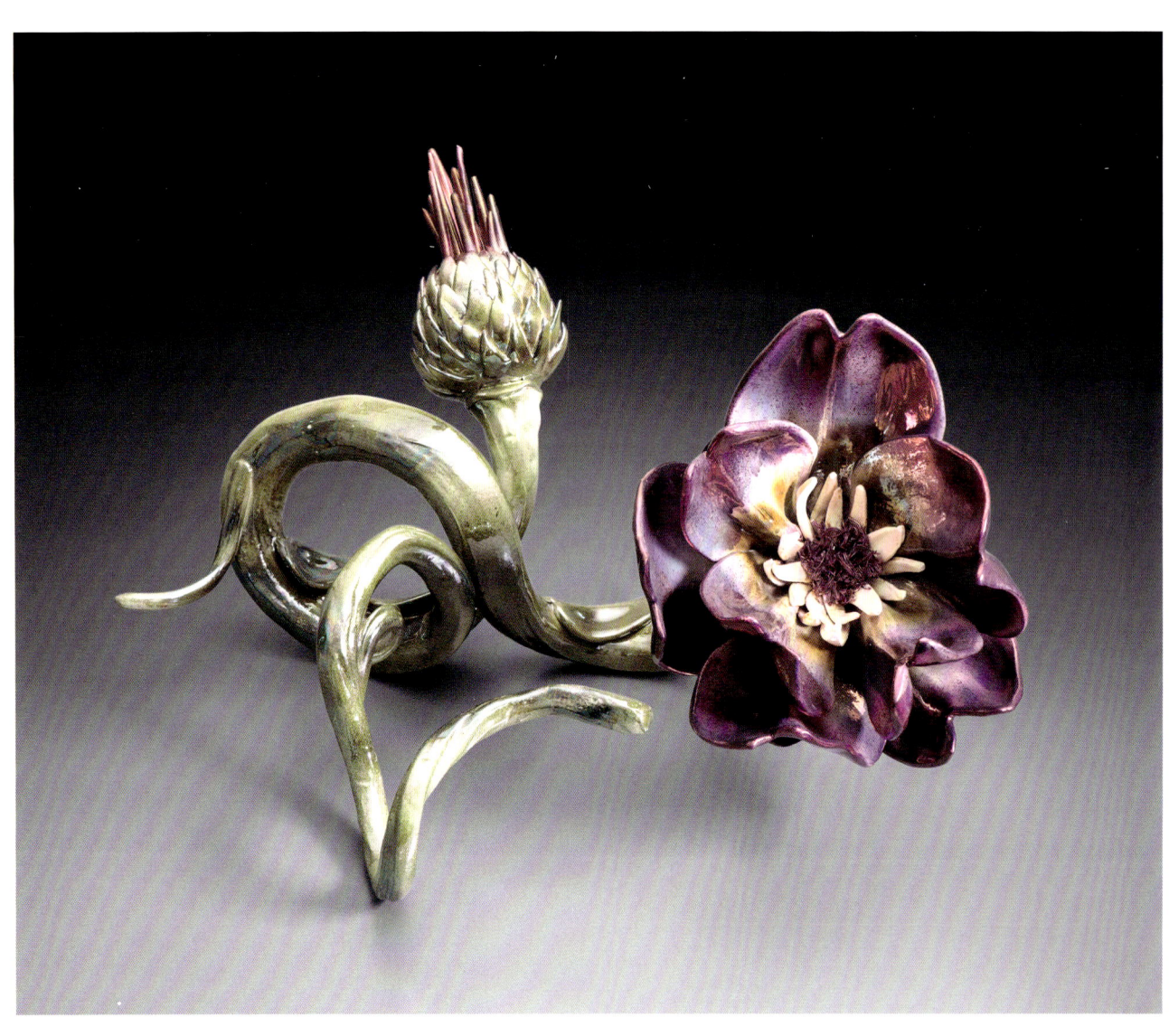

Thistle 2000
Glazed earthenware with luster
28 × 15 × 20 in. (71.1 × 38.1 × 50.8 cm)
Collection Daum Museum of Contemporary Art, Sedalia, MO

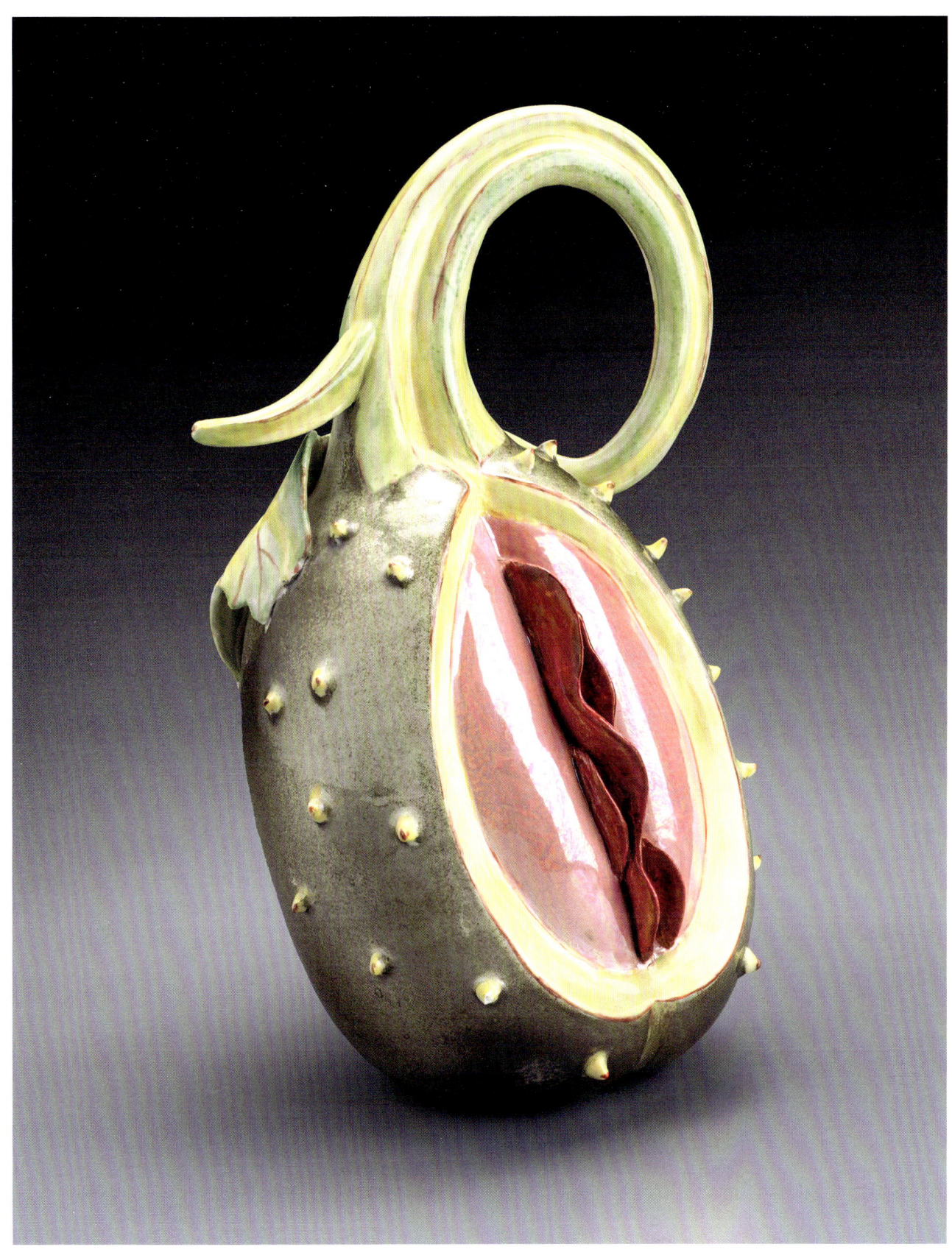

Untitled 2000
Glazed earthenware with china paint and luster
10¾ × 6¼ × 6 in. (27.3 × 15.9 × 15.2 cm)
Collection Andrea Norris

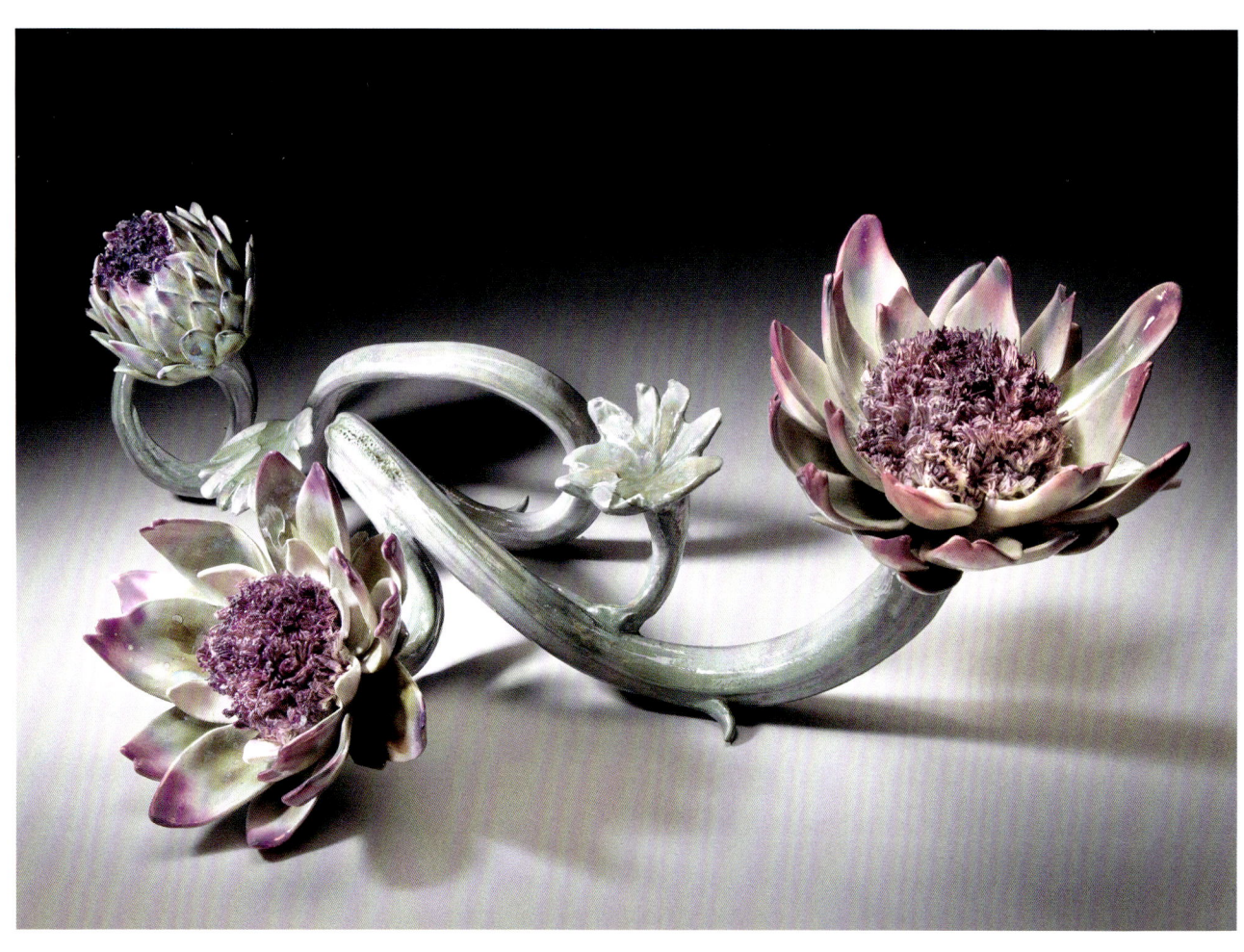

Triple Thistle 2007
Glazed earthenware with luster
28 × 12 × 13 in. (71.1 × 30.5 × 33 cm)
Collection Rachael Blackburn Cozad and Kanon Cozad

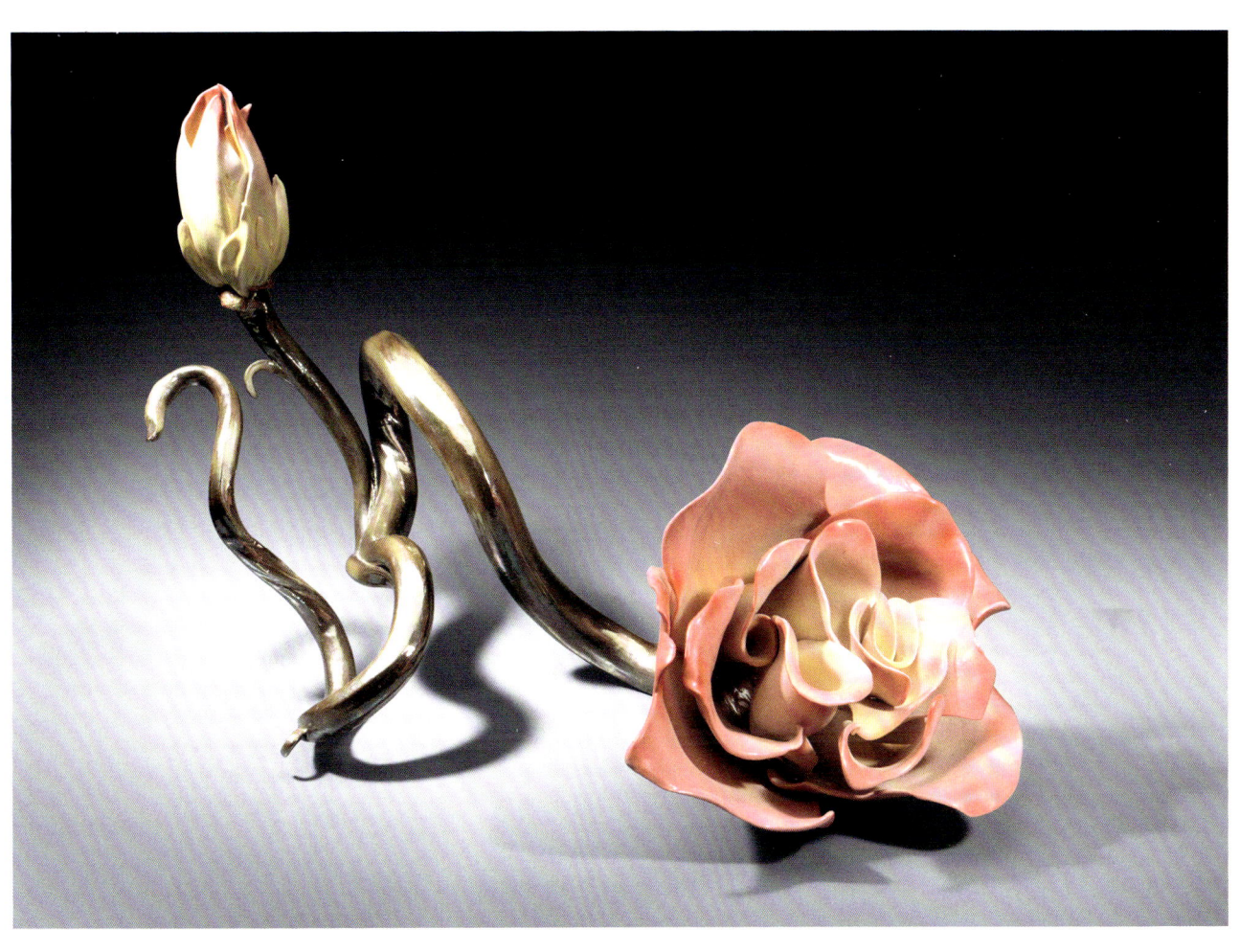

Rose 2015
Glazed earthenware with china paint and luster
21 × 31 × 16 in. (53.3 × 78.7 × 40.6 cm)

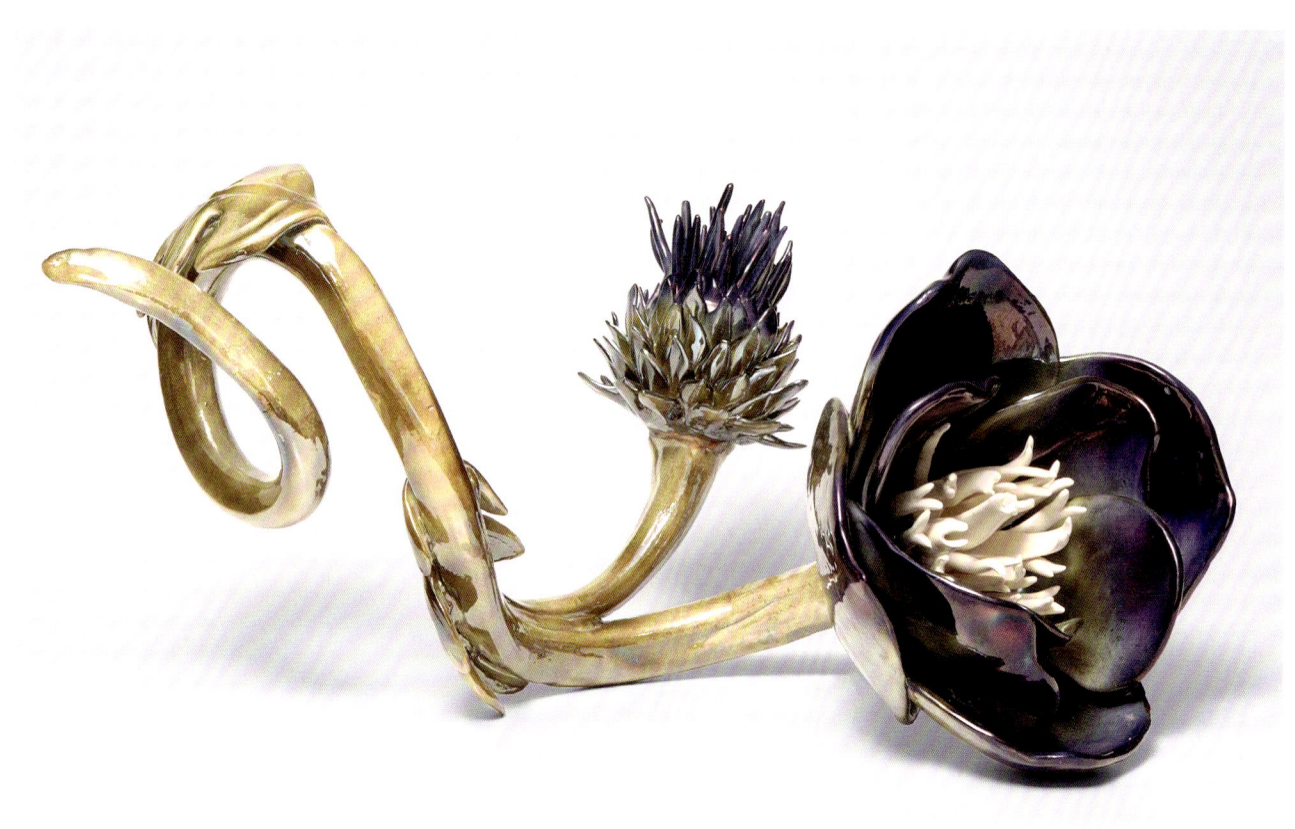

Artichoke 2001
Glazed earthenware with luster
14 × 16 × 24 ½ in. (35.6 × 40.6 × 62.2 cm)
Collection Spencer Museum of Art, University of Kansas, Lawrence, KS

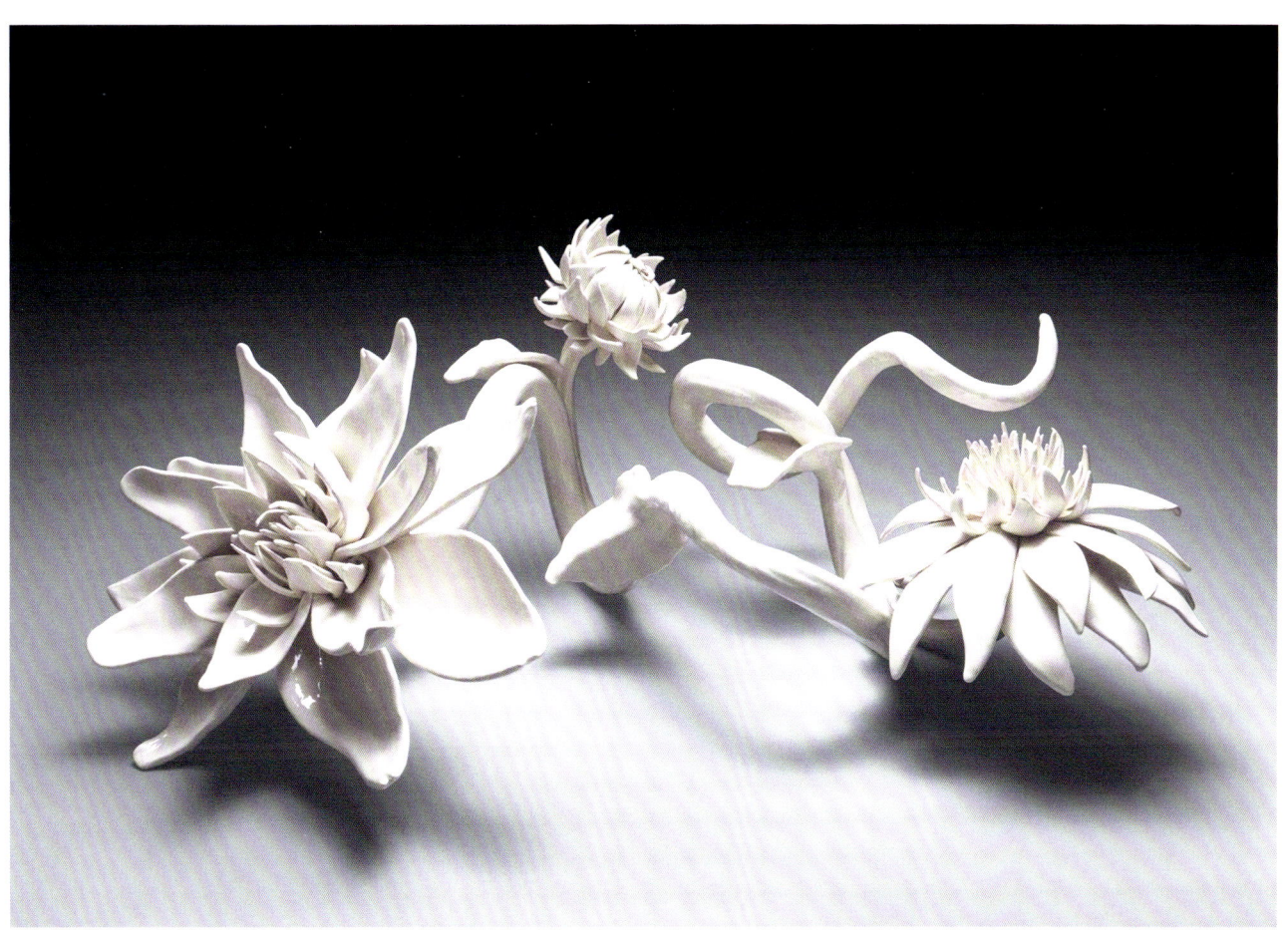

Triple White Zinnia 2003
Glazed earthenware
15 × 43 × 27 in.
(38.1 × 109.2 × 68.6 cm)
Collection Bill and Christy Gautreaux

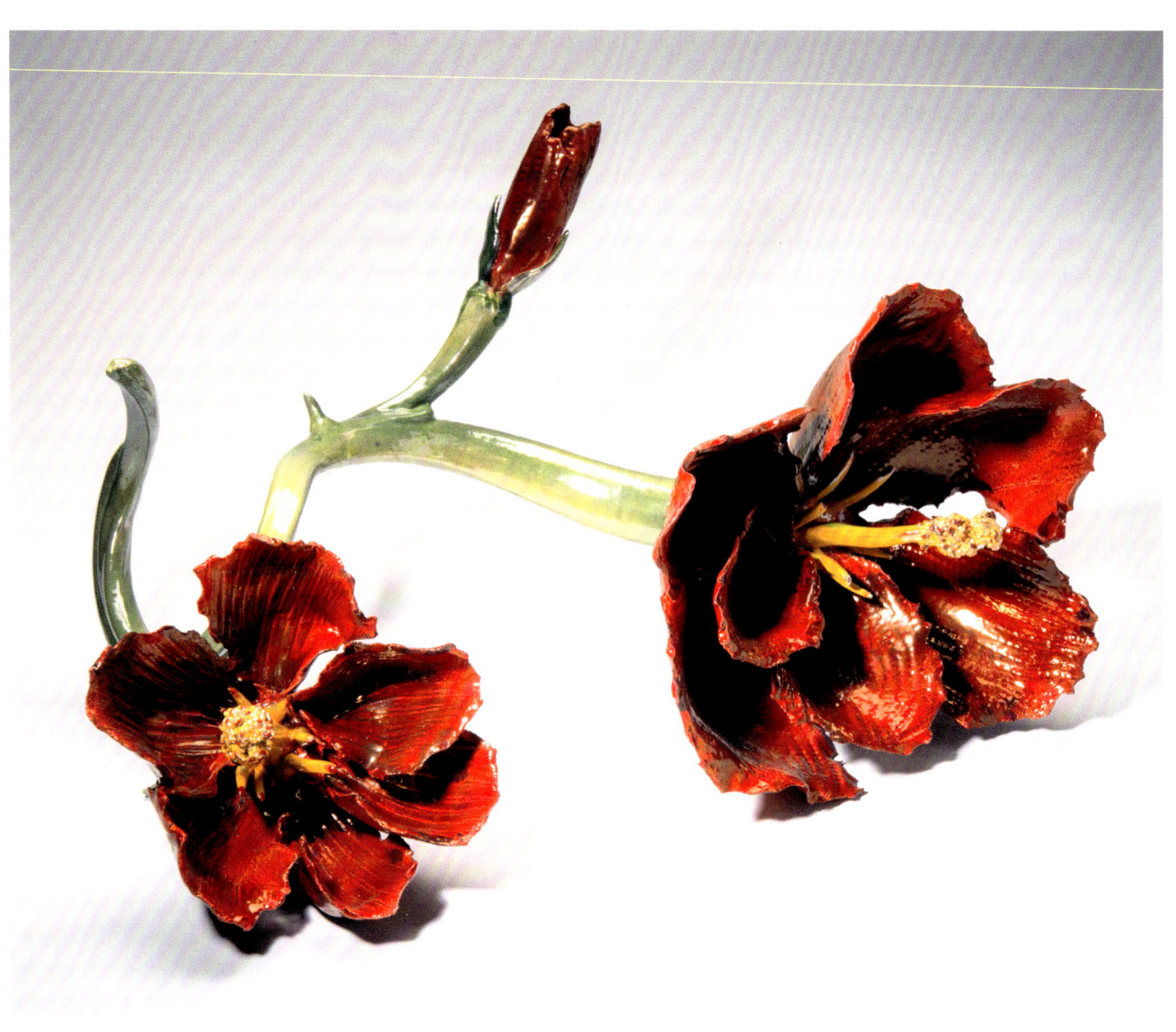

Double Red Hibiscus 2013
Glazed earthenware with luster
12 × 26 × 22 in. (30.5 × 66 × 55.9 cm)

Right page
Untitled 1999
Glazed earthenware with china paint and luster
19 × 9 × 9 in. (48.3 × 22.9 × 22.9 cm)
Collection E.V. Day

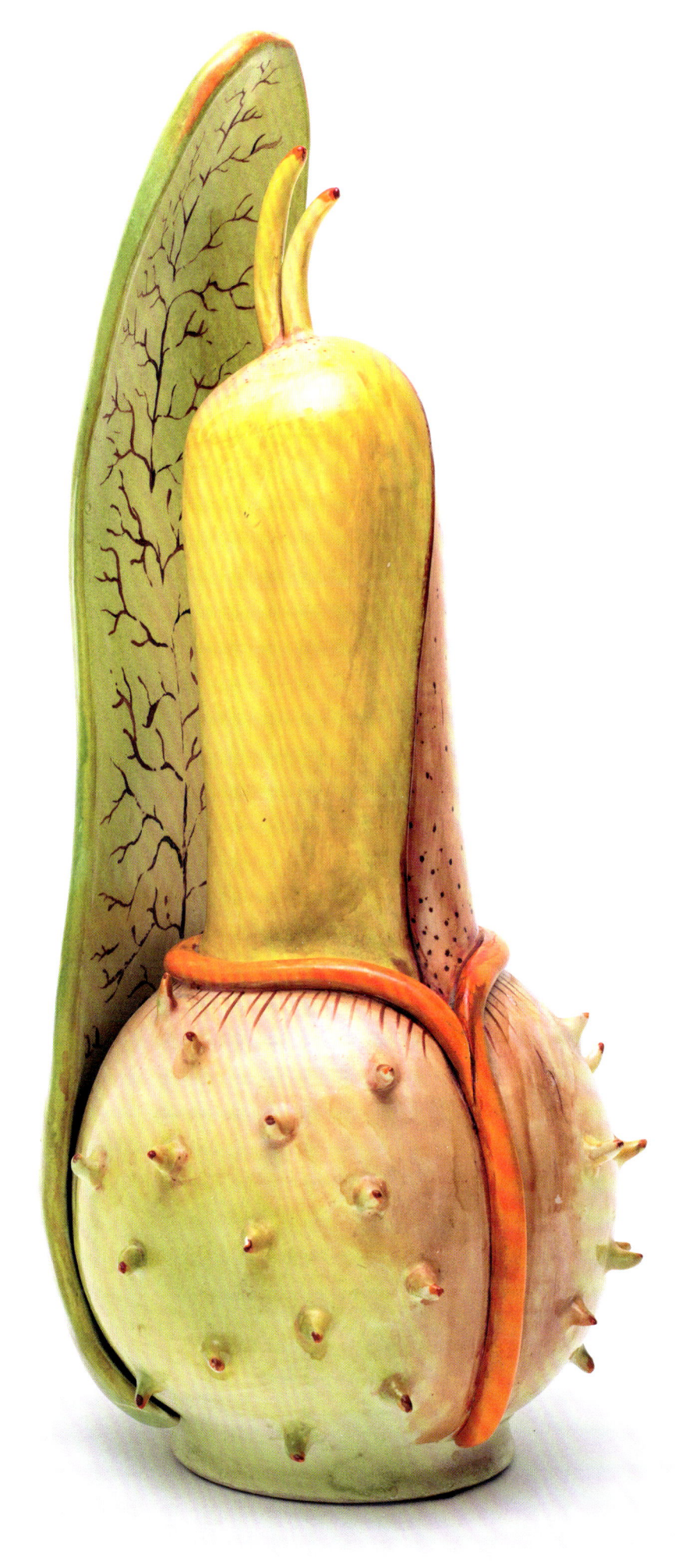

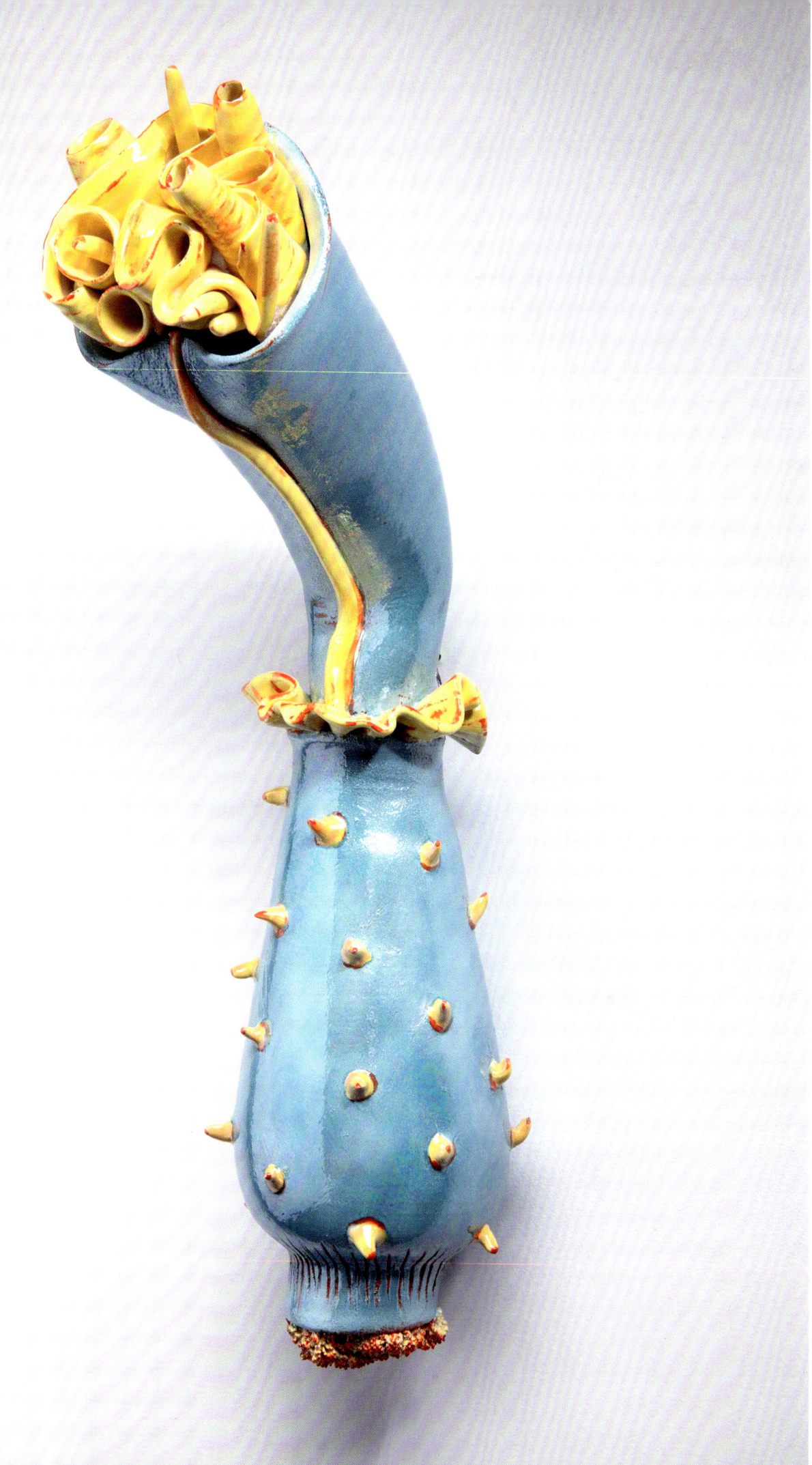

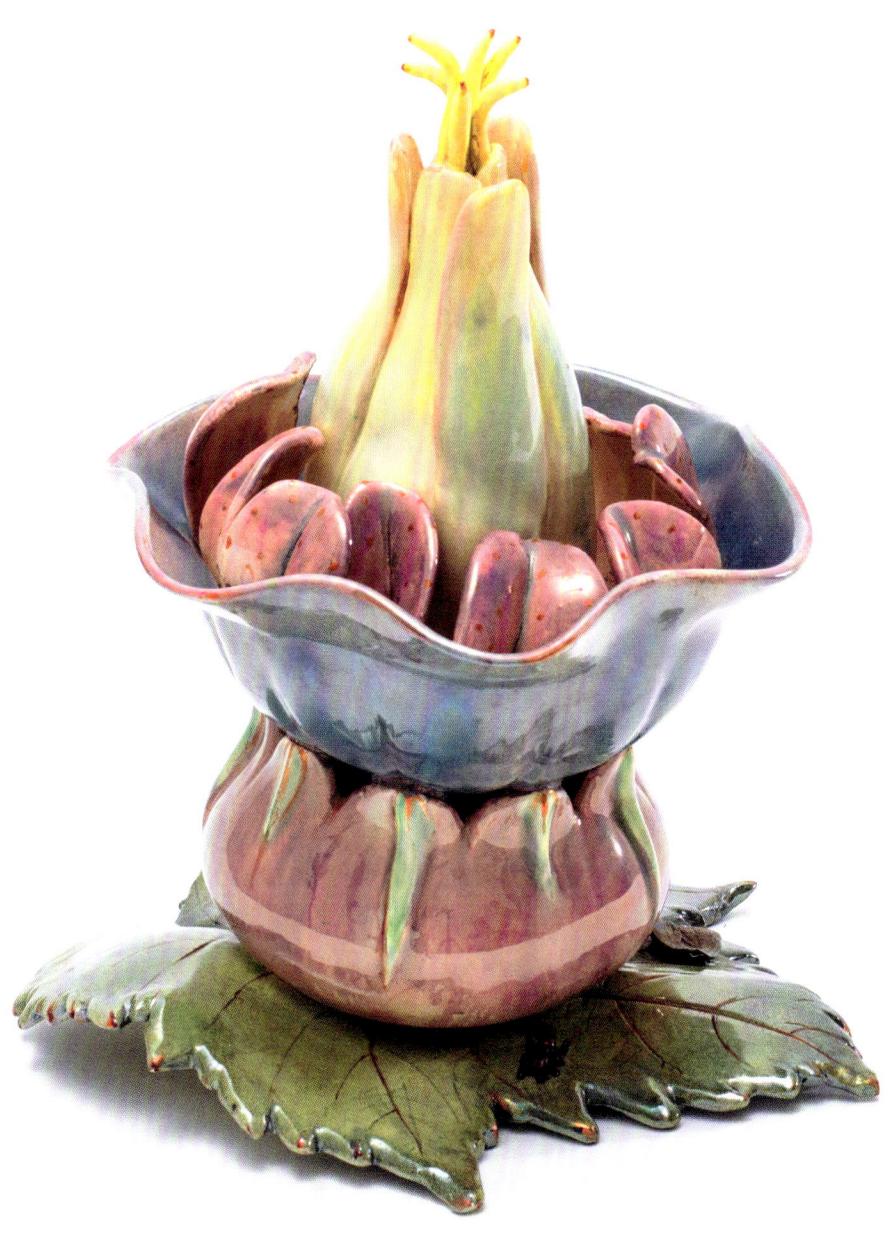

Tubeworm 2007
Glazed earthenware with china paint and luster
16 × 3¾ × 4 in. (40.6 × 9.5 × 10.2 cm)
Collection Rosalind Reed

Wondrous Kiss 2005
Glazed earthenware with china paint and luster
12 × 9½ × 9¼ in. (30.5 × 24.1 × 23.5 cm)

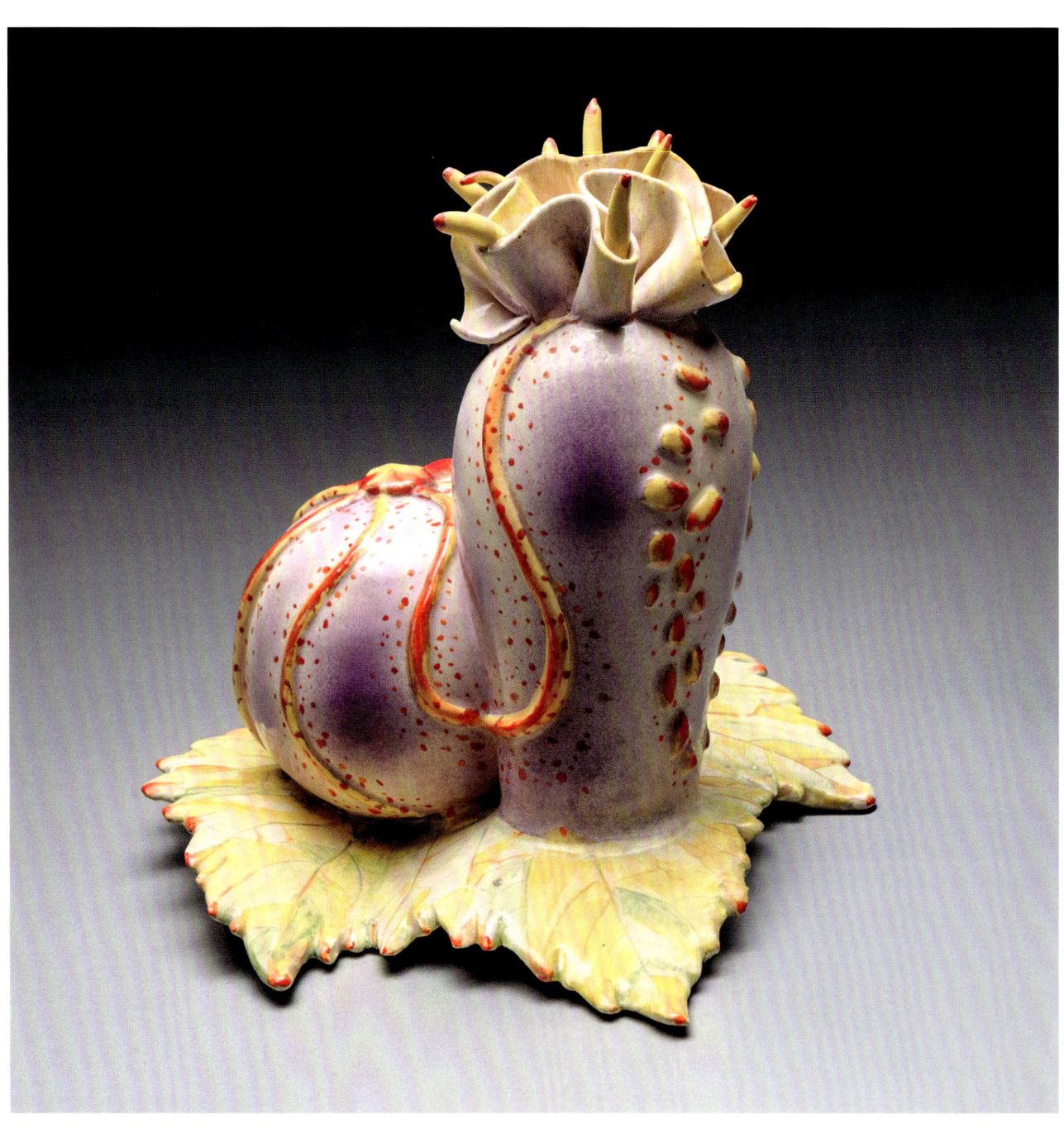

Sea Snail 2002–3
Glazed earthenware with china paint and luster
8 × 8 × 7 ½ in. (20.3 × 20.3 × 19.1 cm)
Collection Doug Drake and Elisabeth Kirsch

Right page
Pinky the Tubacious Tubeworm 2002
Glazed earthenware with china paint and luster
13 × 8 × 8 in. (33 × 20.3 × 20.3 cm)

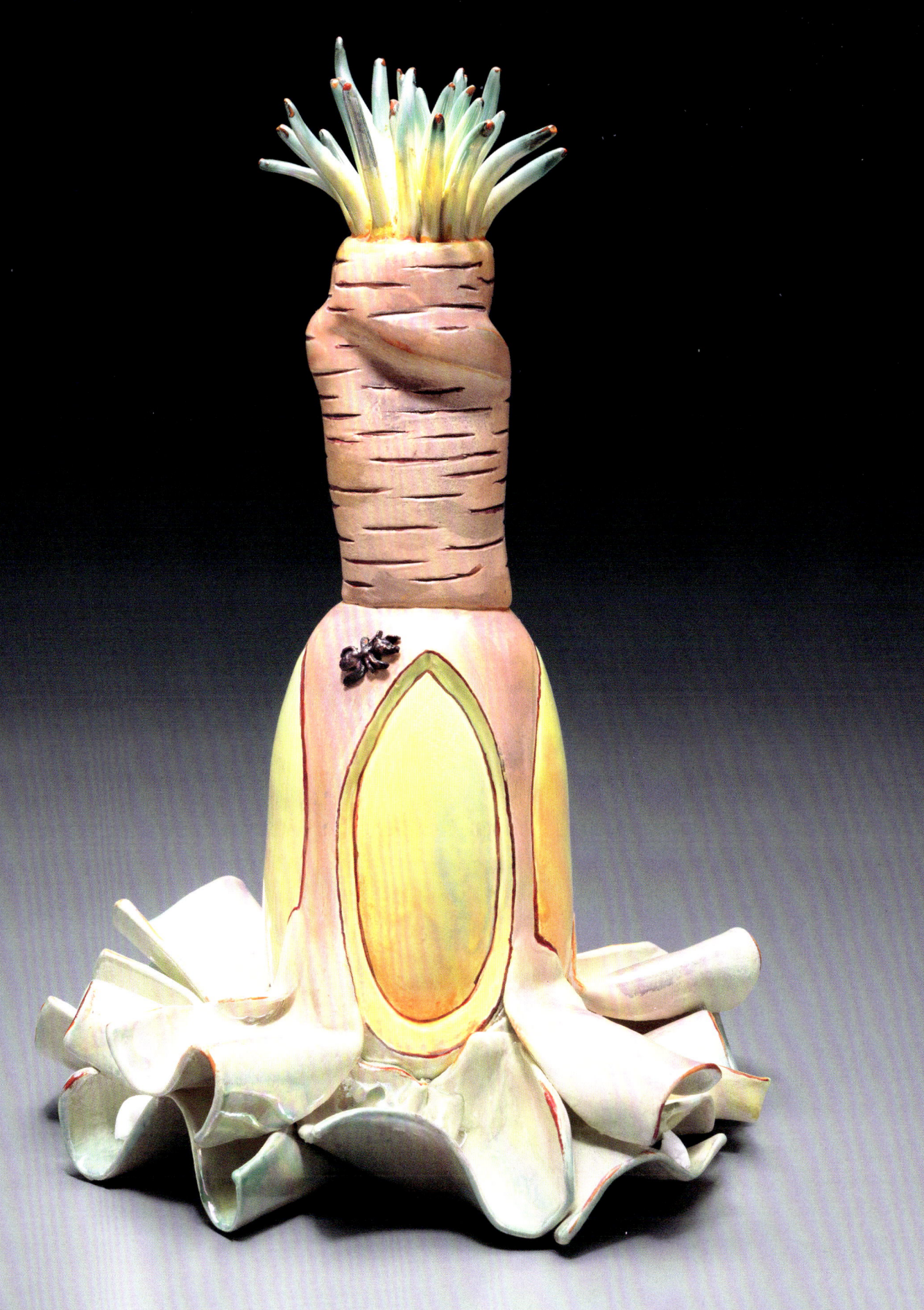

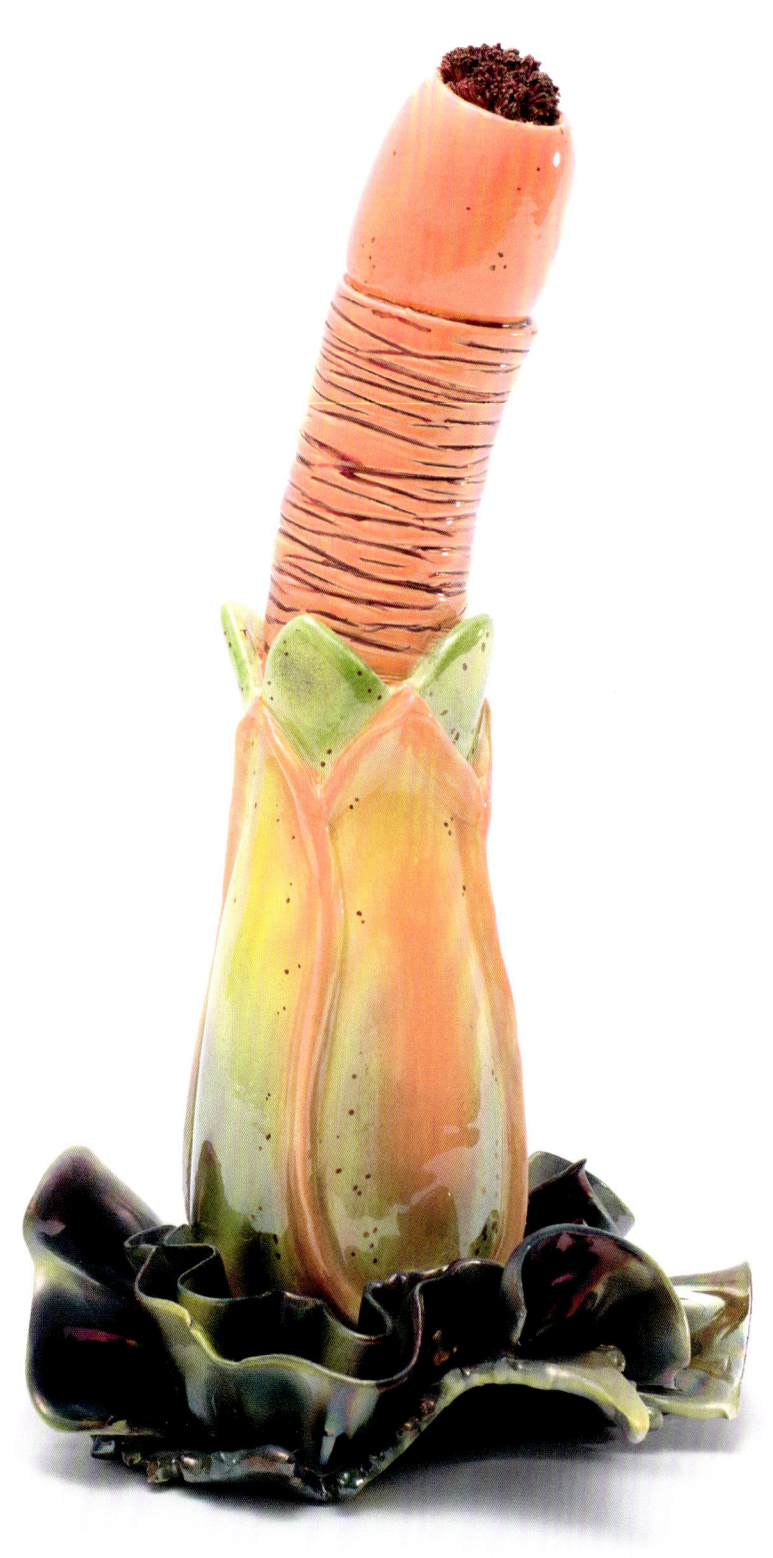

Tubeworm 2002–3
Glazed earthenware with china paint and luster
14 × 8 × 8 ½ in. (35.6 × 20.3 × 21.6 cm)
Collection Rose Dergan, New York

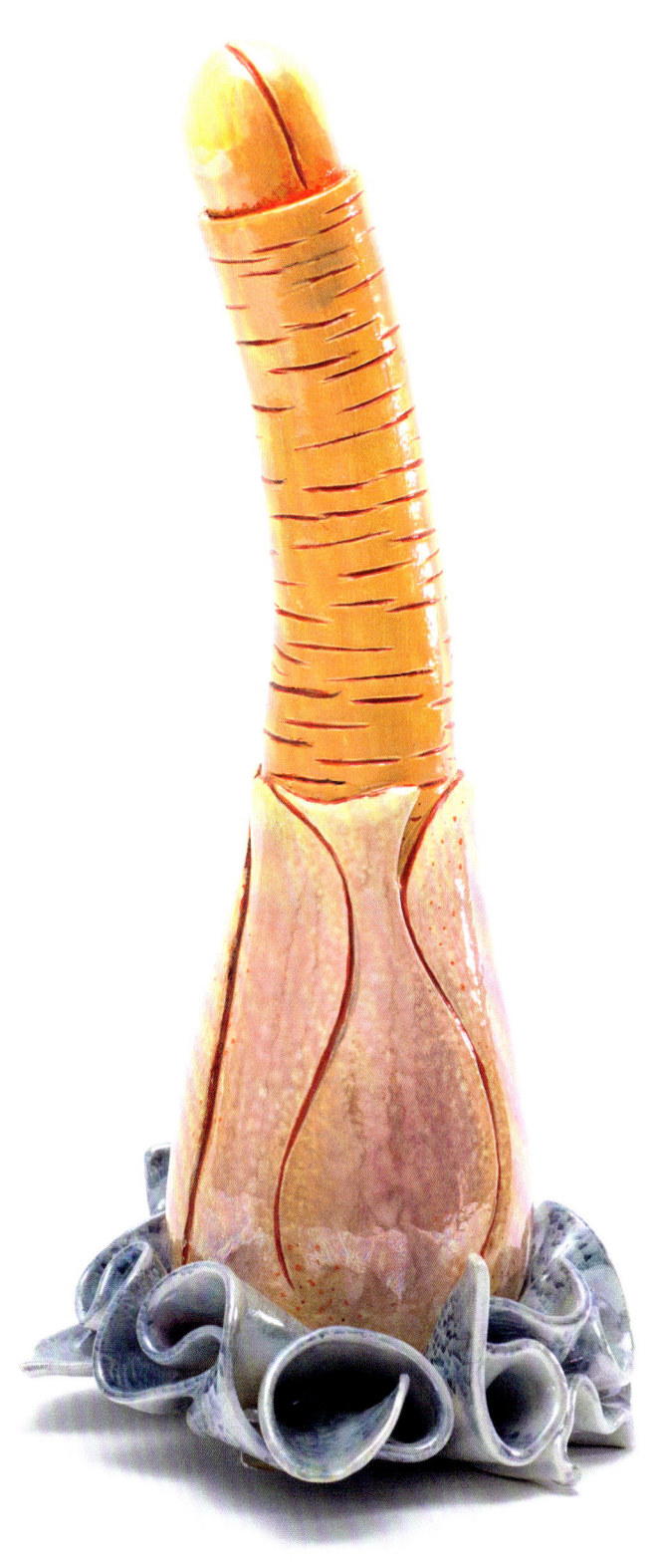

Tubeworm 2004
Glazed earthenware with china paint and luster
17 × 5 × 6 ½ in. (43.2 × 12.7 × 16.5 cm)
Collection Rose Dergan, New York

Right page
Bad Behavior 2001
Glazed earthenware with luster
10 ½ × 10 × 8 ½ in. (26.7 × 25.4 × 21.6 cm)

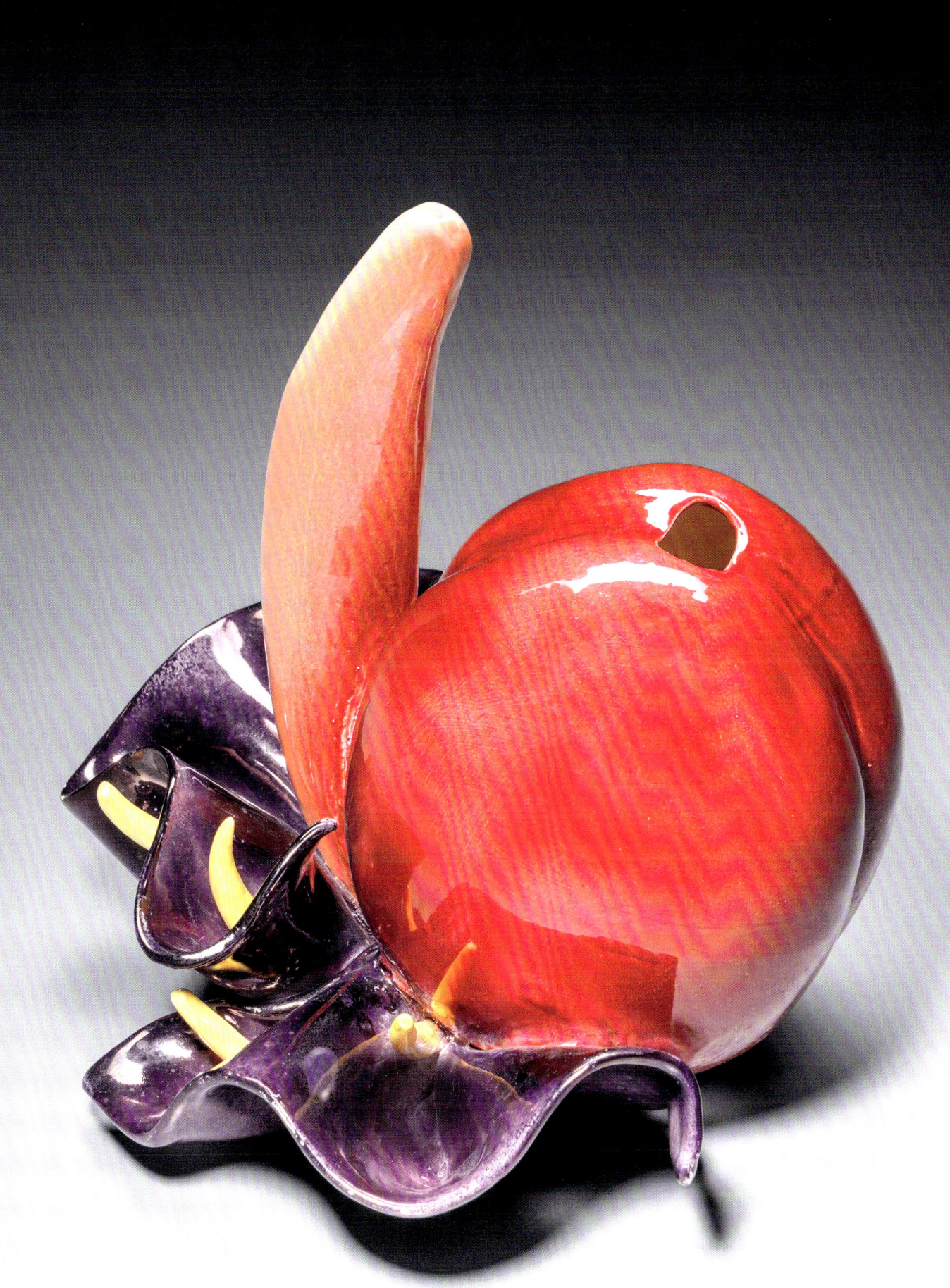

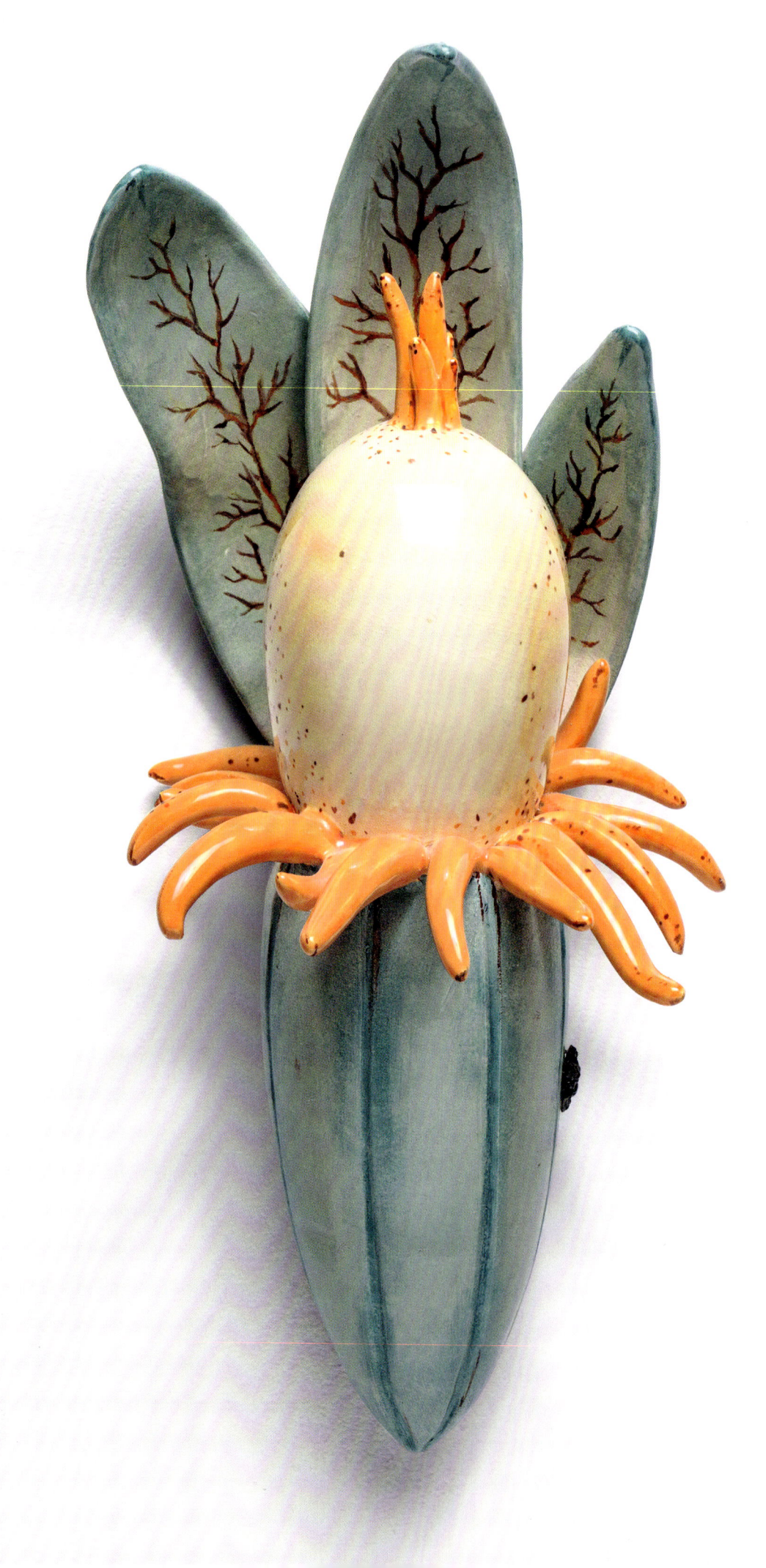

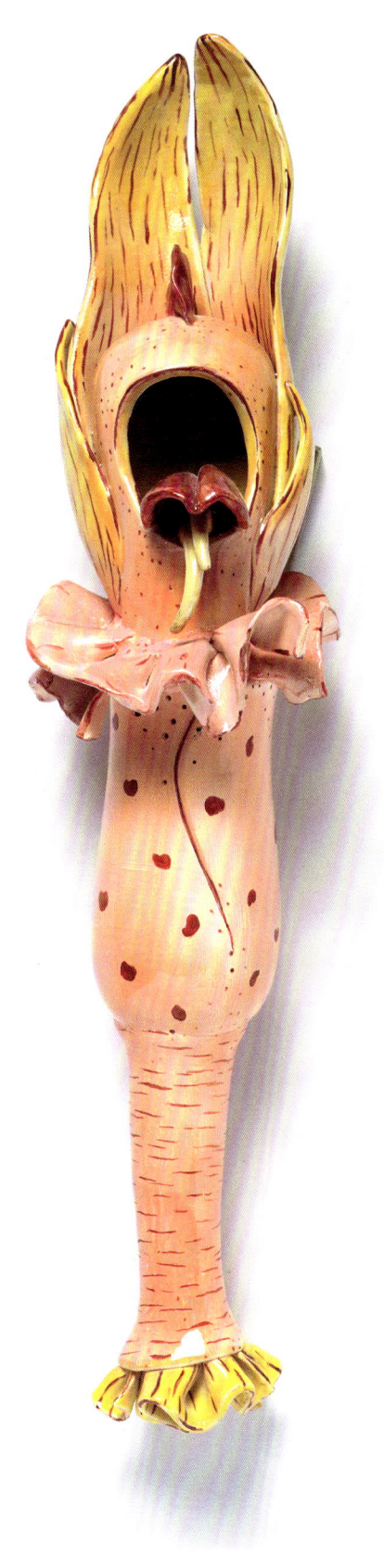

Left page
Untitled Tubeworm 2002
Glazed earthenware with china paint
15 × 7 ½ × 6 ½ in. (38.1 × 19.1 × 16.5 cm)

Circus Tubeworm 2002
Glazed earthenware with china paint and luster
25 ½ × 6 ½ × 8 in. (64.8 × 16.5 × 20.3 cm)

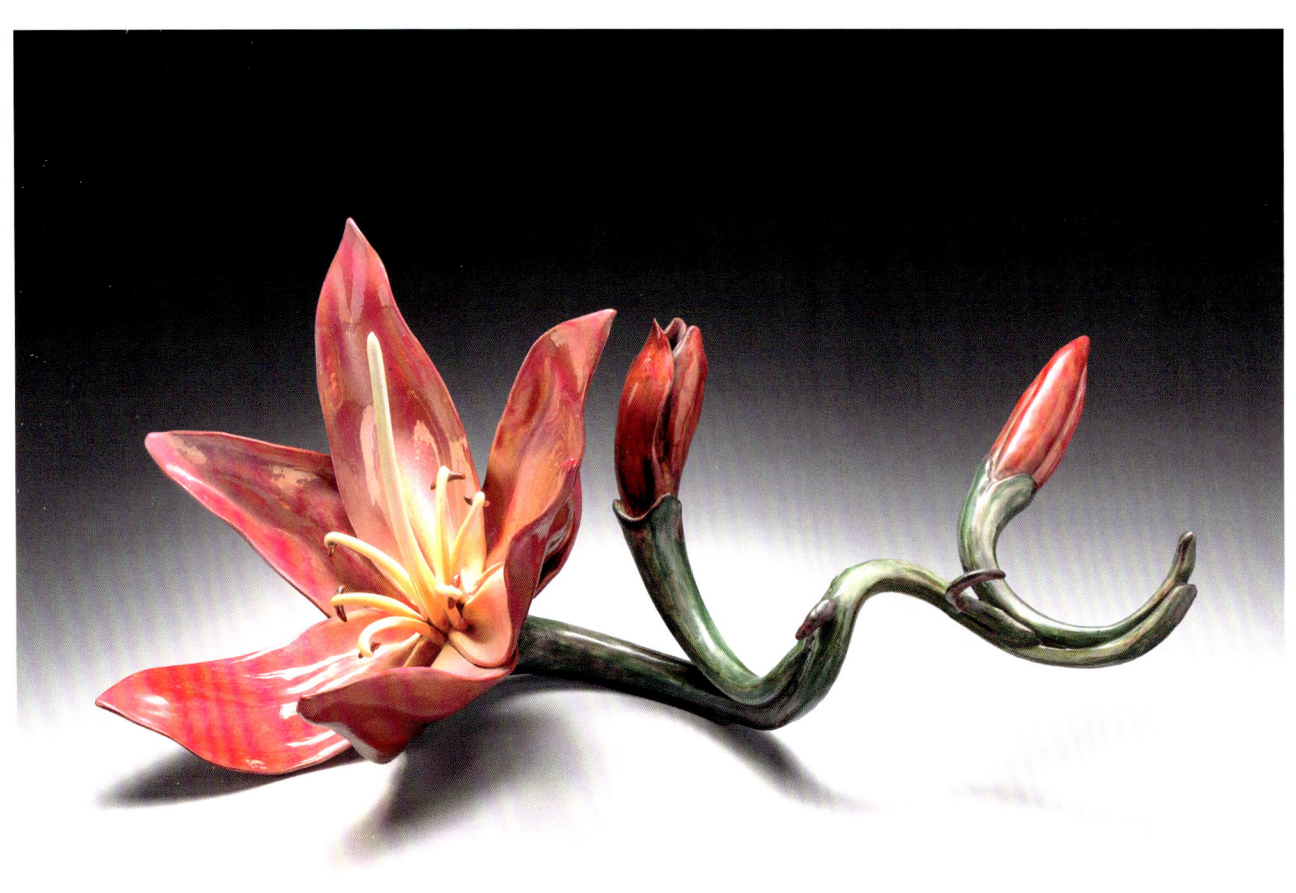

Red Lily 2008
Glazed earthenware with luster and paint
9.25 × 24 × 13 (23.5 × 61 × 33 cm)
Collection Charles and Susan Porter

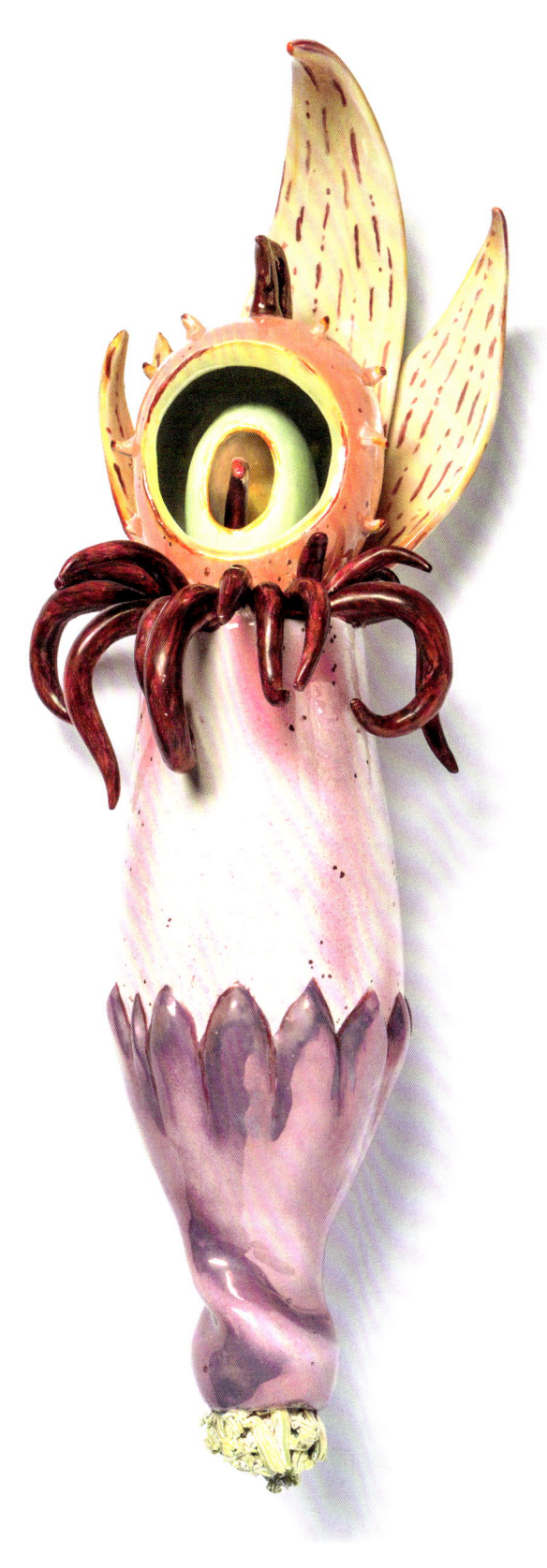

Dame Edna 2002
Glazed earthenware with china paint and luster
17 × 11 × 7 in. (43.2 × 27.9 × 17.8 cm)
Collection Nerman Museum of Contemporary Art,
Johnson County Community College, Overland Park, KS

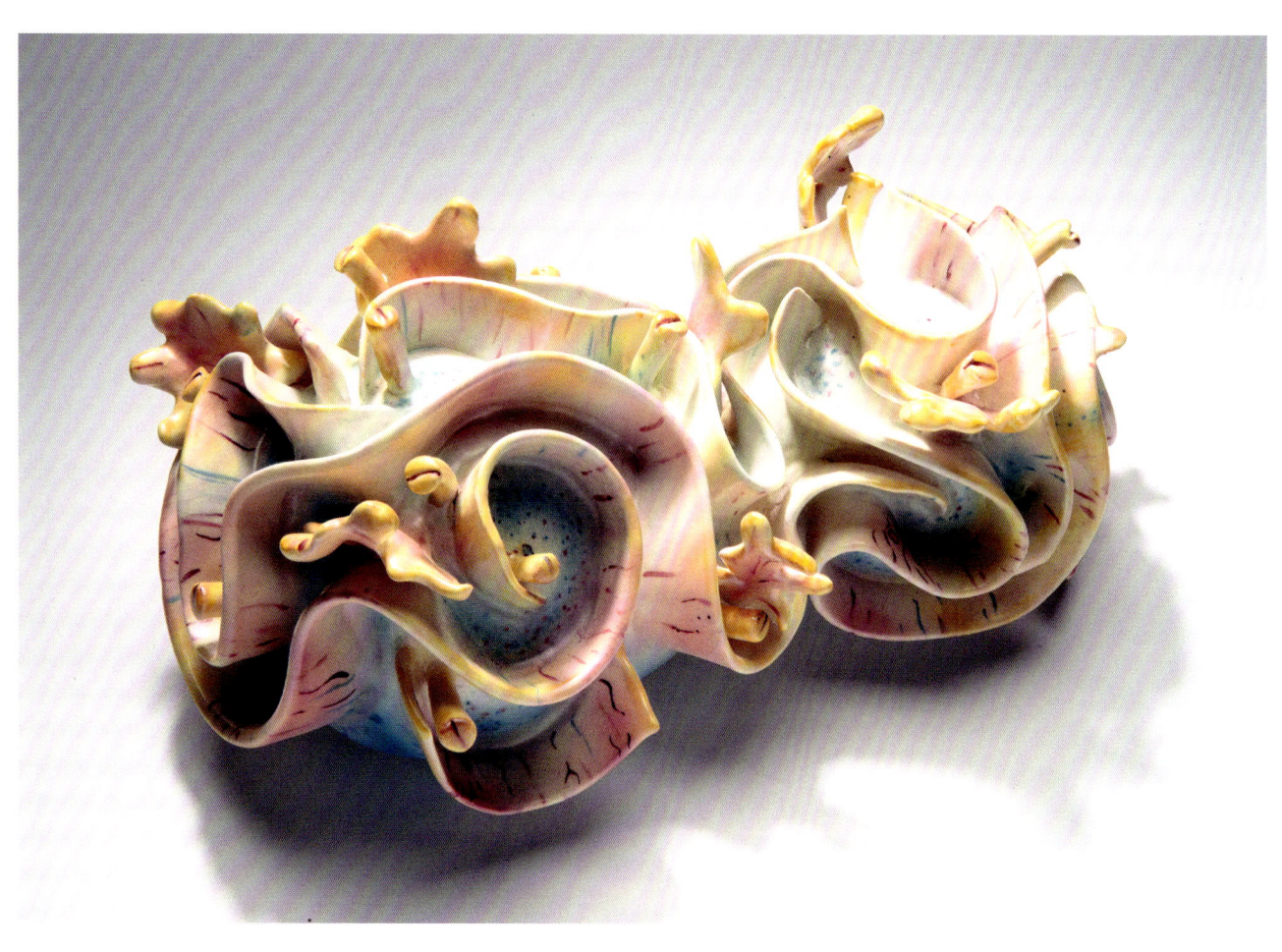

Miami Sea Sponge 2017
Glazed earthenware with china paint
16 × 7 × 8 in. (40.6 × 17.8 × 20.3 cm)
Collection Dr. Jemshed Khan

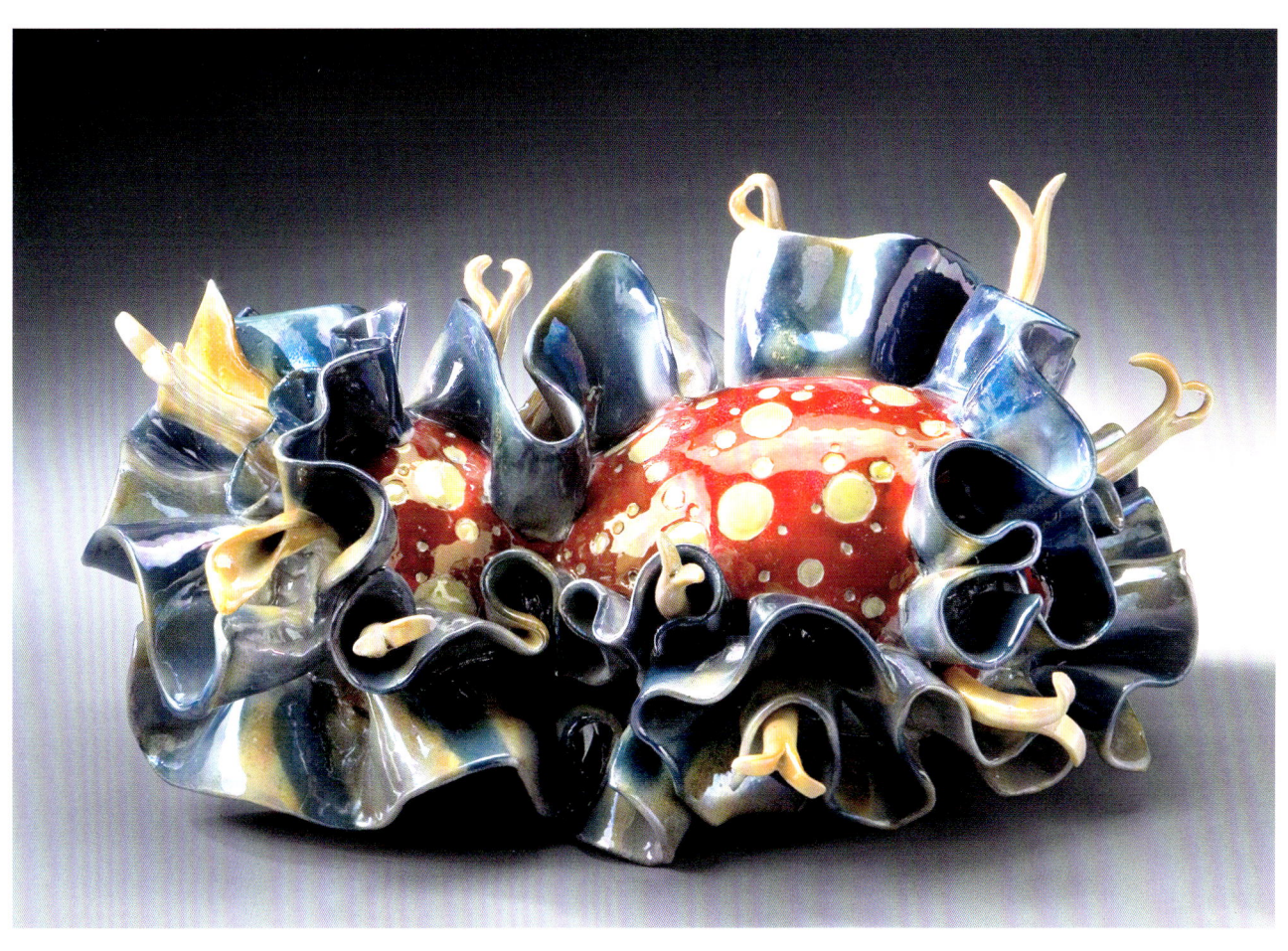

Sea Sponge 2007
Glazed earthenware with china paint and luster
15 ½ × 9 × 6 in. (39.4 × 22.9 × 15.2 cm)
Collection The Nelson-Atkins Museum of Art, Kansas City, MO

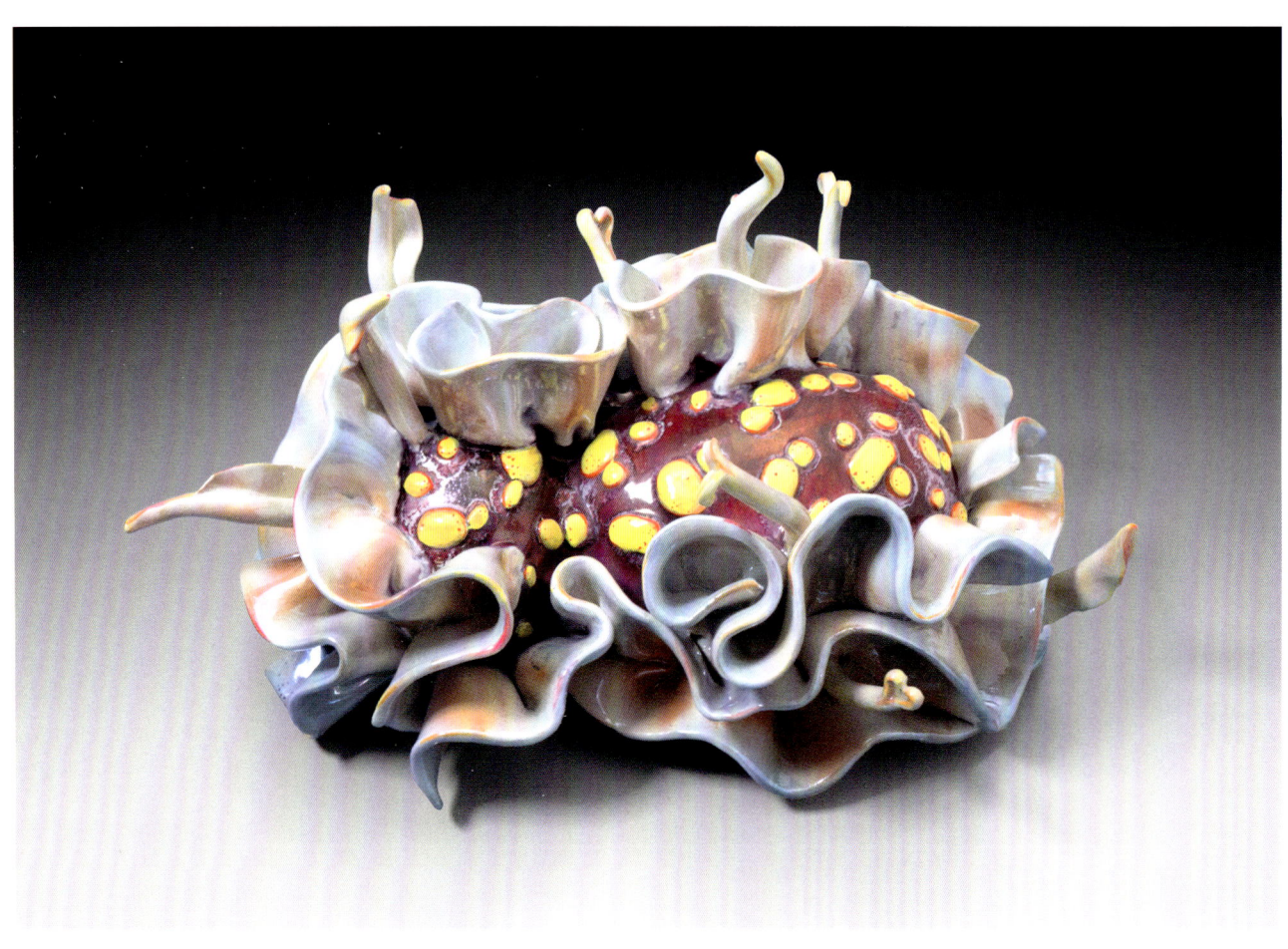

Fire Sponge Tedania Ignis 2004
Glazed earthenware with china paint and luster
15 ¼ × 9 × 6 in. (38.7 × 22.9 × 15.2 cm)
Collection Kemper Museum of Contemporary Art, Kansas City, MO

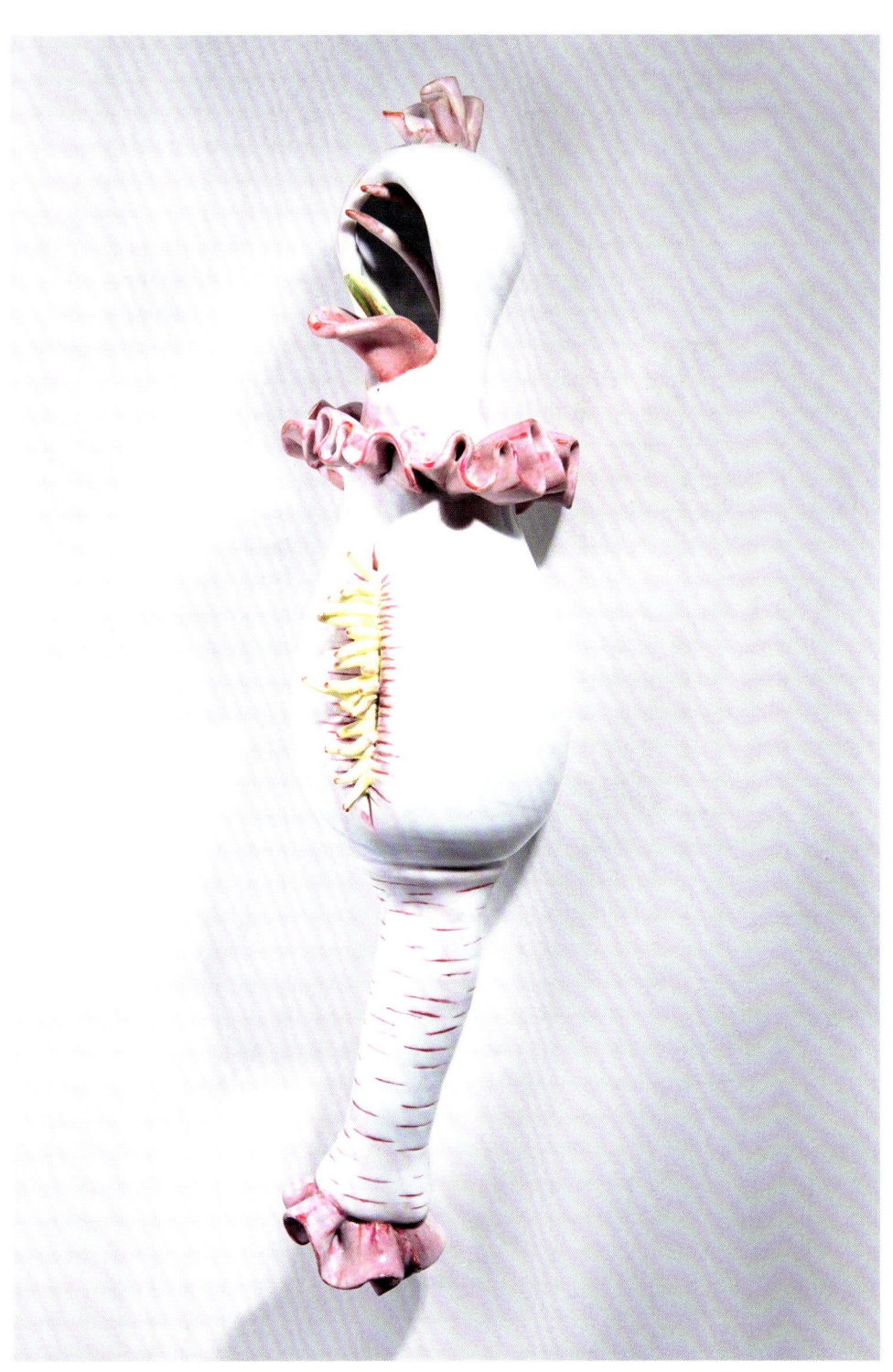

Tenacious Tubeworm 2003–5
Glazed earthenware with china paint
18 × 5 × 4 ½ in. (45.7 × 12.7 × 11.4 cm)

Untitled 2015
Glazed earthenware with china paint and luster
15 ½ × 12 × 19 in. (39.4 × 30.5 × 48.3 cm)

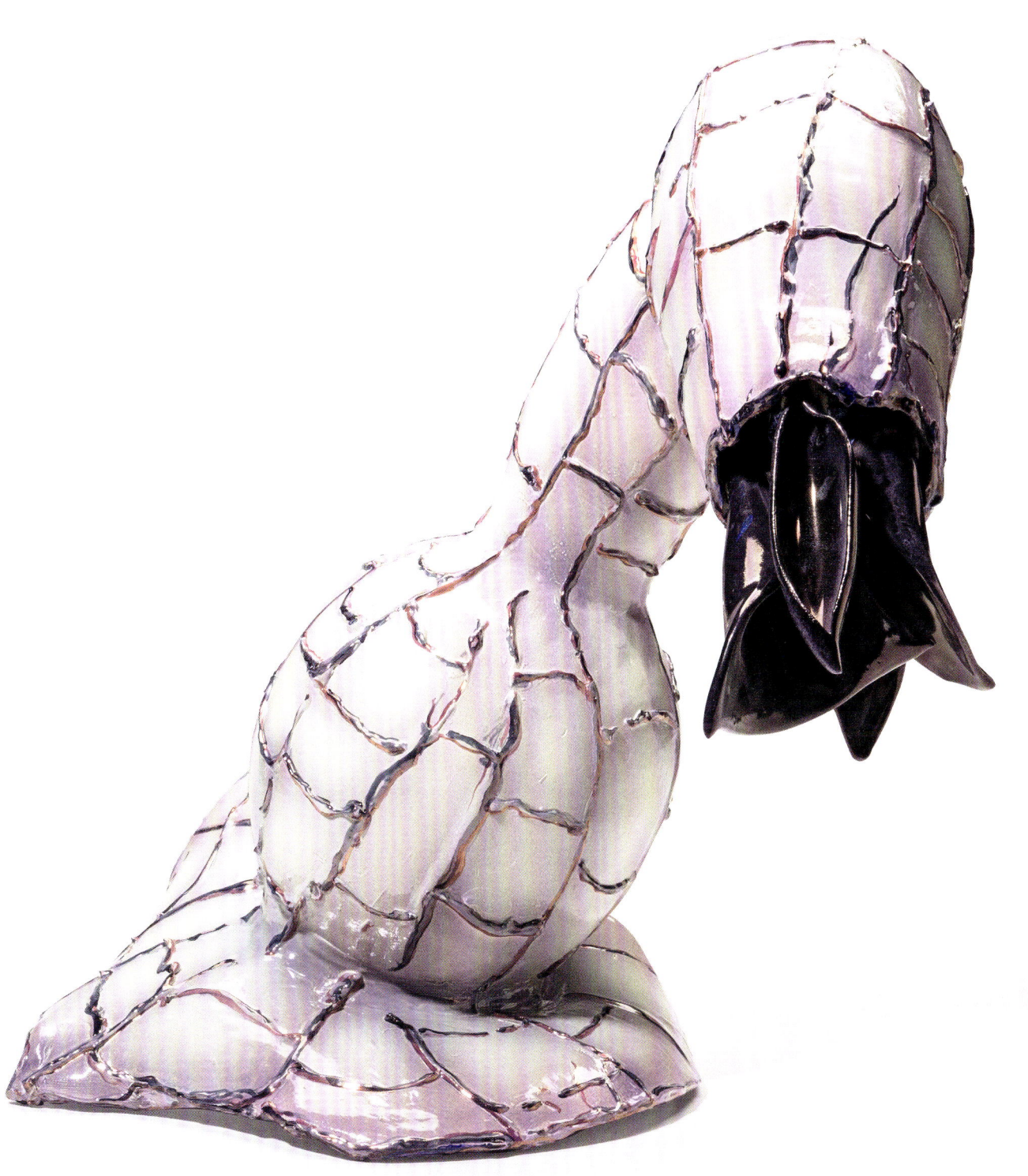

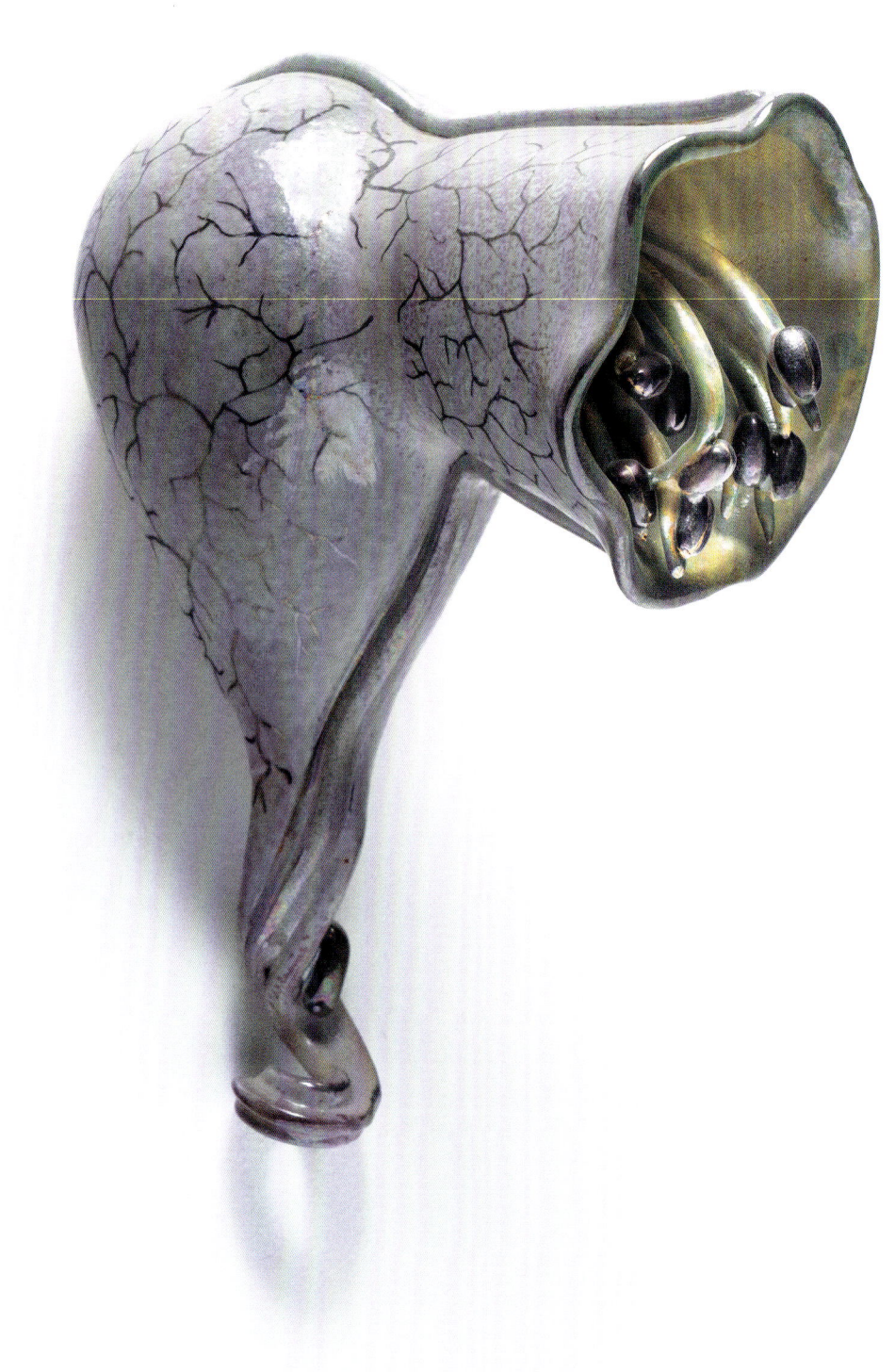

Untitled Tubeworm 2004
Salt fired porcelain with china paint and luster
9 × 4 ¼ × 7 ½ in. (22.9 × 10.8 × 19.1 cm)

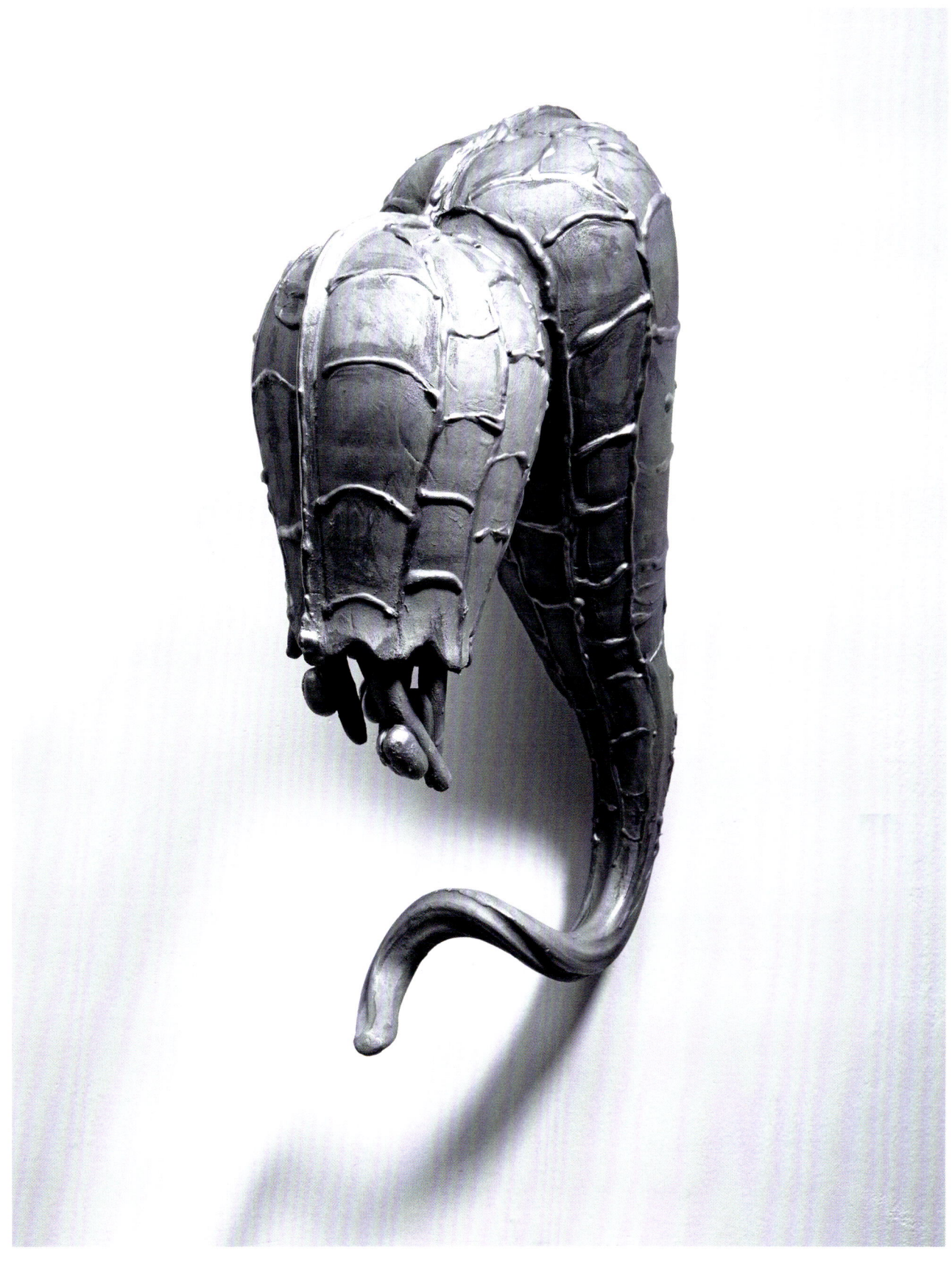

Spanish Tubeworm 2016
Black fired earthenware
12 ½ × 4 ½ × 8 in.
(31.8 × 11.4 × 20.3 cm)

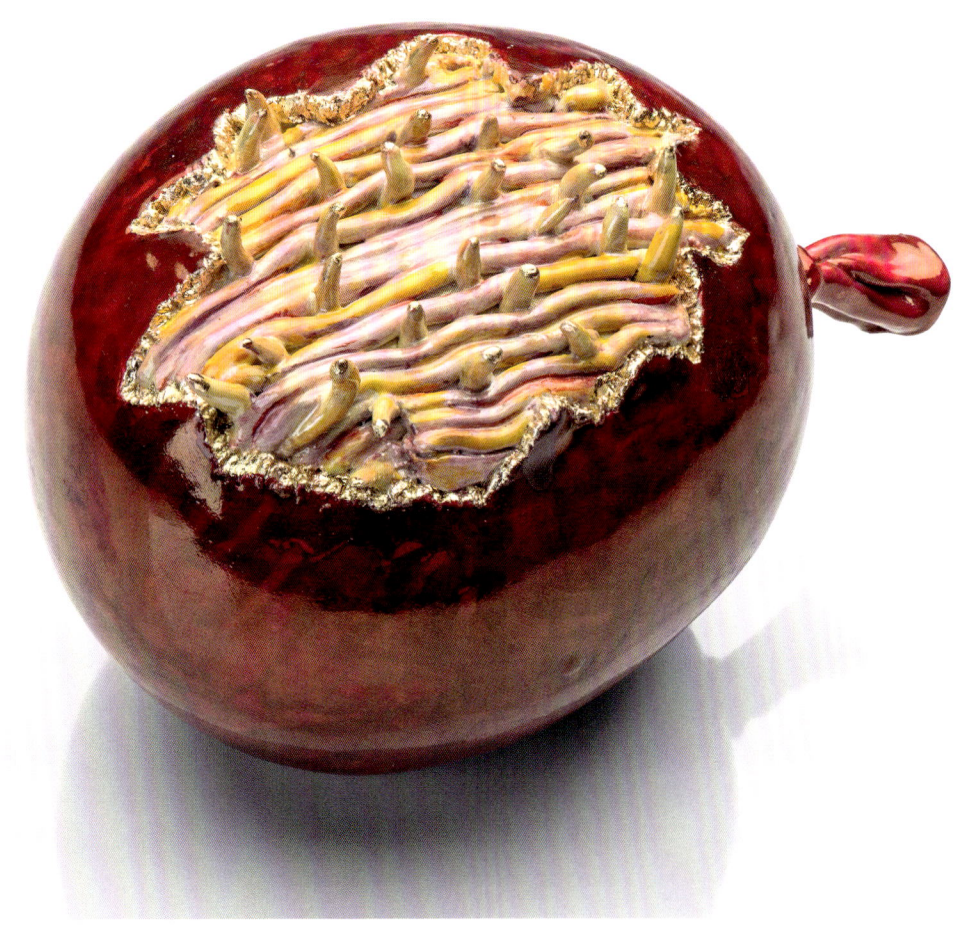

My Desire 2015
Glazed earthenware with china paint, luster and metal leaf
7 × 10 × 7 in. (17.8 × 25.4 × 17.8 cm)

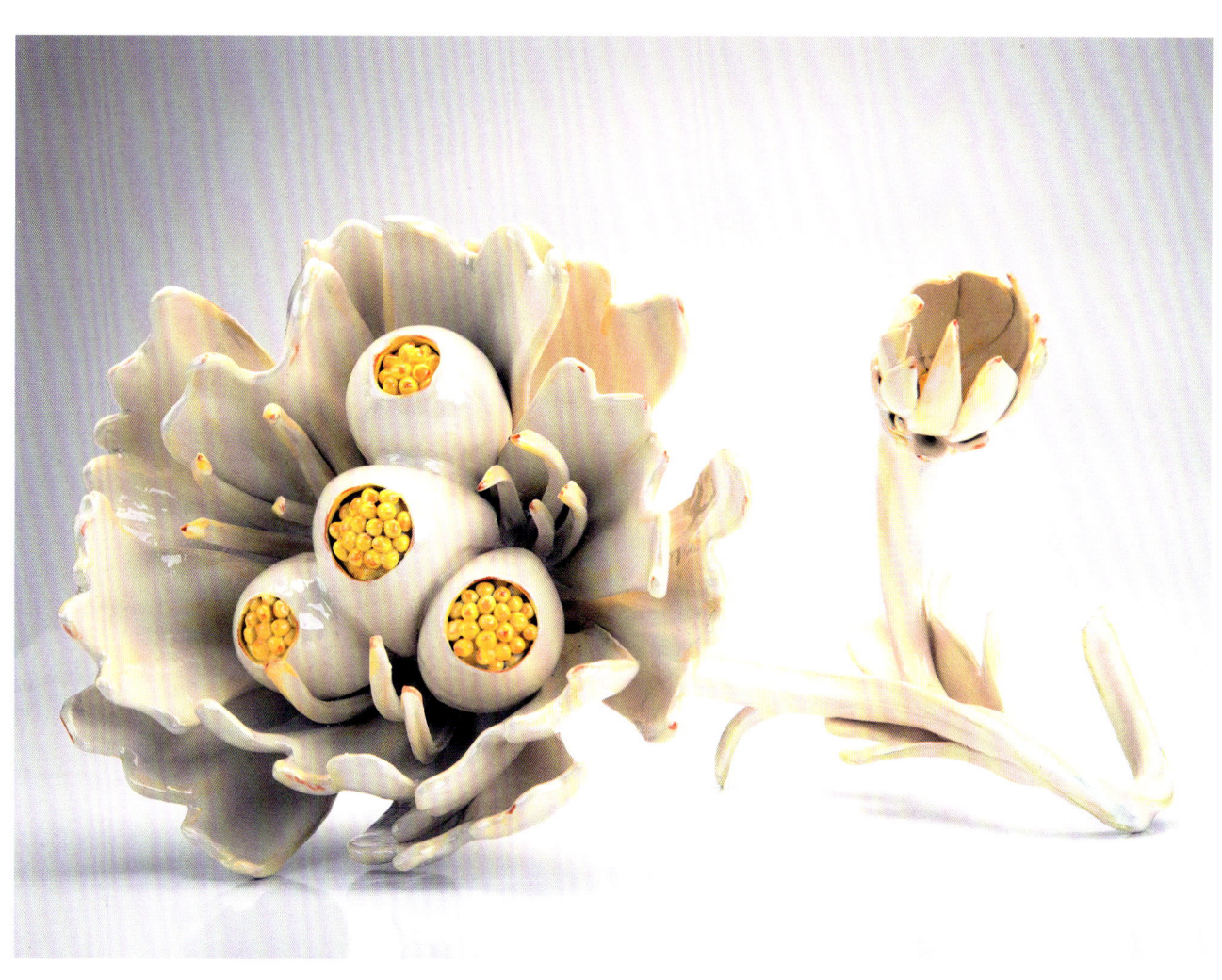

My Desire (White) 2016
Glazed earthenware with china paint
10 × 20 × 14 in. (25.4 × 50.8 × 35.6 cm)

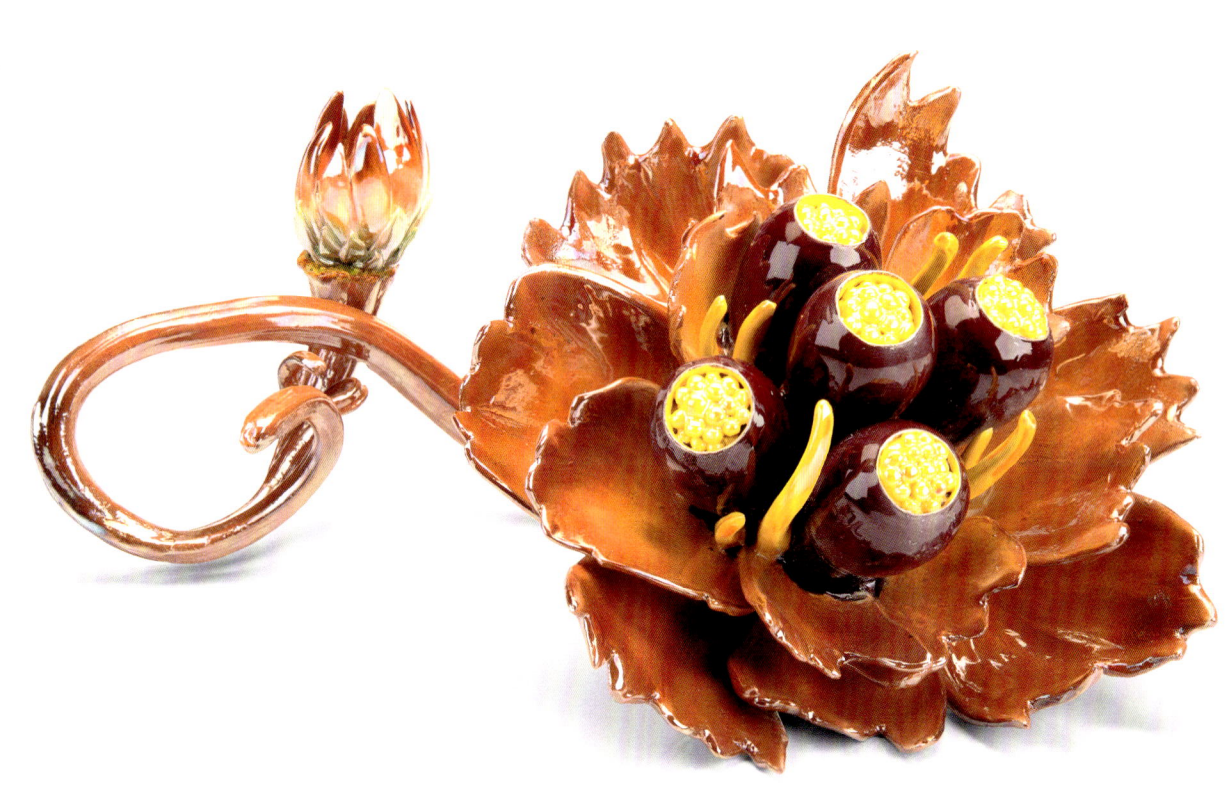

My Desire (Brown) 2016
Glazed earthenware with china paint
11 × 25 ½ × 15 ½ in. (27.9 × 64.8 × 39.4 cm)

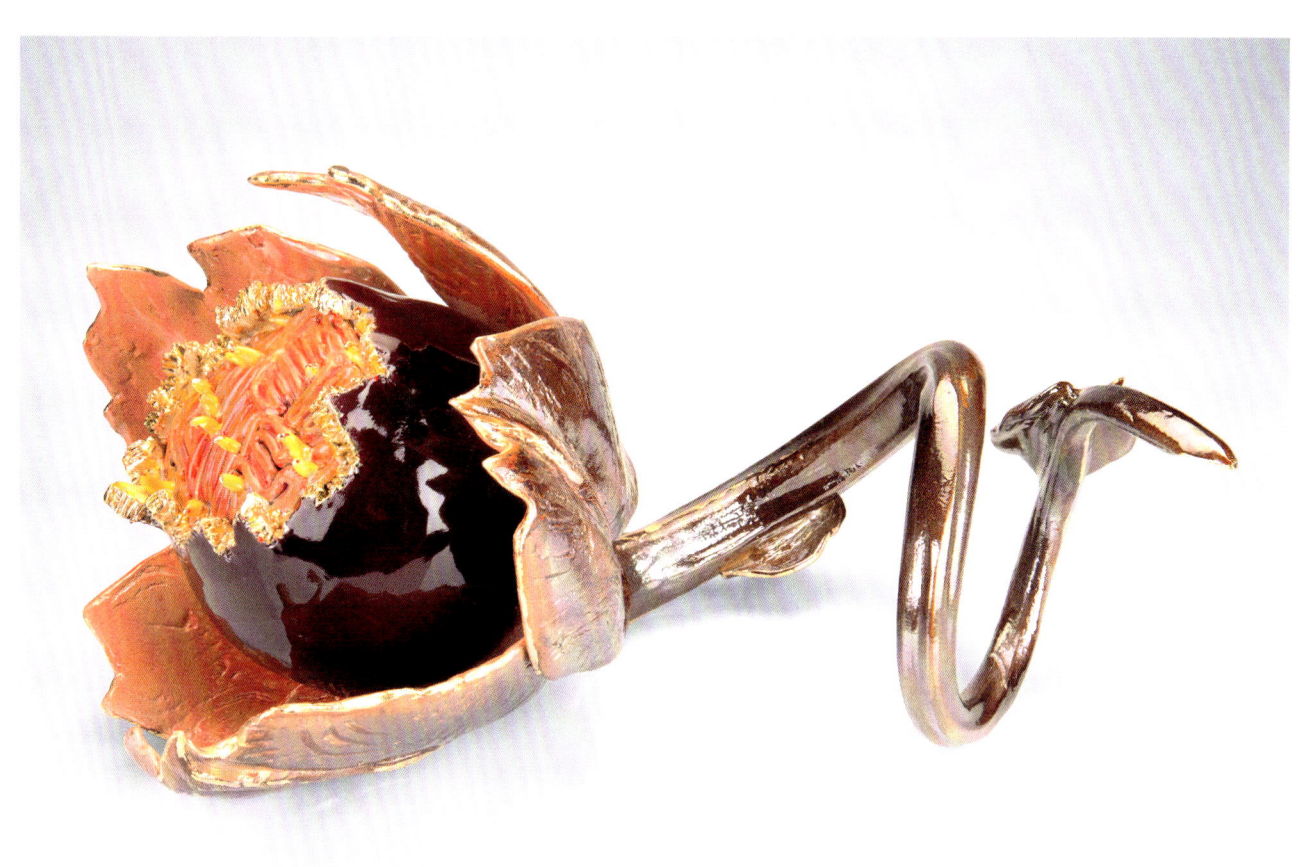

My Desire 2016
Glazed earthenware with china paint, luster and gold leaf
23 × 26 ½ × 2 ¾ in. (58.4 × 67.3 × 7 cm)

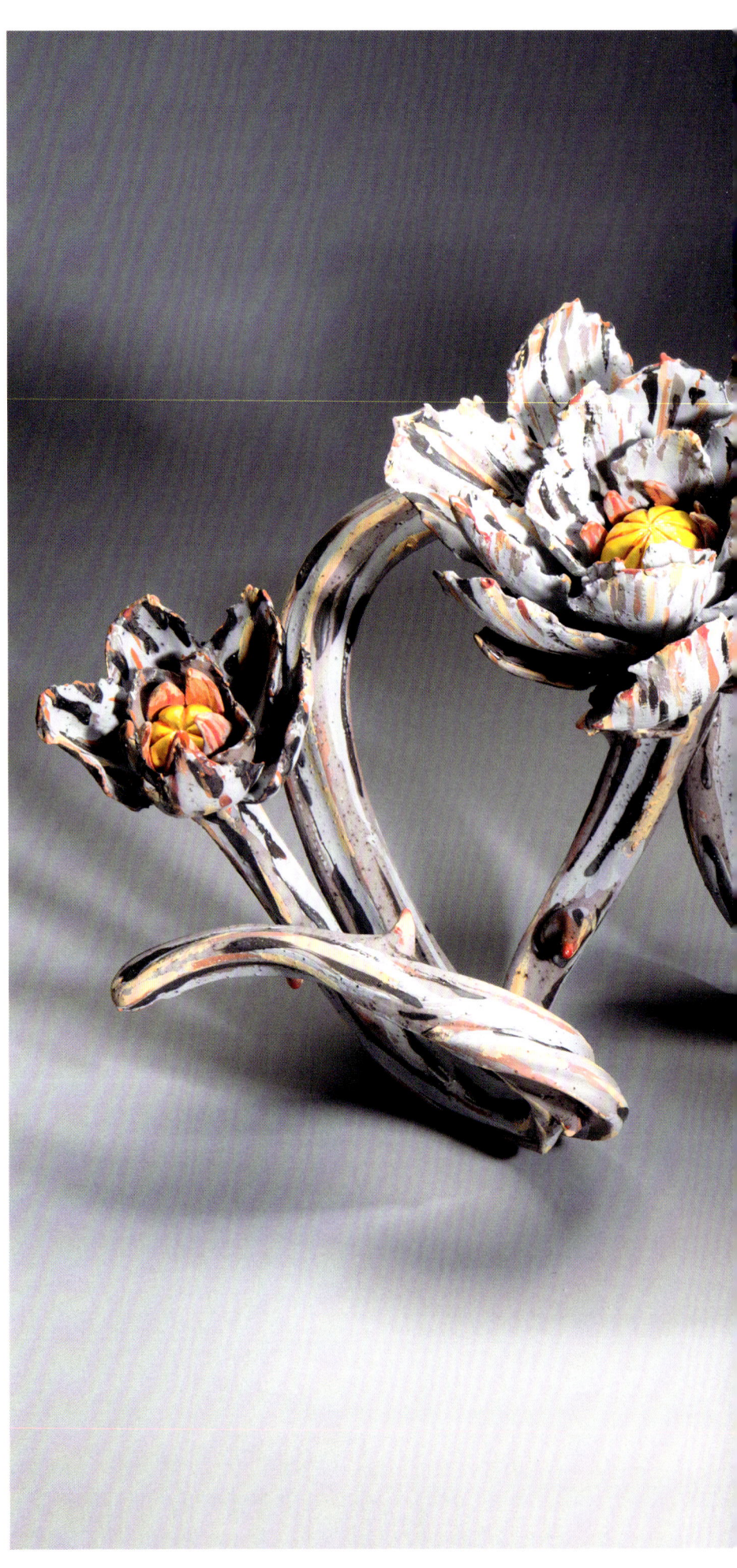

Black Widow 2018
Glazed earthenware with china paint
14 × 31 × 21 in. (35.6 × 78.7 × 53.3 cm)

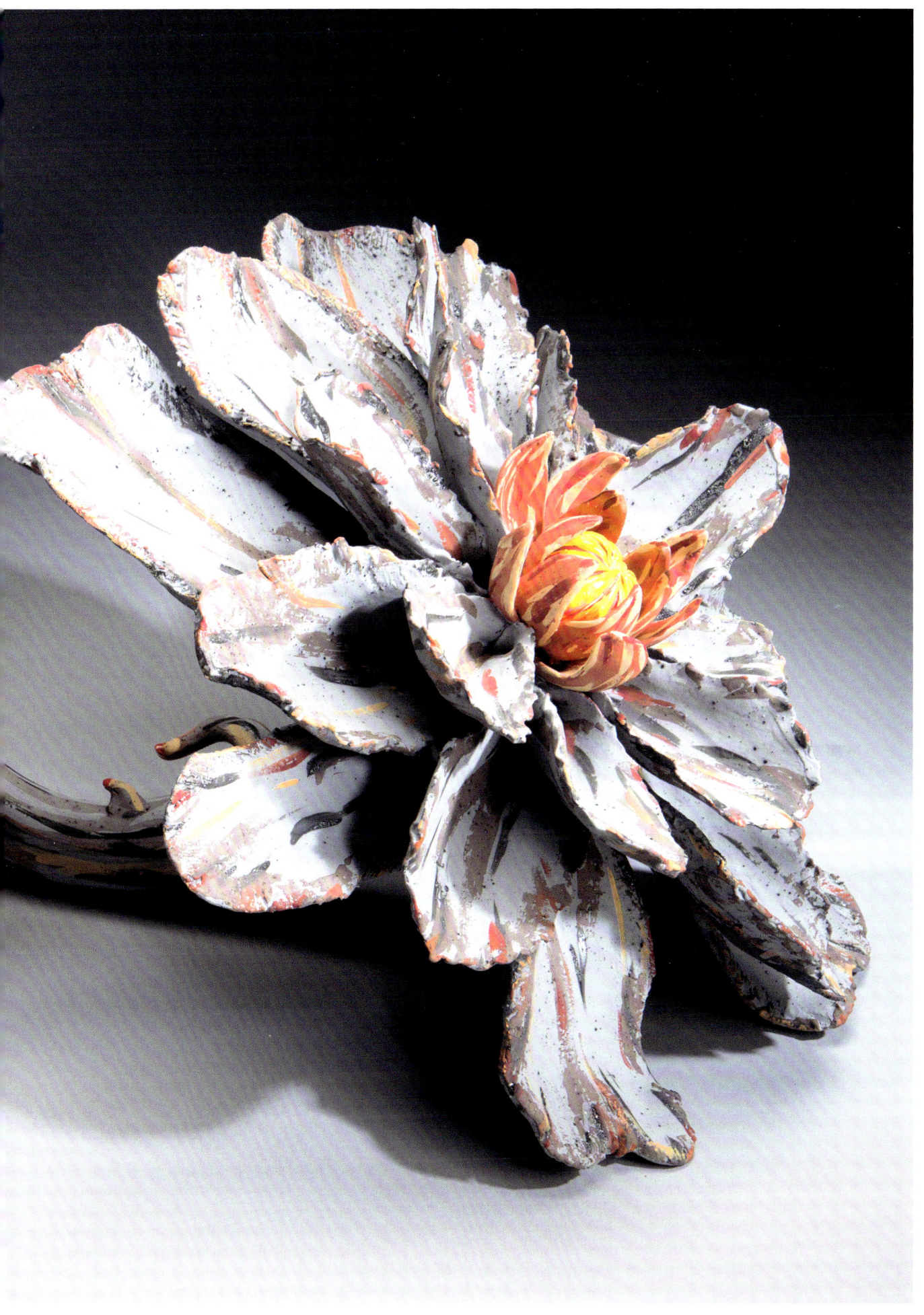

VORACIOUS THINGS:
LINDA LIGHTON AND THE OBJECTS OF DESIRE

by Sydney Stutterheim

n a 2020 lecture presented at the Académie Internationale de la Céramique, Linda Lighton avowed that, throughout her nearly fifty-year artistic career, her "focus has been on desire." Connecting it to what she describes as a life force, Lighton's exploration of the complexities behind the concept of desire is certainly one of the most important themes running throughout her remarkable body of work. Given that the definition of desire is to wish for, or aspire to, something beyond what is presently in reach, it hits our most primal emotions and can culminate in the greatest forces imaginable—the battles of love and war.

These opposing terms, as they mutually constitute the actualization of desire, form the conceptual basis of *Linda Lighton: Love and War, A Fifty-Year Survey, 1975–2025*, the first major retrospective exhibition of Lighton's work, staged at the Nerman Museum of Contemporary Art. Spanning sculptures and drawings made over a half-century, this show considers the ways that Lighton's work explores desire through social, biological, and political manifestations—the ways it can motivate the good as well as the bad; love and war alike. Whether through artworks that delve into the motivations for status and power, or those that revel in the diversity of life while expressing universally shared needs, Lighton cogently visualizes the vast expressions of desire as central to life itself.

There are four types of desire that appear thematically in Lighton's work: intellectual desire, consumer desire, sexual desire, and physical desire. For instance, desire often serves as the motivating force in one's personal ambition for influence and recognition, but may be equally cited as the driving factor in libidinal appetites of erotic lust. There is economic desire, one that materializes as consumer demand, as well as physical desire, understood as the bodily impulses towards procreation, sustenance, or self-preservation. Perhaps paradoxically, desire can play out as the impetus for both consumption and reproduction, creation and decay.

As seen in her powerful, witty, and often poignant work, Lighton understands such contradictions, allowing them to coexist. Yet to put desire so plainly in the foreground of one's artistic work contains a kind of risk. For as much as desire pervades the forces that drive all of existence, its often primal nature means that it remains hidden within contemporary society. Through her life and work, Lighton defiantly, courageously, and joyously refuses this concealment. Her desire to create art exceeds her fear.

Ambition and Desire

The concept of desire powerfully shaped Lighton's personal biography, in terms of both her inherited circumstances and her subsequent life decisions. Born into a well-to-do family in Kansas City, Missouri, during the postwar boom of mid-century America, Lighton entered the world with societal expectations at the ready. Her father, Alfred Lighton, owned the upscale department store Woolf Brothers, which was a family business in the heart of the booming Midwestern garment industry; Alfred inherited the business from his uncle, Herbert Woolf, running the store. The Woolf family was long established in Kansas City, having relocated there in the late nineteenth century, and they ran not only the successful clothing stores, which had branched out as a chain to other nearby states, but also a horse-racing business.

As much financial success as the Lighton family had, their Jewish cultural identity positioned them outside the religious mainstream in Kansas City.[1] Still, her family was active in developing cultural centers in the city and were major supporters of both the visual and performing arts. Despite the noted appreciation for the arts, however, having one of their own family members pursue a career in those fields was another story. Being an artist was something other people did—and this certainly did not pertain to their daughter.

Lighton graduated high school in 1965, at a time when the country was undergoing a radical political and social transformation marked by a shift in generational values. Inspired by these changes to women's roles, Lighton refused to attend the prestigious Kansas City debutante Jewel Ball (which her family helped to fund in its inception) and declared her aspiration to go to art school. However, her parents rebuffed this request, sending her away to the Centenary College for Young Women, a junior college in New Jersey. There, the message was centered on building a life for women inside the home as wives and homemakers for wealthy husbands. Lighton bluntly recalls of her parents' wishes: "They wanted me to look good, keep my mouth shut, serve some hors d'oeuvres, you know? And I think a lot of people wanted that for their kids back then. Didn't look that good to me."[2]

But Lighton was savvy and used the college's proximity to New York City as a way to immerse herself in the epicenter of the contemporary art world. During the year that she attended Centenary, American Pop Art was at its zenith. Andy Warhol's *Silver Clouds* installation opened at the Leo Castelli Gallery in 1966, just as Roy Lichtenstein was selected to represent the United States at the Venice Biennale. The experience of seeing work by these artists firsthand, which Lighton recalls "made a huge impression on me," inspired a major move—first to Lawrence, Kansas, where she worked on an underground leftist newspaper, and on to the West Coast in 1968, where she took up residence in Haight-Ashbury at the height of the hippie movement. At the age of 21, after moving once again, this time to Seattle, Lighton had a daughter.

Despite the vicissitudes of life as a young woman in a dramatically shifting American landscape, Lighton retained her artistic aspirations. Her desire was, quite simply, to be an artist. On the run from familial restrictions—as Glenn Adamson describes in his essay, she was put under an involuntary hold at a mental institution by her conservative father as a result of these ambitions—she attended art school, first at the Factory of Visual Arts in Seattle, then Western Washington State College in Bellingham, Washington, where Funk art and ceramics traditions were at the fore. After living on the Native American Colville Reservation in eastern Washington and meeting her second husband, Lynn, in Idaho, Lighton's desire had come up against practical concerns. Seeking a

better schooling situation for her daughter Rose, Lighton returned to Kansas City.

Amidst the rampant consumerism, neoliberal economic policies, and growing conservatism of 1980s America under the newly elected Republican president Ronald Reagan, Lighton began to probe important questions in her art concerning the social, political, and environmental issues at stake during this period. While 1960s second-wave feminism had spurred a substantial investigation into the ways in which women (largely white middle-class women) were not only legally, but also culturally, marginalized as secondary to men, the 1980s marked considerable reversals for the feminist advancements made in decades prior. One notable exception was in 1984, when the Supreme Court ruled against sex-based discrimination, effectively expanding Title VII of the 1964 Civil Rights Act, a legal safeguard against workplace discrimination. Despite such rulings, however, the 1980s were at the same time shaped by underlying prejudices, harassment, and biases against women. As Susan Faludi exposed in her 1991 book *Backlash: The Undeclared War Against American Women*, the 1980s were defined by a period of increasing pressures on women, whether in the form of pervasive sexual harassment in the workplace, a growing antiabortion movement seeking to regulate women's bodies, rising gender-based income disparities, and the myth of working mothers being able to achieve perfection in their roles within both domestic and workplace settings. Lighton knew of this struggle on a deeply personal level. In thinking through the complexities within her personal experience of being a woman, a mother, and an artist in a Midwestern city far from the stereotypically progressive coasts, her ambition sharpened as these concerns became the thematic focus of her work and practice.

**

In contemporary American society, desire and ambition are equally revered and shunned. Both are at the core of the country's collective identity, with aspirations for gaining or maintaining sex, love, wealth, and health

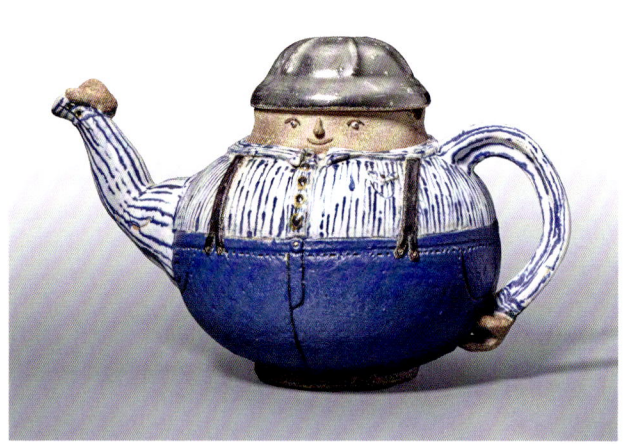

1 **LINDA LIGHTON, Logger Teapot** 1978
Glazed stoneware with underglaze and luster
7 × 11 × 7 in. (17.8 × 27.9 × 17.8 cm)

driving consumer culture and personal decisions alike. Although these motivations are deeply rooted in the nation's character—examples range from nineteenth-century westward expansion in growing the country's physical footprint to modern-day reality television programming centered on the lust for fame, adoration, and money—desire is often treated as something to be hidden.

Basic desires—to create art, to celebrate life, to pursue one's interests, to have bodily sovereignty, to embrace sensuality, and to live without fear of gun violence—are what drives Lighton and her courageous work, which spans the beautiful and grotesque, serious and playful. It is as if she sees the connection between polarities, their mutual imbrication, and the ways that such contrasts necessitate one another in order to exist. Lighton's approach injects her chosen medium with a vitality that challenges the mainstream order. Her entry into making art in the mid-1970s coincided with the historical introduction of postmodernism and, with it, a shattering of the rigorous categorical hierarchies central to the modernist project through the introduction of

video, sound, installation, and performance art. Her work, while reflecting the dual influences of both Pop Art and West Coast ceramic artists with whom she studied, officially or not, importantly presents a distinctly contemporary perspective that defies easy categorization.

As esteemed ceramics scholar Garth Clark has pointed out, there were two main strains of ceramics within a complex, heterogeneous field at the time Lighton launched her artistic career.[3] The first concerns the reinvestment in the vessel as a vital ceramics form; in response to the widespread rejection in the 1960s of the vessel as reactionary or anachronistic, ceramic artists working in the 1980s developed approaches to engage with both fine and decorative art traditions, what critic Peter Schjeldahl has called the "smart pot."[4] The second thread can be traced through the work of Robert Arnason, Viola Frey, and Mary Frank, among others, as ceramic sculpture achieved new heights by such artists fully embracing the clay to create figurative work loosely connected to the "ceramics tradition of the figurine."[5]

Both of these genealogical strands of ceramics come into play in Lighton's early sculptures from the late 1970s and early 1980s. Although she was initially trained as a painter, some of Lighton's earliest works engage with the ceramic tradition of the vessel as a key form. *Logger Teapot* (1978) **(fig. 1)** and *Huntsman Teapot* (1979) both play on the anthropomorphic shape of a teapot by playfully transforming the vessel into smiling, barrel-chested men. Notably, while Lighton would subsequently depart from these more traditional ceramic forms in her practice, we can see the beginnings of her interest in the archetypes of one's occupation, and how these communicate information about the self to the world. These ideas around personal aspirations and desire would return in Lighton's works during the late 1980s, such as her *Building People* series, which centered on surrealistic sculptures in which human figures are depicted with different architectural building types in place of their heads. Lighton has described these works as an exploration of the ways that people become set in their social roles or occupations, which ultimately come to define them. For ex-

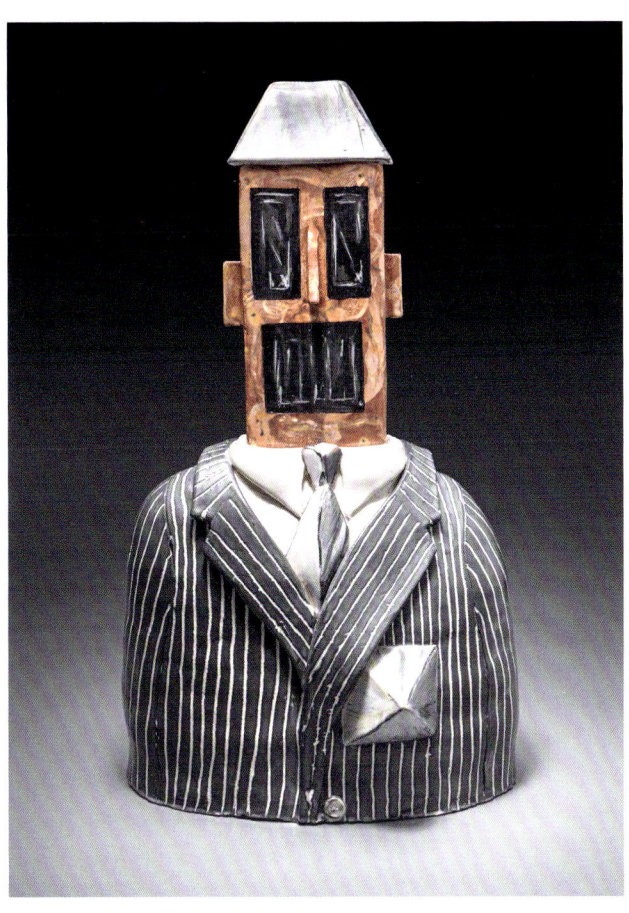

2 **LINDA LIGHTON, Figure in Architecture** 1989
Glazed earthenware with underglaze and china paint
17 × 9 ½ × 6 in. (43.2 × 24.1 × 15.2 cm)

work challenges the latent conservatism around sexuality in contemporary art, while her life has been lived unapologetically in pursuit of forging a path dedicated to making art. Allowing lived experiences to inform her work, Lighton's circumstances—particularly as a young mother estranged from her prominent and conservative family—created such rigid boundaries that it was impossible not to push against them until they shattered open. Certainly, the oft retold quip about well-behaved women not making history resonates here on a deep level. For all of these desires, when thrust against reality, rarely turn out quite as you imagine.

Given the capriciousness of reality, it is perhaps unsurprising that Lighton has pursued a career dedicated to the creation of strikingly memorable ceramic sculptures. For ceramics, as a medium, has a tendency to disobey its maker. It behaves much like desire, seeking to manifest itself in ways that, at times, go against the best-laid intentions. Starting from an artist's initial molding by hand, the clay undergoes multiple sequences of being fired in a kiln. Returning the sculptures to the inordinately hot fire after each layer of china paint, this process lends itself to warping, breakage, and cracks that are unseen until taken out of the kiln; the fragility of the finished object is unlike most other traditional sculptural materials such as bronze or marble.

This fundamental unpredictability meets its match in Lighton. Rather than seeing this capriciousness as a liability, she embraces the willfulness of her medium, working to create her ceramic sculptures with a kind of allegiance forged between herself and her clay. By taking seriously how clay declares its own agenda through the creation process, something approaching a kind of animism emerges. When coupled with all the technical conditions of breakability or possible missteps, there is a unique expression of the fragility of life expressed through the medium. The desire to make art encounters the clay's material desire to remain unformed as a lump of earthen minerals; the battles of love and war, of ambition and dogged defiance, come together in Lighton's singular work.

ample, both *The Judge* (1989) and *Figure in Architecture* (1989) **(fig. 2)** deal with public-facing occupations and the conflict of resolution within one's private identity, conveying a feeling of entrapment through the inclusion of hardened edifices that supplant the subjects' individualized faces.

**

Lighton's works are underpinned by a shared exploration of the ways that desire shapes the world around us. Her pieces often present a critique, but in a way that is playful and continually life-affirming. This has at times come at a cost, both personally and professionally. Her

Pop, Desire, and the Everyday

One of the most obvious ways that desire materializes in contemporary society is through consumption. In the early 1960s, American Pop artists began looking to the imagery of commercial advertising and popular entertainment as the visual embodiment of the country's consumer culture. While canonical Pop Art dominated the New York-based art world during the middle of the decade when Lighton visited the city, there was another strand of art-making running concurrently on the West Coast which Lighton encountered during her early artistic training in Washington state.

In 1961, *Craft Horizons* editor Rose Slivka described the "New Ceramic Presence," a distinctly American branch of artistic work being made on the West Coast by such artists as John Mason and Ann Stockton, who focused on the expressive capabilities of the medium as fine art.[6] Emerging from this new investment into the creative potential of clay, artists like Robert Arneson, Magdalena Suarez Frimkess, and Michael Frimkess began producing painted ceramics that frequently dealt with themes drawn from popular culture and used strategies of play, exuberance, wit, and humor. Although

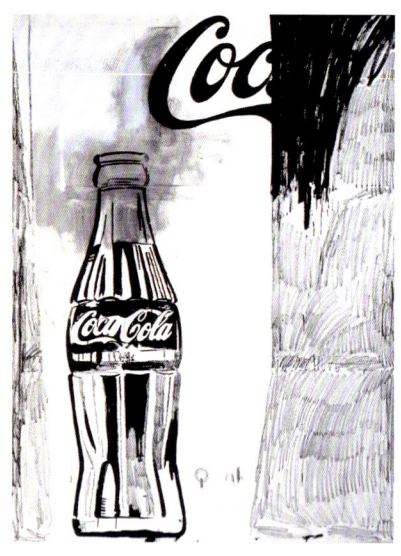

4 **ANDY WARHOL, Coca-Cola [2]** 1961
Casein and wax crayon on linen
69 ½ × 52 ¼ in. (176.5 × 132.7 cm)
The Andy Warhol Museum, Pittsburgh

these ideas, sometimes associated with the Funk art movement, dovetailed with certain contemporaneous tendencies burgeoning in mainstream contemporary art, such as Pop Art's fascination with the signage and imagery of consumer culture, these artists' emphasis on a less polished facture represents a distinct approach characterized by visual distortion and self-deprecation.

In such pieces as *Gas Pump* (1980) **(fig. 3)**, *Legal Pads* (1984), and *Bullet Belt* (1985), Lighton's references to popular culture reflect the influence of Pop Art's preferred subject matter and overall sense of slickly polished refinement, but also the Funk sensibility of a more direct encounter with humble everyday objects rather than their advertised image. In this manner, the unpretentious nature of her subjects, familiar to everyday Americans—such as her gas pump reflective of a time of economic uncertainty spurred by the ongoing energy crisis of the 1970s, or her legal pad's symbolic representation of white-collar labor under late capitalism—might more closely align with the DIY aesthetic found in the early 1960s sculptures by Claes Oldenburg or early Pop paintings by Warhol, for instance **(fig. 4)**.[7]

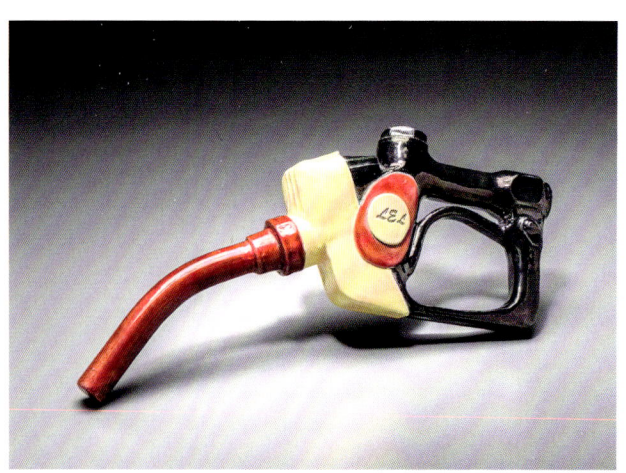

3 **LINDA LIGHTON, Gas Pump** 1980
Glazed earthenware
2 ¼ × 17 ¾ × 8 in. (5.7 × 45.1 × 20.3 cm)

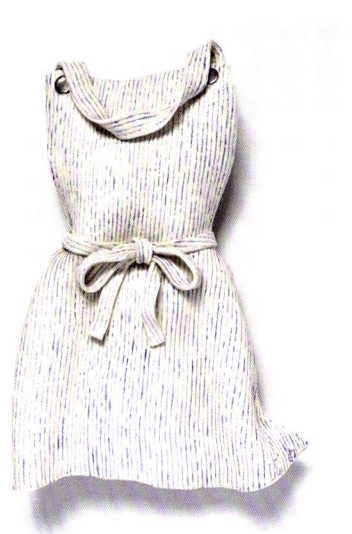

5 **LINDA LIGHTON, Apron** 1987
Glazed earthenware with china paint and luster
21 × 14½ × 4½ in. (53.3 × 36.8 × 11.4 cm)

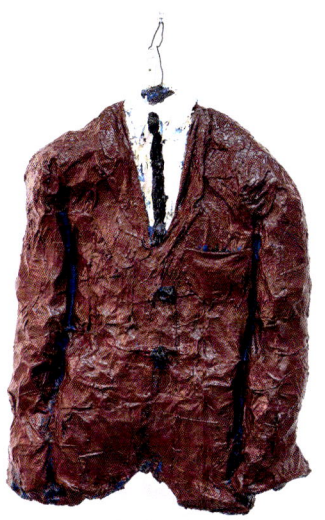

6 **CLAES OLDENBURG, Men's Jacket with Shirt and Tie** 1961
Muslin soaked in plaster over wire frame, painted with enamel
41 ¾ × 29 ½ × 11 ¾ in. (106 × 74.9 × 29.8 cm)
Museum Ludwig, Cologne

With a striking social commentary on the ways cultural tendencies affect the individual, Lighton's work marks a stark contrast in synthesizing—but also extending—elements from both artistic movements. Her uniquely feminist approach expands and sharpens Pop Art's famously ambiguous relationship to politics, drawing out the implications of consumer desire as it shapes American life beyond the cash register, particularly for women. At the same time, her works present a seriousness concerning the use of representational imagery and a refined aesthetic that evolves recent Funk traditions of clay-based sculpture.

In 1981, Lighton began the *Americana* series, a body of ceramic sculptures based on various clothing types: tuxedo, cowboy, denim, apron, lavallière, and so on. Each represents a different occupation or existence: the tuxedo's formalwear communicates an upscale urbanity when compared with the denim workshirt; the home-maker's apron speaks to a labor practice distinct from that of the office secretary's blouse. Some of these were accompanied by accessories imparting a specific occupation, such as a doctor's bag and stethoscope. But even

when left plain, the garments themselves convey information about the lifestyle of the wearer, whose physical presence is starkly absent. Lighton shows the different social roles that may be performed and, relationally, their connection to certain subcultures in American society: the cowboy, the housewife, the professionalized doctor, the manual laborer. In using the garment to signify a greater nexus of social mores, expectations, and yearnings, Lighton underscores the desires pulsating within the American dream in all its varied expressions and lifestyles.

With only subtle undulations to convey mass, the *Shirts* do not display a fleshy body underneath; at the same time, their understated animation activates these sartorial objects beyond mere commodity types. In *Apron* (1987) **(fig. 5)**, Lighton takes an example of attire meant to protect the wearer's street clothes from the calamities of the kitchen while cooking; the domestic, rather than professional, connotations in Lighton's piece are found in the relative cleanliness of the garment, its delicate striped patterning, and lace detail most typically associated with women's fashion at the time.

Twenty years earlier, Oldenburg pursued a similar subject: a suite of sculptures based on people's garments, including underpants, shoes, and indeed, shirts. Just before his introduction of a "soft" sculptural language in 1962, in which he stuffed and sewed canvases into enlarged, but often misshapen, depictions of familiar objects, Oldenburg created various sartorial renderings that assumed the appearance of malleability but were in fact rigid. As seen in *Men's Jacket with Shirt and Tie* (1961) **(fig. 6)**, these pieces are composed of muslin soaked in plaster, which was laid atop wire frames and then painted. The resulting surfaces are highly textured and rough-hewn, with craggy undulations that distort the painterly articulations. The marked contrast between the subject—a man's brown suit jacket and shirt—and its appearance creates an ambiguity regarding the object's symbolic role. That is, seen in this atypical state for a business garment—hardened, wrinkled, and consciously ill-defined, with underlayers of paint peeking out in slivers—the role and function of the suit comes under pressure: it is neither a pristine consumer product nor a garment pre-worn and pre-loved.

Lighton's *Shirts* pivot on similar themes, yet her expression of desire—particularly as it intersects with consumerism—is arguably more complex. In making her sculptures materially seductive, with a glossy sheen and crisp expression of their functionality, she lets the aspirations, hopes, and desires of the implied wearer and garments themselves come forth. Whereas Oldenburg's sculptures of clothing from the early 1960s, such as *Blouse*, *Shirt*, *Two Girls' Dresses*, and *Mu-Mu* (all 1961), were shown within related investigations of the American postwar popular imagination and capitalist consumer culture in Oldenburg's large-format installation *The Store*, Lighton's *Shirts* series appeared at a moment in history tinged with conservative political policies and cultural regression in the United States. Given the cultivation of President Reagan's down-home, country-western persona during his senatorial and presidential campaigns—a feigned public image stemming from his previous career as a film actor—*Denim Shirt* (1981) might perhaps be read

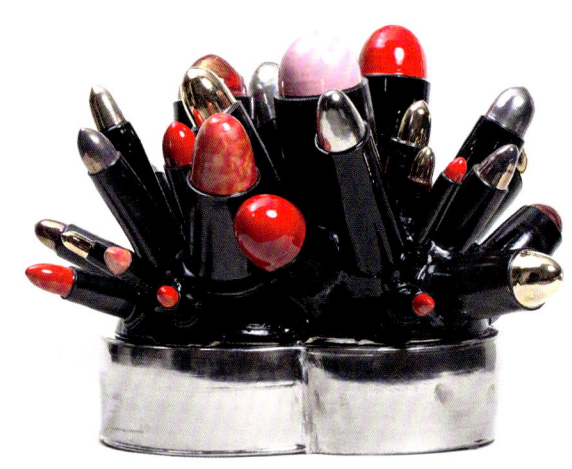

7 **LINDA LIGHTON, Love and War: The Ammunition II** 2011
Glazed earthenware with china paint and luster
26 × 16½ × 18 in. (66 × 41.9 × 45.7 cm)

as a commentary on Reagan's residency in the Oval Office that began that same year, as much as a statement on the quite literally blue-collar roles of American workers around whom Lighton lived in Idaho at the time.

Lighton continued to explore desire as it relates to consumer culture more recently in a radically different body of works, exemplified by *Love and War: The Ammunition II* (2011) **(fig. 7)**. Expanding one of her earlier sculptural forms—a lipstick made to emphasize its morphological similarities with a bullet—this piece features an eruptive array of lipstick-bullets, set on a platform, pointing in various directions, as if assuming a crystalline or floral arrangement composed of these manufactured inorganic objects. Some of the tips are tinged red or pink, drawing out the references to makeup, while others feature silver, brass, or gold reminiscent of the metals found on weapons of war. Here, Lighton draws connections between the seemingly innocuous consumption of beautification tools with the devastation effected by the military-industrial complex and its hold on American economic and political policy. "These works were about the landscape of war," Lighton once explained. "No one has to make lipsticks that look like a dick or a bullet. Women are using weapons of their own. One [bullet] gets you an oil field, and the other [lipstick] bags you a man."[8]

A similar point is made in *Modern City State #3* (2017), where Lighton emphasizes the similarities between the fundamentally seductive nature of weaponry, such as guns, alongside the glamour and appeal of beauty. Her ongoing critique of gun violence has figured prominently in her work of recent years; her advocacy for gun control finds perhaps its greatest expression in *I Don't Want a Bullet to Kiss Your Heart* (2012), her large-format sculpture composed entirely of ceramic guns cast from actual semi-automatic weapons and painted in a putrid yellow. Certainly, the economies of desire—how Americans are consumers of beauty and violence, love and war—represents a significant thread in Lighton's career, one that features prominently in this exhibition.

The Personal Is Political:
Feminism, Sexuality, and Desire

In his essay "Hard Targets: Male Bodies, Feminist Art, and the Force of Censorship in the 1970s," art historian Richard Meyer discloses the history of an important, but lesser known, branch of 1970s feminist art in which the male body—and phallic imagery in particular—was featured as a means of visually declaring heterosexual female pleasure as integrally tied to feminist concerns.[9] American women artists who made such "erotically audacious" art had, as Meyer explains, undergone substantial censorship while attempting to produce, exhibit, and sell their work. In 1973, artist Anita Steckel formed a New York-based women artists' collective centered on the creation of "sexually explicit art" known as the Fight Censorship (FC) group; members included Louise Bourgeois and Joan Semmel, among others.[10] Through public appearances and the distribution of a press release based on a manifesto written by Steckel, the FC group

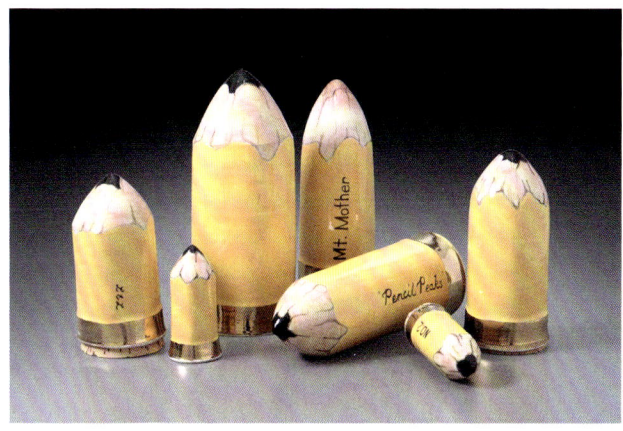

8 **LINDA LIGHTON**, **Pencil Peaks** 1978
Glazed earthenware with china paint, luster and cork
Overall: 9 × 17 × 10 in. (22.9 × 43.2 × 25.4 cm)

forcefully declared the right, and significance, for women artists to create works featuring sexual subject matter, pointing out its centrality in the enjoyment and propagation of life itself. Steckel's press release closed with the following provocative comparison: "If the erect penis is not 'wholesome' enough to go into museums—it should not be considered 'wholesome' enough to go into women. And if the erect penis is 'wholesome' enough to go into women, then it is more than 'wholesome' enough to go into the greatest art museums."[11]

By the end of the 1970s, not much had changed in terms of accepting the visualization of sex and nudity from a woman's perspective in the mainstream art world. Yet this did not deter Lighton, who—independently from, but informed by, the New York feminist art movement—developed strategies for creating artwork that explored women's perspectives on gender dynamics using wit and sexuality. Drawing from a Pop and Funk-inspired sensibility but infusing it with a feminist perspective, Lighton developed a visual language still in use within her practice today that reconceptualizes sexuality and desire as a formidable source of strength and power.

One of the ways that Lighton advances these ideas is by friskily evading explicit representations, instead transmogrifying both familiar everyday objects and un-

nocence. This latent sexuality embedded in *Pencil Peaks* explores, among other things, how the female body is still often feared, hidden, and controlled.

In the *Globe* sculptures, another body of early work dating from the late 1970s, Lighton dramatizes the duality of attraction and repulsion frequently at play in the reception of artworks depicting female genitalia made by women. The self-contained forms of these spherical orbs are ruptured by prominent protrusions that cleave the smooth surface, erupting into an unexpected amalgam of colored entrails that are exposed through vulva-shaped excisions. The glaze and luster materials that Lighton uses here create a sense of gleaming refinement related to her ongoing exploration of consumer desire—the longing for shiny new things that contrasts with the unidentifiable, almost alien viscera rendered in mint green, butter yellow, and soft pink.

By severing the protective membranes of these vessel-like forms, Lighton eradicates the separation between things meant to remain unseen and seen, creating a mediation on the relationship between restraint and growth. In so boldly emphasizing the base corporeality of these quasi-organic objects, which remain undefinable in familiar terms, she solicits at once disgust and desire through lustrous surfaces and technical prowess. This approach aligns Lighton's work with another sculptor working with ceramics in a different context: Ken Price. Whereas Price's egg-shaped sculptures from the 1960s, which also featured enigmatic protrusions and fissures, retain a modernist neutrality, Lighton's ceramic sculptures assert a decidedly feminist perspective in their excavation of the extraordinary, but often unfamiliar, ways the human figure can be represented—particularly in the case of women's bodies. This aesthetic estrangement, in which unease is courted by unnerving the perception of the familiar, also recalls the strategies enacted by artists associated with historical Surrealism, in particular the biomorphic volumes in the work of Jean Arp and Constantin Brancusi, for instance.

The phallic nature of sculptures by Lighton such as *Bad Behavior* (2001) **(fig. 9)** or *Tubeworm* (2002) engages

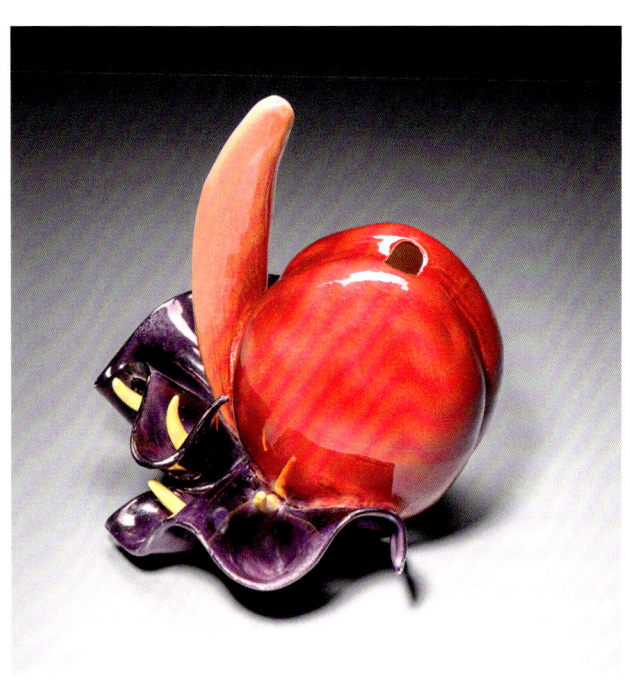

9 **LINDA LIGHTON, Bad Behavior** 2001
Glazed earthenware and luster
10½ × 10 × 8½ in. (26.7 × 25.4 × 21.6 cm)

usual living creatures into artistic surrogates for human genitalia. This is achieved through varying degrees of candor. In *Pencil Peaks* (1978) **(fig. 8)**, seven stout ceramic sculptures of pencils are loosely arranged in a group. Despite their larger-than-life scale, these depictions of writing tools appear worn down through apparent use; their vertical orientation exposes the soft curve of their lead tips and the almost veiny appearance of the wood. Presented as mere nubs, with individual variations amongst the sharpness of their tips, the pencils lose their scholastic references, becoming something almost bodily.

Hidden among the black-tipped pencil peaks—a clue given, perhaps, by the work's title—is one notable variation. In one of the pencils, a soft, flesh-toned pink appears in the place of the graphite. Suddenly, the pencil becomes an upturned breast, with a rosy nipple shattering the pretense of the work's youthful, school-aged in-

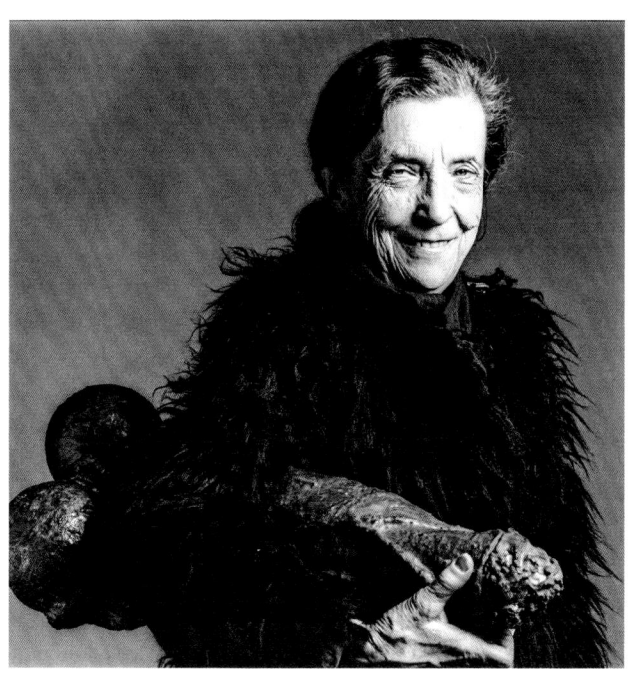

10 **ROBERT MAPPLETHORPE, Louise Bourgeois** 1982
Gelatin silver print
20 × 16 in. (50.8 × 40.6 cm)

with a feminist legacy of depicting male genitalia in a way that rather joyfully celebrates sexual desire and the bodily impulses toward sex. Her refusal to couch such imagery in more demure terms recalls the rebellious spirit of Louise Bourgeois, whose 1968 sculpture *Fillette* took the latex material associated at the time with American process artists working on abstract sculptures and applied it over a plaster support rendered in the shape of a large penis (fig. 10). The resulting work's flesh-like surface and mode of exhibition display—disembodied and hung on a meat hook by its tip—produced an often polarized reaction from critics and audiences, one that was playfully embraced by the artist.[12]

Another way that Lighton looks at women's desire is through her clever sculptural investigations of household cleaning products as symbolic of domestic labor and its imbrication with sexual power. Beginning in 1986, she introduced a series of sculptures celebrating objects

associated with household upkeep—tasks and responsibilities that typically fall to women in heterosexual relationships. By highlighting these often-overlooked responsibilities and tools, at times literally placing such items atop pedestals, Lighton achieves her ambition behind such works, which she describes as "to qualify women's iconography and give it the credibility it deserves."[13] Through works like *S&M Cleaning* (1987), in which she clads domestic cleaning paraphernalia, such as polishing spray, plastic gloves, and toilet cleaner, in what appears to be black latex and accessorized metal spikes, Lighton asks the viewer to consider the significance of such often gendered tasks as integral to the negotiation of domestic lifestyles, whether in terms of sexual or practical exchanges of time, energy, and attention.

This artistic spotlight on women's traditional roles in maintaining a household and the tools needed to successfully achieve such tasks dovetails with the motifs and imagery deployed by some of Lighton's Pop Art influences. For instance, the visual language of manufactured cleanliness is perhaps most memorably expressed through Warhol's reproductions of mass-produced commercial bulk packaging for Brillo soap pads, a cleaning product familiar to American consumers in the 1960s (fig. 11). While Lighton also explores the subject of domestic cleaning supplies, as seen in works like *The First Lady* (1986) (fig. 12) and *Daddy's Hungry* (1987), the expansion of her inquiry into the symbolism of the objects themselves and the gendered nature of such tools reflect an evolution of Warhol's 1960s Pop agenda, which focused more heavily on the branded imagery of mass advertising rather than the use of such commodities and the gender dynamics imbedded within.

Painted in a patriotic color palette of red, white, and blue emblematic of the American flag, *The First Lady* comprises a dustpan, an Ajax-style cleaning powder shaker, a spray bottle, liquid soap, and a roll of paper towels. These are positioned on a banner-accented round platform, which is reminiscent of those used at political rallies for aspiring candidates to greet cheering audiences. While carefully painted in a manner loosely

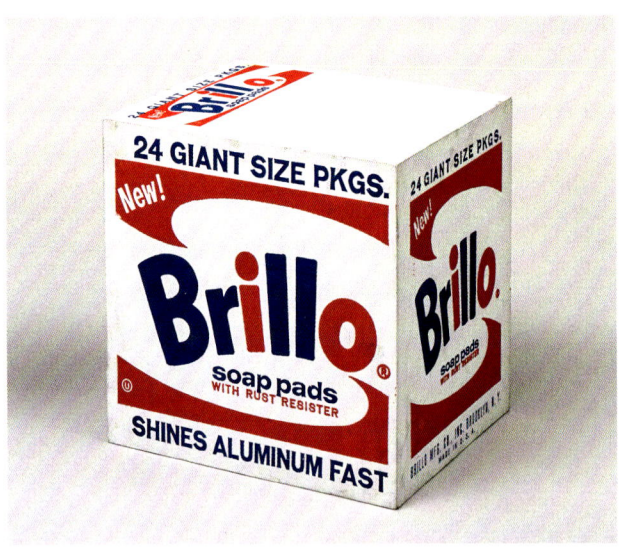

11 **ANDY WARHOL, Brillo Box (Soap Pads)** 1964
Synthetic polymer paint and silkscreen ink on wood
17 ⅛ × 17 × 14 in. (43.5 × 43.2 × 35.6 cm)
The Museum of Modern Art, New York, NY

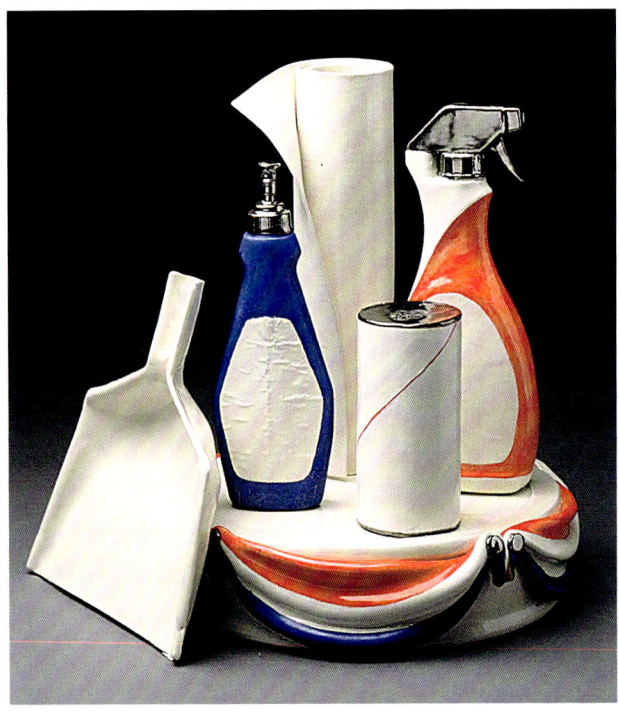

12 **LINDA LIGHTON, The First Lady** 1986
Glazed earthenware with china paint and luster
14 × 9 ½ × 13 in. (35.6 × 24.1 × 33 cm)

alluding to familiar commercial packaging, Lighton has removed all references to a specific brand, instead leaving ghostly white blanks in the place of a label or logo. The combination of the—quite literally—whitewashed treatment of cleaning products typically kept out of view, coupled with the title alluding to the president's wife, *The First Lady* conveys a subtle, but still forceful, critique of women's roles both within American politics and the public realm, as well as the hidden world of domestic labor. This concept of being placed upon a pedestal, but one not necessarily indicative of personal aspirations or desires, speaks to an experience familiar to many women, particularly in the context of the conservative culture wars in 1980s America.

In *Daddy's Hungry*, Lighton reconfigures many of these same items as found in *The First Lady*—such as cleaning spray and dish soap—but presents them within what appears to be a commonplace paper bag, encircled by a brown leather belt. However, the sculptural scene is anything but ordinary, as the items are all presented with a glossy black surface that resembles patent leather or latex and is accented with silver studded hardware. This rather brilliant use of glaze, china paint, and luster transforms the unremarkable nature of these domestic cleaning products into a realm of fetishized objects and introduces the suggestion of sexual play within the presumed negotiation of household duties. Such associations are alluded to in the work's title, which could be read as innocuous or erotic, depending on one's perspective. Desire is seen here as something repressed, whether in terms of personal aspirations being stifled through the typical role for women within the domestic sphere, or in terms of a sexual predilection for certain sexual deviancy that is kept under wraps for social acceptability. Yet, as Lighton seems to imply in *Daddy's Hungry*, desire can also be wielded as a kind of power, rethinking the possibilities of tools within women's reach to achieve access and control over their own longings.

Lighton addressed this iconography of domestic maintenance throughout her series *And She Did Not Live Happily Ever After... but She Did Live*. Inspired by her reevaluation of her domestic role in the wake of her daughter leaving for college in 1987, Lighton began thinking about how women's identities are formed and shaped. She wrote, "Generally speaking, these are traditionally wife, child-bearer, mother and homemaker. These are normal, socially endorsed and approved, society defined roles." She continued: "I'm sure we no longer lie to ourselves about the creativity of housework. ... We are trying to explode the myth of those roles."[14]

Such recourse to visualizing the tools and practices necessary in building and sustaining a household was an important motif of feminist artists like Mierle Laderman Ukeles, whose practice of "Maintenance Art" involved performing in public processes of largely uncompensated upkeep (such as dressing children or cleaning the floor), which would typically only be visible in the background of domestic and civic realms (fig. 13). In her "Manifesto for Maintenance Art 1969!" Ukeles articulated the gendered differences between the conventional male roles as artistic "creators" versus women's contributions in performing everyday tasks that upheld, and often perpetuated, the illusion of unfettered creative production. With a perspective similar to that of Lighton's, she writes, "Maintenance is a drag; it takes all the fucking time (lit.). The mind boggles and chafes at the boredom. The culture confers lousy status on maintenance jobs = minimum wages, housewives = no pay."[15] In presenting tasks of support or preservation like cleaning, cooking, and caring for others as an alternative, but equally significant, art practice, Ukeles sought to undermine the cultural valuation of a conventionally male system of labor, which often centered on the avant-garde destruction of what came before in the name of creation and "progress."[16]

Lighton similarly sought to reconfigure the hierarchies of value regarding production, seeking ways of elevating the ordinary objects and labor that often remain unseen within society. In a related body of works known as the *Trash* sculptures, Lighton depicts consumer debris and litter, such as soda cans, plastic bottles, and egg cartons. The inverse of the cleaning products, these gor-

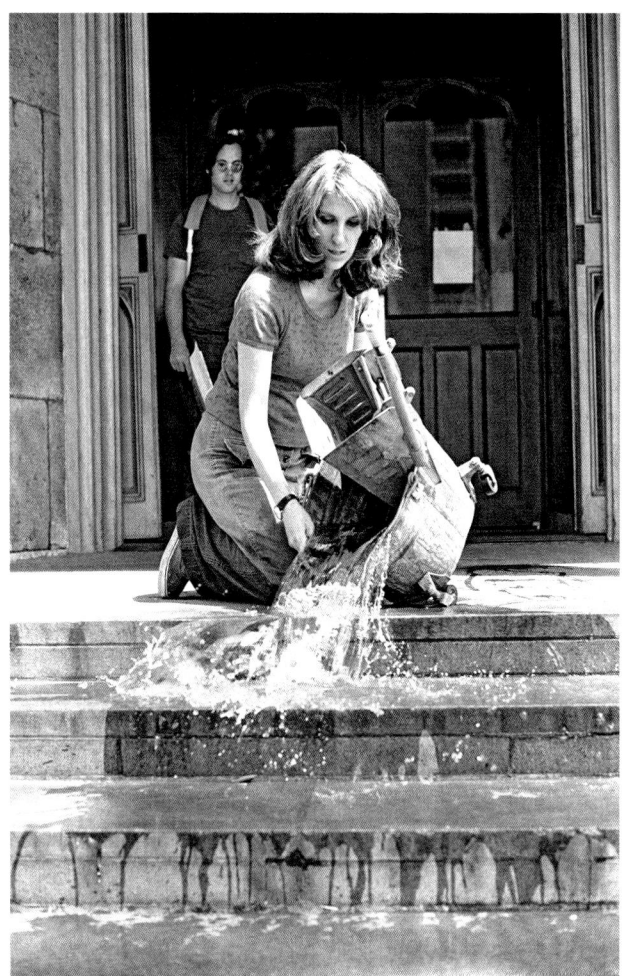

13 **MIERLE LADERMAN UKELES,**
Washing/Tracks/Maintenance: Outside July 23, 1973
Performance at Wadsworth Atheneum, Hartford, CT
(part of *Maintenance Art* performance series, 1973–74)

geously rendered sculptures express another form of often invisible labor: that of environmental preservation.[17] One of the earliest pieces from this series, *Recycle Your Trash* (1980), comprises an array of commonplace objects—a crumpled soda can, a gnawed apple core, a gleaming silver quarter, and a sealed bag that, due to a large tear at the base, nonetheless has its contents spilling out. Arranged to appear haphazard, as if discovered on an urban sidewalk, *Recycle Your Trash* dramatizes the

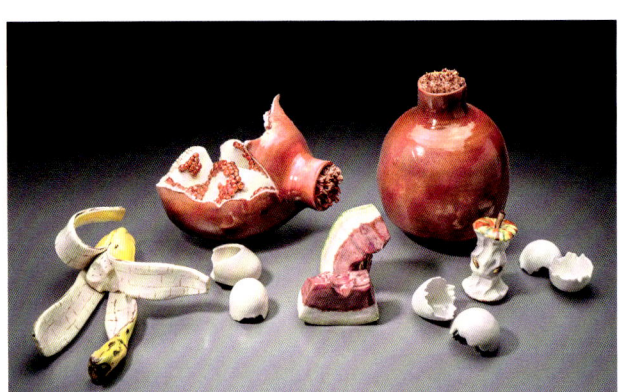

14 **LINDA LIGHTON, Compost** 2004
Glazed earthenware with china paint and luster
Overall: 10 × 43 × 12 in. (25.4 × 109.2 × 30.5 cm)

sense of opening and spillage that trash conceptually occupies as it accumulates in the spaces of our lives. Significantly, this work was made to celebrate the institution of recycling centers in the United States, as the 1970s environmentalism movement in the United States pursued governmentally supported policies—such as the 1976 Federal Resource Conservation and Recovery Act—that attempted to preserve the Earth's resources by dealing with the preponderance of human waste.

While the feminist slogan "the personal is political" gained traction among second-wave feminists in the 1960s—coinciding with the period in which the domestic, the familiar, and the everyday became subjects in Pop, but also at times Process, Minimalist, and Conceptual art—much of the work made by male artists invoked merely the imagery of the domestic realm and its quotidian objects, rather than its potential political dimensions.[18] By contrast, women's work, bodily representations, and perspectives were, and continue to be, at the core of Lighton's sculptures. Evolving motifs and themes first developed in 1960s feminist art into more nuanced investigations of the perpetuation of gender disparities through 1980s America into the present day, Lighton presents women's desire as a potent source of strength that can go to battle against the values of a male-dominated society.

Natural Desire and Self-Preservation

A substantial segment of Lighton's work centers on biological forms—flowers, such as lilies, thistles, and roses; marine creatures, including anemones, tubeworms, and sea snails; or seeds and pods. These sculptures, while exquisitely beautiful objects made with a striking technical ability, also powerfully communicate ideas related to reproduction, sustenance, and related physical desires that are shared by all living things. As the artist wrote in an undated statement about these works: "these bulbs, pods, and organic forms are about life unfolding, families, birth, growing, shedding old skins, emerging, branching out, and death." She was quick to add: "Of course, sex is an important part of it all."[19]

This iteration of natural desires, exemplified by the 2004 sculpture *Compost*, is key to understanding Lighton's body of work featuring organic forms and contextualizing them within her broader practice (**fig. 14**). With a rich palette of burgundy, snow white, vermilion, and yellow, *Compost* depicts an array of edible foods, such as eggs and watermelon, strewn haphazardly and shown in varying states of consumption. Larger than life-size, the individual components otherwise replicate precise details of the provisions—the banana peel is bruised in places, irregular bite marks define the shape of the apple core, and an extraordinarily rendered pomegranate is shown both intact and broken open, its seeds clustered in magnificent arrangements. Notably, each of these foods is structured with an outer membrane and contains the possibilities for its reproduction—whether seeds or the embryonic parts of an egg—within itself. Here, Lighton gives visibility to the overlooked, and elevates the ordinary by emphasizing the basic, fundamental desires underpinning all living things.

In works like *Rose* (2015), an undulating stem culminates in two flowering ends: one a blooming rose, the other a bud with petals tightly contained. Here, Lighton conveys the sense of temporal progression from different stages of life cycles through these dichotomous, but related, segments of the flower's anatomical system. A similar emphasis, this time on the universal needs across varied species coexisting on Earth, is expressed in *Spanish Tubeworm* (2016). Here, the black fired ceramic process creates a sense of stillness; it conjures an image of the natural world under attack by man-made disasters like oil spills and climate change. Despite all of our violence, Lighton seems to say, life wants to endure.

Lighton further emphasizes the fundamental connection between the ecological and social world through such works as *Untitled* (1987) **(fig. 15)**. This sculpture is significant in that it anticipates certain formal elements that would later recur in Lighton's pieces, such as the folding of thin yet broad, petal-like protrusions that wrap around a central "body." Resembling at once arms touching a figure in a self-protective gesture as well as botanical leaves shielding an inner entity, this basic form would be expanded in Lighton's later *Diva* series, for instance. Yet here, this gesture creates a highly expressive affect, one that animates the abstract shape with a sense of life force and almost alien agency. It also, perhaps more pertinently, draws out the similarities between the way humans engage in physical acts of self-reassurance, assuming postures and modes of touch that are quite similar to those found in plants or animals. The biological world is as hard as it is delicate, using strategies similar to those invoked by humans to protect the softness into which desire—for life, love, success, recognition, and legacy—likes to burrow.

Often the socially imposed gender distinctions that she investigates in human relations find a seductive resolution in the slippage of sexual difference in the organic realm. Her sculptures of *Bulbs*, for instance, contain all necessary components to create life within itself; botanical hermaphroditism is pervasive, and perhaps connects Lighton's interest in such forms to her more obviously anthropomorphic subjects. These self-sufficient beings have nature on their side as they defiantly declare their independence to pursue life cycles autonomously.

Begun in the early 2000s as a celebration of women in her life whom she believed to remain largely free from internalizing societal judgment, Lighton's *Divas*—a suite

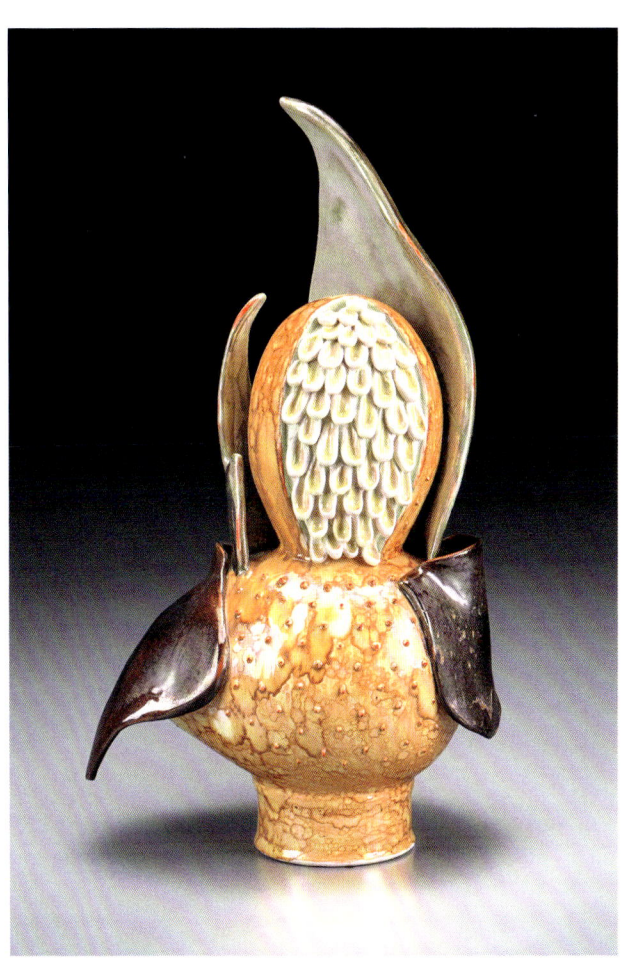

15 **LINDA LIGHTON, Untitled** 1987
Glazed earthenware with china paint and luster
19 × 11 × 9 in. (48.3 × 27.9 × 22.9 cm)

of anthropomorphized rare orchids with boldly individualized personalities **(fig. 16)**—embody self-assuredness and the celebratory joy of personal expression. Yet they also exemplify the proximities between the desires to create and destroy, to reproduce and to end life, in a single being. Such a point is echoed by Elizabeth Kirsch, who wrote, "The majority of these entities are hermaphrodites, sprouting cavernous vulva and tumescent penises all in one self-contained, cheerful organism. They beckon seductively to anyone who comes near as they simultaneously threatened to slurp one down whole."[20]

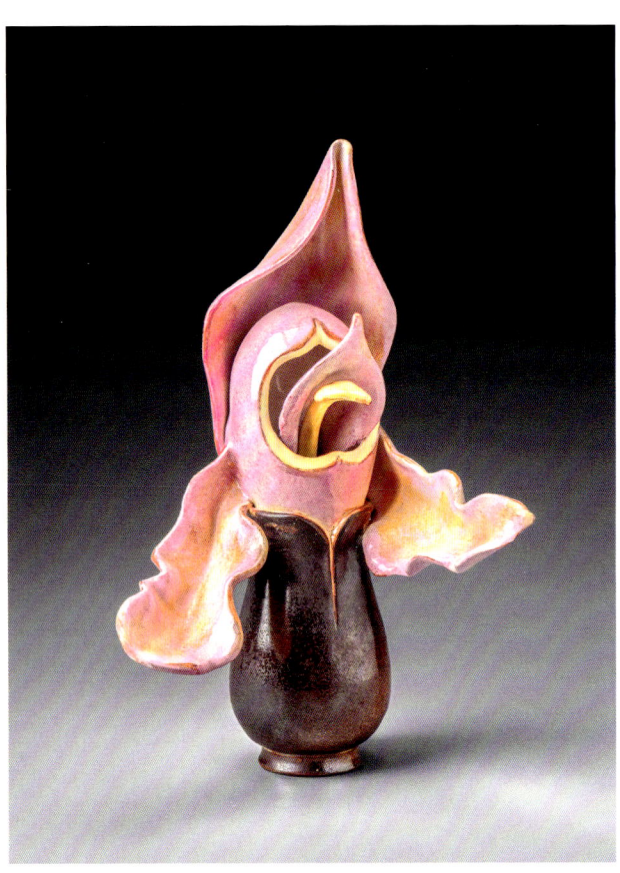

16 **LINDA LIGHTON, Diva Yael** 2000
Glazed earthenware with china paint and luster
12 × 7 ½ × 7 in. (30.5 × 19.1 × 17.8 cm)

cavities, often accompanied by protrusive forms. For instance, in many of her *Divas*, tongue-like projections emerge from hollowed spaces that together create the appearance of an expressive vocalization. The angles at which the *Divas* are positioned often project beyond their ruffled bases, contributing further to the sense of inner-outer relations.

A related trope within these explorations of biological desire is Lighton's preoccupation with mortality, whether in terms of poetically making sense of these inevitable transitions or her more politically minded sculptural examinations of weapons and war. Works like *Transition* (1998) visualize the former rather abstractly; here, a central form, painted yellow, appears to emerge from within a peach-hued enclosure composed of petal-like layers. As the exterior delicately unfurls, two thin projections appear at the uppermost opening; entangled, they wrap around one another as if in a romantic embrace. The sense of passage, from one state to another, is immanent in *Transition*, as the work's compositional elements seem to defy their rigid materiality.

The innate desire to sustain and perpetuate life comes to the fore in another important body of Lighton's work. While her sculptures dealing with the social or political impact of gun violence might, at first, be seen as distinct from her conventionally gorgeous sculptures of flowers and sea creatures influenced by the natural world, both are rooted in the concept of desiring survival and self-preservation. Lighton's political engagement has grown over the course of her career, taking on more overt articulations in sculptures: either depictions of, or casts made from, actual weapons. The desire to destroy—the destructive impulse—is linked to that of survival and, as such, the way in which Lighton visually ties these two forms of desire together in such works as *La Petite Mort* (2016), *Allegretto con Moderato (Medium)* (2016) (fig. 17), and *Camouflora*, is powerful and poetic.

Combining two of her major bodies of work—her flower sculptures, which revel in the profound diversity of biological life, and her conflation of the tools men and women stereotypically use to gain power, such as guns

Lighton's work centered on inhuman organic life-forms might also articulate the connection between the natural desires, such as hunger, thirst, procreation, and longevity, and the appetites for economic, intellectual, and cultural consumption. Spillage is a recurring formal device in her sculptures that alludes to the overflow of emotion, lust, and desire—the insatiability at the core of human existence. Whether a form of surplus that comes from porous physical boundaries or a more conceptual indeterminacy—between inorganic and organic matter, or the discrepancies between inner psychology and outward personas presented to the social world—much of Lighton's work pivots on the dichotomy between inside and outside. This can also be seen in her extensive use of

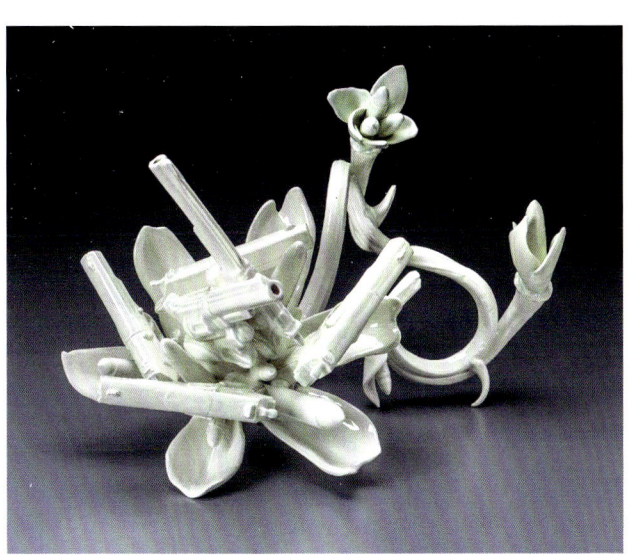

17 **LINDA LIGHTON, Allegretto con Moderato (Medium)** 2016
Glazed earthenware
12 ½ × 22 × 14 in. (31.8 × 55.9 × 35.6 cm)

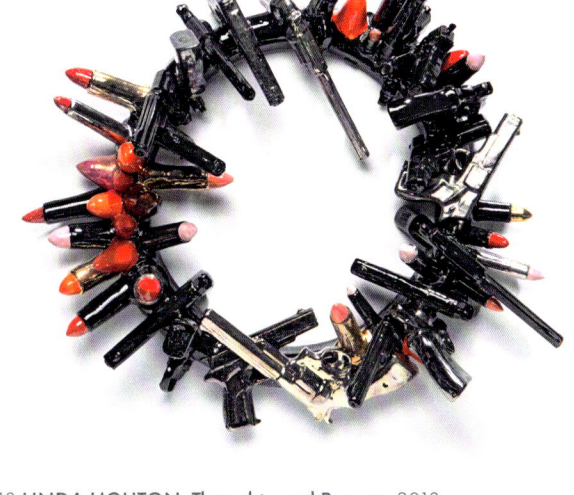

18 **LINDA LIGHTON, Thoughts and Prayers** 2018
Glazed earthenware with china paint and luster
24 × 27 × 8 ½ in. (61 × 68.6 × 21.6 cm)

and makeup—these sculptures contain bullet-cum-lipsticks in the place of flower stamens and pistils. In so doing, Lighton alludes to the flowering abundance of both objects—the proliferation of sex and violence growing like weeds across America. In *Cause and Effect*, pieces of semiautomatic weapons and gas pumps are presented as if a profusion of flowering plants projecting from a base; this presentation is also reminiscent of the abstractly organic *Flowering Bulb* from 1986. Similarly, in *Thoughts and Prayers* (fig. 18), Lighton adopts a wreath shape, replacing plants with guns in a statement on both the almost domesticated familiarity of these objects and their adjacency to life.

Desire Unleashed

Over the last fifty years, Lighton has explored various themes and subjects spanning consumer culture, social roles, political activism, and biological diversity. Across this range, however, desire continually pulsates through her sculptures, giving shape to her celebration and cri-

tiques of lived experience. For this singular artist, differences are minimized in favor of what is universal: all living things desire autonomy, sustenance, pleasure, and longevity.

In 2023, Lighton returned to her *Shirts* series in her piece *Sweatshirt*, using a form first introduced at the start of her practice in the early 1980s. Depicting a light gray cotton sweatshirt that hangs limply on the wall, with its hood collapsed forward, this garment takes on an expanded resonance today in the wake of the Black Lives Matter movement and the broader cultural reckoning regarding the ongoing racism against Black Americans. Specifically, the work calls to mind the 2012 murder of Trayvon Martin, a seventeen-year-old African American boy who was shot and killed in Sanford, Florida, while wearing a hooded sweatshirt; this garment later became a symbol of protest against racism across the United States. The fact that Martin died at the hands of a gun, the source of much of Lighton's activism, both within and outside her artistic practice, brings yet another level of understanding to her recent reinvestigation of these earlier forms.[21]

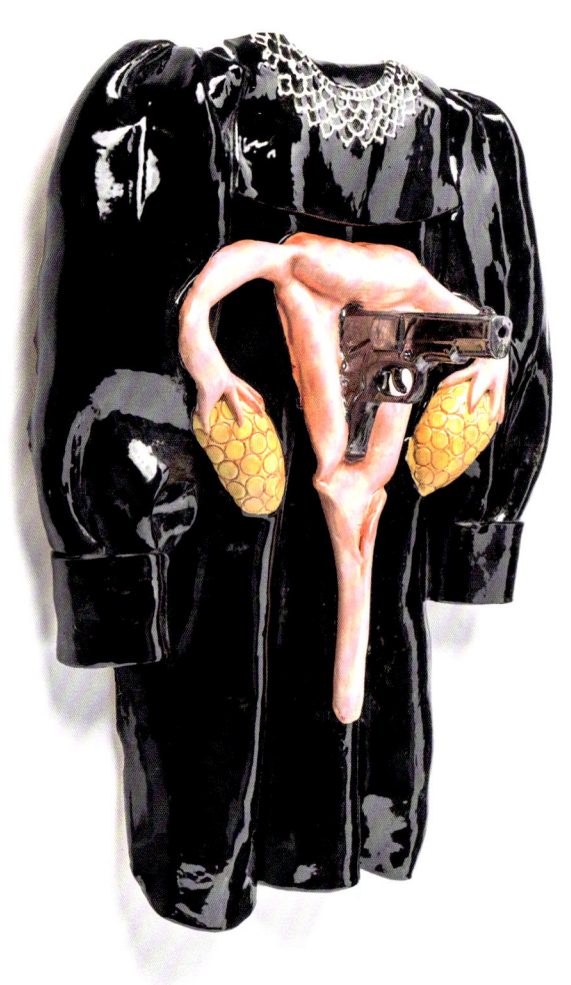

19 **LINDA LIGHTON, Supreme Justice** 2023
Glazed earthenware with china paint and luster
22½ × 18 × 8 in. (57.2 × 45.7 × 20.3 cm)

Lighton's *Sweatshirt* demonstrates the way that this series, and her work more generally, continues to evolve in light of cultural shifts and pressing societal issues concerning race, class, and gender. In *Supreme Justice* (2023) **(fig. 19)**, Lighton replicates the gown worn by Supreme Court justices. Yet certain details conjure a specificity—notably, the iconic black robe features a delicate lace collar emblematic of the late justice and feminist icon Ruth Bader Ginsburg, who died in 2020. In this piece, Lighton includes a gun, pointed outward from a detailed rendering of female reproductive organs.

With the Supreme Court's shocking 2022 reversal of *Roe v. Wade*—the 1974 case that established women's right to their own bodily sovereignty—in mind, *Supreme Justice* articulates the ways in which the law continues to restrict and regulate women's bodies, and also reminds us of the dangers still present long after women's rights were thought to be legally determined. The orientation of the gun toward the viewer expresses the unfathomable contrast between the lack of regulation of guns in the United States and the increasingly tight control under which women's bodies are placed. Therefore, the interconnections between the multiple forms of desire that I argue are integral to Lighton's oeuvre come together in *Supreme Justice*: a desire for personal freedom and choice; a desire to love how, why, and whom we want; a desire to embrace ambition, achieve greatness, and break molds; and a desire to pursue life without fear of unnecessary violence. For these desires are really what the crux of love and war is about.

Notes

1 In a 2011 interview, Lighton recalled how the Jewish community in Kansas City was ostracized through much of the 1960s, often discouraged from working as doctors at public hospitals, living in certain neighborhoods, or joining local country clubs. https://speakingkc.org/sites/default/files/transcriptions/MVSC-GARMENT-Lighton-Linda.pdf

2 Lighton, https://speakingkc.org/sites/default/files/transcriptions/MVSC-GARMENT-Lighton-Linda.pdf

3 Garth Clark, "American Ceramics Since 1950," in *American Ceramics: The Collection of Everson Museum of Art*, ed. Barbara Perry (New York and Syracuse: Rizzoli and Everson Museum of Art, 1989). The fact that famed critic Clement Greenberg delivered the keynote lecture at the annual Ceramics Symposium in 1979—certainly one of the high points of contemporary art's embrace of ceramics within the mainstream art world—speaks of the transformation underway in this medium regarding its acceptance as "high" art.

4 Peter Schjeldahl, quoted in Garth Clark, "American Ceramics Since 1950," in *American Ceramics: The Collection of Everson Museum of Art*, ed. Barbara Perry (New York and Syracuse: Rizzoli and Everson Museum of Art, 1989), 206.

5 Garth Clark, "American Ceramics Since 1950," 206.

6 Rose Slivka, "The New Ceramic Presence," *Craft Horizons* 21, no. 4 (July/August 1961): 31–37.

7 While both would later be regarded as key figures in the mainstream, "high" Pop movement, their works in the early 1960s—Warhol's hand-painted *Coca-Cola [2]* and Oldenburg's *The Store*, both from 1961, come to mind—were notably less pristine meditations on the postwar American commercial culture.

8 Linda Lighton quoted in Elizabeth Kirsch, "Dangerous Beauty," *Review* (August 2006): https://www.lindalighton.com/dangerous-beauty-2006.

9 Richard Meyer, "Hard Targets: Male Bodies, Feminist Art, and the Force of Censorship in the 1970s," in *WACK! Art and the Feminist Revolution* (Los Angeles: Museum of Contemporary Art, 2007), 363.

10 Fight Censorship press release, March 1973, as quoted in Meyer, "Hard Targets," 366.

11 Anita Steckel, quoted in Meyer, "Hard Targets," 366.

12 See, for instance, William S. Rubin, "Some Reflections Prompted by the Recent Work of Louise Bourgeois," *Art International* 13, no. 4 (April 1969): 19–20.

13 Lighton, "*Love and War: The Ammunition* Statement," undated.

14 Lighton, Artist Statement, *And She Did Not Live Happily Ever After... but She Did Live*, November 6, 1987, Batz/Lawrence Gallery, Kansas City, Missouri.

15 Mierle Laderman Ukeles, "Manifesto for Maintenance Art 1969!," 2.

16 The solution, according to Ukeles, might involve positing forms of labor that maintained or protected such so-called "advancements"—which were often associated with women's domestic activities—as equally valuable; this was to be explored in an ultimately unexecuted exhibition that she titled *Care*. As she proposed in her manifesto, Ukeles planned to perform household tasks of upkeep and domestic labor in the context of an art museum, thereby situating such behaviors as a kind of process-based performance art. While her peers in the New York contemporary art world—such as Robert Morris and Richard Serra—were staging works in which the actions and procedures of the creative process were prominently featured as integral components of the finished piece, Ukeles's conscious fore-grounding of domestic processes was a feminist gesture that struck a notable contrast with the presumed neutrality of the actions undertaken by the white male artists, who remained the modernist universal subject *par excellence*.

17 This notably connects to another of Ukeles' projects—her long-standing work with New York City's sanitation department.

18 The difference between the ability of male and female artists to create work free from gendered commentary or gender-based interpretations in the work's reception is a significant point that can only be briefly discussed in the present essay. Oldenburg's "soft sculptures" used not only the fabric materials and techniques like sewing associated at the time with women's work, but also their creation necessitated technical labor performed by his then wife Patty Muschinski. Similarly, the supposed universal male subject behind Warhol's invocation of cleaning supplies in his *Brillo Boxes* or the emphasis shifted to process in late-1960s works by Serra and Morris meant that these artists could use traditionally feminine media or references to the domestic sphere without a political or social dimension that would be the case in works created by women artists.

19 Lighton, undated exhibition statement, 3421.

20 Elizabeth Kirsch, "Dangerous Beauty," *Review* (August 2006): https://www.lindalighton.com/dangerous-beauty-2006.

21 As Adamson explains in his essay for this catalogue, Lighton—a resident of one of the country's worst cities for gun violence—has worked tirelessly to advocate for gun control through both official and unofficial channels.

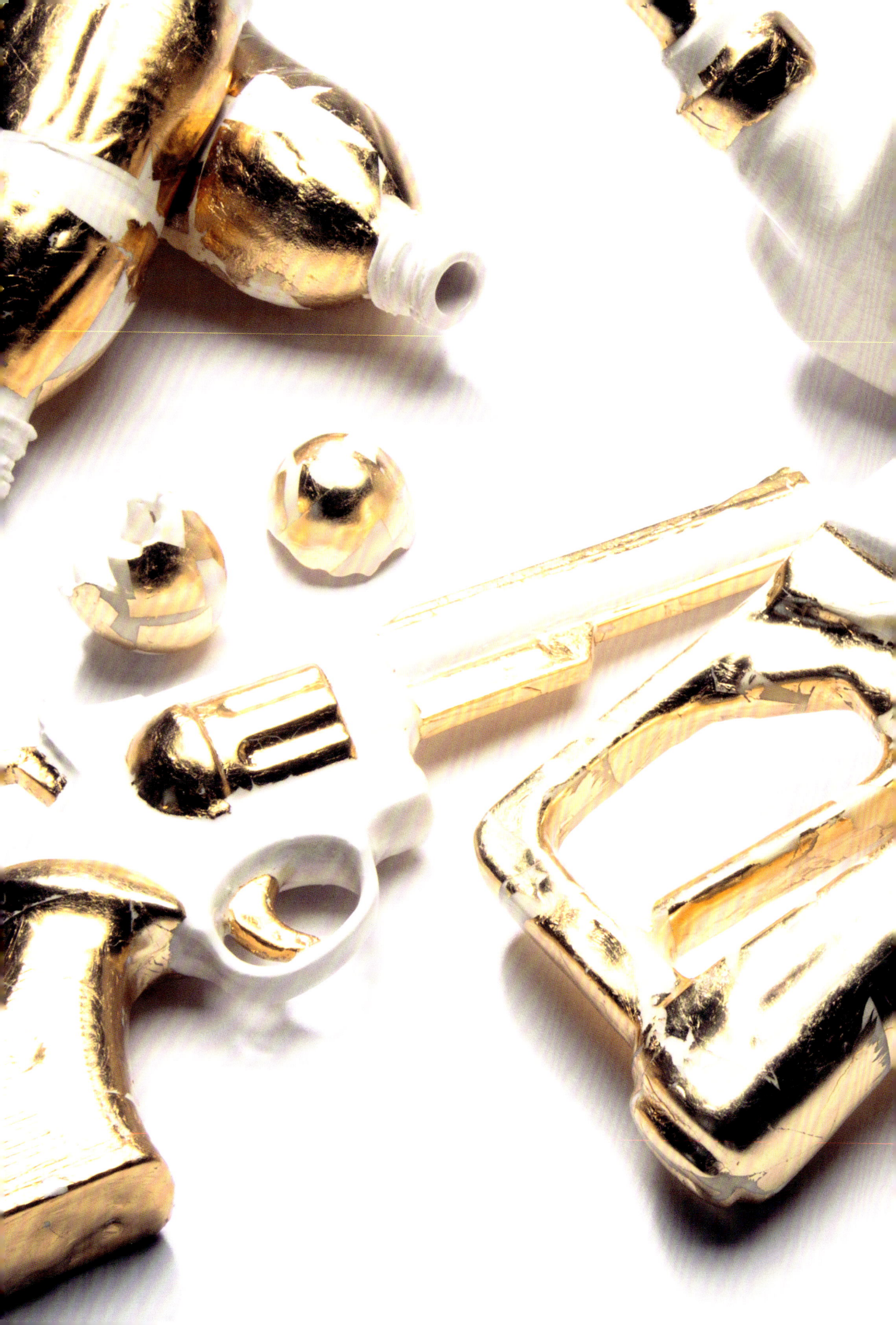

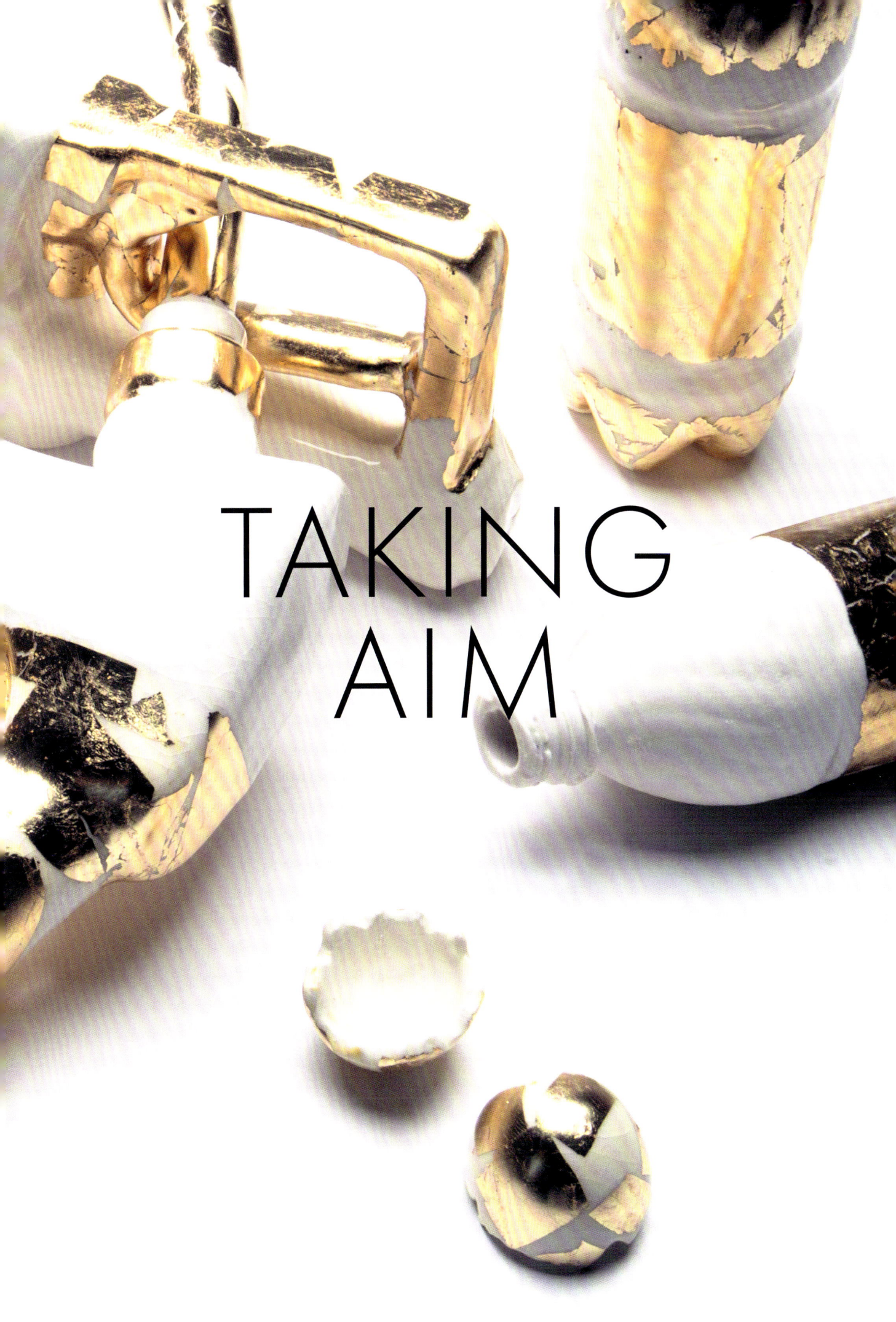

TAKING
AIM

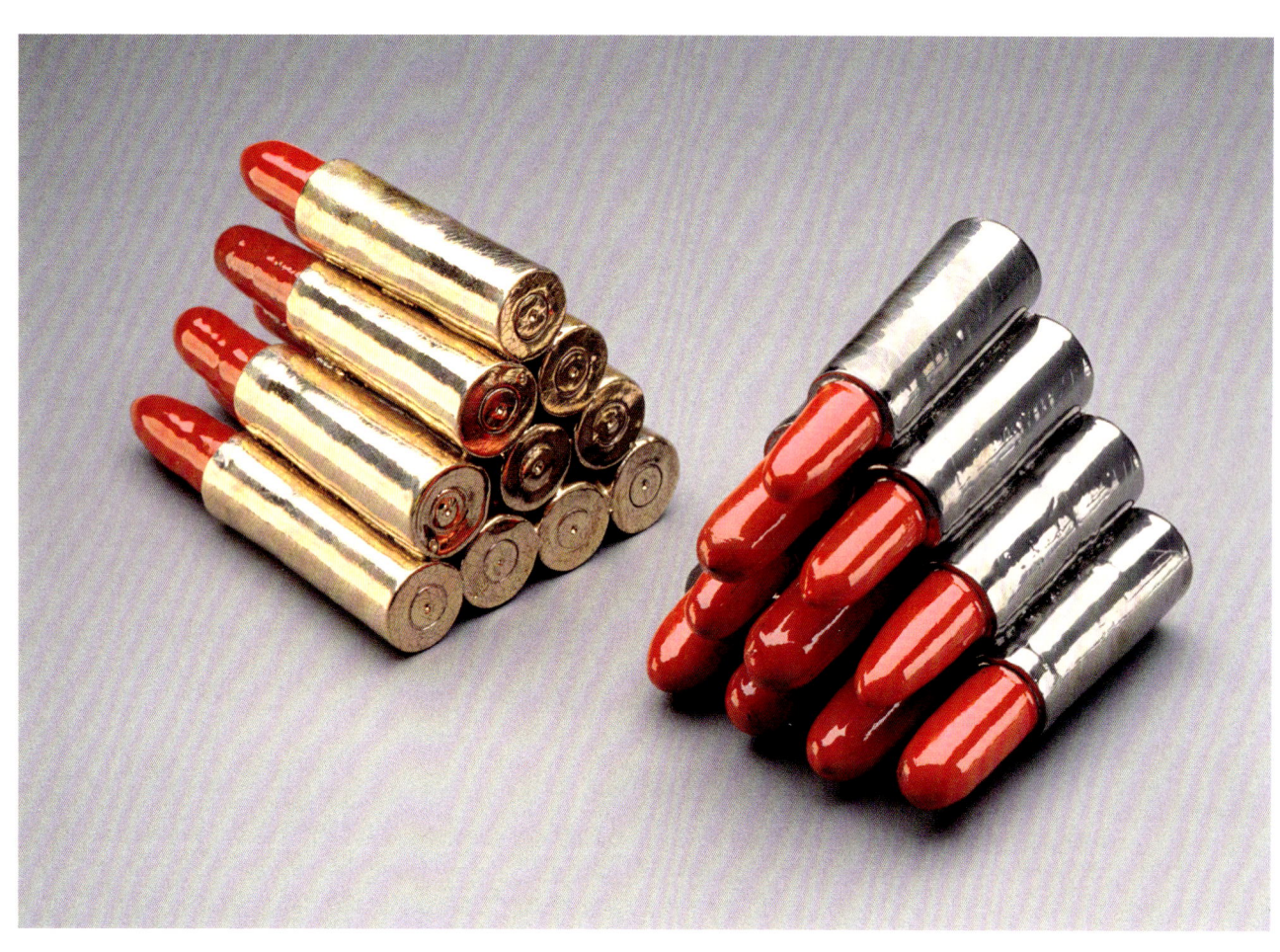

Love and War: The Ammunition 1986
Glazed earthenware with china paint and luster
Each: 5 × 6 × 5¾ in. (12.7 × 15.2 × 14.6 cm)
Collection Jean O'Brien

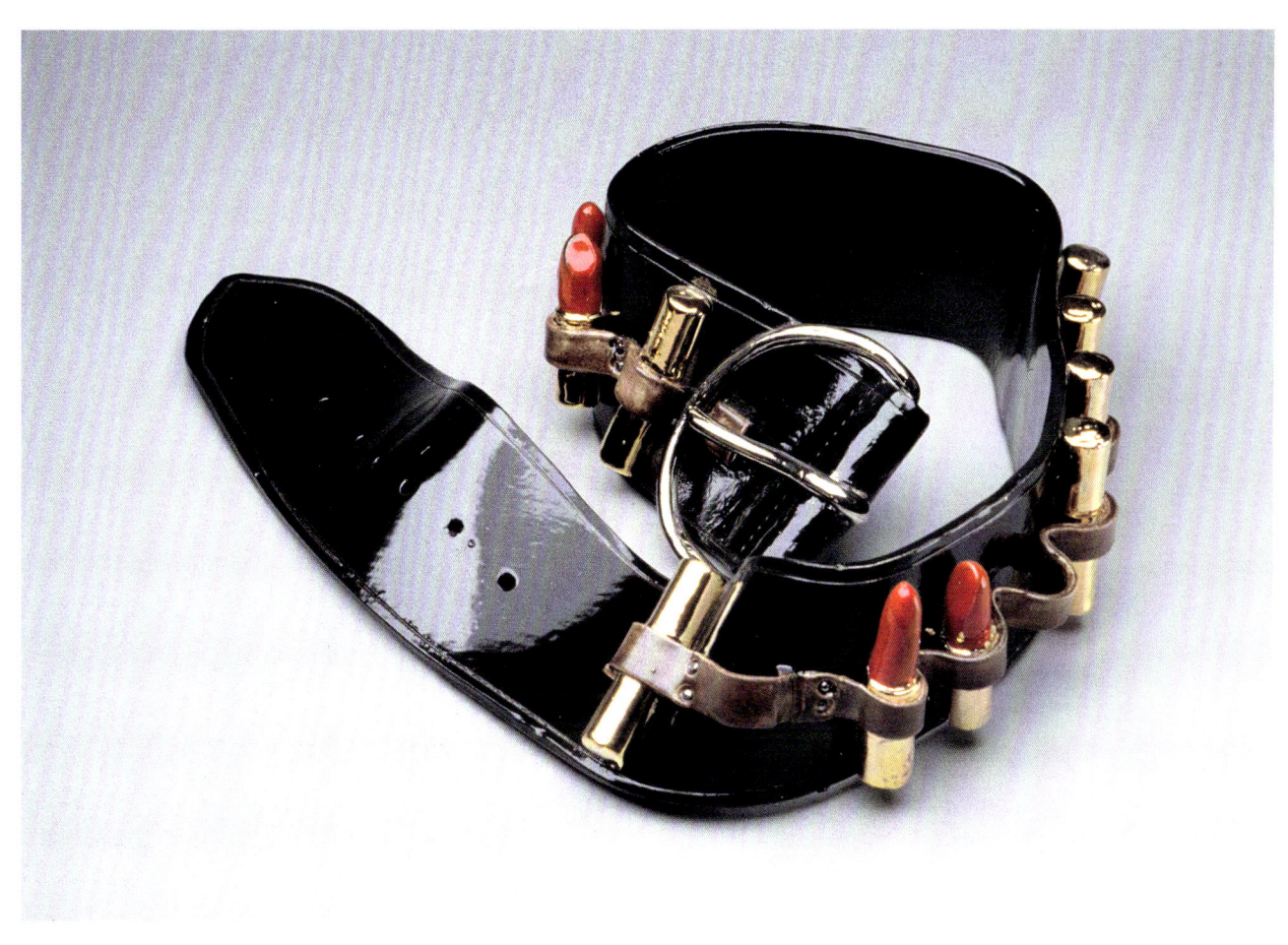

Bullet Belt 1985
Glazed earthenware with china paint, luster and wood (not pictured)
4 × 15 × 15 in. (10.2 × 38.1 × 38.1 cm)
Collection Crocker Art Museum, Sacramento, CA

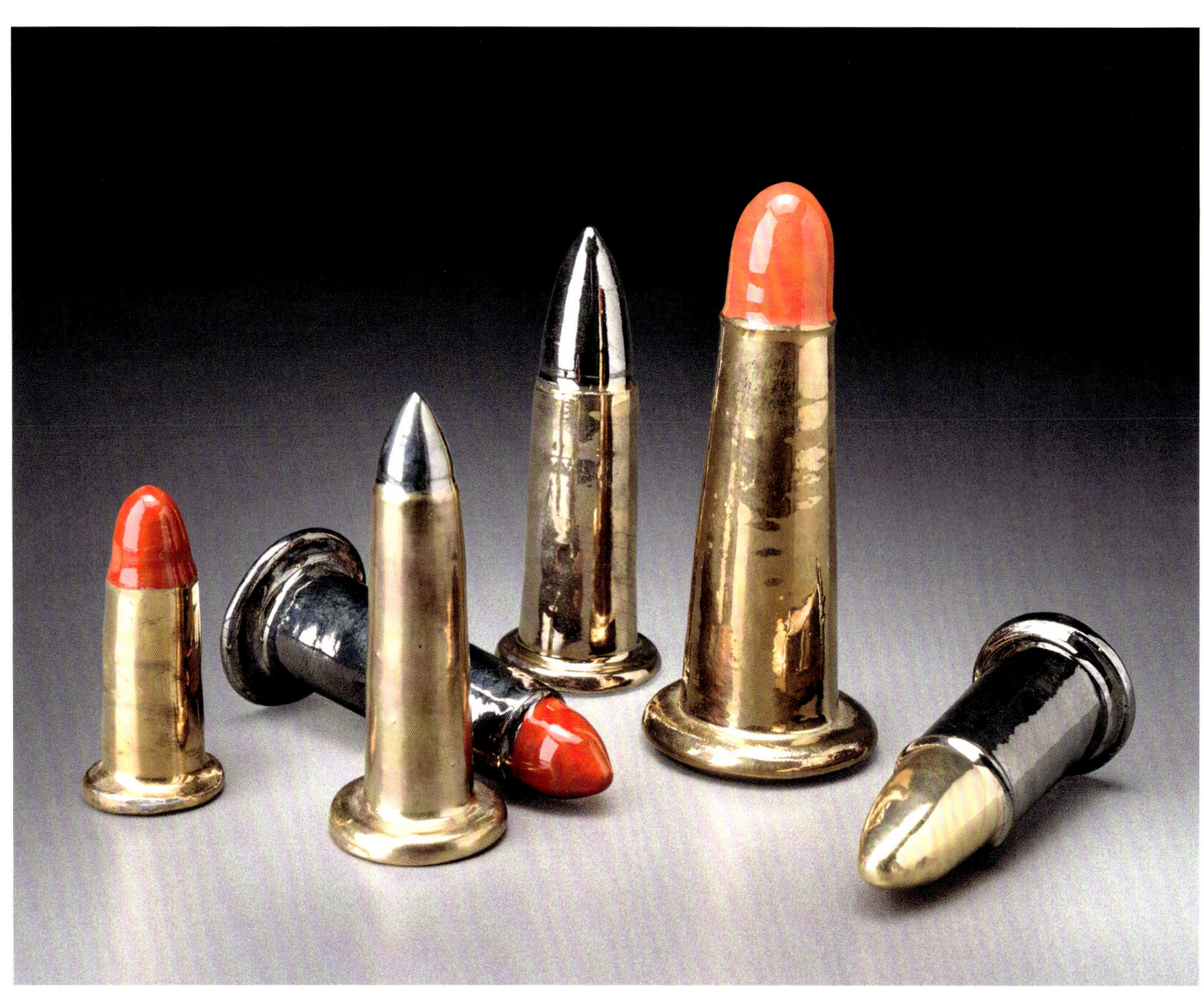

Lipsticks and Bullets 1985–2024
Glazed earthenware with china paint and luster
6 × 9 × 8 in. (15.2 × 22.9 × 20.3 cm)

Right page
44 Magnum Mandala 2011
Glazed porcelain with paint and steel
28 ½ × 19 ½ × 4 in. (72.4 × 49.5 × 10.2 cm)

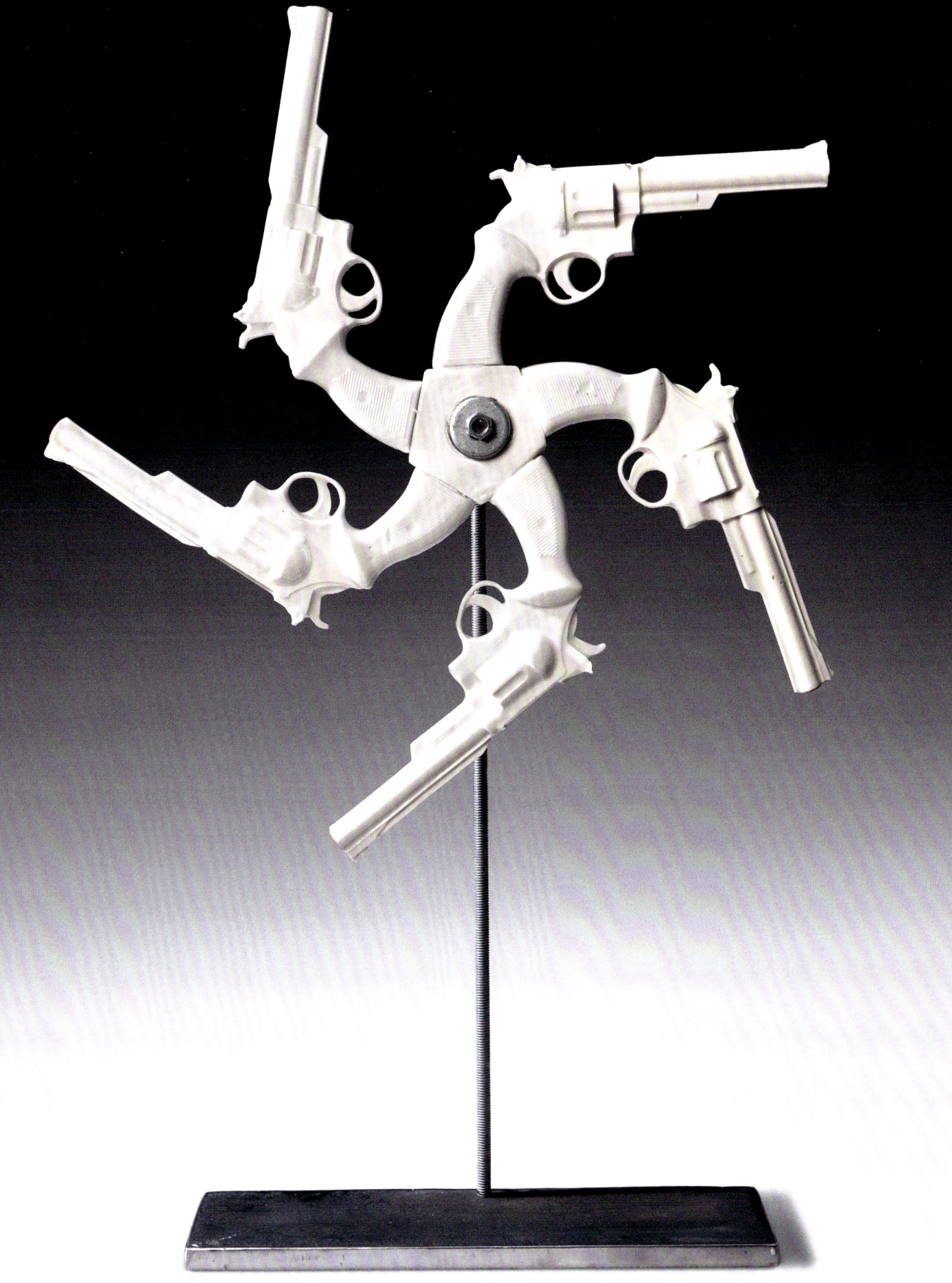

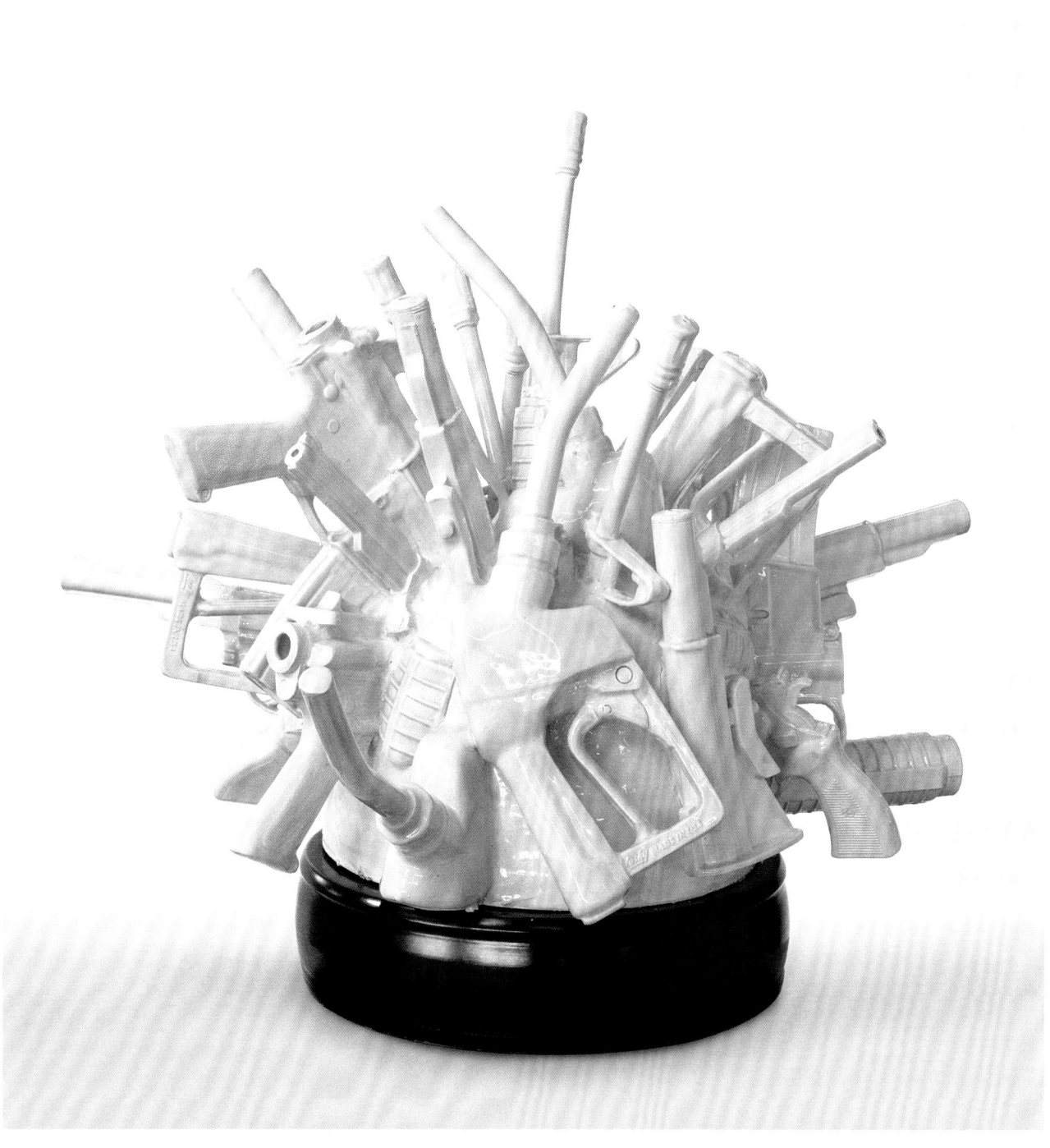

Cause and Effect 2011
Glazed earthenware
24 × 28 × 22 in. (61 × 71.1 × 55.9 cm)

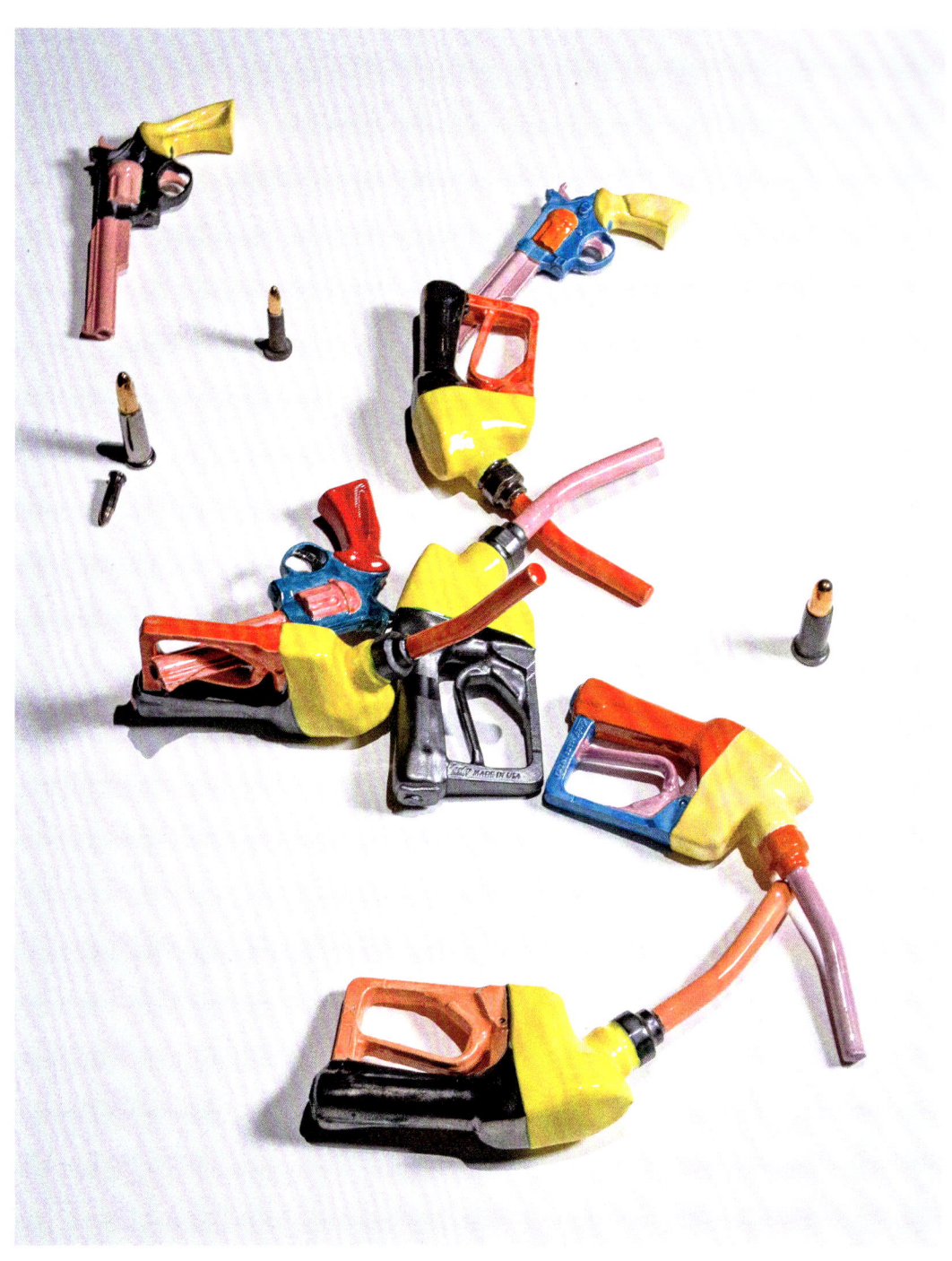

Candy Coated Fear and Greed 2011
Glazed earthenware with luster
Overall: 9 × 22 × 32 in. (22.9 × 55.9 × 81.3 cm)

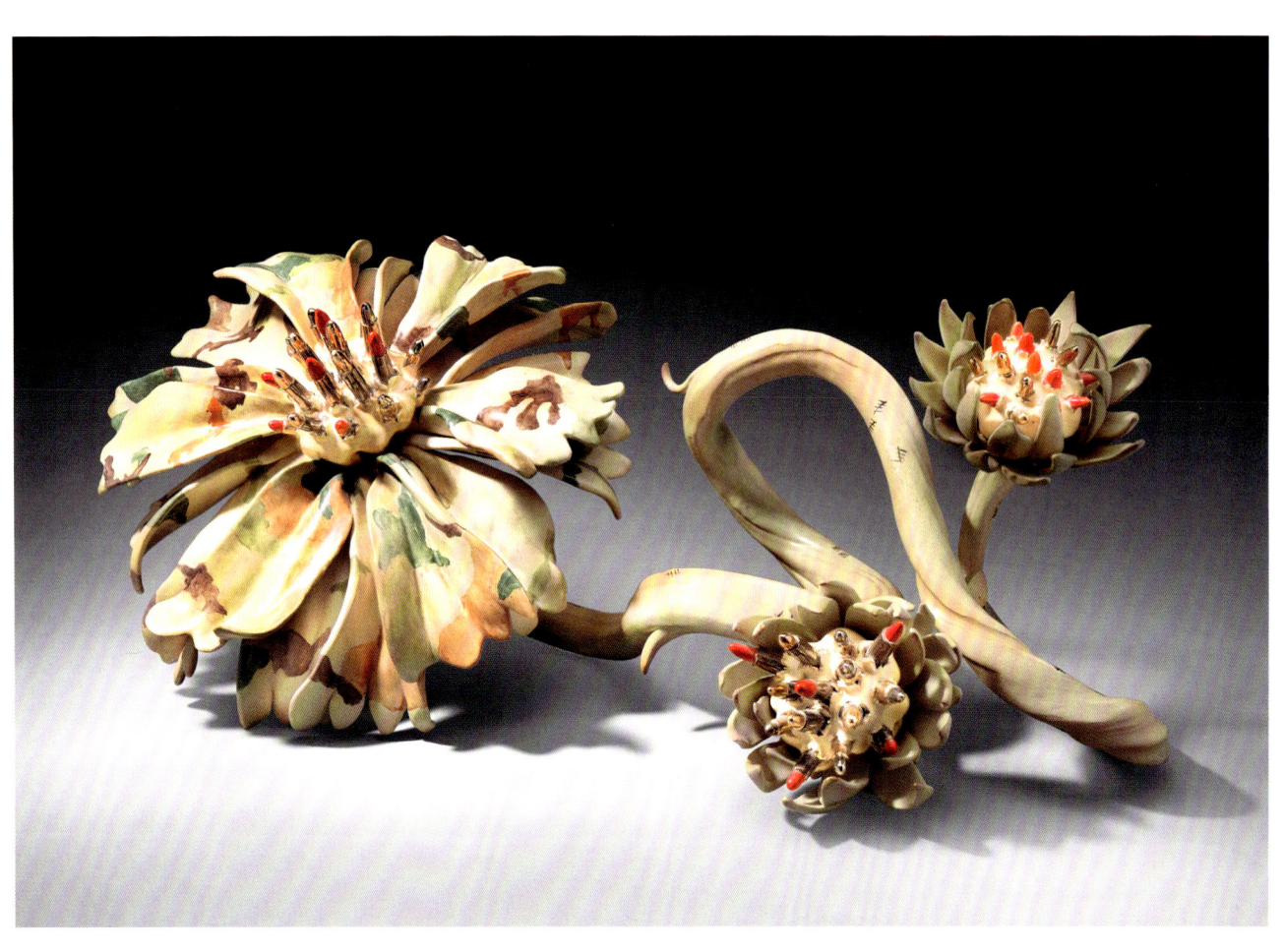

Camouflora 2004
Glazed earthenware with china paint and luster
15 × 35 × 20 in. (38.1 × 88.9 × 50.8 cm)

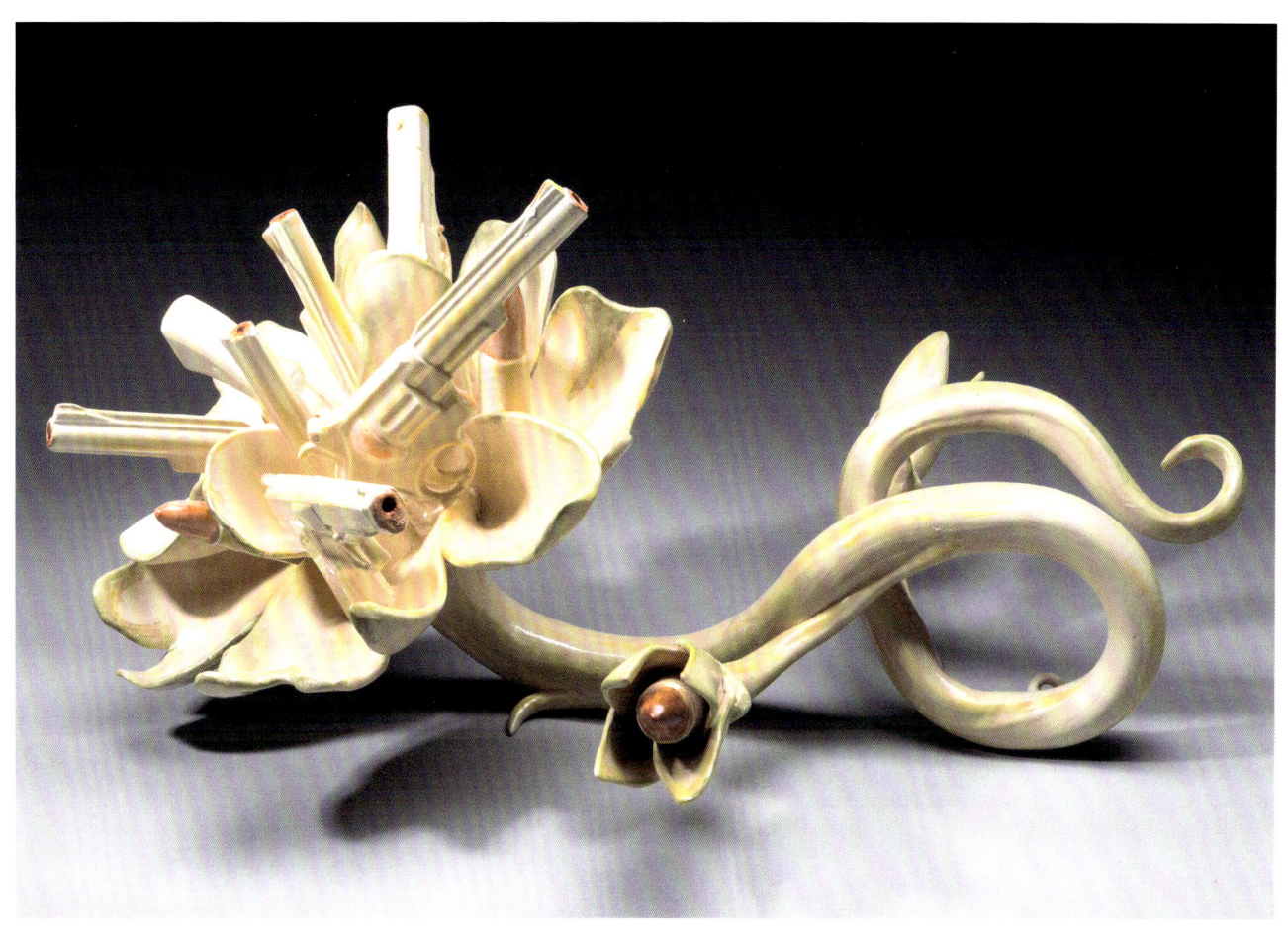

La Petite Mort 2016
Glazed earthenware with china paint and luster
14 ½ × 29 × 18 in. (36.8 × 73.7 × 45.7 cm)

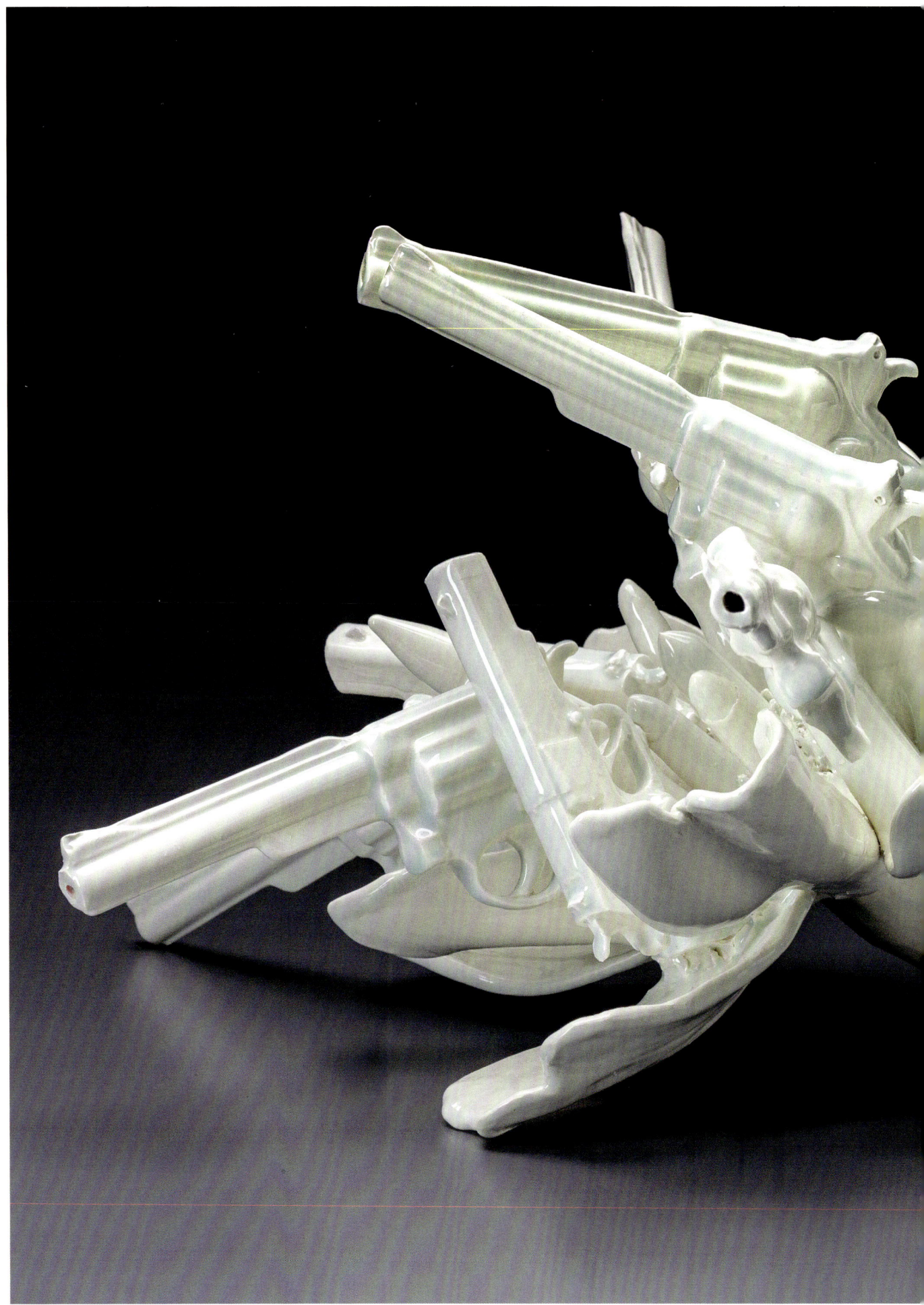

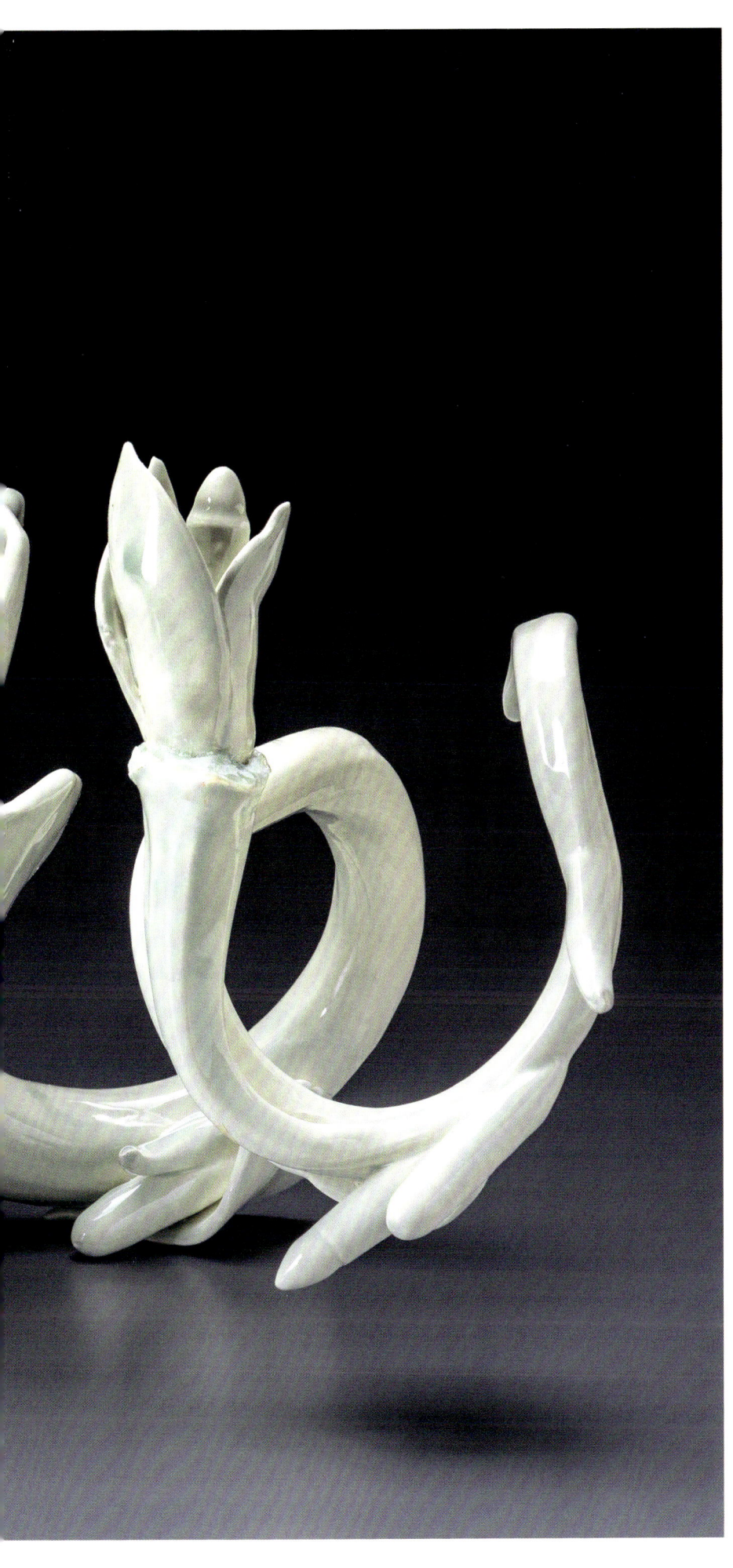

Allegretto con Moderato 3 2014
Glazed earthenware
26 × 12 × 19 in. (66 × 30.5 × 48.3 cm)
Collection Rod Parks

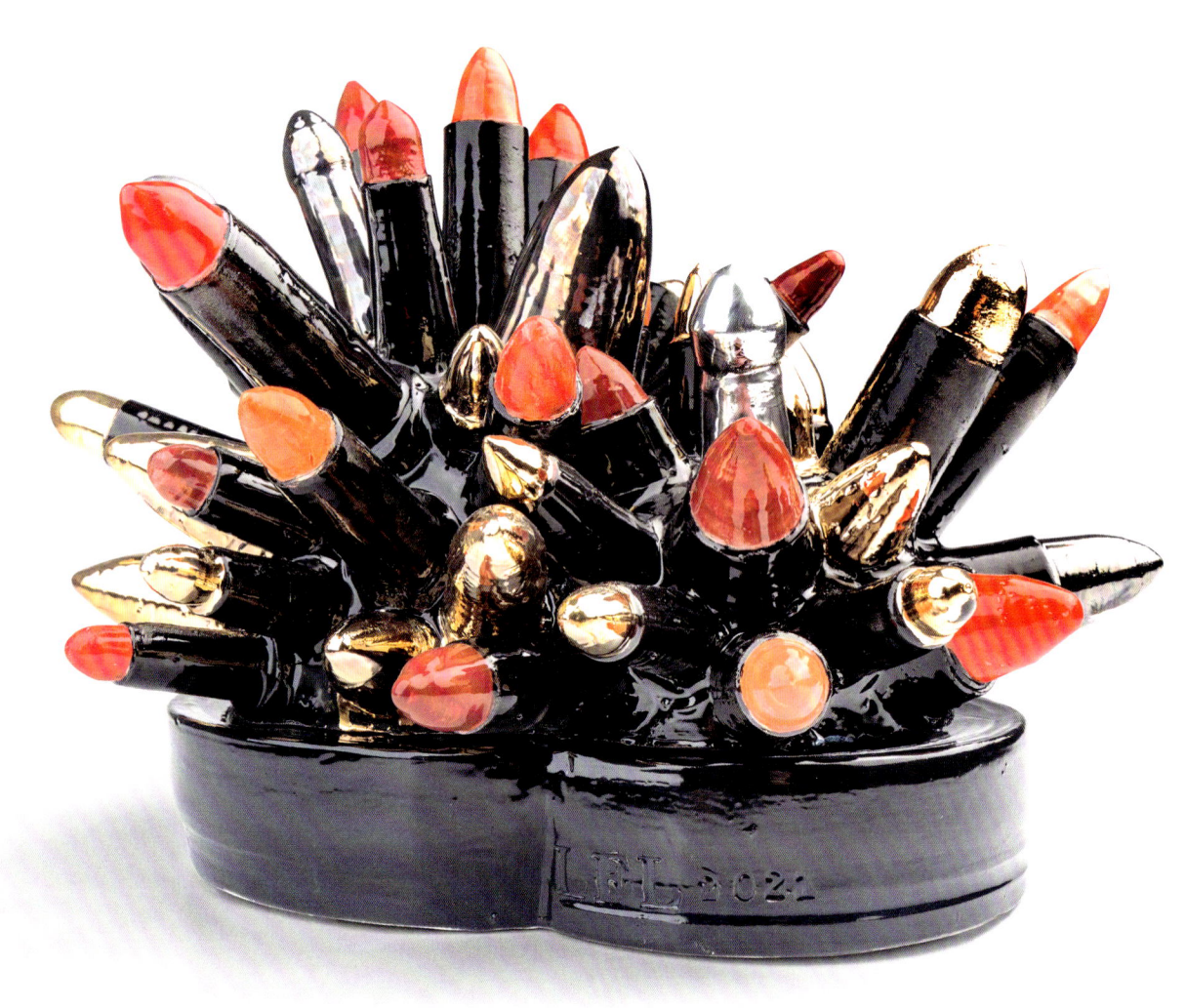

Love and War: The Ammunition (Petite) 2021
Glazed earthenware with luster and mirror paint
11 × 14 × 13 ½ in. (27.9 × 35.6 × 34.3 cm)

Right page
Camouflora Small 2004
Herend porcelain with china paint and luster
9 × 22 × 14 in. (22.9 × 55.9 × 35.6 cm)

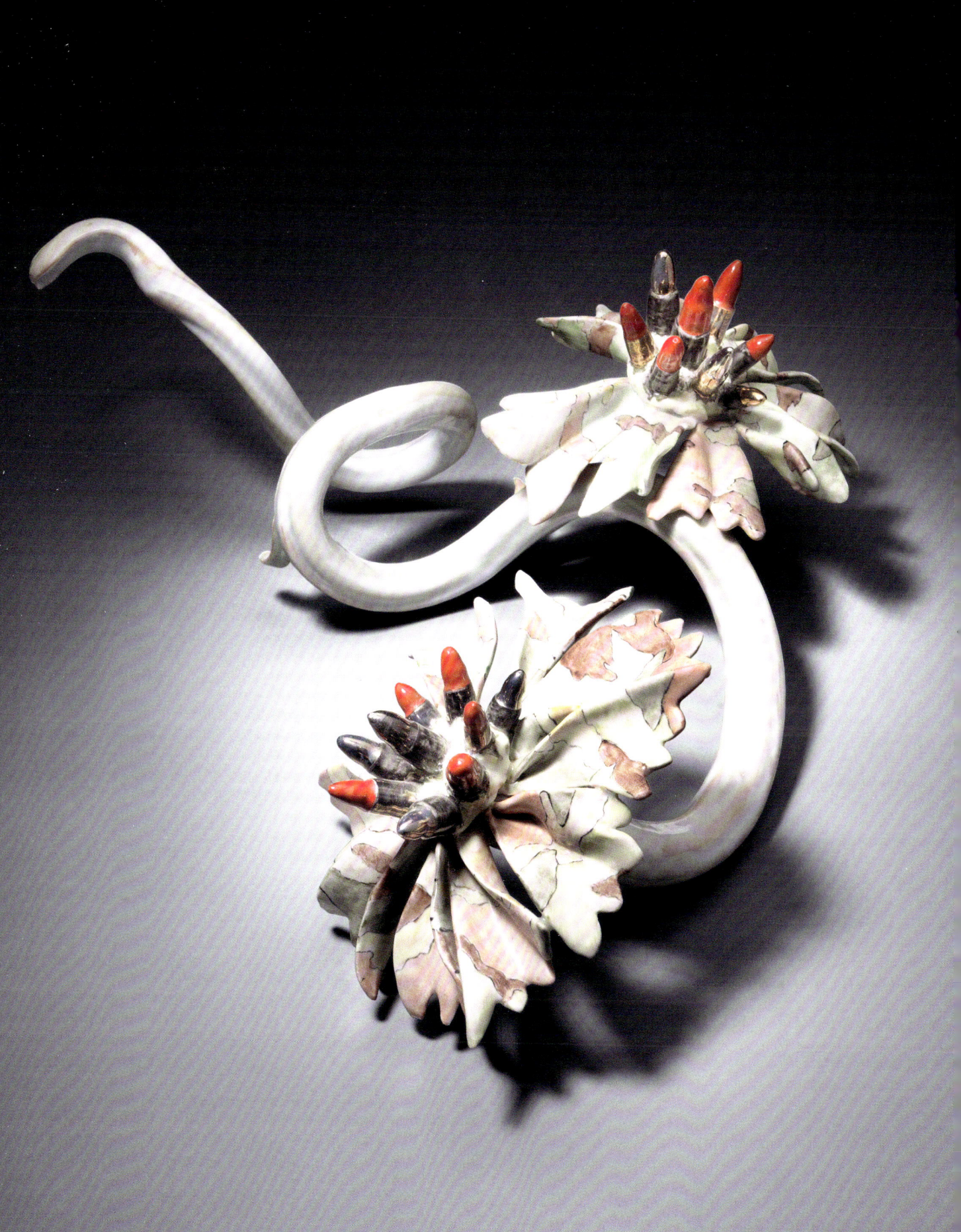

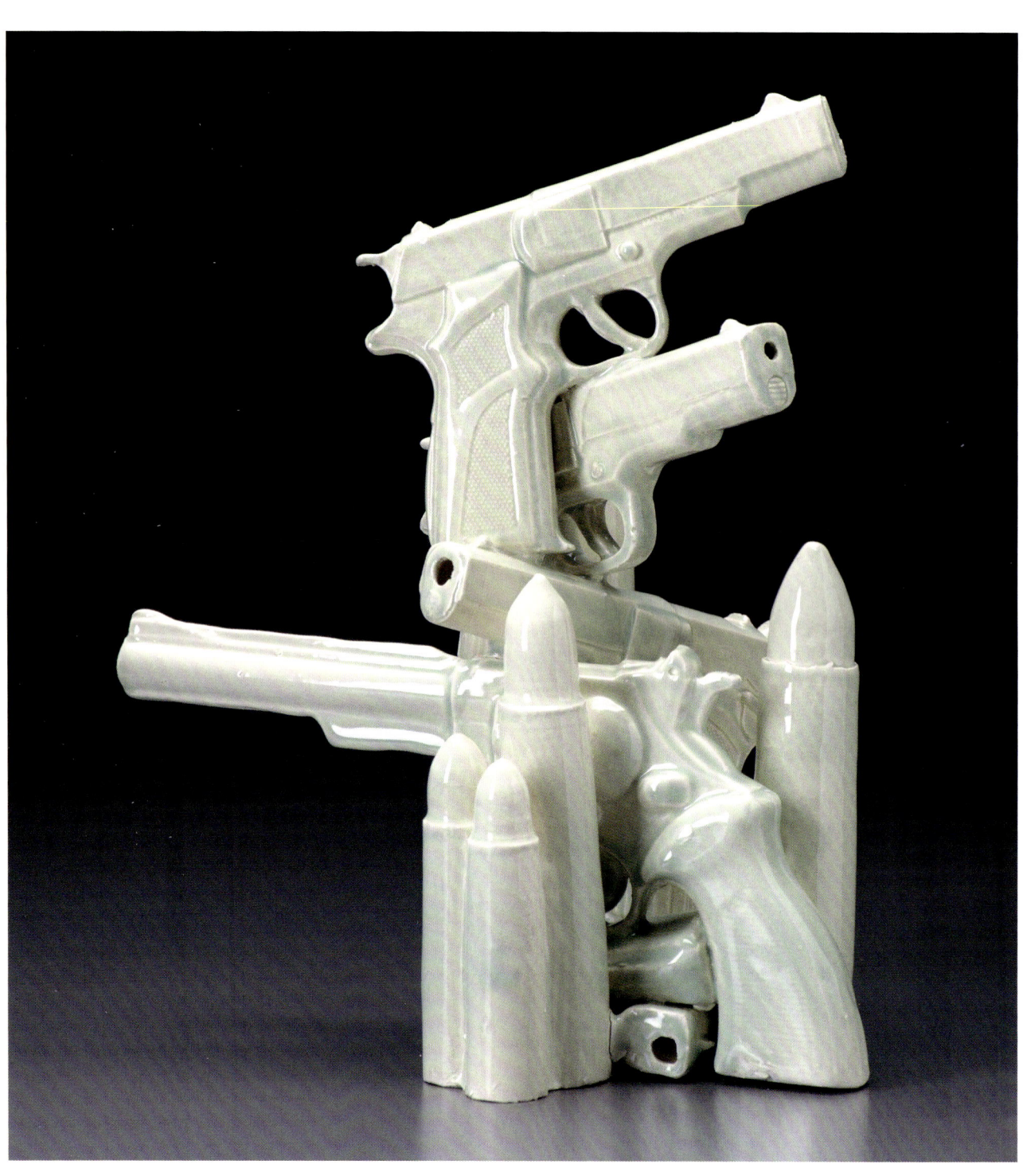

Hands Up Don't Shoot #2 2015
Glazed earthenware
12 × 10 × 9 in. (30.5 × 25.4 × 22.9 cm)

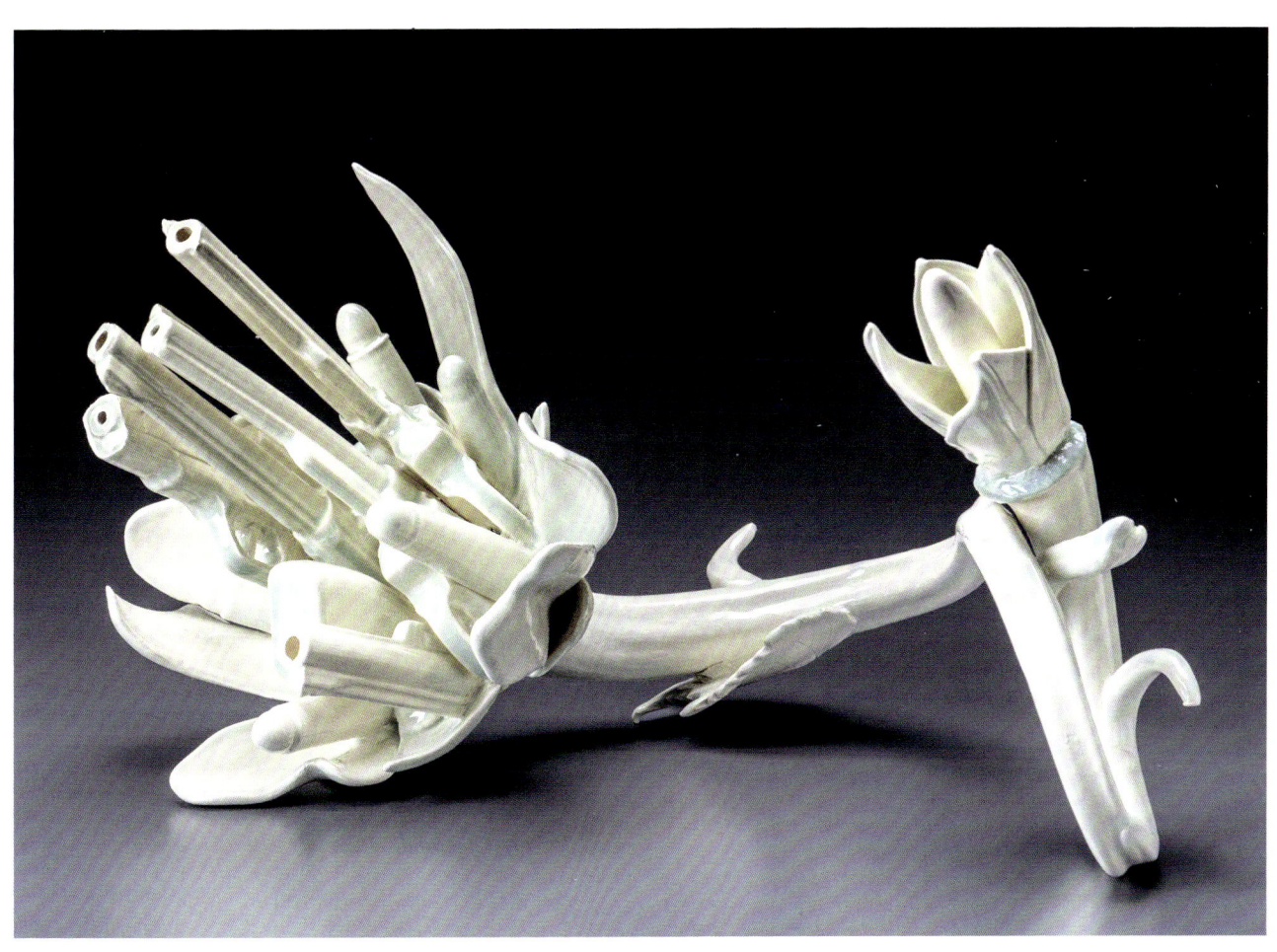

Allegretto con Moderato (Small) 2016
Glazed earthenware
10 × 18 × 15 ½ in. (25.4 × 45.7 × 39.4 cm)

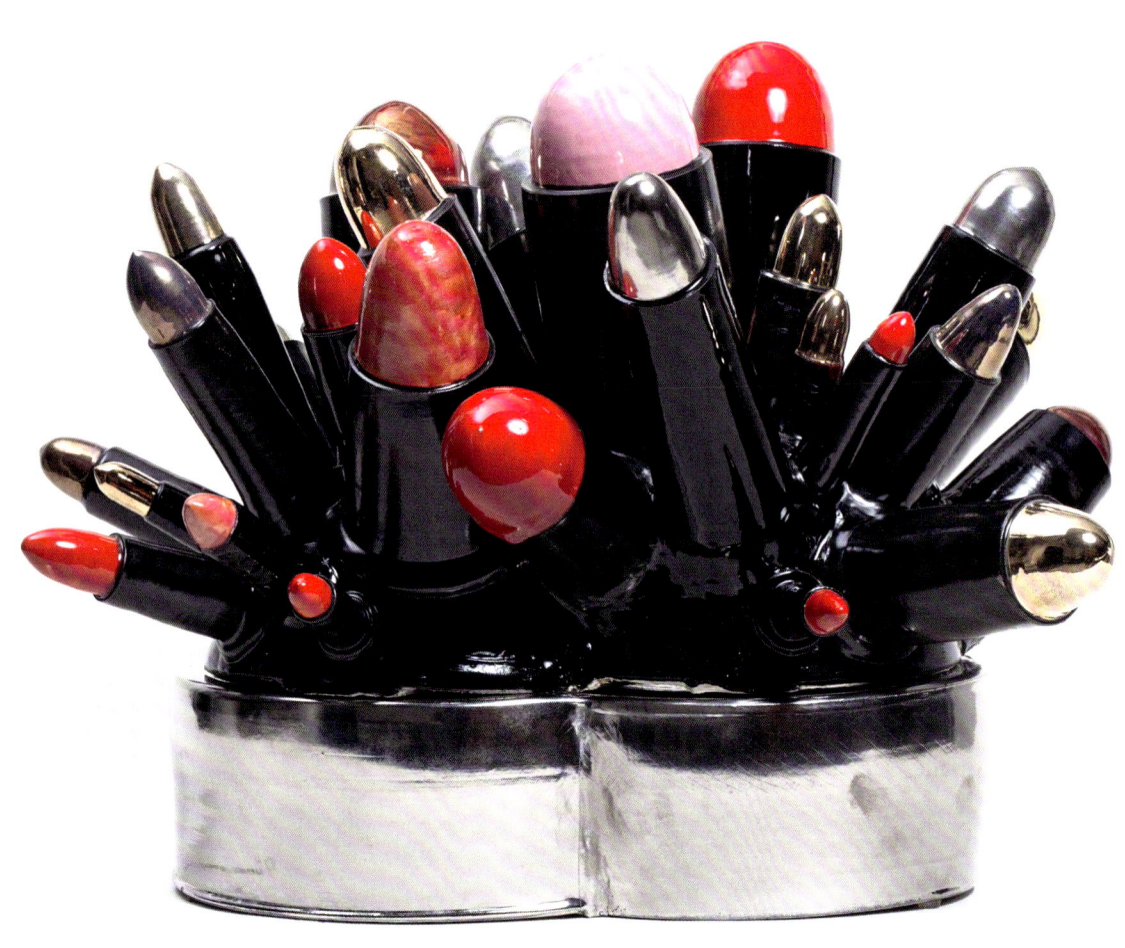

Love and War: The Ammunition II 2011
Glazed earthenware with china paint and luster
26 × 16 ½ × 18 in. (66 × 41.9 × 45.7 cm)

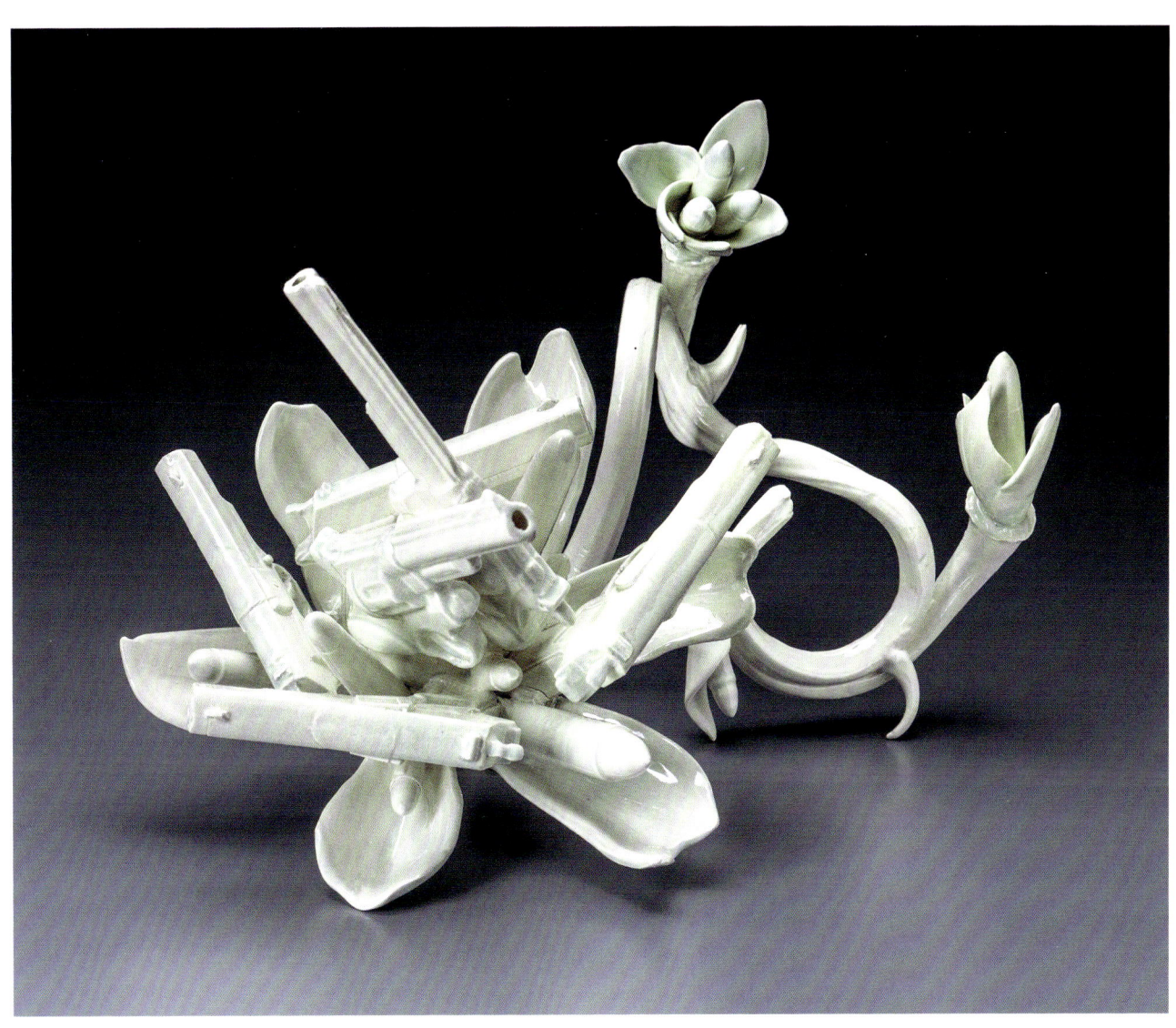

Allegretto con Moderato (Medium) 2016
Glazed earthenware
12 ½ × 22 × 14 in. (31.8 × 55.9 × 35.6 cm)

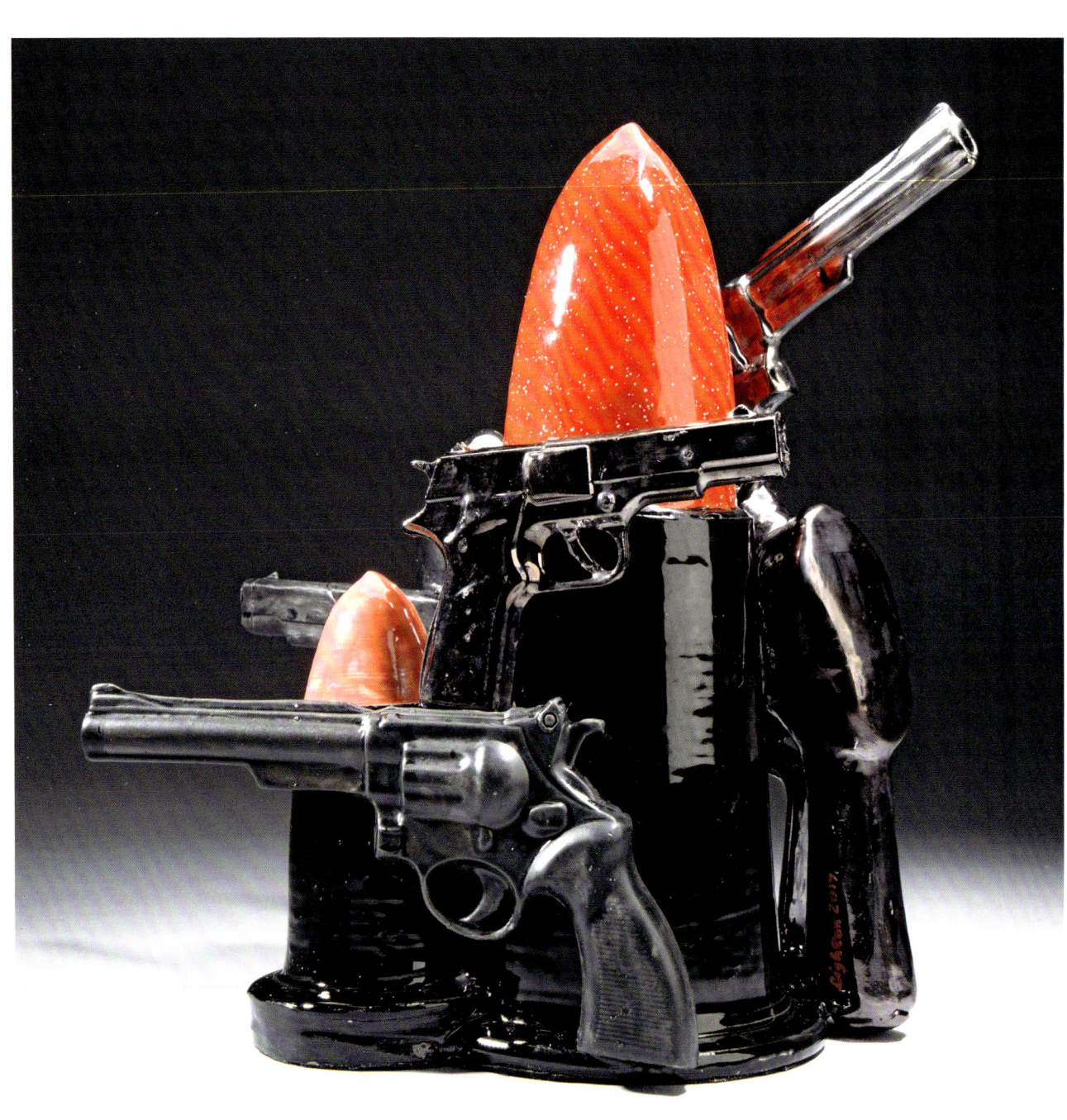

The Modern City State #3 2017
Glazed earthenware with luster
15 × 14 × 11 in. (38.1 × 35.6 × 27.9 cm)

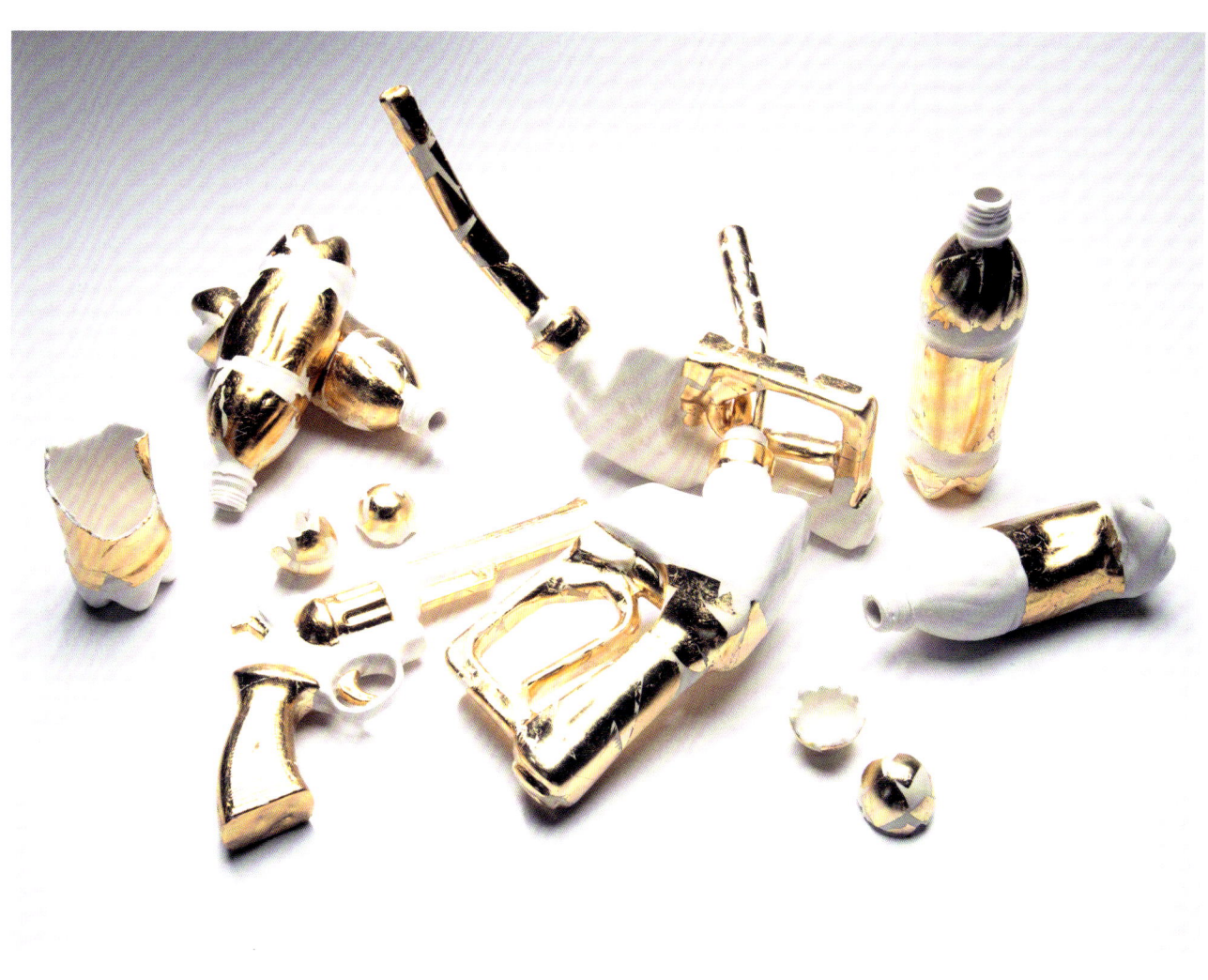

Trump Trash 2017
Glazed earthenware with gold leaf
24 × 22 × 9 in. (61 × 55.9 × 22.9 cm)
Collection Laura E. Robinson

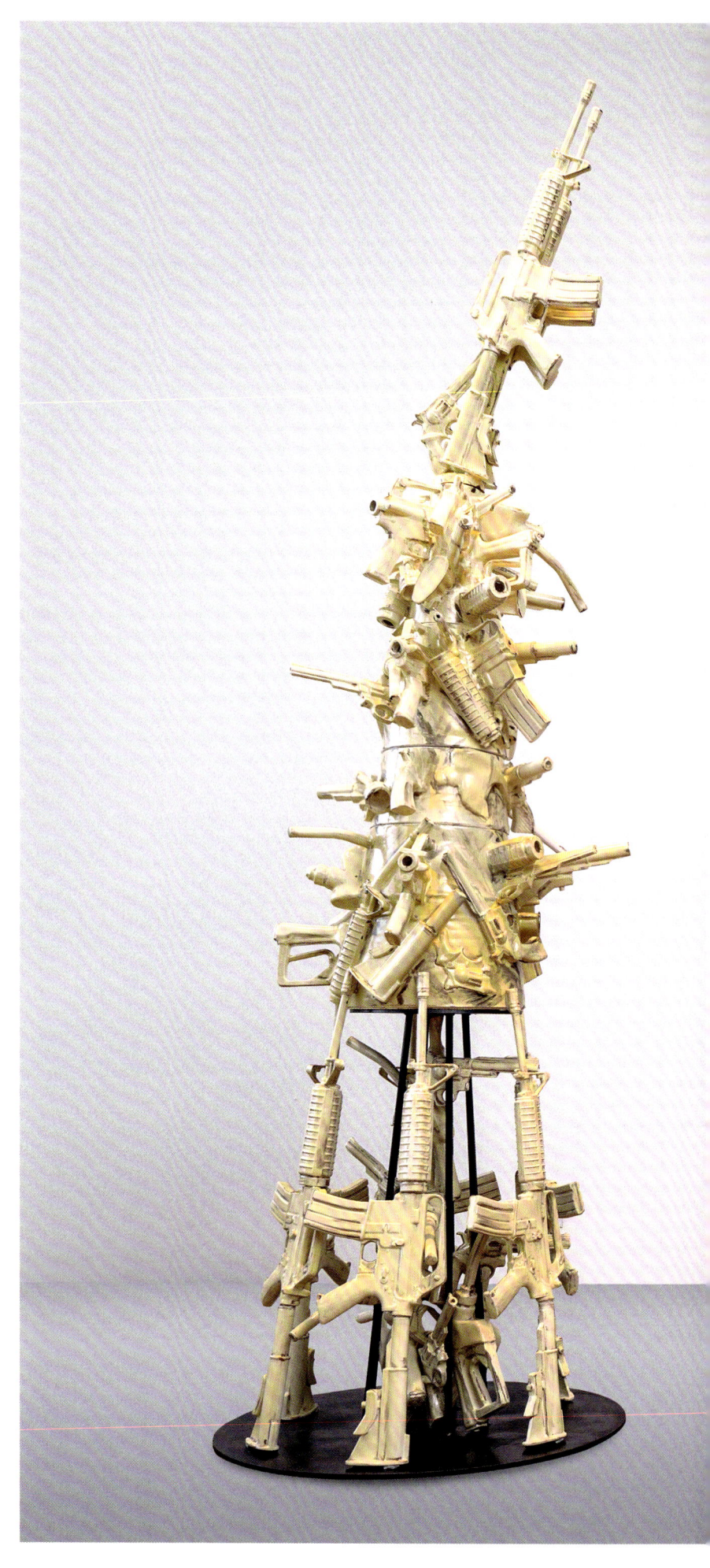

I Don't Want a Bullet to Kiss Your Heart
2012
Glazed earthenware with paint and steel
101 × 96 × 28 in. (256.5 × 243.8 × 71.1 cm)

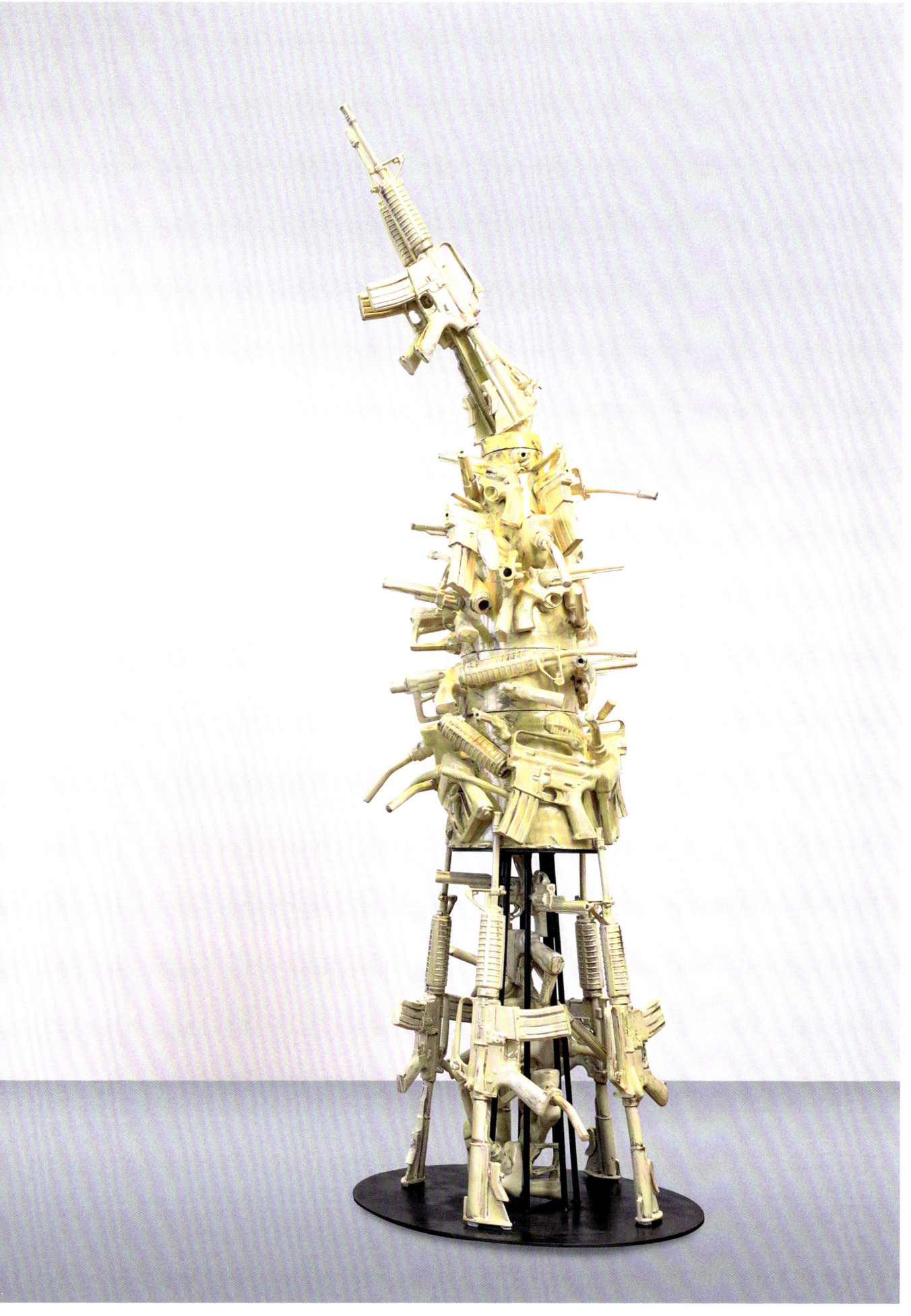

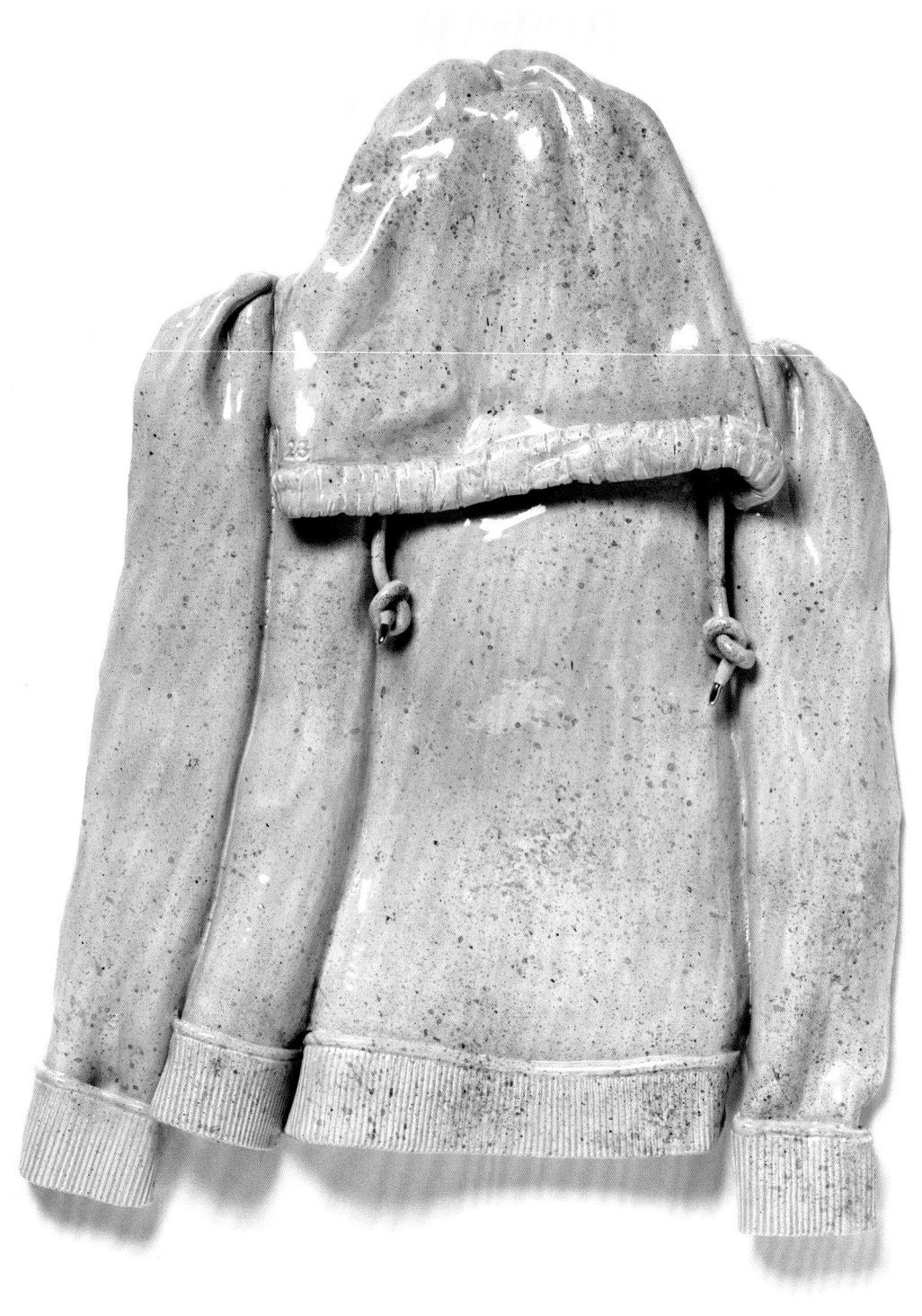

Sweatshirt 2023
Glazed earthenware with luster
25 × 18 ½ × 3 in. (63.5 × 47 × 7.6 cm)

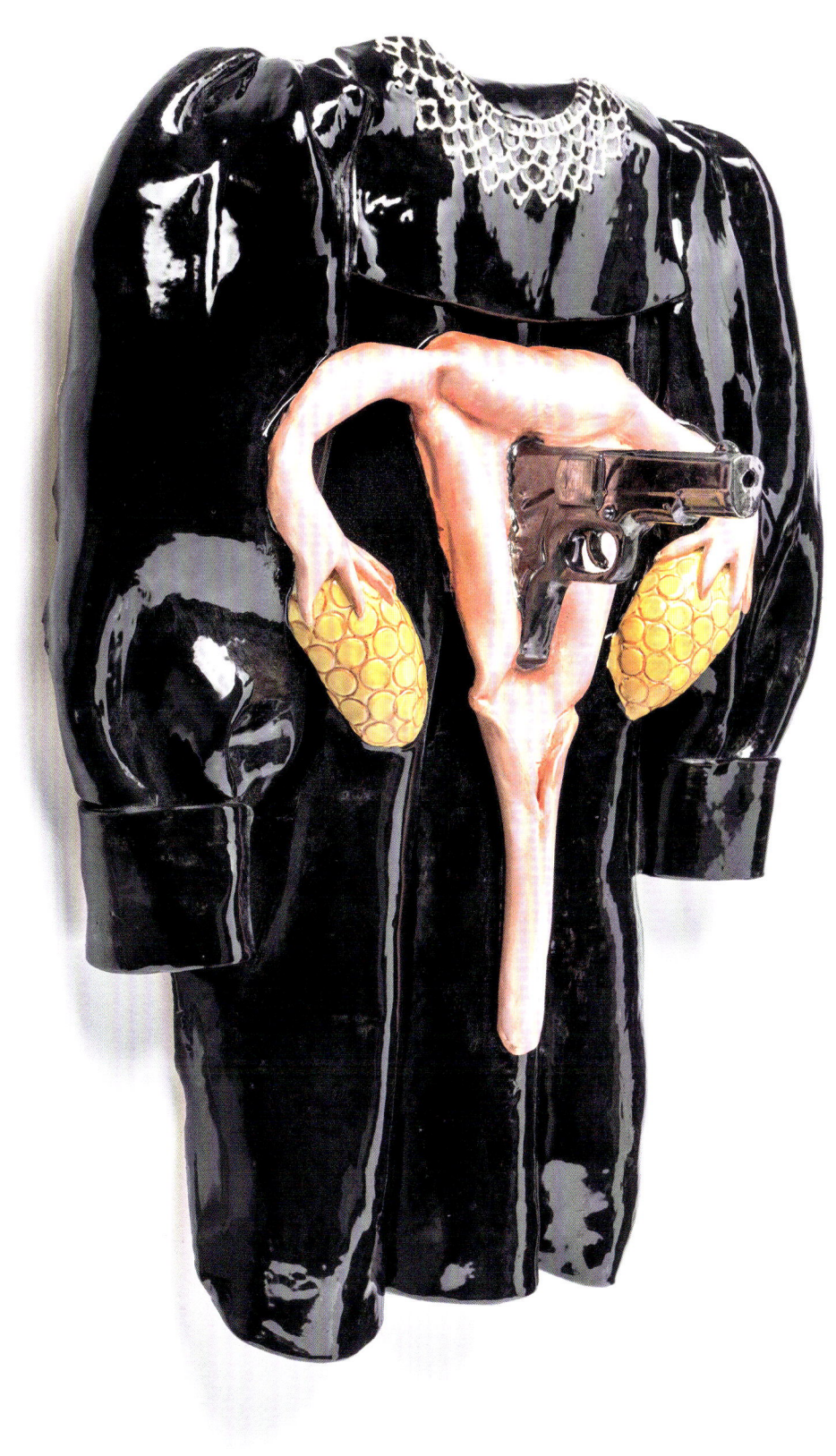

Supreme Justice 2023
Glazed earthenware with china paint and luster
22 ½ × 18 × 8 in. (57.2 × 45.7 × 20.3 cm)

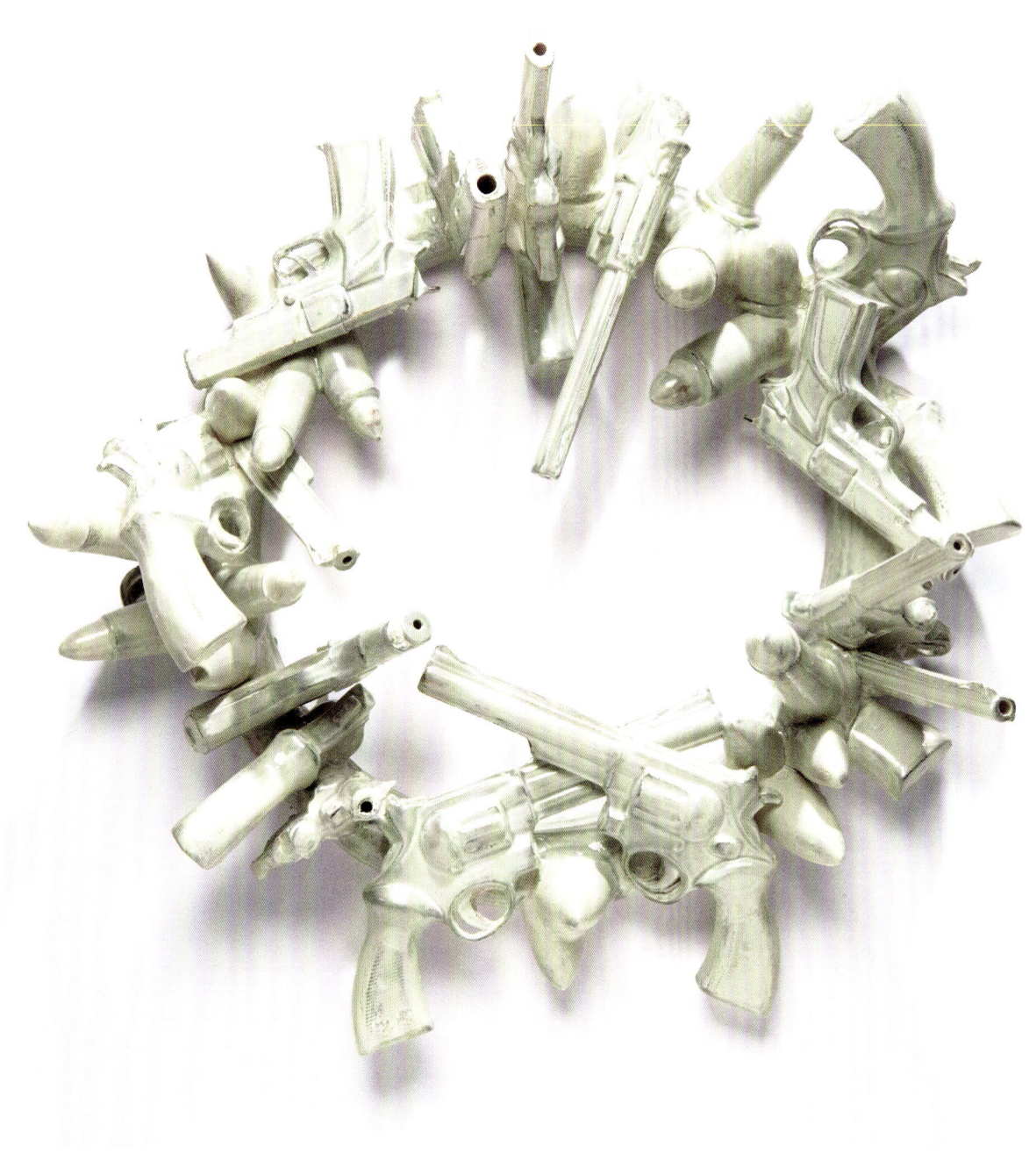

Thoughts and Prayers 2 2018
Glazed earthenware with paint
24 × 24 × 10 in. (61 × 61 × 25.4 cm)

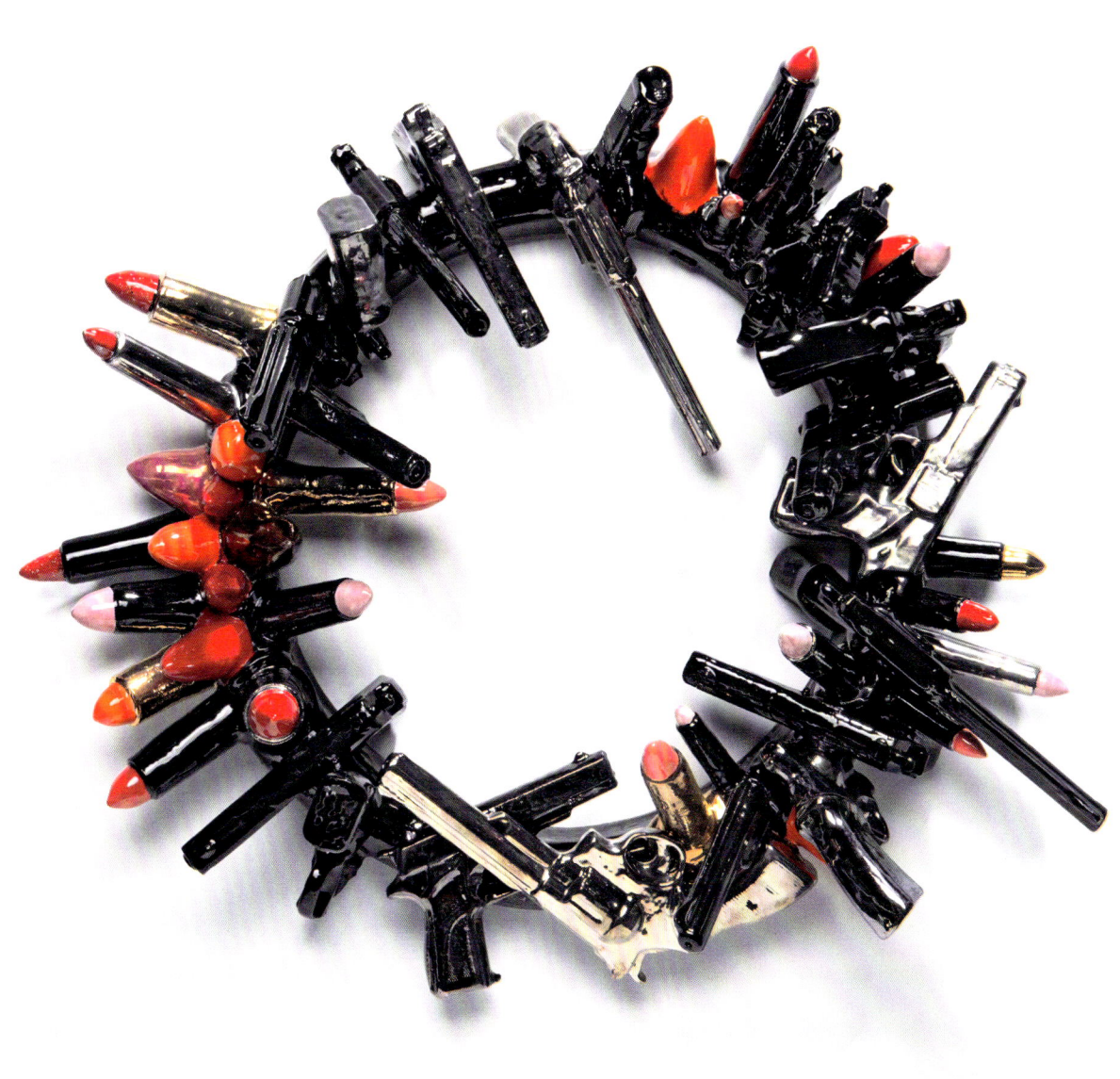

Thoughts and Prayers 2018
Glazed earthenware with china paint and luster
24 × 27 × 8 ½ in. (61 × 68.6 × 21.6 cm)

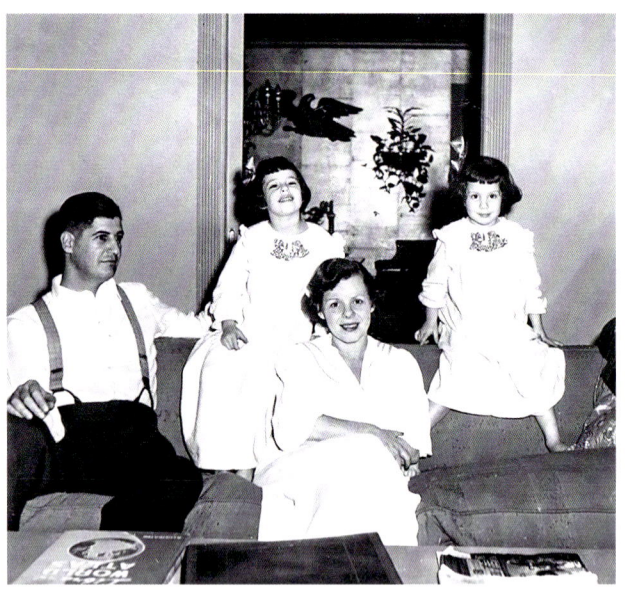

Lighton's father, Alfred; her sister, Jeanne; her mother, Jean; and Linda (far right), at home, c. 1951

1948

March 10: Linda Elise Lighton is born in Kansas City, Missouri, the second daughter of Alfred Woolf Lighton and Jean, née Schoenberg.

Jean's mother's family, the Lehmans, helped cement the city's reputation as a cultural capital of the Midwest by opening the Orpheum Theatre, a premier vaudeville venue, in 1898. Jean's father, Albert Schoenberg, owned a successful commercial real estate business.

The Woolfs emigrated from England to the United States around 1860, settling in Leavenworth, Kansas. Alfred and Samuel Woolf established Woolf Brothers, a prosperous men's clothing business, which they moved to Kansas City following the Civil War. By 1962, when Linda's father inherited the company from his uncle, Herbert Woolf, it had become a chain of department stores with locations well beyond Missouri. His mother, Gertrude Woolf Lighton, was a patron of the arts who established Lighton Studios, an artistic and literary hub, which became the

headquarters of the Kansas City Society of Artists, as well as a trustee of the Kansas City Art Institute. As the second vice president of the Friends of Art group at the William Rockhill Nelson Gallery of Art (now the Nelson-Atkins Museum of Art), Gertrude shaped the institution's collection of modern art through key acquisitions.

The family is affluent and well-connected. Linda grows up with material comforts and social conventions she later rejects.

1951

Linda enters the all-girls Sunset Hill School, which she will attend until the age of eighteen.

Her brother, Robert Woolf Lighton, is born. Her elder sister, Jeanne, was born in 1945.

1954–1962

Early influences on Linda's creative development include her grandmother's porcelain collection—she vividly remembers dusting the Staffordshire model dogs, Sèvres figurines, and late-nineteenth-century dishes—

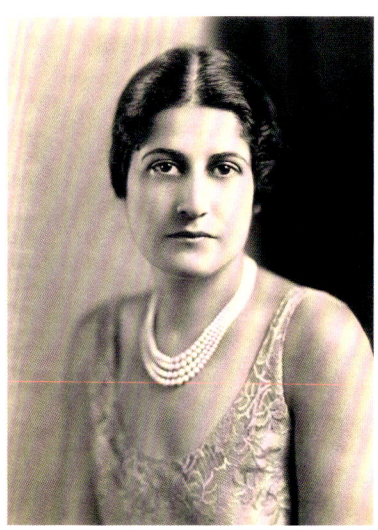

Gertrude Woolf Lighton, Linda's grandmother, c. 1920s

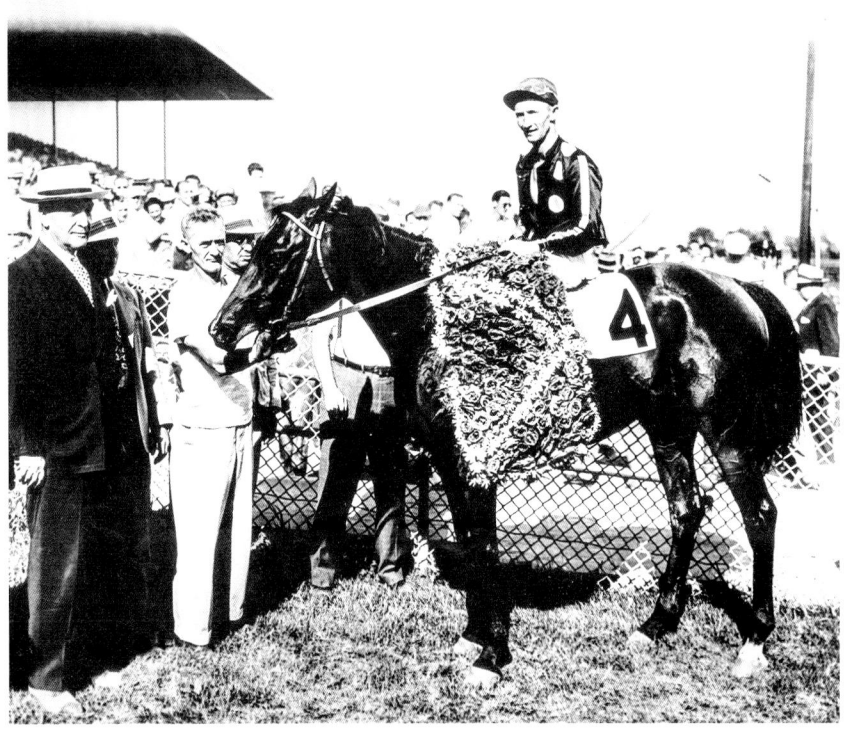

Herbert Woolf (far left), Linda's great-uncle, from whom her father inherited Woolf Brothers, pictured here with his horse, Lawrin, in the Kentucky Derby Winner's Circle at the Churchill Downs racetrack in Louisville, Kentucky, 1938

and her uncle, the sculptor Richard Hollander. Linda grew up playing in his garage studio among the pieces of metal and wood he transformed into dynamic abstract compositions. Hollander, who was married to Alfred's sister, Gertrude, remained an inspiration and sounding board for Linda until his death in 1991.

Linda's parents also directly shaped her appreciation of beauty, art, and culture. Jean and Alfred were consummate hosts who surrounded themselves with lively, creative personalities. Leading fashion designers such as Geoffrey Beene and Bill Blass and modeling agency founder Eileen Ford were frequent guests at Woolf Brothers dinner parties hosted at their home. Jean orchestrated exquisite meals and designed her homes with

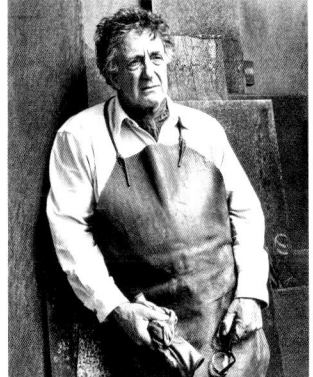
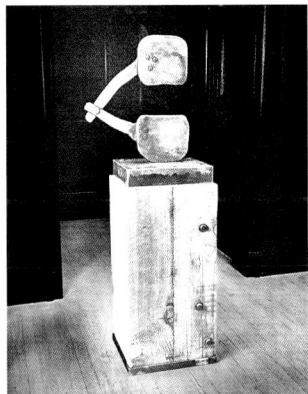

Linda's uncle, artist Richard Hollander, photographed by Richard Loftis, 1982; and one of his steel sculptures

such flair as to garner coverage in *Architectural Digest* and *Better Homes and Gardens.*

1963

Summer: Attends a Spanish language course at the Monterrey Institute of Technology in Mexico. Her first exposure to a culture dramatically different from her own, the trip ignites an enduring wanderlust and passionate curiosity about other ways of life.

1964

Returns to Monterrey for a second year and dates Allan Soehl, who also becomes an artist. She doesn't learn much Spanish, but does pick up a sense of adventure and a fondness for cigarettes.

1965

Summer: Attends the School of Fine Arts at Fontainebleau (École des Beaux-Arts de Fontainebleau) at Fontainebleau Palace, the hunting lodge and vacation home of Louis XIV and Napoleon, among other French rulers. She draws from live models daily and attends wonderful concerts organized by the celebrated conductor and composer Nadia Boulanger, who teaches music. Dates Matthias D'Huarte, a successful young artist from Paris. Together, they explore the castle, sneaking into a lavish theater and its loges with faded silk and cobwebbed chandeliers, and travel far beyond its walls. They visit Constantin Brancusi's studio in Paris, when it was still possible to walk among the sculptures and sit on the chairs; Calder's studio in the south of France; and the studio of Op Art pioneer Victor Vasarely, who tells Linda she needs to draw every day if she wants to become a good artist and gives her a scarf. The rich pinks and purples of French paint and textile dyes, unlike any colors she had encountered back home, make a lasting impression.

1966

Graduates from high school along with eighteen girls she has known since first grade. Hoping to attend the Kansas City Art Institute, Linda meets with the president of the school (an audience likely arranged by her father), who discourages her. "The guy put his hand on my shoulder, and he said, 'Honey, don't you have a boyfriend? You're never going to make art,'" she recalls. "I assume Alfred was paying him to say that." She doesn't apply and attends her parents' choice—Centenary Junior College for Women in Hackettstown, New Jersey—instead.

Centenary is a quick bus ride from New York City, and Linda makes regular trips to see contemporary art, including Ellsworth Kelly, Claes Oldenburg, Roy Lichtenstein, and Andy Warhol exhibitions at the Sidney Janis Gallery. She even sits through the entirety of *Empire* (1965), an eight-hour experimental film by Warhol. The Pop artists, who examine and play with everyday objects and consumer goods, become enduring influences.

"Pop is really reflecting what's going on in America at that time and that was really important for me. Humor is a great access point—that's how you get in."

One of Warhol's photographers invites Linda to visit the Factory during a chance meeting in Central Park, but she is too shy to go.

1967

Returns to Kansas City after just one year at Centenary. Instead of moving back to her parents' home with its maids, chef, and chauffeur, she finds a job in a flower shop and rents an apartment of her own. Even more controversial is her refusal to be a debutante. With these rebellions, Linda makes it clear she is not interested in the life her parents have been grooming her to lead. "I thought that money was the root of all evil," she said, reflecting on the oppressive rules and scrutiny under which she was raised. "No matter what I did, I was never

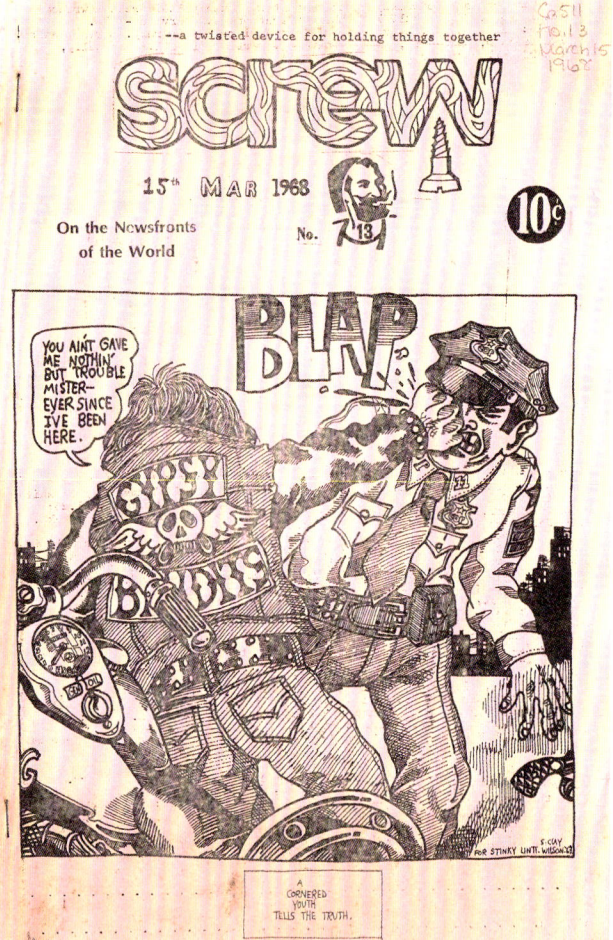

The Screw: A Twisted Device for Holding Things Together, cover, March 15, 1968

good enough. Who raised me? Who bought me a bra? Who told me about my period? It was the housekeepers, and I loved them dearly. That was where the humanity was."

Meets Joe Dergan, a hairdresser and marijuana dealer, at a sit-in protesting the Vietnam War in a city park. He moves into her apartment on 39th Street, near the Kansas City Art Institute.

1968

Alfred visits the apartment and finds a note on the door: "Do Not Disturb: We're taking LSD." Furious, he forces his daughter back to the family home and locks her in her room. She is nineteen and unable to leave. Alfred beats her with a wooden canvas stretcher until she is black and blue. One night, Linda sneaks to the basement and calls Joe. "He just goes, 'I'm coming to get you.' And so I meet him outside in the middle of the night, and we drive to Oklahoma and get married." Linda is nineteen; Joe is twenty-four.

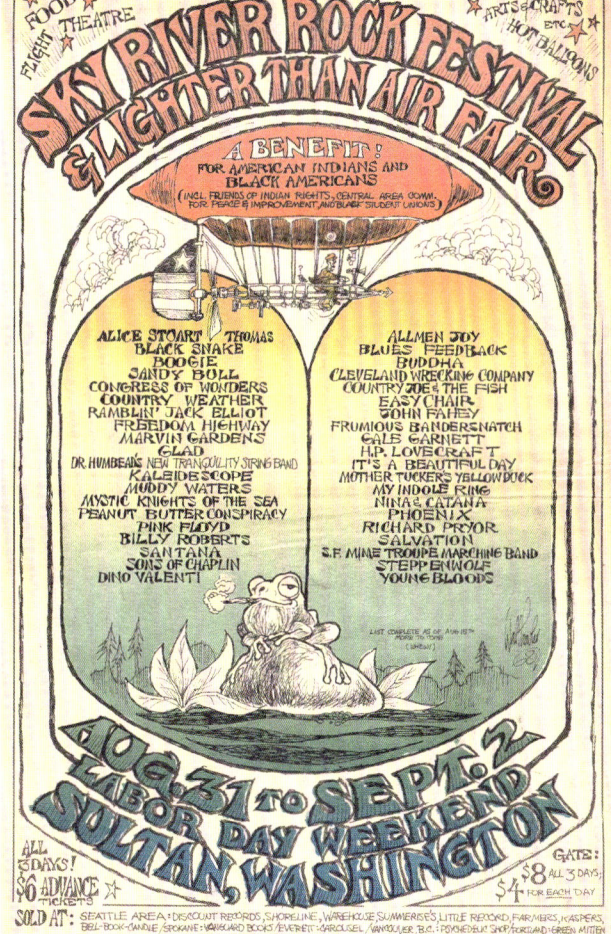

Advertisement for the first Sky River Rock Festival and Lighter Than Air Fair, August 31 – September 2, 1968. This was a benefit organized for Native Americans and Black Americans.

The newlyweds move to Lawrence, Kansas, where they live with a friend and work on *The Screw: A Twisted Device for Holding Things Together*, an underground, counterculture newspaper whose issues include illustrations by R. Crumb and an interview with one of the earliest Vietnam War draft dodgers. Police regularly raid the office. Linda regularly participates in anti-war marches.

Alfred comes to the house with Kansas City police chief (and future FBI director) Clarence Kelley. He knocks on the door, punches Joe, and kidnaps Linda.

Linda is detained in a private mental institution, sedated, and presumably given shock treatments. (Alfred and his close friend, psychiatrist Albert Preston, sit on the board of the hospital.) Linda is unable to make or receive phone calls. Neither her parents nor siblings visit. "I was diagnosed with an Oedipal complex, of all things."

"I lost a few weeks without knowing what was going on. There weren't any books. You couldn't go outside. I tried to meditate. It was pretty terrifying."

Unable to afford a lawyer, Joe enlists a psychiatrist at University of Missouri – Kansas City to help find her. He obtains a writ of habeas corpus, and a judge determines that Linda's detainment is unlawful. Alfred appeals. Linda is transferred to St. Mary's, a state mental hospital. She appears in court five times, but remains institutionalized due to Alfred's appeals.

Finally released, Linda files a court order against her father and decides to get as far away as possible from Kansas City. She and Joe hitchhike to Salt Lake City, where some friendly Mormons cook them dinner; then they catch a bus to the Haight-Ashbury district of San Francisco. There, they move in with a ("very nice") drug dealer at Casa Madrona, a four-story apartment building around the corner from the Hells Angels and the Grateful Dead and down the block from Jefferson Airplane and Janis Joplin, whom they often see perform. They share the building with the Steve Miller Band and a woman who makes clothes for Jimi Hendrix. Linda and Joe help build geodesic domes in the Bay Area.

Within a year, though, San Francisco begins to feel dangerous and increasingly bleak. Linda survives by panhandling and testing LSD before it is sold on the street. She moves to Seattle with Joe. There she helps friends avoid the draft by making them satin loincloths, so examiners will assume they're gay, and feeding them meals designed to sabotage their medical exams: "Lots of salt and egg yolks! Messes up your blood!"

Summer: Helps organize the Sky River Rock Festival and Lighter Than Air Fair. Thousands attend this historic event—the first major, multi-day rock festival—at a raspberry farm on the Skykomish River outside Sultan, Washington. Acts include Santana, Big Mama Thornton, James Cotton, Richard Pryor, and Country Joe and the Fish. The Grateful Dead appear on the last day, unscheduled but eager to perform. Linda picks them up from the airport, where they set off fireworks on the tarmac.

1969

February 21: Roseann Dergan, Linda's only child, is born in Seattle, Washington.

Linda and Joe move to Taos, New Mexico, where they live in a house with a dirt floor, and then to a wooden cabin in Arroyo Seco. Their social life is rich—friends include Wavy Gravy and the Merry Pranksters—but they are not. Linda receives $15 a month through welfare. Surrounded by various intentional communities—groups of people

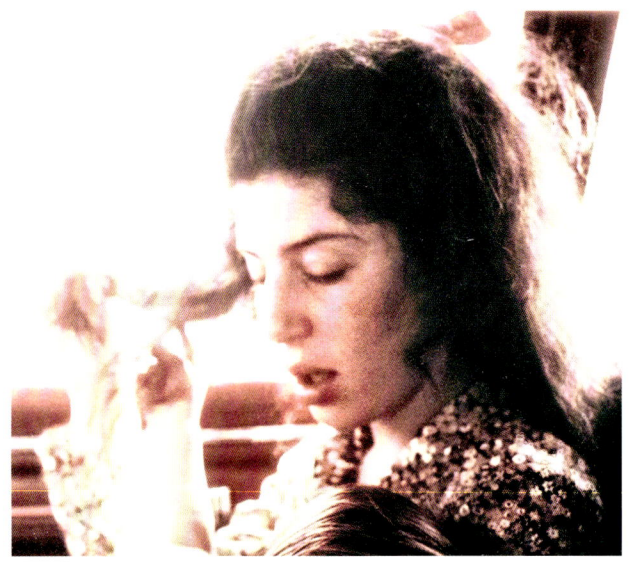

Linda in New Mexico, 1970

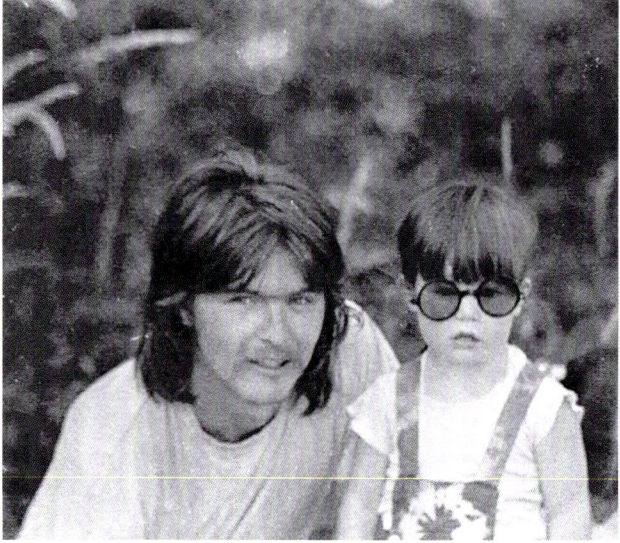

Joe and Rose, 1970

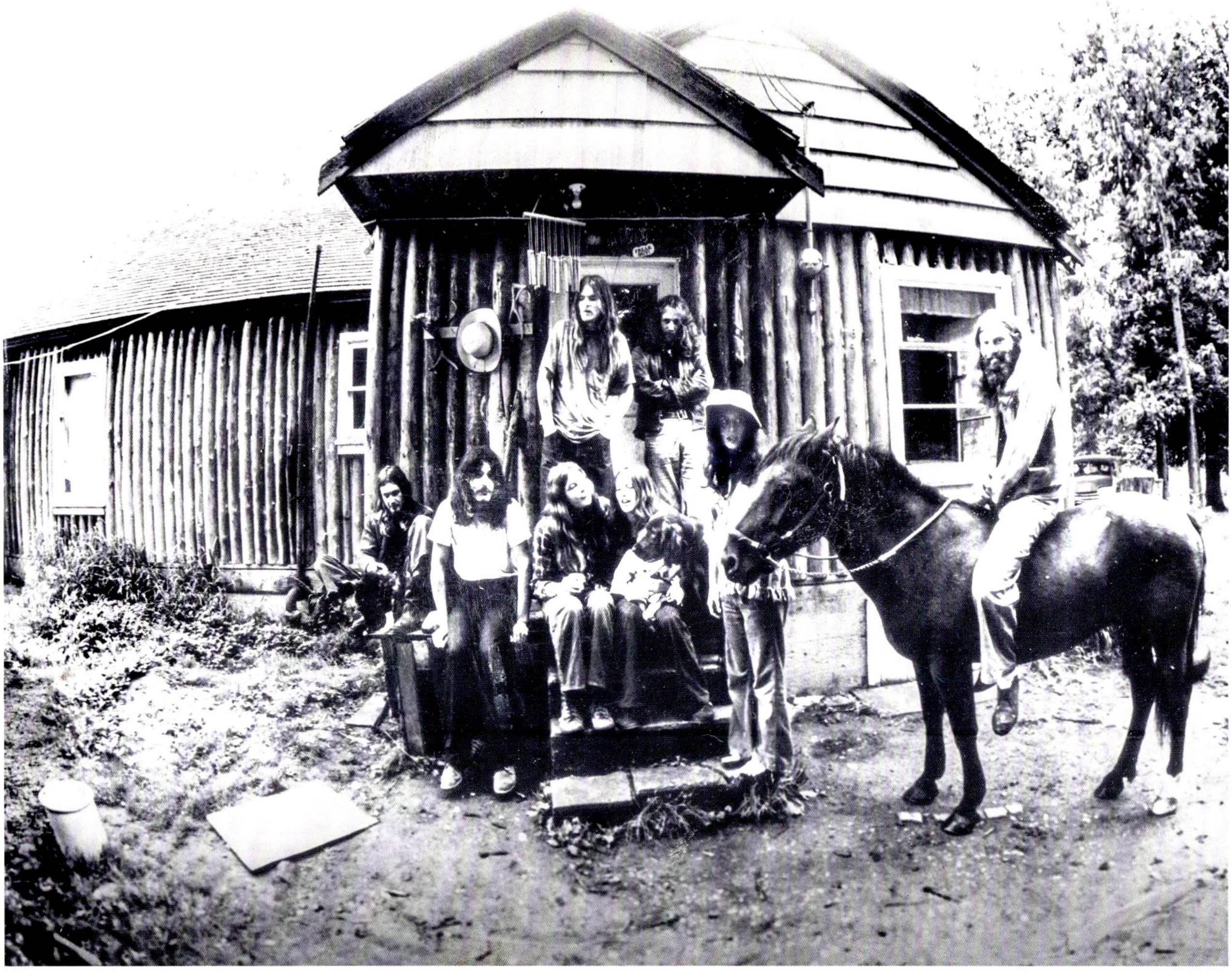

Joe, standing rear left, and Linda in hat, standing front right, at their communal house in Bothell, Washington, 1970

pursuing alternative, communal ways of living together—she grows increasingly interested in the Back to the Land movement and plant-based medicine. They move back to Seattle after a stray coal burns down their cabin.

December 6: Attends the Altamont Speedway Free Festival, where the Hells Angels, who were hired to work security, fatally stab concertgoer Meredith Hunter during a set by the Rolling Stones. Linda and Joe give a ride to Sue "Ruby" Blankenburg, who has run away from home to attend the concert. Blankenburg becomes a lifelong friend.

After a short time living in Bothell, she rents the defunct Rainier Yacht Club in Seattle with Joe and a large group of friends, including Ruby Blankenburg.

1971

Moves to a communal house on a farm in Duvall, Washington. While living in Duvall, Linda takes painting classes at the Factory of Visual Arts, an alternative art school. She soon discovers clay is a better fit for her restless energy. "I'm really ADD," she says. "Who wants to look at a white canvas? With clay, it's everything all over the place all at once!" Her instructors include Patti Warashina, David Furman, Mark Burns, Margaret Ford, and Anne Currier, all talented graduate students at Washington University who teach ceramics at the Factory as part of their degree. David, who makes humorous trompe l'oeil sculptures of workmen's tools, minigolf courses, and food, becomes a close friend and influence on Linda's approach to clay and pop culture. She learns china painting, which allows her to apply translucent layers of color, which she prefers to the opacity of most glazes. Drawn to the Back to the Land movement's ideals of self-sufficiency, she plans to make her own dishes, but makes a flying fish car hood ornament and a bottle in the shape of an ear of corn instead. She studies at the Factory through 1974.

1973

Parents Jean and Alfred Lighton separate. They divorce three years later, in 1976.

Joe briefly moves back in with Linda in Duvall, but his drug deals continue. He stores kilos of hash, enough to make a sofa, which they cover with a blanket. One night, burglars break in, tie up Linda and Rose, and steal the drugs at gunpoint. Linda is convinced karma will get them back, but the money is gone. She breaks up with Joe, whose addictive personality and various bad habits have grown unmanageable.

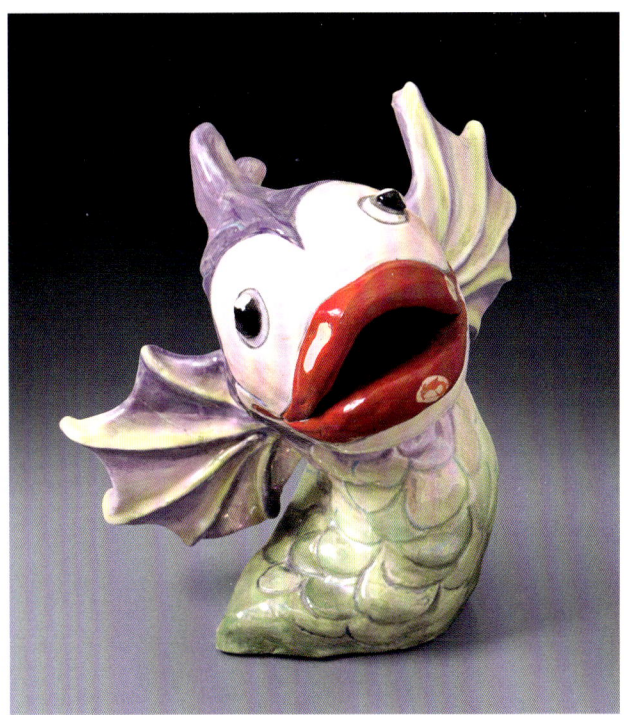

Linda Lighton, *Flying Fish*, c. 1972, glazed earthenware, china paint and luster, 7 ½ × 8 × 6 ½ in. (19.1 × 20.3 × 16.5 cm). A car hood ornament, it is Lighton's first ceramic sculpture.

Linda seeks the advice of Yogi Bhajan in New Mexico, who encourages her to meditate every day for a month. On the final day, David Furman, who is moving to California, offers her his rental outside Bothell, Washington. She leaves Joe for good and moves into the house with her friend Ruby Blankenburg.

1974

Divorces Joe.

A friend introduces her to Tim Brazzil and members of the Rainbow Family, a loose network of people interested in communal living, who are looking for land. Linda introduces them to her friend John Bixler, one of the Sky River organizers, who owns property on the Colville Indian Reservation, home to twelve confederated tribes, in north central Washington. Linda and some members of the Rainbow Family buy two hundred acres for a song and move there together. A long-standing interest in the Back to the Land movement becomes a way of life.

Linda, Tim, and Rose live in a lean-to made of salvaged wood, corrugated metal, and a tarp; the structure has no floor, three walls, and a fourth side open to the elements. There is neither running water nor electricity. With Tim, Linda digs a well, tills a vegetable garden, makes soap, and raises horses, turkeys, pigs, chickens, and goats (she is a

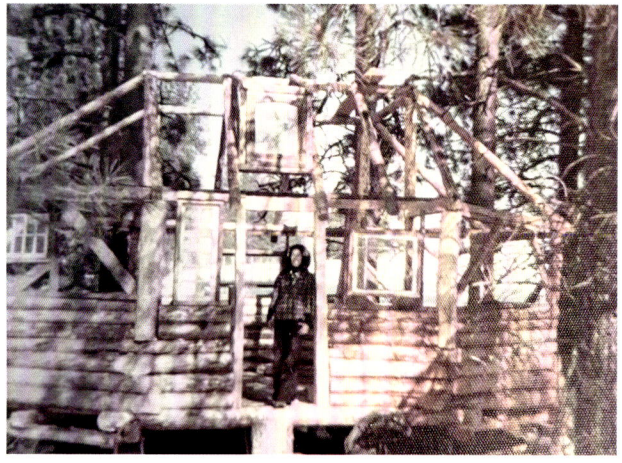

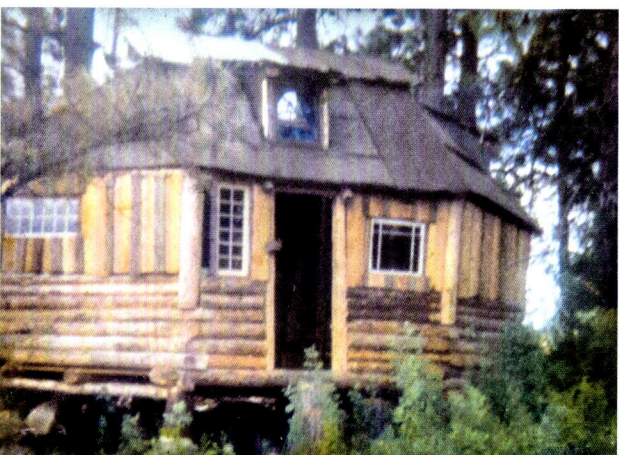

Lighton in the eight-sided log cabin she designed and built on the Colville Indian Reservation near Nespelem, Washington, 1974

The eight-sided log cabin, near completion, 1975

vegetarian until they kill the pig, Mrs. Nixon). She hunts elk and deer and tans the hides to make clothes and moccasins. Still, food is scarce. For six months, the group survives on rice and beans. To make money, Linda and Rose pick fruit in Yakima and Wenatchee, Washington.

Linda and Tim find work with the US Forest Service thinning trees. While logging in Fruitland, Washington, the family lives in an abandoned mine for several weeks.

"I spent a summer splitting cedar rails. My shoulders got so big I couldn't get a leotard over them!"

Tasked with clearing parts of an old-growth forest afflicted with parasitic mistletoe, Linda cuts down a large tree, its trunk twice as big as she can reach around. She feels so terrible that she quits the job that day. She still considers this the worst thing she's ever done.

Designs and builds an eight-sided house from standing dead timber, without using nails or power tools. By winter, the house has a floor, walls, and roof, but no insulation, and it is bitterly cold. On the days Rose goes to school, she rides to the bus stop on Skis, a wild Shetland pony Tim tamed, as the snow is sometimes five feet deep.

Linda and Tim move in with another couple for the winter, as it's too cold to live in the lean-to or the unfinished house. Ultimately, Linda discovers that living one's life as art leaves very little time to actually make art.

1975

Fall: Linda returns to school, taking ceramics classes at Western Washington State College (now Western Wash-

ington University) in Bellingham, Washington, through 1976.

Sells her first work—the untitled bottle in the shape of an ear of corn she had made at the Factory of Visual Arts—to Gerry and Gene Strauss, friends of her parents.

First solo exhibition at Gemini Gallery in Bellingham, Washington.

1976

Moves with Tim to Troy, Idaho, so he can pursue work as a logger.

She attends the University of Idaho, earning straight As and a spot in the Mortar Board society. She makes anthropomorphic teapots—a lumberjack, a weight lifter, a farmer—that reflect her interest in Americana and the ways in which the clothes we wear and tools we carry signal our professions and roles in society.

Impressed by her drawings and ceramics, Frank Cronk, her professor, suggests she attend graduate school at Washington State University in Pullman. She meets with the chair of the Fine Arts Department, but he tells her they already have a woman and turns her down.

Moves to a large pink house on a hill in the small lumber and farming community of Deary, Idaho (population 411). Her first standalone studio is in a canning shed beside the house (the kiln is in the living room).

Joe Dergan dies in a car accident in Puyallup, Washington, where he lived.

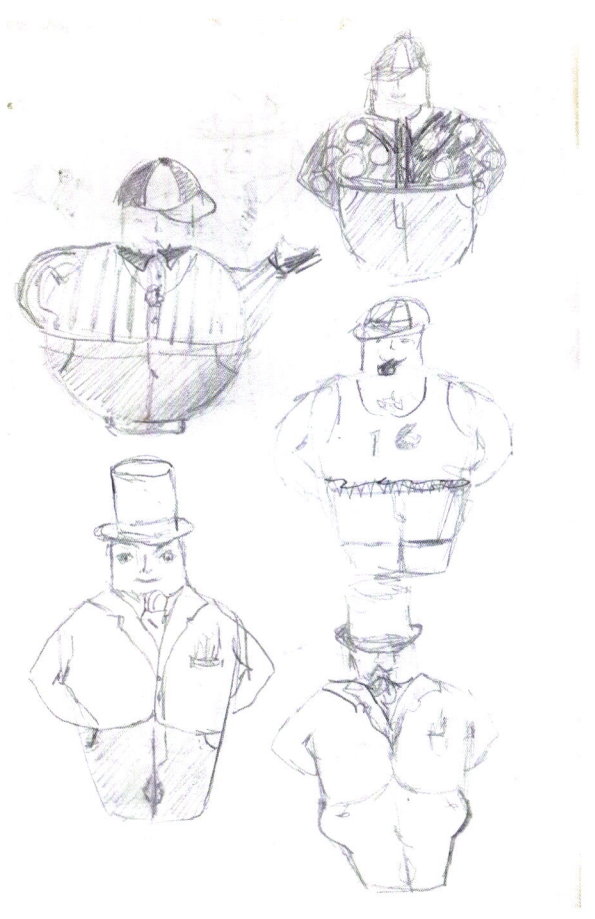

Lighton's drawings of figurative teapots: a referee, a jockey, a weight lifter, and a huntsman, c. 1977

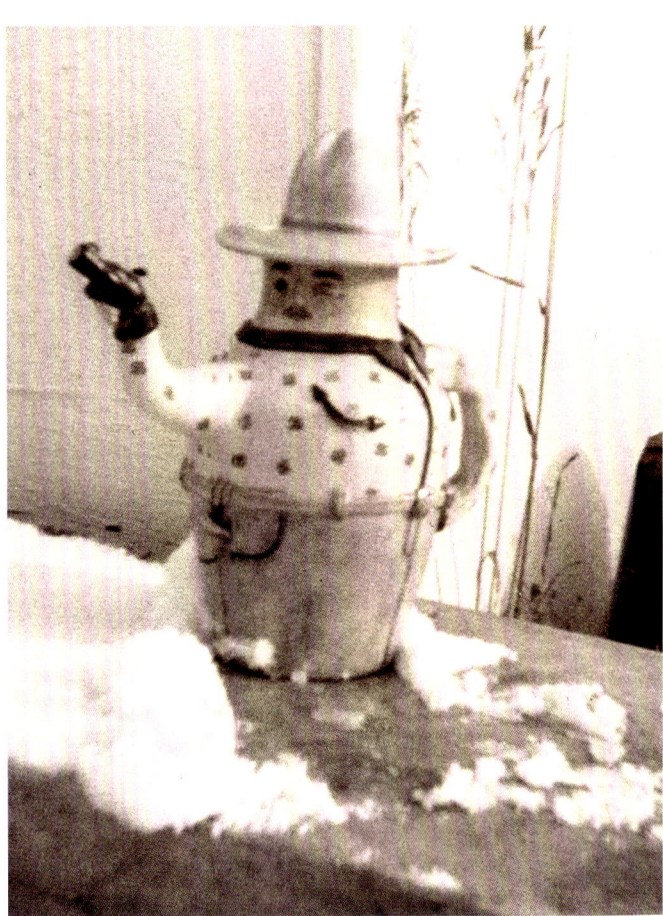

Linda Lighton, *Cowboy Teapot*, c. 1978

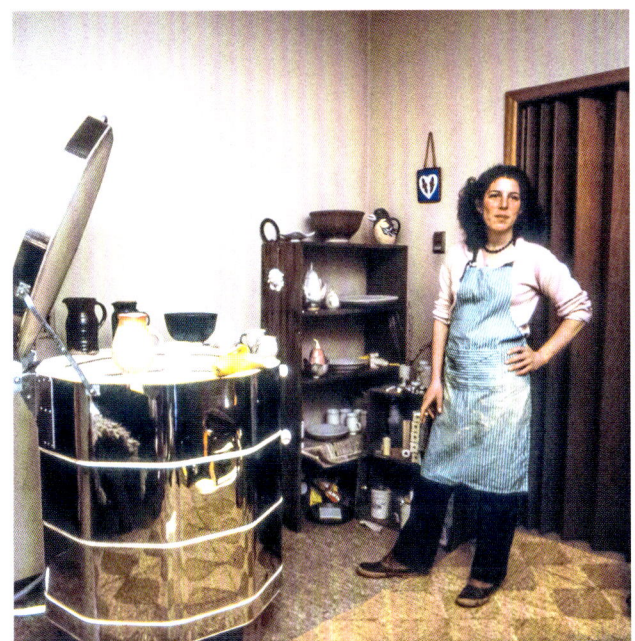

Lighton with her kiln and recently fired work, in the living room, Deary, Idaho, c. 1978

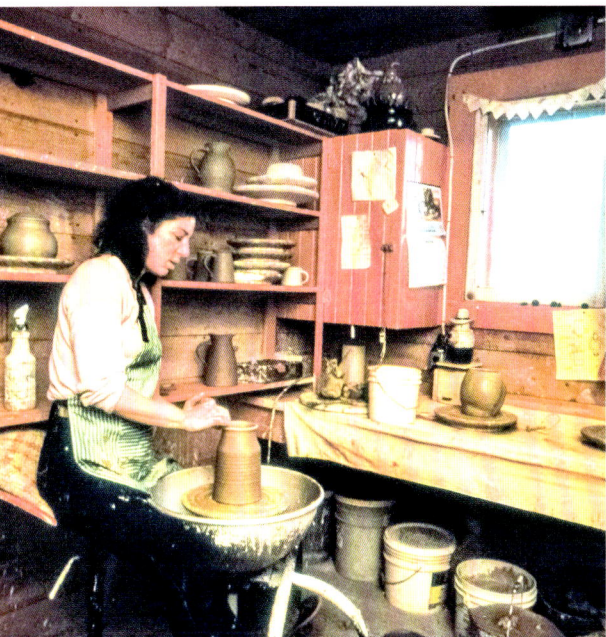

Lighton in her studio in Deary, throwing a vessel, c. 1978

1977

Alfred Lighton is mugged in a parking garage during an evening out with friends in Kansas City. The group hands over their wallets, but Alfred pursues the thieves. They shoot him in the neck, paralyzing him from the neck down. After extensive therapy, he is eventually able to walk with a cane.

1978

Exhibits bowls made using *neriage*, a Japanese technique for combining different-colored clays, in *Container Show*, a group show at the Cheney Cowles Museum in Spokane, Washington (now the Northwest Museum of Arts and Culture).

1979

First solo exhibition at L'Omega Gallery in Kansas City, where she will be the subject of a single-artist exhibition every year through 1983, mounting five shows in total. The first exhibition, which includes figurative teapots, bananas, and pea pods, attracts critical praise and sells out. (Linda had hoped to show her series of *Globes*, a series of lusterware with vaginal slits containing provocative contents, but the gallery owner, David L. Stewart, deemed them "too sexual" for his clients (pp. 80–81). He nonetheless remains a champion of her work.) With these sculptures, Linda demonstrates her talent for china painting, a technique typically used for decoration she uses instead to achieve rich, layered colors and subtle gradients. Bruce Hartman, who assisted at the gallery in 1980, later becomes the founding director of the Nerman Museum of Contemporary Art.

Summer: Decides to leave Deary, Idaho, so Rose can attend a better school. She considers living in Seattle, but, recalling her Washington friend group's enthusiasm for drugs, chooses Kansas City instead.

1980

Summer: Meets Lynn Adkins outside Deary, Idaho, at the wedding of her friends Diane Derr and David Adkins. Lynn, the groom's brother and a former intelligence officer in the US Army, is the school psychologist and director of special education for the rural Whitepine School District in northern Idaho.

Winter: Marries Lynn on December 27. They return to Deary after the wedding and live outside town in a saltbox house Lynn had built himself, where Linda has a separate studio. There she begins the *Americana* series, which portrays professional and blue-collar workers and housewives, sometimes through the tools of their trade

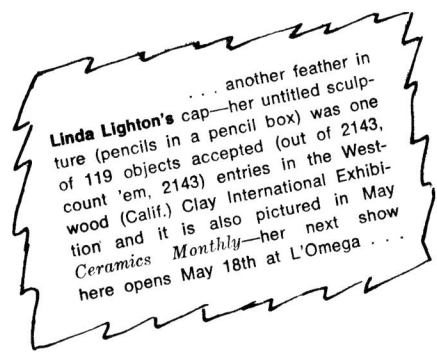

The Independent   MAY 3, 1980

. . . another feather in Linda Lighton's cap—her untitled sculpture (pencils in a pencil box) was one of 119 objects accepted (out of 2,143, count 'em, 2143) entries in the Westwood (Calif.) Clay International Exhibition and it is also pictured in May *Ceramics Monthly*—her next show here opens May 18th at L'Omega . . .

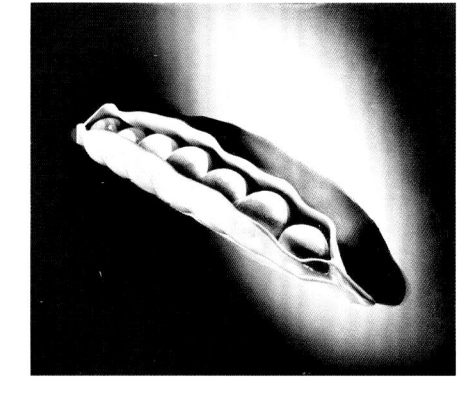

MAY 18 - JUNE 22

Linda Lighton
Psycho-Ceramics

Announcement in *The Independent* (Kansas City), May 3, 1980

Linda Lighton: *Psycho-Ceramics*, L'Omega Gallery exhibition catalogue, 1980

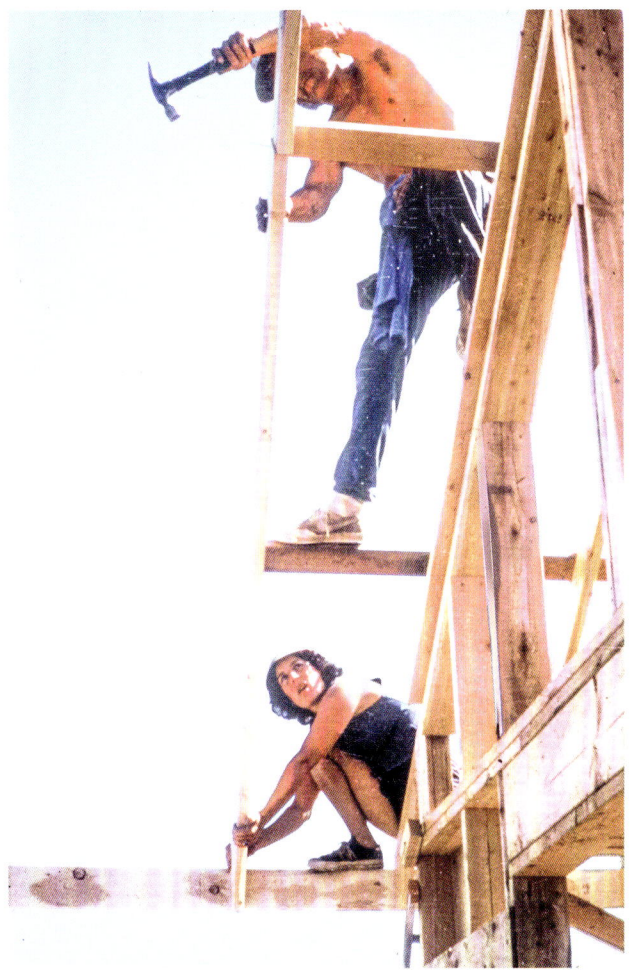

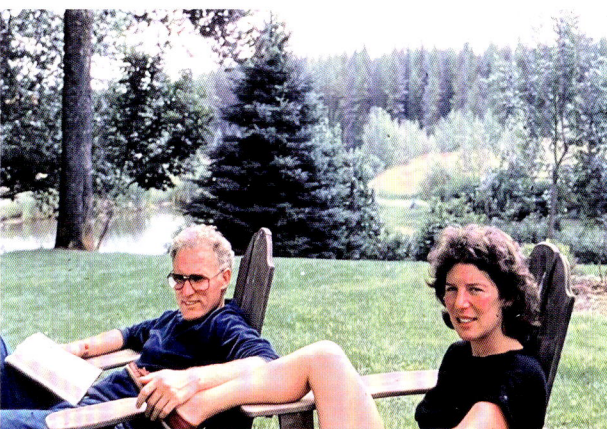

Lynn and Linda at their house outside Deary, Idaho, c. 1981

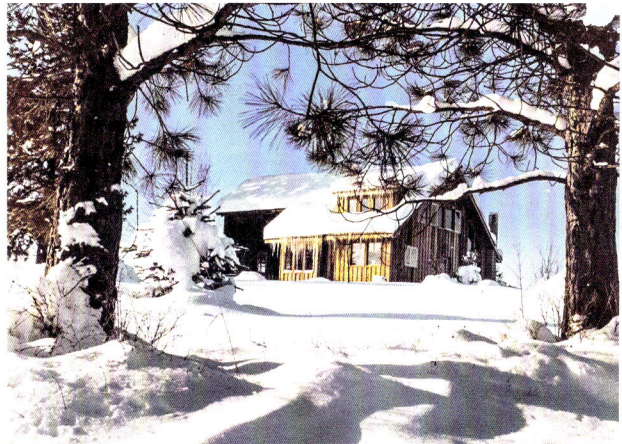

Linda, and Lynn's brother, David, working on the addition to the house in Idaho, 1981

The house outside Deary, showing the addition built by Lynn and Linda

(a battered black valise, for instance, embodies the country doctor on a house call) and the quotidian issues they face, from static cling to the price of gas. The series continues through 1987.

"I feel that humor plays an important role and is often an overlooked aspect in art."

1981

Lynn and Linda design and build an addition to the saltbox house, installing plumbing and wiring themselves. They remove the façade and double the footprint. The redesign wins an honorable mention in the Met Home of the Year competition the following year.

1982

Fall: Moves back to Kansas City, where there are better schools for Rose. Linda's studio and kiln are in the basement. Lynn briefly works at Woolf Brothers, the retail company founded by Linda's great-grandfather, but transitions to real estate, eventually owning and managing a group of residential rental buildings.

Solo exhibition at the Cheney Cowles Museum in Spokane, Washington.

Begins campaigning with Sybil Kahn and Myra Morgan to institute the One Percent for Art program, which requires that public building projects allocate one percent of construction costs to public art. Although the program has technically been in place in Kansas City for years, it has been used to underwrite landscaping and lighting instead of contemporary art.

Exhibits shirts and tools from the *Americana* series at Art Attack Gallery in Boise, Idaho. José Luis Rodriguez Guerra, one of the gallery's founders, is an artist, migrant farm worker, union organizer, and member of the Seattle Art Commission. The gallery shows West Coast artists, including Peter Voulkos, Sam Francis, and Luis Jiménez.

1984

Begins studying the tea ceremony at the Urasenke School of Chanoyu in Kansas City, continuing through 2016. Her interest stems, in part, from the phenomenal collection of Japanese ceramics at the Nelson-Atkins Museum in Kansas City, where the vessels are installed in a spare, tranquil space, and her interest in Japanese aesthetics. She becomes fascinated by the history of the tea ceremony and its philosophy, in which life, art, food, and architecture are all connected.

December: Her mother, Jean Lighton, dies of skin cancer at age 69.

1985

November: *Beyond Ourselves,* Batz/Lawrence Gallery, Kansas City. Exhibits works created in response to her mother's death, in which pyramids missing their tops symbolize transitions and a sense of infinity (pp. 88–89). Sometimes, she notes, it's necessary to break apart an old monument in order to enter a new phase (pp. 91–92).

"In physics we learn that you can't destroy matter. Perhaps a metamorphosis from life to death to life happens. So I have built monumental forms and then broken out of them."

Begins writing for the *National Council on Education for the Ceramic Arts Journal.* She will be a regular contributor through 1994.

1986

Thanks to Linda's work with Sybil Kahn and Myra Morgan, a new administrator is hired to ensure that the One Percent for Art program is, in fact, used for contemporary art commissions in Kansas City.

1987

July: Her daughter Rose moves to New York to attend New York University.

September: Returns to college at the Kansas City Art Institute, enrolling in the Ceramics Department chaired by Ken Ferguson. Asked to make a vessel, she creates a *Building Person,* a wry comment on how bodies are containers for selves and cities are containers for bodies. Her professor and peers miss the symbolism, and the feedback is harsh. Confident in her work, she transfers to the

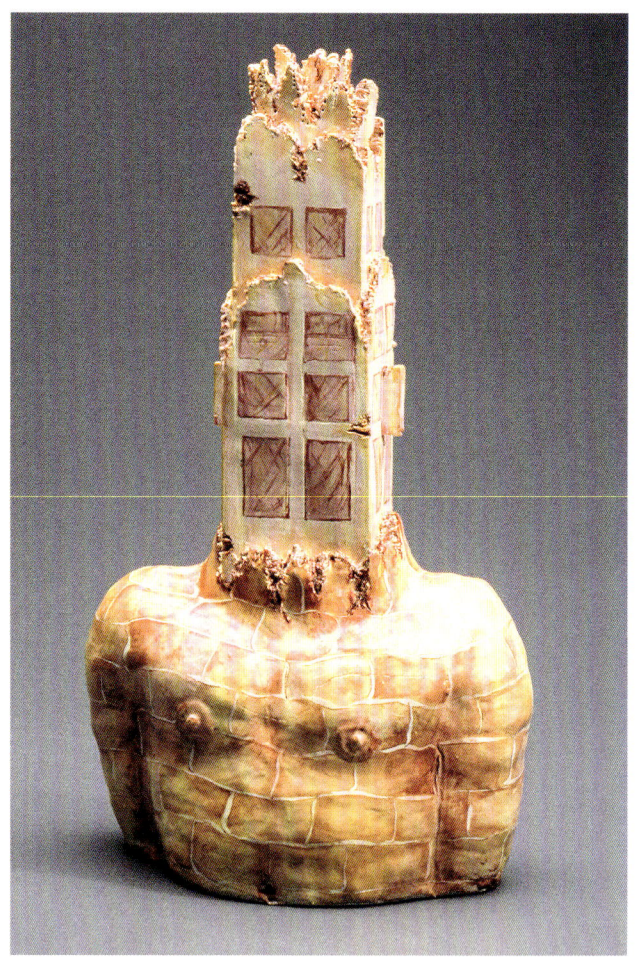

Linda Lighton, *Body Building, Urban Armour,* 1987, glazed earthenware and china paint, 21 × 12 × 6½ in. (53.3 × 30.5 × 16.5 cm)

Sculpture Department chaired by Dale Eldred, where she finds a more welcoming, experimental environment. Dale tells his students that they can do anything, work as big as they want, and that there are no rules.

November: Solo exhibition at the Batz/Lawrence Gallery of works from the series *And She Did Not Live Happily Ever After... but She Did Live.* Reflecting on her purpose in the absence of Rose, she realizes she is no longer a "mother" in the daily sense she has been for the past eighteen years. "It is no longer an effective identity," she writes. Women's roles, in the broader cultural sense, have also transformed. "I'm sure we no longer lie to ourselves about the creativity of housework," she writes. "We clean from a different viewpoint now. It is no longer an end in itself. We are now trying to explode the myth of these roles." Addresses these personal and societal shifts through still-life tableaux with contemporary elements. The works include *Static Cling* (1983), a trompe l'oeil pile of rumpled laundry, and *What the Bridal Consultant Never Tells You* (1987; p. 43), a still life composed of household cleaning products, both glazed white.

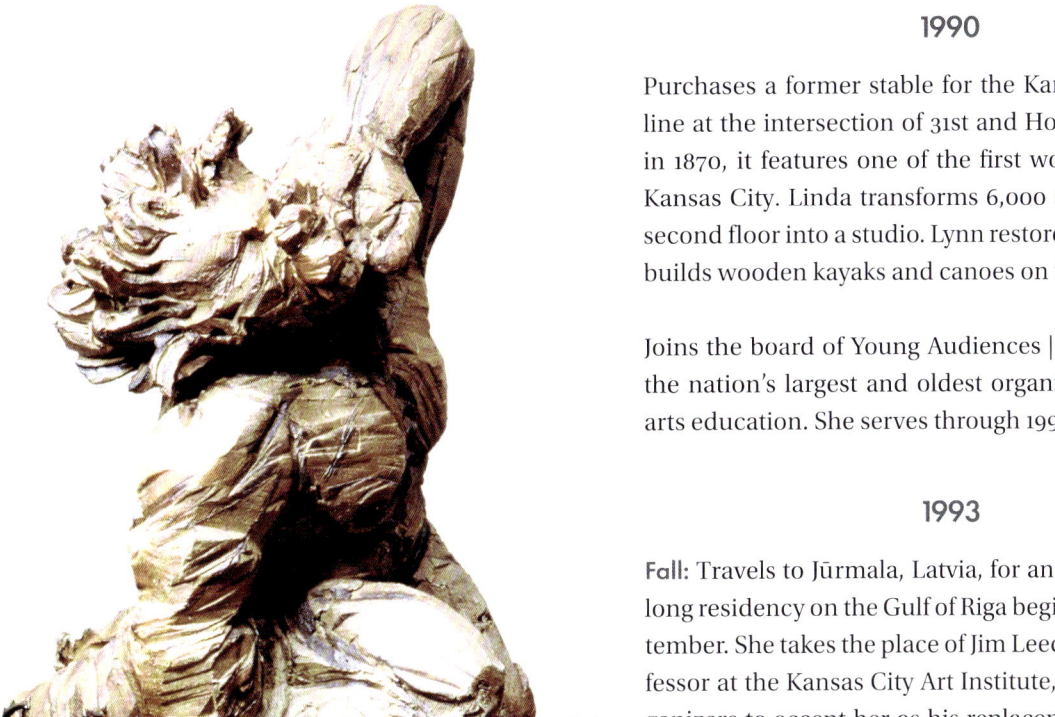

Linda Lighton, *Anguish*, 1989, stoneware, 28 × 24 × 23 in.
(71.1 × 61 × 58.4 cm)

"I am trying to strike a balance between a funky, hands-on approach and the delicate quality of European porcelain. I would like the art to speak about life over the knowledge of art."

Becomes a founder, executive board member, and major fundraiser for the Kansas City Contemporary Arts Center (now the Leedy-Voulkos Art Center).

1989

Graduates with honors from the Sculpture Department of the Kansas City Art Institute.

Makes figurative work using a wooden two-by-four, knife, cheese cutter, and ceramic carving tool. Unlike previous series built by hand or thrown on the wheel, these works are beaten and carved.

Linda Lighton, Dorry Gates Gallery, Kansas City, Missouri. Shows *Crystalline Pencil* (1977), but Dorry hides it from some visitors, convinced it's too sexy.

1990

Purchases a former stable for the Kansas City streetcar line at the intersection of 31st and Holmes Streets. Built in 1870, it features one of the first wooden elevators in Kansas City. Linda transforms 6,000 square feet on the second floor into a studio. Lynn restores vintage cars and builds wooden kayaks and canoes on the ground floor.

Joins the board of Young Audiences | Arts for Learning, the nation's largest and oldest organization devoted to arts education. She serves through 1999.

1993

Fall: Travels to Jūrmala, Latvia, for an impactful month-long residency on the Gulf of Riga beginning in mid-September. She takes the place of Jim Leedy, her former professor at the Kansas City Art Institute, who urges the organizers to accept her as his replacement. "I have been impressed by her sincere devotion to her art and her professional attitude," he wrote. "Her art is her life, and she lives it daily." She is the US representative among sixty artists from countries around the world specializing in craft media, including ceramicists, textile artists, and enamelers. During much of the Soviet era, painting and sculpture had been subject to state demands and brutal censorship, while artists using less prestigious media—such as clay, fiber, and enamel—enjoyed greater freedom.

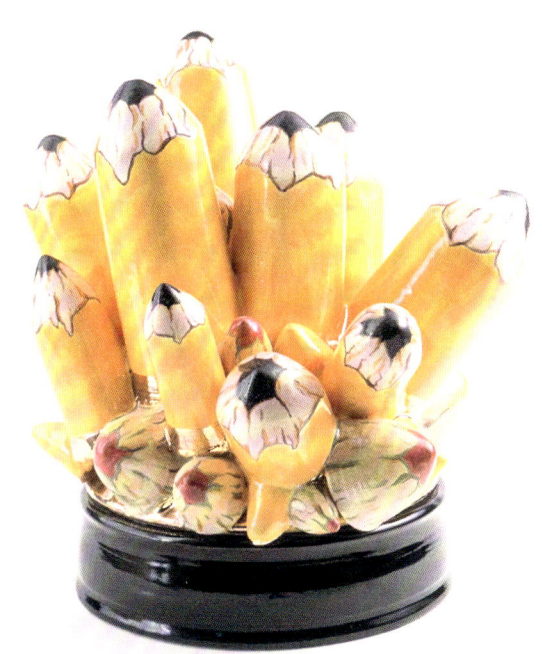

Linda Lighton, *Crystalline Pencil,* 1977, glazed earthenware with china paint and luster, 15 × 14 × 14 in. (38.1 × 35.6 × 35.6 cm)

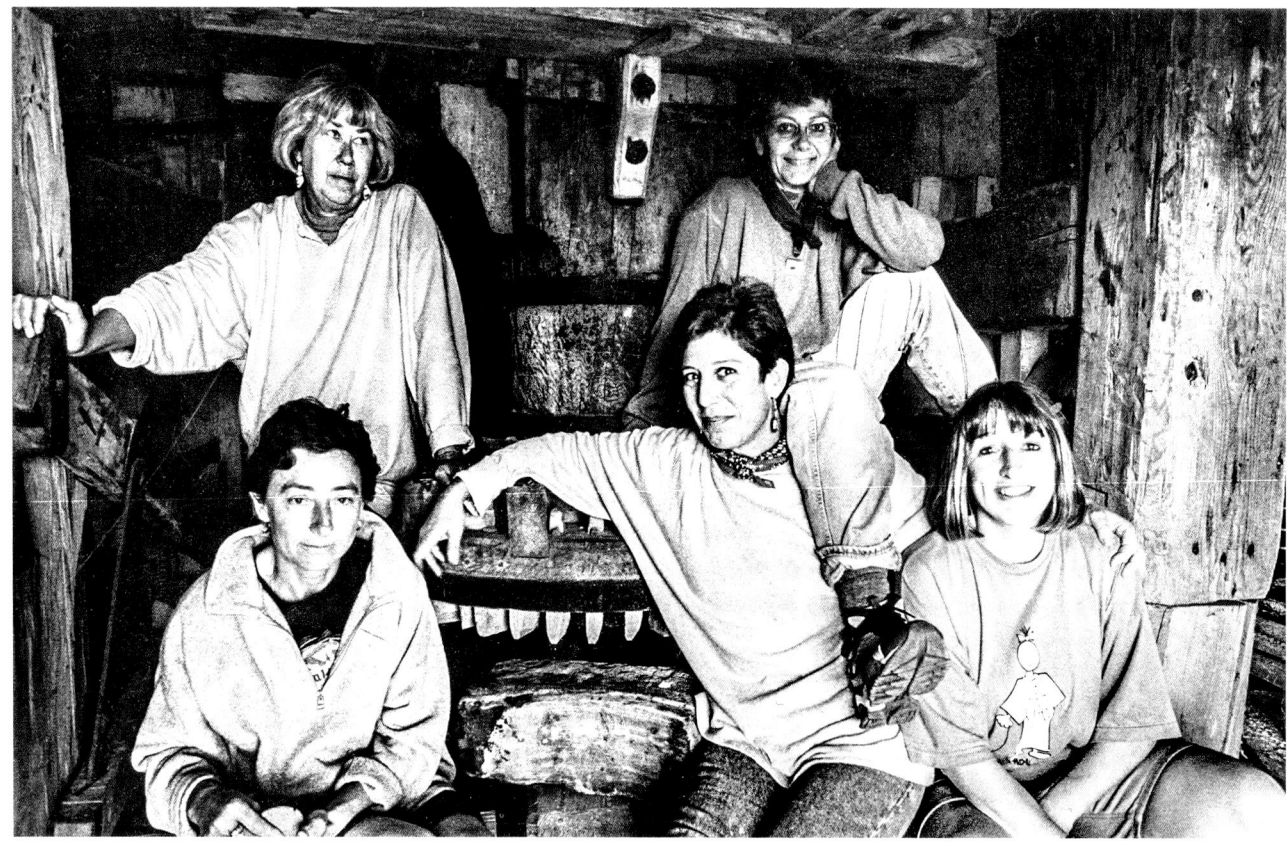

Lighton (center) in Latvia with fellow artist residents Bebe Walsh, Jytte Gaihede, Hara Angelidis, and Yvonne Melhuish, 1993

Latvia feels incredibly foreign. There is no heat or hot water when Linda arrives, and electricity is scant. Paper and other art materials are scarce, as is food. "Everything's black and white," she remembers. "It's so gray there. And my jeans would have wrapped around every man twice—everybody was skinnier than anything. There wasn't anything to eat."

Still, the people she meets are warm, thoughtful, and eager to see contemporary art. Interviews with artists in Latvian and Russian regularly appear on television and radio programs and in local newspapers. Exhibition coverage is a standard part of the evening news. Her time there convinces her of the power of art to bridge cultural differences. She becomes close friends with artists Pēteris Martinsons and Ilona Romule, both Latvian, and Hendrik Schink, who is German. Looking back, she remembers "the joy of making art with other people; it is a language without words." Stunning, too, is the generosity of the residency. It doesn't cost participants money, nor does it require the artist leave a work behind, unlike many residencies in the United States.

The residency culminates with an exhibition on the beach. She exhibits *Latvian Security Guard* (1993; p. 48),

a sculpture combining the seventeenth-century Powder Tower in Riga and the local green police uniform, as well as several "sex toys," heart-shaped sculptures with movable pieces that can be placed inside vaginal slits surrounded by thorns.

"Thank you for helping me to have a wonderful time in Jurmala. Thank you for helping me to communicate and for so many good laughs.

I am overwhelmed to leave behind so many lovely Latvians with so little, while I just step into the world with so much stuff and so many choices. I feel a great relief to come back here and such a sadness for [the] many extras and services my new friends are deprived of. I wish (want) to help in some way but I am not sure what is appropriate. Do you have any ideas?"
— Letter to Hendrik Schink after the residency

She begins to imagine a residency program of her own.

Tea ceremony lecture and presentation, Japanese Language Festival, Rockhurst College, Kansas City, Missouri. Linda goes on to lecture on and present the Japanese tea ceremony at venues including the Consulate General of Japan (1994), US Department of Agriculture (1997), Nelson-Atkins Museum (1999), and the Japanese Language Festival, University of Missouri – Kansas City (1997–2000).

1994

Solo exhibition curated by Hendrik Schink at Galerie Zopf in Rheinsberg Castle in Rheinsberg, Germany. Nam June Paik and Joseph Beuys have concurrent exhibitions. From there, Linda takes the train across Poland to Lithuania.

Attends the International Bone China Symposium at the Jiesia Bone China Factory in Kaunas, Lithuania. She spends August and half of September learning to work with bone china, an extremely fragile clay that must be fired inside molds, responding to the theme of "non-traditional teapots" with nineteen other local and international artists. It's a rare opportunity—there are only a handful of bone china factories in the world—but it's also the most challenging residency of her career.

Kaunas had been occupied by Russia until 1988. It was a "closed town" during the Soviet period, subject to severe restrictions and rigorous checks on residents and visitors. It had only recently opened when Linda arrives. The bone china factory where she works is across from a prison and an hour-long walk from the housing project where she stays. Everything is in Cyrillic and her translator, who is openly antisemitic, refuses to help her after she tells him she's Jewish. Every day, trucks deliver cow bones, often bloody, to the factory to make the clay.

Nonetheless, Linda creates *Branch Tea Set* (1994), a bone china tea set with handles and finials in the shape of wooden branches, which also form the border of the

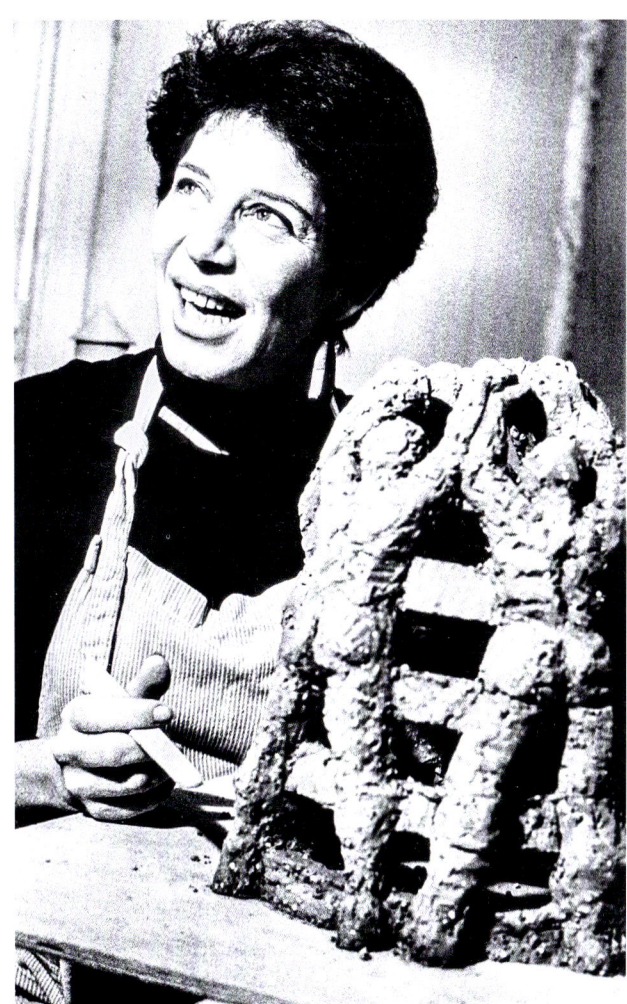

Linda with a maquette for a figurative gazebo, in Latvia, 1993

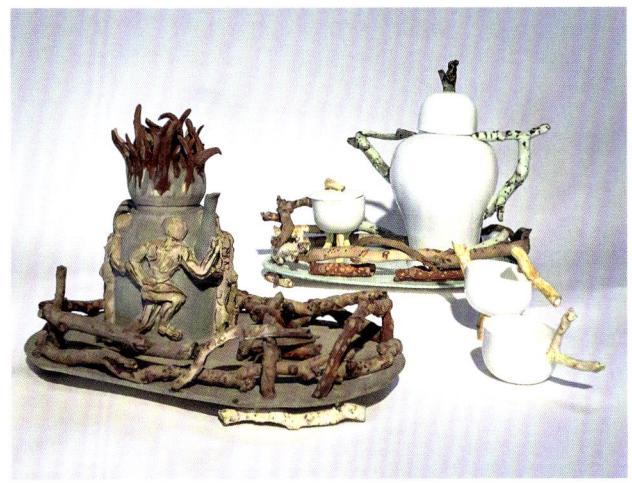

Musing on Global Village Tea Set, made from local Lithuanian clay, and *Branch Tea Set*, made from bone china in Lithuania

tray, and *Musing on Global Village Tea Set* (1994), made with a coarser local clay from Kaunas. A ring of figures dance around a teapot with a flaming lid, a metaphor for the global community. The residency concludes with an exhibition, *Ideas in Bone China*, at the Museum of Contemporary Art in Kaunas, Lithuania, which travels to the Museum of Applied Art in Vilnius and the Museum of Applied Art in Riga.

Bill Clinton presents Young Audiences, the arts education organization she supports as a board member, with a National Medal of Arts.

1995

Linda Lighton, Morgan Gallery, Kansas City, Missouri. Linda shows maquettes for figurative fountains and gazebos made of clay. The gallery is an important Midwestern hub for contemporary art from both coasts. Robert Rauschenberg and Jasper Johns show there, as do the ceramic artists Robert Arneson, Ken Ferguson, and Peter

Voulkos. Linda continues to show with Myra Morgan through 1999.

Works on a proposal for a bistate cultural tax to fund arts and culture in the Kansas City metropolitan area. Thought to be the first of its kind in the US, the tax (one eighth of a cent collected in Missouri and Kansas), passes in 1996. Over the next five years, between 1997 and 2002, the tax raises $121 million for the arts and facilitates the restoration of Union Station, the city's historic rail hub, and the creation of a new science museum inside the space.

1996

Summer: Attends the International Workshops of Ceramic Art in Tokoname, one of Japan's most important ceramics regions. Known for hard-fired, red-brown vessels with dark green natural wood ash glaze, Tokoname is home to one of the Six Ancient Kilns of Japan, which remain in use today. Linda uses a white and granular local clay to produce flowers and eggplant bulbs. She is one of sixteen participants from North America, Europe, and Asia who arrive in late July. The workshop culminates a month later with an exhibition at the annual Tokoname Ceramic Festival. More than 200,000 people visit.

At the end of the trip, Linda develops peritonitis and is rushed to the hospital for an emergency oophorectomy. Lynn travels to Japan to be with her. Linda spends a month recovering in the maternity ward.

1997

Summer: Curates *Wild Woman Salon* with Lynn Huber (July 11 – August 30) at Morgan Gallery in Kansas City, Missouri. The show includes Patti Warashina, Sylvia Plimack Mangold, and Miriam Schapiro, among forty-odd women artists.

1997–1998

Attends classes at Sogetsu School of Ikebana in Kansas City, learning the Japanese art of flower arrangement.

1998

Summer: Attends the 2nd International Ceramics Symposium at the Artists' Union of Latvia in Zvārtava, Latvia (August 4–23), led by her friend, the prominent Latvian ceramic artist Pēteris Martinsons, at Zvārtava Castle, a center for arts education, workshops, and art symposia.

Linda is one of thirteen foreigners accepted and the only artist from the United States. Gives china-painting demonstrations and creates work in the soda wood-fire kiln and raku kiln. She leaves several works behind for the Latvian Artists' Union. The president of Latvia attends the residency exhibition (August 21 – September 4) at the Gallery of the Artists' Union of Latvia.

1999

Linda's father, Alfred Lighton, dies of cancer on January 20.

Linda and Lynn buy a house in Friday Harbor on San Juan Island in Washington, where her friend and former housemate Ruby Blankenburg lives. The nudibranchs and tubeworms underneath the docks, with their audacious forms and brazen colors, inspire new bodies of work. Lynn takes up sailboat racing in earnest, and the couple becomes active on the Northwest regatta circuit, competing fifteen times in the Swiftsure Lightship Classic. The race, which begins and ends in Victoria, British Columbia, can last up to three days.

Sensuality Is Its Own Reward, Morgan Gallery, Kansas City, Missouri. The show includes large flowers and sensual bulbs.

"I want them to reveal the spirit rather than the physical in our daily lives. These bulbs, pods and organic forms are about life unfolding, families, birth, growing, shedding old skins, emerging, branching out and death. Of course, sex is an important part of it all."

2000

Embarks on the *Divas* series, in which anthropomorphic interpretations of rare Pacific Northwest orchids embody strong women and the generative power of sexuality.

"I want to make gorgeous, elegant and sublime work, but I have seen the world. I need to laugh. I want to reveal a bit of the terror and vulgarity in life. I know that sex and nature are driving forces and must be acknowledged as such."

Linda Lighton, Kansas City Jewish Museum, Overland Park, Kansas.

Joins the Advisory Board of the National Council on Education for the Ceramic Arts (NCECA), serving through 2003.

Submits work to the First World Ceramic Biennale, the main event of the World Ceramic Exposition and one of the medium's most prestigious international competitions. An enormous event, it includes every genre of ceramics from the figurative to the functional, the traditional to the mass-produced. Her work is selected among entries from more than seventy countries and wins an honorable mention. Six million visitors attend the Biennale exhibitions in Icheon, South Korea (August 10 – October 28).

Donates *Diva* (2001) to the Icheon World Ceramic Center, Kyonggi Province, Korea.

September: Tours Korean ceramic exhibitions, museums, cultural sites, and studios before participating in the International Ceramic Symposium, a three-day bilingual scholarly meeting devoted to the past, present, and future of ceramic arts.

2002

Inspired by her experiences abroad, especially her time in Latvia, Linda establishes the Lighton International Artist Exchange Program (LIAEP).

"If you go to another country and you can't speak the language, you have to rely on people and then you really make true friends with them. And that's how I got the idea to start the Lighton International Artist Exchange Program."

The program provides support for mid-career visual artists and arts professionals, Midwestern artists in particular, to travel to residencies and artist communities abroad and for international visual artists to come and work in the United States. With LIAEP, Linda hopes to foster the kinds of lasting friendships and fresh perspectives she found through her own experiences abroad. Funds the project with assistance from the Kansas City Community Foundation, which manages charitable giving to nonprofit organizations. (Upon his death, her father, Alfred, had left all his money to the Kansas City Community Foundation.) Janet Simpson, executive director of the Kansas City Artists Coalition, is LIAEP's first director and helps launch the program.

"Artists are great ambassadors. They speak a language without words. By going to a foreign country we can put a face on America that is not seen in the news."

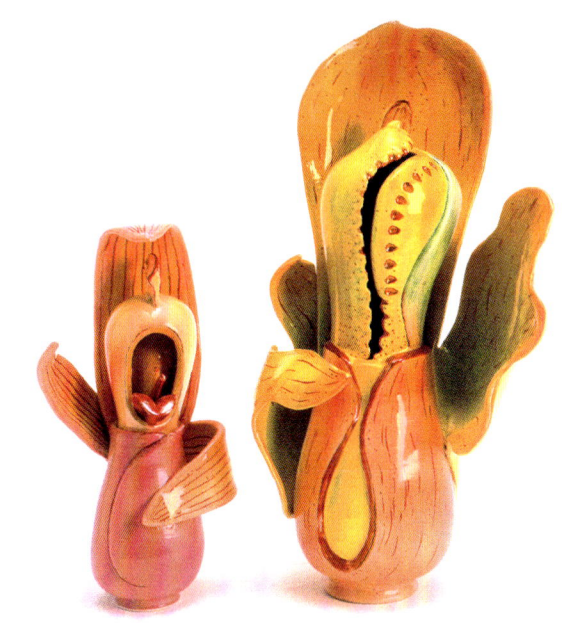

Linda Lighton

Invitation to *Linda Lighton and David Furman: Male/Female* at Belger Arts Center, Kansas City, Missouri, 2002

March: First international residency brings Pēteris Martinsons from Riga, Latvia, to Kansas City. Pēteris presents an exhibition at the Kansas City Artists Coalition and gives lectures and workshops at local universities and a slide presentation at NCECA. More than 3,000 visitors see his exhibition or attend an event.

Linda Lighton and David Furman: Male/Female, UMKC Belger Arts Center, Kansas City, Missouri (March 13 – May 23). Exhibits works from the *Divas* series.

2003

The Spencer Museum of Art, Lawrence, Kansas, acquires *Artichoke* (2001; p. 108).

Daum Museum of Contemporary Art, Sedalia, Missouri, acquires *Thistle* (2000; p. 104).

Summer: Travels to Hungary for a month-long residency at the International Ceramics Studio (Nemzetközi Kerámia Stúdió), a center for ceramic art on the Great

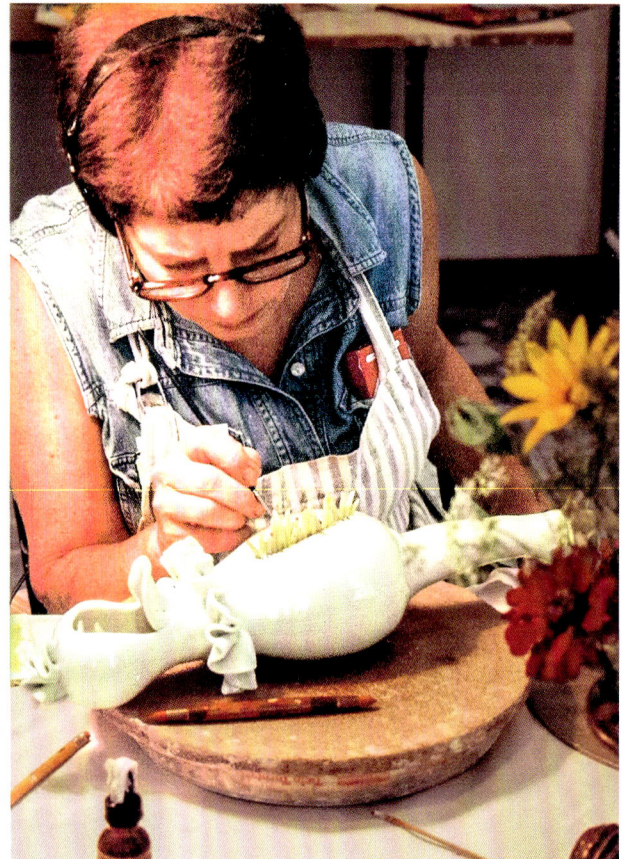

Lighton applying china paint to *Tenacious Tubeworm* at her studio in Kecskemét, Hungary, 2003

"These works are not about angst, anxiety, resistance, or strife; they are about the gentle spiral of life unfurling. These flowers are about the fecundity of life, growth, birth, maturity, opportunity and hope, chance, the dance of life, and regeneration."

August 26 – September 4: Attends the International Academy of Ceramics General Assembly in Icheon and Seoul, South Korea, as an invited guest. Visits exhibitions, cultural events, performances, artist studios, museums, and lectures on Korean art.

December: The Nerman Museum of Contemporary Art, Overland Park, Kansas, acquires *Diva Marilyn* (2000; p. 58) and *Dame Edna* (2002; p. 123).

"I am interested in the life force, a dangerous beauty that entails seduction, sexual prowess, moaning hormones. I want to celebrate the spirit of life, edging toward figuration, beckoning seductively, shouting, singing opera for recognition, and beckoning the viewer to come closer, come hither."

Hungarian Plain in Kecskemét, Hungary, established in 1976 by Hungarian artists who felt culturally and ideologically isolated by the Soviet regime. LIAEP provides grants for four other artists, two Europeans and two from Kansas City, to attend as well. Linda works with Limoges and Herend porcelain and begins work on *Tenacious Tubeworm* (2003–5; p. 127), which she finishes in Kansas City, and *Camouflora Small* (2004; p. 169), a flower with a bullet stamen. The museum and gallery of the International Ceramics Studio acquires a large flower for its collection.

Linda and Janet Simpson meet with the mayor of Kecskemét and the administration of the residency and together implement an exchange program with the United States. LIAEP sponsors two artists to work at the residency every year for the next three years.

2004

February: *Hothouse Exotica* at Sherry Leedy Contemporary Art, Kansas City, Missouri. Linda shows several large works from the *Flowers* series.

2005

February through March: First artist-in-residence at the Benyamini Foundation for Ceramic Art in Tel Aviv, Israel. Her time there concludes with an exhibition, in which she shows a *Flower*, a *Diva*, and a *Bulb*. Leads a master class on china painting and luster techniques, including a lecture on the history of china painting and its contemporary applications, and a class on combining nylon fiber with clay in the Negev Desert. Linda learned the second technique from the feminist ceramic artist Marilyn Levine, who was an important influence on her work. Combined with nylon, the clay behaves like fabric and can be manipulated into forms it wouldn't normally tolerate.

The trip reminds her of the importance of travel and her reasons for establishing LIAEP: "[Being in a new place] helps you get in touch with all your senses and see things as if for the first time. This enlarges you as an artist and by making a foreign friend we are making peace, one person at a time."

Linda is awarded membership in the International Academy of Ceramics, a selective association of professional ceramic artists which is based in Geneva, Switzerland.

Joins the Visual Arts Consortium in Kansas City, an organization dedicated to making Kansas City a magnet for artists and arts professionals. The organization provides support and planning for the Nelson-Atkins Museum Bloch Building addition, the Lyric Opera of Kansas City, the Nerman Museum of Contemporary Art, and the downtown Power & Light District, including the Kansas City Convention Center.

2006

Participates in three major exhibitions abroad: the Bienal Internacional de Ceràmica de Manises at the Museu de Ceràmica de Manises in Valencia, Spain; the 20th Icheon Ceramic Festival in Icheon, South Korea, and *World Clay: IAC Members Exhibition* at the Latvian National Museum of Art in Riga.

2007

Completes a one-month residency in Fuping, China, where she uses Tang tomb clay and historical green and orange glazes. The residency is supported by I-Chi Hsu, a major supporter of the ceramic arts in China, who established the Fuping Pottery Village, an international ceramic arts center with museums dedicated to individual countries. Linda creates work for the new American museum, which opens July 4, using local materials and facilities.

Visits Beijing, the Forbidden City, the Great Wall, and the Terracotta Army of Qin Shi Huang, as well as various ceramics collections and manufacturing hubs, including the Shanxi Art Museum, Yaozhou Kiln Museum, the historic Chen Lu pottery village, the "ceramic capital" of Jingdezhen, and Shanghai. The trip has a profound impact on her work, from the sinuous forms and recesses of

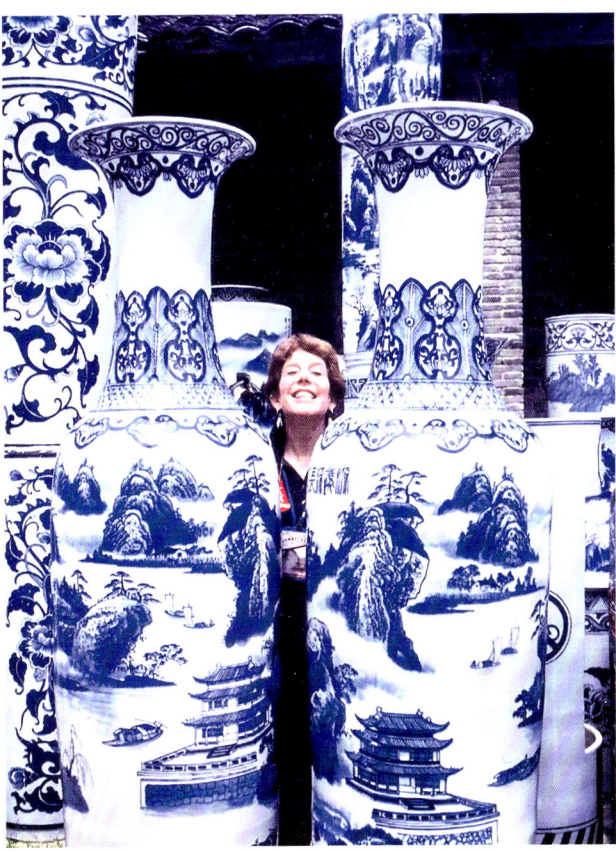

Lighton in Jingdezhen, the eastern Chinese city known as the "ceramics capital" of China, 2007

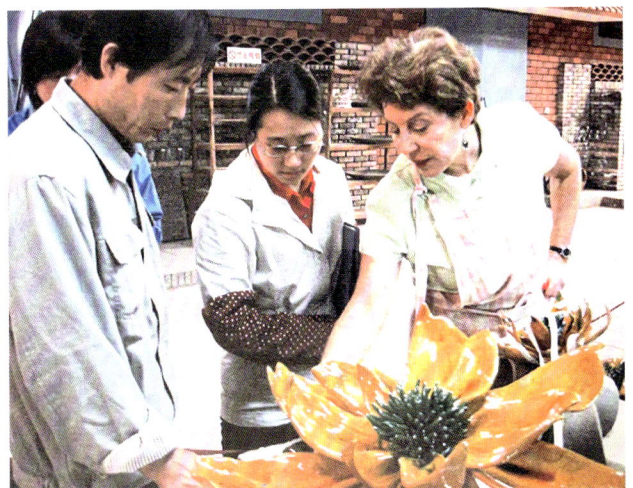

Lighton with a large flower sculpture she created at her studio in Fuping, China, 2007

the scholars' rocks to the intricacy of the jewelry and adornment of everyday clothing. She carries the radiant shades of Tang Dynasty tomb pottery into her own work as well as the luminous jade and sea-foam greens of the celadon in Chen Lu.

The Kemper Museum in Kansas City, Missouri, acquires *Mapped Flower* (1995; p. 99).

2008

Boundless Joy, Carter Art Center Gallery, Metropolitan Community College – Penn Valley, Kansas City, Missouri (January 31 – March 14).

"My sculptures are defined by their sensuality, fertility and empowered sexuality."

The Nelson-Atkins Museum of Art acquires *Sea Sponge* (2007; p. 125) and *Diva Laura* (2001; p. 60), an homage to Laura Hockaday, a social justice advocate and writer for the Kansas City magazine *The Independent*.

Musée Ariana, Geneva, Switzerland, acquires *Diva Kay* (2001), a gift of the International Academy of Ceramics.

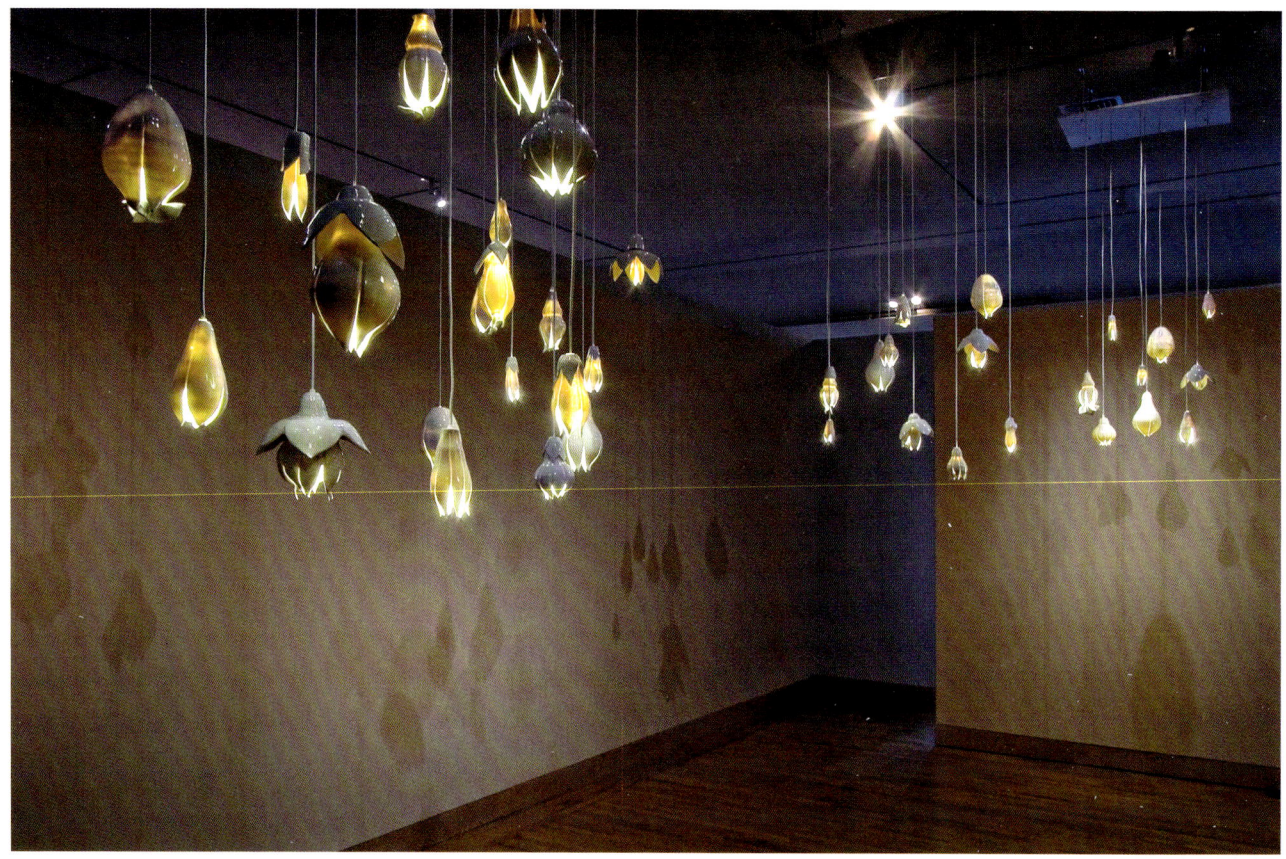

Lighton's immersive *Luminous* installation at Greenlease Gallery, Kansas City, Missouri, 2010

September: International Academy of Ceramics Art Show, Xi'an Exhibition Center, Xi'an, China.

2009

Receives the 2009 Missouri Arts Award, the state's highest honor for individuals and institutions who have made profound and lasting contributions to the cultural and artistic landscape of Missouri. Governor Matthew Blunt and First Lady Melanie Blunt present the award in Jefferson City, Missouri.

Receives an Inspiration Grant, an award designed to support ambitious projects involving growth, risk, and change, from the Metropolitan Arts Council of Kansas City. The grant supports *Luminous*, an exhibition held the following year.

2010

The Spencer Museum of Art, Lawrence, Kansas, acquires *White Trash* (2003).

Spring: *Luminous*, Greenlease Gallery, Rockhurst University, Kansas City, Missouri (April 9 – May 15). The works reflect Linda's concept of the enduring life force we all possess and honor the memory of her close friend, patron and confidante, Richard Nadeau. "When one dies, their energy doesn't go away, it just loses color and vibrancy. It loses sex appeal, but it's in the ether. It's still there," she says. The exhibition incorporates recorded music by Paul Rudy, Coleman Hawkins, Samuel Barber, and György Ligeti, as well as scent (vetiver, lavender, neroli, and cucumber) to enhance seventy hanging sculptural lights that resemble fuchsia flowers. The room is painted blue to evoke depth and night, with one peach wall suggesting innocence. The *Luminous* series conveys an ethereal sense of grace, far from the mundane concerns of the material world. To achieve the desired translucency, Linda mixes the clay herself so that it can vitrify, or partially transform into glass, inside the kiln. The process is delicate and temperamental.

Fall: Her husband Lynn witnesses a fatal shooting at a gas station near the studio at 8:30 a.m. on a Monday. Two men die. Linda begins researching gun violence and discovers that Kansas City is the fifth most dangerous city in the country, with three murders a week. Determined to effect change, she speaks with the police commissioner and her congresspeople, who urge her to help maintain a public dialogue.

Embarks on the *Taking Aim* series, a reflection on power, gender, and desire—integral aspects of guns and gun violence, as well as long-standing themes in her work. She combines contrasting qualities—feminine and masculine, sinister and beautiful, natural and artificial, vulnerable and resilient—to capture the seductive and repellent nature of violence. Raising awareness around guns remains one of her ongoing missions.

2011

The American Museum of Ceramic Art, Pomona, California, acquires *White Lily* (c. 1994–95).

Summer: Participates in the 2nd International Symposium and Exhibition of Overglaze Paintings at Anadolu University in Eskişehir, Turkey (June 20 – July 21). Artists from fourteen countries work alongside university students and faculty for two weeks, exchanging ideas and techniques. Linda creates *Flags of the World* (2011), a gas pump with maps including all the countries represented at the symposium. The exhibition opens on July 1 at Anadolu University Faculty of Fine Arts Exhibition Hall.

Completes first works in the *Taking Aim* series: *Cause and Effect* (p. 162) and *44 Magnum Mandala* (p. 161), which she casts using a mold taken from a realistic gun that shoots rubber bullets.

2012

Summer: *Buy My Bananas*, Kate Werble Gallery, New York (June 22 – August 2), curated by Julia Trotta, granddaughter of feminist art historian Linda Nochlin. The show takes its title from a photograph Nochlin took depicting a nude man holding a tray of bananas—a companion piece to a nineteenth-century pornographic photo of a woman selling suggestively placed apples. Shows two *Tubeworms* (pp. 116–17) from the early 2000s and *Wondrous Kiss* (2005; p. 113). Kathe Burkhart, Sarah Lucas, Lee Lozano, and Rachel Harrison are among the other artists.

Fall: With Anna Calluori Holcombe, Laura Addison, and Joe Bova, curates *New World: Timeless Visions*, the biennial membership exhibition of the International Academy of Ceramics, at the New Mexico Museum of Art in Santa Fe (September 7–26). Linda shows *Mapped Flower* (1995; p. 99) and *44 Magnum Mandala* (2011; p. 161).

Taking Aim, Sherry Leedy Contemporary Art, Kansas City, Missouri (November 2 – December 22).

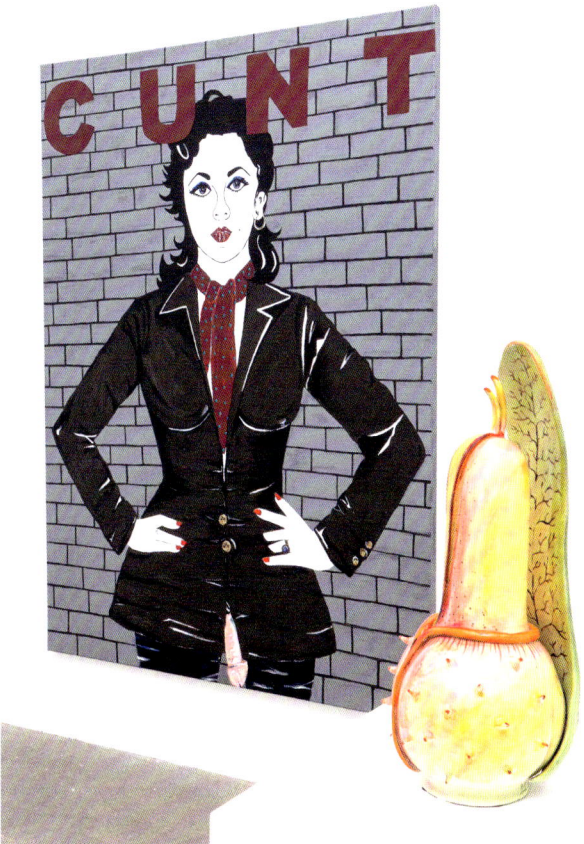

Kathe Burkhart's *Cunt* and Lighton's *Untitled*, 1999, in *Buy My Bananas*, Kate Werble Gallery, New York, 2012

Includes *I Don't Want a Bullet to Kiss Your Heart* (2012; pp. 176–77), one of her most ambitious projects to date: it is comprised of twenty-one parts that fit together to form an archway nearly nine feet tall composed of cast guns (.44 Magnums) and cast semi-automatic weapons (AR-15s). As she is preparing for the show, both her studio and the gallery are vandalized and strafed by gunfire. Although these events are not connected, they reinforce the prevalence of gun violence in Kansas City and the United States writ large. The police department assigns two officers to guard her during the opening as a precautionary measure. Her friend and filmmaker Don Maxwell documents the two-year process of creating *I Don't Want a Bullet to Kiss Your Heart* for a short film titled *Witness*, scored with an aria by Victoria Botero.

"An artist's job is to visualize what is happening in society. … What I see is an explosion of over 370 million guns in this country. A profusion of guns has not made us safer, or more civil. It has not strengthened our institutions but is destroying them."

Begins a concerted effort to persuade her congresspeople and mayor to address gun violence.

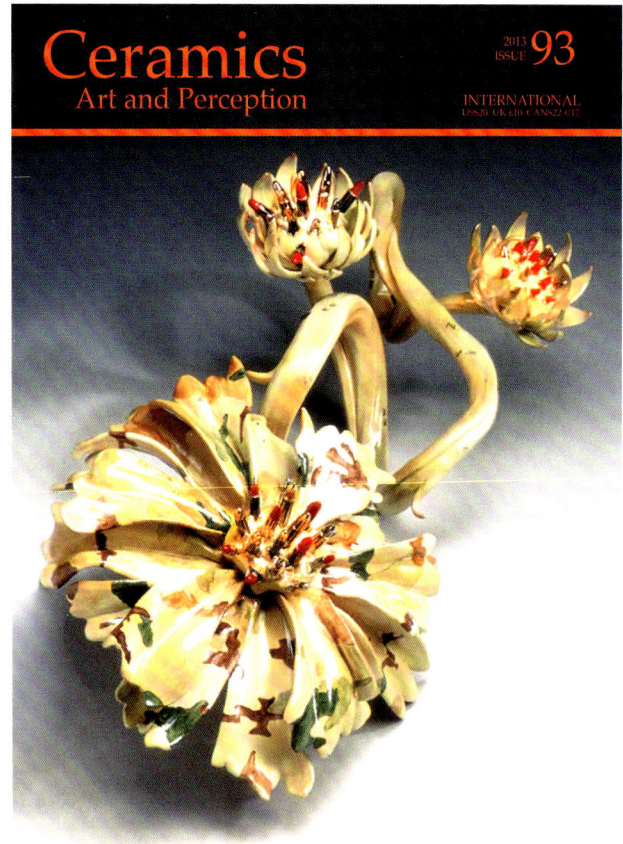

Lighton's *Camouflora*, 2004, on the cover of *Ceramics: Art and Perception*, 2013

At every exhibition of the *Taking Aim* works, she includes petitions against gun violence for visitors to sign. Collaborates with Grandmothers Against Gun Violence and Moms Demand Action.

2013

Summer: Tours the Silk Road with seventeen artists on a trip organized by I-Chi Hsu (June 15–30), visiting Tibet, the Gobi Desert, and Buddhist temples.

Camouflora (2004) is on the cover of *Ceramics: Art and Perception*, issue 93, in which *Taking Aim*, her exhibition at Sherry Leedy Contemporary Art, is favorably reviewed by art historian Tanya Hartman.

2014

Fall: *Hands Up, Don't Shoot: Artists Respond*, Alliance of Black Art Galleries (October 17 – December 20). Over 100 artists participate in exhibitions protesting gun violence at eighteen venues throughout St. Louis City and County in response to the killing of Michael Brown, a young unarmed Black man shot by police officer Darren Wilson in Ferguson, Missouri. Linda contributes work to the exhibition at the 10th Street Gallery in St. Louis.

Makes flowers with guns growing out of the center inspired by her trip to China, the birthplace of gunpowder and celadon, during a residency at the Red Lodge Clay Center, Red Lodge, Montana (pp. 166–67).

2015

Winter: Participates in *Women to Watch 2015: Focus on Women, Art & Nature*, an exhibition at Epsten Gallery (founded as the Kansas City Jewish Museum) in Overland Park, Kansas (February 8 – March 22). The show, mounted in conjunction with the *Women to Watch* exhibition series at the National Museum of Women in the Arts in Washington, DC, brings together works addressing sexuality, politics, and gender with references to the natural world. Linda shows *Camouflora* (2004; p. 164), *Untitled (Floral Pistil)* (2014), and *Cause and Effect* (2011; p. 162), a crystalline formation sprouting white clay casts of guns and gas pumps. Gallery staff cover this work with a sheet, concerned it will offend the residents of the retirement community in which Epsten Gallery is located—the home was the site of deadly shootings in April 2014. Linda feels betrayed when the work, which protests gun violence, is eventually removed.

Summer: At the invitation of sculptor Kwan Wu, Linda spends August in residency in his studio in Foshan, Guangdong Province, China. Donates six important works to Shiwan Ceramic Museum in Foshan to celebrate "2015 Conversation – China & America Ceramics Week."

2016

Curates *Desire*, an exhibition including thirty-seven artists representing twenty-two countries on six continents, at the Belger Arts Center in Kansas City, Missouri (February 5 – May 21). Linda asks artists to encapsulate, in their works, what desire means to them. She exhibits *My Desire* (2016; p. 135) and publishes an accompanying catalogue.

March: Receives an Outstanding Achievement Award from the National Council on Education for the Ceramic Arts (NCECA) in recognition of her assistance in organizing the annual NCECA conference in Kansas City, as well as *Desire,* the exhibition she curated to coincide with the conference.

LINDA LIGHTON
Sex and Death

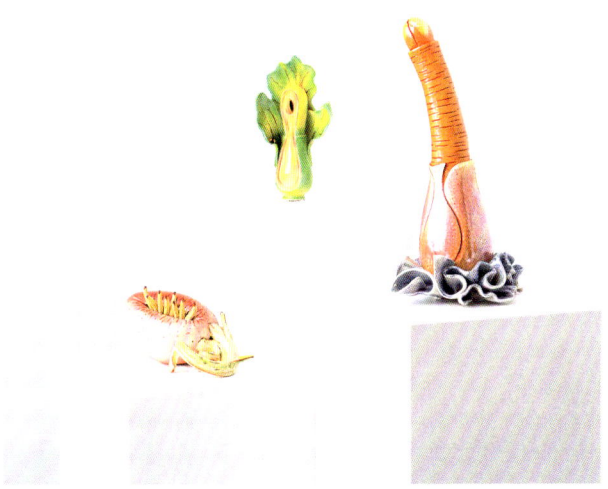

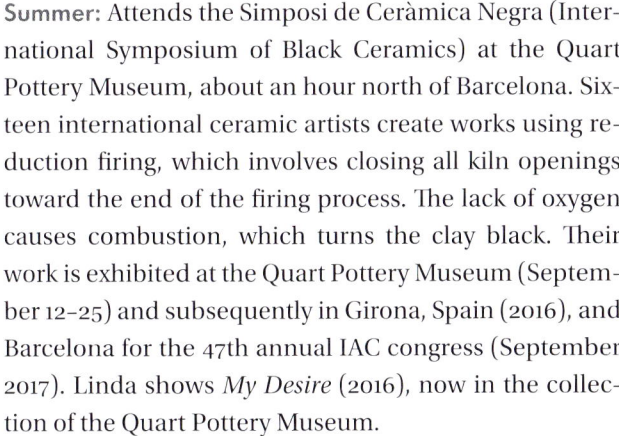

Linda Lighton: Sex and Death, Patrick Parrish Gallery, New York, 2015

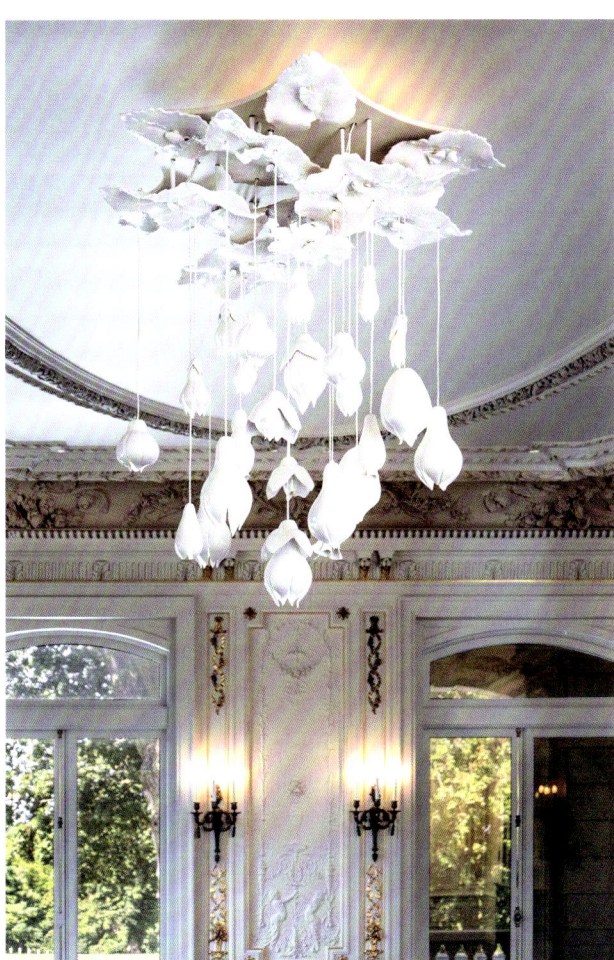

Lighton's *Luminous* chandelier commission, installed at the Kansas City Museum, Kansas, 2021

Summer: Attends the Simposi de Ceràmica Negra (International Symposium of Black Ceramics) at the Quart Pottery Museum, about an hour north of Barcelona. Sixteen international ceramic artists create works using reduction firing, which involves closing all kiln openings toward the end of the firing process. The lack of oxygen causes combustion, which turns the clay black. Their work is exhibited at the Quart Pottery Museum (September 12–25) and subsequently in Girona, Spain (2016), and Barcelona for the 47th annual IAC congress (September 2017). Linda shows *My Desire* (2016), now in the collection of the Quart Pottery Museum.

Fall: *Linda Lighton: Sex and Death*, Patrick Parrish Gallery, New York (September 8 – October 8).

2018

Linda Lighton: Thoughts and Prayers, Kim Weinberger Fine Art, Kansas City, Missouri. The title work—a wreath of black and silver guns with black, red-tipped bullets resembling lipsticks—evokes the allure of weapons as well as their human cost (pp. 180–81).

Nelson-Atkins Museum of Art, Kansas City, Missouri, acquires *Echinacea* (1998; p. 98).

2019

Taking Aim: Power, Gender and Firearms, Human Rights Institute Gallery, Kean University, Union, New Jersey (February 5 – May 9). To accompany the exhibition, Linda produces a booklet with facts about gun violence in the US.

Participates in the 3rd International Art Symposium at Muğla Sıtkı Koçman University in Bodrum, Turkey. The art school has beautiful facilities overlooking the Aegean Sea, where Linda works with ceramic artists from around the world.

2020

Commissioned to make *Luminous* (2020), a chandelier with twenty-five porcelain lights resembling blooming flowers, for the restoration and reopening of the Kansas City Museum, Kansas City, Kansas.

203

"Everything I've ever made is about transitions. How can we get to the next place with grace and style? Change can be painful—shedding old skins like a locust, or a cotton boll opening to release the white fluff inside, revealing something new and delicate."

— Linda Lighton, in conversation with Judith Fertig, in Kansas City (March 1, 2020)

2022

44 Magnum Mandala (2011) is on the cover of *Artillery*, a contemporary art magazine based in Los Angeles. The issue includes an overview of Linda's life and work by curator and art historian Elizabeth Kirsch titled "Psycho Ceramics."

Unveils *Ode to the Tallgrass Prairie* (2022), a monumental china painting on ceramic tiles at the new Kansas City International Airport, commissioned by One Percent for Art. Measuring four feet tall and twenty feet wide, the installation celebrates prairie flora and fauna from hawthorns to honeybees. The process is extremely technically demanding (many of the tiles are painted and fired five times to achieve the desired colors). During the pan-

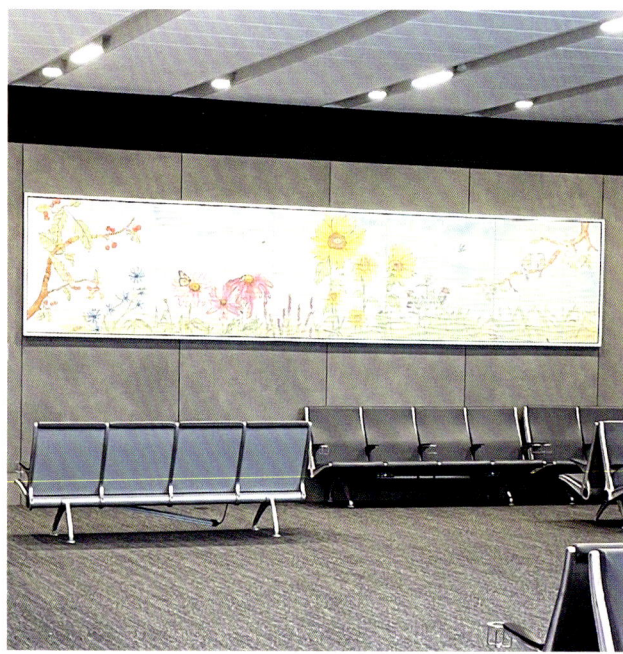

Linda Lighton, *Ode to the Tallgrass Prairie*, 2022, ceramic tile, china paint and luster, in wood-and-metal frame, 48 × 240 in. (121.9 × 609.6 cm), Kansas City International Airport

demic, Linda works in the studio every day for six months to complete the project, which involves extensive research. Airport visitors can scan a QR code to read about the plants and animals in the mural, and even about recipes for food and for traditional medicine.

"I found recipes for the original maraschino cherry that is wild in our region and how to cook cicadas. I learned that the female firefly lures the males and eats them to produce a smell that protects them from other insects, and that echinacea is helpful for lung problems."

2025

To date, Linda has been the subject of more than sixty single-artist shows and has participated in hundreds of group exhibitions on three continents.

The Lighton International Artists Exchange Program has sent 201 artists to residencies in 56 countries, including parts of the Arctic Circle.

Linda continues to live and work in Kansas City, where she remains a vocal advocate of gun control and the arts.

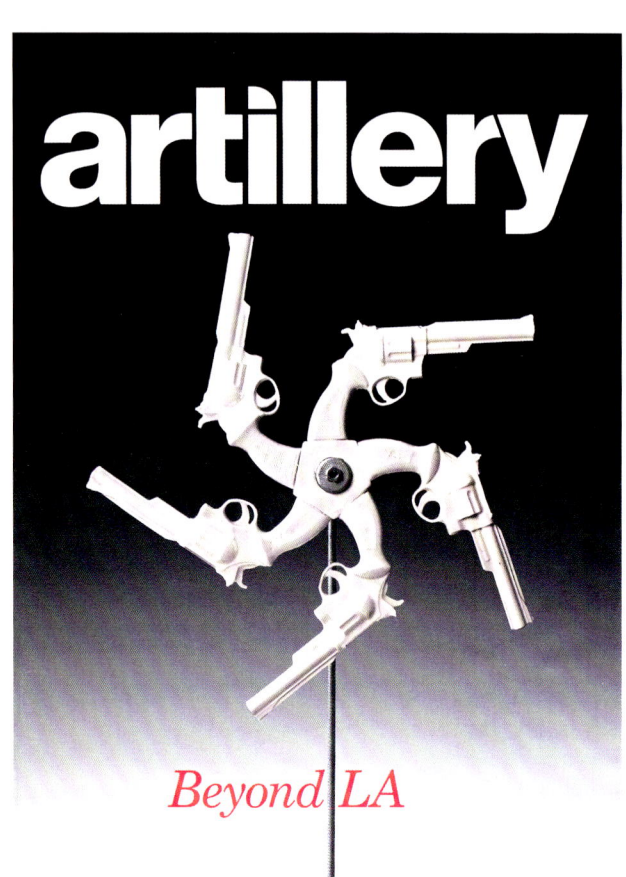

Lighton's *44 Magnum Mandala*, 2011, on the cover of *Artillery* magazine, 2022

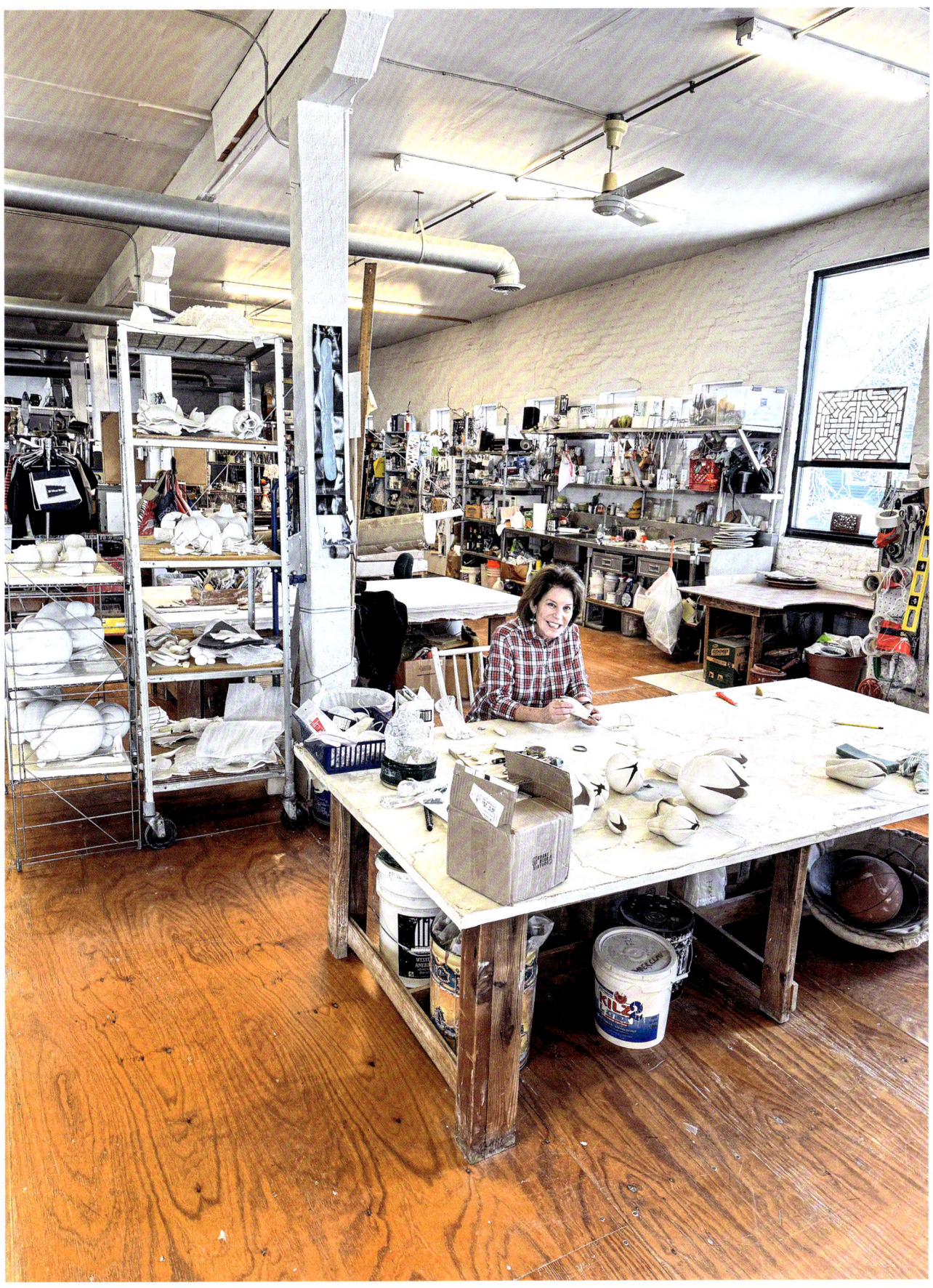

Lighton in her studio working on elements of a *Luminous* installation, 2025

IMAGE CREDITS
AND COLLECTIONS

All artworks are from the collection of the artist unless otherwise noted.
All Linda Lighton artwork photography by EG Schempf except pp. 75, 76 (*Tubeworm*), 78–79, 111, 113, 116, 117 by Maris Hutchinson; pp. 144, 172, 203 (Patrick Parrish installation) by Clemens Kois.
All chronology images not mentioned are taken from the private archive of the artist.

Page 11   Collection San José Museum of Art
Gift of the Lipman Family Foundation, 2006.20
© Estate of Robert Arneson / Artists Rights Society (ARS), NY. Courtesy San José Museum of Art

Page 12   Smithsonian American Art Museum, Washington, DC
Gift of the James Renwick Alliance, 1994.37.1
Photo Credit: Smithsonian American Art Museum, Washington, DC / Art Resource, NY / © Patti Warashina

Page 13 left   Smithsonian American Art Museum, Washington, DC
Gift of Helen Williams Drutt English and H. Peter Stern in honor of the 35th anniversary of the Renwick Gallery, 2007.47.5
Photo Credit: Smithsonian American Art Museum, Washington, DC / Art Resource, NY / © Mark Burns

Page 13 right   The Metropolitan Museum of Art, New York, NY
Gift of R. Thornton Wilson, in memory of Florence Ellsworth Wilson, 1943 (43.100.24)
Image © The Metropolitan Museum of Art. Image source: Art Resource, NY

Page 15 left   The Nelson-Atkins Museum of Art, Kansas City, MO
Gift of the Friends of Art, F75-11
© Estate of Marilyn Levine. Image courtesy of Nelson-Atkins Digital Production & Preservation, Gabe Hopkins

Page 16   The Museum of Modern Art, New York, NY
The Sidney and Harriet Janis Collection
Digital image © The Museum of Modern Art. Licensed by SCALA / Art Resource, NY

Page 17   Yale University Art Gallery
Gift of the Colossal Keepsake Corporation
© Estate of Claes Oldenburg

Page 18 left   Image courtesy of Adrian Sassoon, London
© Photography by Sylvain Deleu
© Kate Malone

Page 18 right   Courtesy of Joan B Mirviss LTD.
Photography by Richard Goodbody

Page 19   Smithsonian American Art Museum, Washington, DC
Gift of the Woodward Foundation, 1978.34
Photo Credit: Smithsonian American Art Museum, Washington, DC / Art Resource, NY

Page 20   The Metropolitan Museum of Art, New York, NY
Charlotte C. and John C. Weber Collection
Gift of Charlotte C. and John C. Weber, 1992 (1992.165.19)
Photo: Seth Joel. Image copyright © The Metropolitan Museum of Art. Image source: Art Resource, NY

Page 21   Photo by Charles Porter

Page 58   Collection Nerman Museum of Contemporary Art, Johnson County Community College, Overland Park, KS
Gift of Norman and Elaine Polsky

Page 60   The Nelson-Atkins Museum of Art, Kansas City, MO
Gift of Richard and Virginia Nadeau in honor of the 75th anniversary of the Nelson-Atkins Museum of Art, 2008.43

COLOPHON

Published on the occasion of

Linda Lighton:
Love & War, A Fifty-Year Survey, 1975–2025
December 13, 2025 – May 3, 2026

Nerman Museum of Contemporary Art
Johnson County Community College
12345 College Blvd
Overland Park, KS 66210
nermanmuseum.org

NERMAN MUSEUM STAFF
Assistant Preparator   Jacob Banholzer
Executive Assistant   Adriana Brown
Community Relations Manager   Mary Anne Matos
Assistant Registrar   Bailey McCulloch
Manager, Learning and Academic Engagement
Katherine Morse
Executive Director and Chief Curator
JoAnne Northrup
Chief Preparator and Exhibition Designer
Andrew Schell
Guest Curator, *Linda Lighton: Love & War,*
A Fifty-Year Survey, 1975–2025
Sydney Stutterheim
Registrar   Whitney Williamson

CATALOGUE
Editors   Rose Dergan and Sydney Stutterheim
Authors   Glenn Adamson, Sara Morris, and
Sydney Stutterheim
Contributors   JoAnne Northrup, Zoë Lescaze,
and Rose Dergan
Special thanks   Ross Redmon, Linda Lighton Studio
Publication Manager; Ryan Wilks; Darlina Goldak;
and Whitney Williamson
Copy Editor and Proofreader   Michael Pilewski
Senior Editor, Hirmer Publishers   Elisabeth Rochau-
Shalem
Publication Manager   Rainer Arnold
Designer   Edgar Endl, booklab, Munich
Lithographer   Reproline Mediateam, Munich
Printer   Optimal Media, Röbel/Müritz
Paper   Gardamatt Art 170 g/m²

Most notable thanks to JoAnne Northrup, Executive
Director and Chief Curator of the Nerman Museum for
her substantial and continued support on this project.

Published by

Hirmer Verlag
Bayerstraße 57–59
80335 Munich
Germany
hirmerpublishers.com

Printed and bound in Germany

The Deutsche Nationalbibliothek lists this publication
in the Deutsche Nationalbibliografie; detailed bibliogra-
phic data is available on the Internet at https://dnb.de.

ISBN 978-3-7774-4429-1

Front cover   *Nude Descending a Staircase,* 2007
(see page 62), and *Tinkerbelle,* 2007 (see page 63)
Back cover   *44 Magnum Mandala* (detail), 2011
(see page 161)
Page 2   *Bullet Belt,* 1985 (see page 159)
Pages 4–5   *Bananascape,* 2020–21 (see page 55)

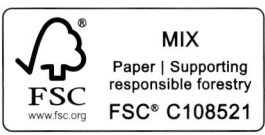